The Expert T

Rex Black, Leo van der Aalst, James L. Rommens

The Expert Test Manager

Guide to the ISTQB Expert Level Certification

Rex Black
www.rbcs-us.com / rex_black@rbcs-us.com

Leo Van Der Aalst
http://leovanderaalst.nl / info@leovanderaalst.nl

James L. Rommens
jimrommens@yahoo.com

Editor: Michael Barabas
Project manager: Lisa Brazieal
Proofreader: Stephanie Pascal, Patricia J. Pane
Layout and type: Josef Hegele
Cover design: Helmut Kraus

ISBN: 978-1-93395-294-9

© 2017 by Rex Black, Leo van der Aalst, James L. Rommens

Rocky Nook Inc.
1010 B Street, Ste. 350
San Rafael, CA 94901

www.rockynook.com

Library of Congress Control Number: 2015958931

Contents

Introduction

The Industrial Revolution is commonly said to have started with the invention of the steam engine in 1712, which means that this book was written shortly after the 300th anniversary of the Industrial Revolution. This period has been one of ever-accelerating technological progress, a period that has brought with it tremendous increases in human health, wealth, convenience, and life span. We are truly fortunate to live in such times, when many people take for granted things that even the emperors of Rome, Egypt, and China could not obtain.

At the beginning of the last quarter of this 300-year period—that is, 75 years ago—Konrad Zuse built what is arguably the first computer. It was primarily mechanical rather than electrical, but it was a programmable computer none-theless, which meant that it had a program. It carried out calculations on data stored in memory, based on software, and read from a paper tape. Sadly, history does not record whether the world's first software program contained a defect.

Over the last 75 years, software has grown in size, complexity, interconnec-tivity, and influence on our lives as perhaps no other innovation has. Software has truly been one of humankind's most remarkable inventions, even in the context of this remarkable period of human progress.

In spite of that growth—or perhaps more accurately in part because of it—the software colossus we have built for ourselves nevertheless has feet of clay. Software is built primarily by manual effort. True enough, the effort is a mental one, not a physical one. However, like all work done by fallible human beings, the manual creation of software inevitably leads to defects in that software, the outcome of mistakes made by the people creating the software. At some point in the future, the means of engineering software may catch up with the other forms of engineering in which we humans engage, but for the moment we must contend with the fact that the software that is increasingly integrated into every aspect of our lives, solving ever more complex problems, comes out of the cre-ation process with a lower level of quality than is needed.

Testing has been one response to these quality problems. While aphorisms such as "You can't test quality into software" are certainly true, it is also true that no one has yet devised a software development process that does not include software testing and still delivers a high level of quality. Software testing is an essential element of any reasonable software quality strategy.

While testing simple software is relatively simple, testing complex software is complex. As with any complex activity, it is not sufficient to unleash dozens of people without any structure, process, or methodology, even if those people are very talented software testers. Testing of software and systems, especially complex ones, must be managed.

If you are one of those lucky people managing testing, especially testing as part of large, complex projects or even programs, this book is for you. We will discuss defining the objectives and strategies of testing; managing testers, test teams, and testing service providers; working effectively within the larger organization; applying project management best practices; evaluating and reporting test results to project teams; the various business domain and project contextual factors that influence testing; and how to evaluate the effectiveness and efficiency of the testing process.

Naturally enough, this book is for experts. We assume that you have been in the software business for a number of years and involved in managing software testing for five years or more. We expect that you have been involved in multiple projects, or even programs, all the way to their completion. If you're like most of us seasoned test managers, you have seen some of those endeavors succeed, while others have failed. Some of these failures may have resulted from quality problems that remained submerged and unseen until testing started, and if so, you know all the drama and disappointment that can accompany such doomed undertakings.

This book will help you navigate future projects, including those that don't go as planned. The topics covered in this book will help you see problems coming earlier, respond more effectively, and alert others to the unfolding situation. After reading this book, you'll know why practices that worked in one situation might not work in other situations, and you'll know how to tailor practices, templates, and methodologies to a given situation. You'll know how to manage your relationships with colleagues, peers, and superiors. You'll know how to inspire, lead, and manage your teams. You'll know how to measure the success of your testing processes and how to identify opportunities for improvement.

In addition to serving as a guide to better test management, this book follows the International Software Testing Qualifications Board (ISTQB) Expert Test Manager syllabus, version 2011. As such, it is a natural sequel to one of Rex Black's other books on test management, *Advanced Software Testing: Volume 2, 2nd edition* (Rocky Nook, 2014). That book follows the ISTQB Advanced Test Manager syllabus, which is the prerequisite to the Expert Test Manager syllabus. If you have read that book, you will find familiar concepts expanded upon here. However, this book is a standalone entity, and you need not have read *Advanced Software Testing: Volume 2* to benefit from reading this book. We do assume, though, that you are an experienced test manager who has applied industry best practices to your work and that you are looking to further advance your knowledge and practices.

Because of this book's alignment with the ISTQB Expert Test Manager syllabus, it is also an ideal resource for people who are preparing for the ISTQB Expert Test Manager exam. Rex Black is one of the primary authors of that syllabus, as well as the chair of the ISTQB working group that produced it, so he has a deep understanding of the material. We'll make sure to discuss the key points for each chapter in depth. Each chapter includes sample exam questions that cover all of the learning objectives defined in it, and each of the 63 learning objectives is covered by a question. Like the actual Expert Test Manager exam questions, many of the sample questions in this book are based on realistic scenarios, where you have to assume the perspective of a test manager in a given situation. For convenience, these scenarios are named in the book. The scenarios are also numbered. Please note that the number assigned is the order in which the scenario was introduced in the book, and remains constant across all chapters.

To make exam preparation easier, we have generally followed the organization of the ISTQB Expert Test Manager syllabus. However, in certain cases we found we could improve the flow of the material or combine material presented in two or more sections into a single section. So, the mapping of sections of this book to the syllabus is not identical, but the chapters and the major sections do correspond.

In addition to the other resources, there is an appendix that describes the exam and discusses the official ISTQB Expert Test Manager sample exam provided by the ISTQB. The authors of this book were involved in the sample exam project (Rex was one of the authors), and we have used our experience creating Expert Level questions to build this additional resource for you. This appendix opens with a description of the different levels of learning objectives present in the Expert Test Manager syllabus and an explanation of how they affect the exam. If you are using this book to prepare for the exam, we recommend you read that first section of Appendix A before you start reading Chapter 1.

Whether you are reading this book to pass an ISTQB exam or simply to learn more about being a better test manager, we hope you find the resources you need in the following pages. One of the nice features that software has brought us is the possibility of reading a book as an interactive experience. If you want to discuss this book or topics in it with us, simply send an email to info@rbcs-us.com. Try to be as specific as possible in your question or comment. We'll respond to you and the wider testing community on our blog on http://www.rbcs-us.com/blog. We look forward to hearing from all of you, our fellow expert test managers.

Rex Black

With 35 years of software and systems engineering experience, Rex Black is president of RBCS (www.rbcs-us.com), a leader in software, hardware, and systems testing. For almost 25 years, RBCS has delivered training, consulting, and expert services for software, hardware, and systems testing and quality.

Employing the industry's most experienced and recognized consultants, RBCS builds and improves testing groups and provides testing experts for hundreds of clients worldwide. Ranging from Fortune 20 companies to start-ups, RBCS clients save time and money through higher quality, reduced risk of production failures, improved product development, improved reputation, and more.

Rex has authored more than a dozen training courses, many of them ISTQB accredited. These materials have been used to train tens of thousands of people internationally, directly through RBCS on-site, virtual, public, and e-learning courses, as well as through a worldwide network of licensed training partners in Europe, Africa, the Middle East, Australasia, East Asia, and Southern Asia. In addition to for-profit training courses, Rex has presented an hour-long, monthly, free webinar for more than seven years; this webinar series has reached more than 40,000 registrants. Rex has written more than 50 articles, presented hundreds of papers, workshops, webinars, and seminars, and given more than 100 keynotes and other speeches at conferences and events around the world.

Rex is the past president of the International Software Testing Qualifications Board and of the American Software Testing Qualifications Board. He remains active in the ISTQB and the ASTQB. He leads the Agile Working Group, is the coordinator for the Advanced Test Manager and Expert Test Manager syllabus teams, and participates as an author and reviewer in a number of other syllabus teams as well.

Rex is the most prolific author practicing in the field of software testing today. His popular first book, *Managing the Testing Process*, has sold more than 100,000 copies around the world, including Japanese, Chinese, and Indian releases, and is now in its third edition. His other books on testing, *Agile Testing*

Foundations, Advanced Software Testing: Volumes I, II, and III, Critical Testing Processes, Foundations of Software Testing, Pragmatic Software Testing, Fundamentos de Pruebas de Software, Testing Metrics, Improving the Testing Process, Improving the Software Process, and *The Expert Test Manager* have also sold tens of thousands of copies, including Spanish, Chinese, Japanese, Hebrew, Hungarian, Indian, and Russian editions.

You can find Rex online at the following coordinates:

Blog: www.rbcs-us.com/blog
LinkedIn: https://www.linkedin.com/in/rex-black
Facebook: www.fb.me/TestingImprovedbyRBCS
YouTube: https://www.youtube.com/user/RBCSINC
Twitter: @RBCS, @MisterSDET, @LaikaTestDog

If you'd like to discuss Rex's work or RBCS's services, those are great ways to catch up with him.

Leo van der Aalst

Leo van der Aalst (www.linkedin.com/in/leovanderaalst/) is Dutch and studied chemistry, mathematics, physics, and biology. However, he switched to IT almost 30 years ago. After having gone through the classic IT path—from programmer to program manager—he became a specialist in the testing area, in which he held functions such as test manager, test advisor, research and development manager, line manager, and Agile coach.

Leo applied his knowledge and experience in the project and test management field during a number of international projects and consultancy trajectories (in the US, Germany, Denmark, and Austria). He also likes to share his knowledge with other people by writing books and articles, and giving presentations and workshops.

Leo is coauthor of TMap NEXT for result-driven testing, TMap NEXT Business Driven Test Management, TMap Human Driven and TMap NEXT in Scrum books. He has written many articles (e.g., "Software Testing as a Service - STaaS"), which can be found through his website (www.leovanderaalst.nl).

Leo is past professor of software quality at Fontys University Eindhoven in the Netherlands, a much sought-after teacher of test training, and a regular speaker at national and international conferences. Leo is an accredited trainer for courses as Certified Agile Tester (CAT), ISTQB Agile Tester, and TMap Suite Test Engineer and Test Master.

Besides all this, Leo is development lead of the ISTQB Foundation and Advanced Agile Tester Syllabi (which are chaired by Rex Black), member of the programme committee of the (Dutch) National Software Quality Conference, fellow of SogetiLabs, and member of Capgemini Expert Connect.

James L. Rommens

Jim Rommens (www.linkedin.com/in/jimrommens) is a seasoned, accomplished project manager, having worked at major companies in industries such as telecommunications, energy, medical systems, and health care. After beginning his career in PC support and software development, Jim moved to management positions, including those of project manager as well as supporting project managers in various project management offices. He has assumed other roles, such as business analyst and tester, making him well-versed in the various roles of the SDLC (software development lifecycle).

Jim has a truly eclectic background with many varied interests, including project management, quality management and customer service, teaching and training, writing and editing, and career development and mentoring others.

For most of his adult life, Jim has maintained a strong interest in continuing education and possesses two graduate degrees (MS in computer science and MA in theological studies) and an undergraduate business degree in market research and industrial and organizational psychology, and has achieved further certification and training as a Project Management Professional (PMP), Certified Scrum Master (CSM), Certified Tester Foundation Level (CTFL), and CTFL – Agile Tester Extension. Jim's interests have also extended to quality and efficiency areas with a Lean Sigma Technician certification and public speaking as a Dale Carnegie graduate.

Jim incorporates key learnings and experiences from these various fields in his teaching classes as an adjunct instructor from the associate level to the graduate level for both online and classroom-led courses in the areas of project management, quality, and computer systems.

Jim's prime motivators in life, extending beyond career and job, follow the acronym *APV*—the *a*bility to do a job well, the *p*assion to do high-quality work, and the *v*alue inherent in his work for others. This work for others transcends the business world into various service and volunteer opportunities, including previously held church roles such as that of deacon, serving at a nursing home through one-on-one visits, playing group games, delivering church sermons, tutoring inner-city students, and packing and delivering meals for the elderly and shut-ins.

Rex Black's Acknowledgements

A complete list of people who deserve thanks for helping me along in my career as a test professional would probably make up its own small book. Here I'll confine myself to those who had an immediate impact on my ability to write this particular book.

First of all, I'd like to thank my colleagues on the American Software Testing Qualifications Board, the International Software Testing Qualifications Board, and especially the Expert Test Manager Syllabus Working Party, who made this book possible by creating the process and the material from which this book grew. Not only has it been a real pleasure sharing ideas with and learning from each of the participants, but I have had the distinct honor of twice being elected president of both the American Software Testing Qualifications Board and the International Software Testing Qualifications Board. I continue to work on both boards. When I think about how the ISTQB program and its syllabi have had a measurable impact on testing around the world, with more than 500,000 exams delivered worldwide, I'm proud of my involvement with the program.

Of course, the Expert Test Manager syllabus could not exist without the material it builds upon, specifically the ISTQB Advanced Test Manager and Foundation syllabi. I had the honor of being part of those working parties as well, including leading the Advanced Test Manager syllabus development. I thank them for their excellent work over the years, creating the fertile soil from which the Expert Test Manager syllabus and thus this book sprang.

In the creation of the materials that make up this book, Jim, Leo, and I have drawn on all the experiences we have had as authors, practitioners, consultants, and trainers. I have benefited from individuals too numerous to list. I thank each of you who have bought one of my previous books, for you contributed to my skills as a writer. I thank each of you who have worked with me on a project, for you have contributed to my abilities as a test manager. I thank each of you who have hired me to work with you as a consultant, for you have given me the opportunity to learn from your organizations. I thank each of you who have taken a training course from me, for you have collectively taught me much more than I taught each of you. I thank my readers, colleagues, clients, and course attendees, and I hope that my contributions to each of you have repaid the debt of gratitude that I owe you.

For around 25 years, I have run a testing services company, RBCS. From humble beginnings, RBCS has grown into an international consulting, training, and expert services firm with clients on six continents. While I have remained a hands-on contributor to the firm, more than 100 employees, subcontractors, and business partners have been the driving force for our ongoing success. I thank all of you for your hard work for our clients. Without the success of RBCS, I could hardly avail myself of the luxury of writing technical books, which is a source of pride for me but not a whole lot of money. Again, I hope that our mutual successes have repaid the debt of gratitude that I owe each of you.

And where would I be without three of the most wonderful women in the world? I thank my wife, Laurel, and my daughters, Emma and Charlotte. I'm proud of RBCS, my books, and my work with the ISTQB, but Emma and Charlotte take the cake. My wife and business partner does the hard work of running the company and the family while I speak at conferences, write books, and work with our clients. Laurel, Emma, and Charlotte, you are my lucky stars.

As regular readers know, my family and I love dogs. We love their emotional honesty, their loyalty, their ability to fully inhabit the moment, and their willingness to work for the greater good of the team. Our pack currently includes Kibo, Roscoe, and Mmink. We have also, during the writing of this book, fostered two working dogs in training, Eeland and Vvittoria. Good dogs, all.

Leo van der Aalst's Acknowledgements

People close to me know how much I love to write, in particular to share my thoughts and knowledge, so when Rex gave me the opportunity to coauthor this book I immediately said yes. Rex, thank you very much for asking me to be a coauthor of this book.

When I mention Rex, I must mention Jim at the same time. Jim provided me with very helpful hints on improving both the content of the chapters and my Dutch English. And, of course, Rex did the same. Their appreciation and interest proved a huge stimulus. Moreover, not only did the content improve from their very helpful comments, but personally I've learned a lot about the English language as well!

Me coauthoring this book would not have been possible without the support of the management team of Sogeti. In particular, I wish to thank Marco van den Brink, Hans Kapteijns, and Berend Roukes, who gave me the leeway needed to contribute to this book.

The person who suffered the most from my writing activities is for sure my wife, Carla. Although I knew we had made other commitments certain evenings and weekends with family, friends, and so on, often I went down to my study to process and write down the ideas that popped up in my head just before we would have left our house. Thank you, Carla, for supporting me in my writing activities.

I worked on this book with great enthusiasm. Whether you are an experienced test manager or an inexperienced tester, I hope this book offers you a clear story on how to best manage testing in all its aspects and inspire you with many ideas, detailed information, tips, and real-life stories. I—and I'm pretty sure this applies to Jim and Rex as well—am proud of the result and hope you, our reader, will agree.

James L. Rommens' Acknowledgements

I am very much grateful to Rex Black and humbled by the opportunity he has given me to coauthor this book. Writing a book has been one of my dreams; little did I know, after connecting with some friends in my network list in December of 2015, where I noted my part-time teaching work and interest in writing a book, that Rex would immediately contact me to help write a portion of this book. I learned a lot over the past year regarding the publishing process and how truly difficult yet satisfying the experience can be. In fact, as Rex would note, I've contracted the writing bug, with an interest in future writing projects, based primarily on my experiences working on this book. And so, I am very much indebted to Rex for taking the chance and allowing me to fulfill one of my dreams. I had known Rex for several years while I was the testing liaison within our project management office where I formerly worked. It was through Rex's courses that I was able to study for both the Foundation and Advanced Test Manager exams and often encouraged others at work to pursue them as well.

I would also like to thank Leo van der Aalst, our coauthor, for helping me to learn more about Agile and for providing helpful hints on metrics.

I also am indebted to my wife, Cynthia, and our four daughters, Lauren, Nicole, Kristen, and Kaitlyn, who have put up with me holed away while working on this book and other work-related projects. Thank you, ladies; I love you all.

My dogs, Grace, Michael, and Mina, have also been patient but, as long as they get food and attention (generally in that order), they are happy.

Lastly, I thank God for providing everything I needed to contribute in a small way to this book.

1   Test Missions, Policies, Strategies, and Goals

Keywords: analytical test strategy, consultative test strategy, methodical test strategy, model-based test strategy, operational profile, operational profiling, process-compliant test strategy, reactive test strategy, regression-averse test strategy, standard-compliant test strategy, test mission

1.1   Introduction

Learning objectives
No learning objectives for this section.

Let's start this book by considering four simple questions you can ask about your current (or last) project or program:

- What is the purpose of testing?
- What specific objectives are you trying to accomplish?
- How would you know if you had accomplished those objectives, and how do you measure success?
- How does each of the activities in your test plan and schedule relate to those objectives?

These are simple questions, but they don't have simple answers. In fact, in most organizations, these questions do not have answers at all, at least not answers that are clearly articulated and uniformly understood by project or program participants and stakeholders.

This absence of clear purpose, destination, objectives, and success criteria is a significant problem. In our work with clients, we find these kinds of ambiguities and disagreements are the most frequent cause of serious, sometimes career-ending, difficulties for test teams and their managers. To paraphrase the simile used in the syllabus, a test effort on a project or program is a serious

> **ISTQB Glossary**
>
> **test mission:** The purpose of testing for an organization, often documented as part of the test policy. See also *test policy*.
>
> **test policy:** A high-level document describing the principles, approach, and major objectives of the organization regarding testing.

business, a journey that serves a purpose (the test mission), that must have objectives and a destination (the test policy), and that requires a map (the test strategy).

In this chapter, we will talk about how to resolve the ambiguities and disagreements about the test mission, the test policy, and the test strategy.

1.2   Mission, Policy, and Metrics of Success

Learning objectives

LO 2.2.1   (K4) Discuss the quality goals of the organization, and define a test team's mission consistent with those goals.

LO 2.2.2   (K6) Define, describe, and evaluate test objectives, priorities, and test goals that might have long-term effects on the software, quality, and dependencies (organizational, economical, and technical).

LO 2.2.3   (K3) For a given situation, define effectiveness, efficiency, and satisfaction metrics for the test process, identifying opportunities for improvement.

The International Software Testing Qualifications Board (ISTQB) program defines testing expansively. Static testing (via reviews and static analysis) is included as well as all levels of dynamic testing, from unit testing through to the various forms of acceptance testing. The test process is defined to include all necessary activities for these types of testing; planning; analysis, design, and implementation; execution, monitoring, and results reporting; and closure.

What is the point of all this work? We could do all of these activities in a fashion that is technically correct but still fail to deliver any value to the business. That might seem surprising, but we have performed a number of assessments for clients where their internal testing processes functioned reasonably well but their work and deliverables were not valued by any of the key stakeholders. The managers of these test groups typically had failed to identify the stakeholders or, worse yet, in spite of being aware of the stakeholders, failed to work collaboratively with them to determine how to connect the testing process to something valued by each of them.

1.2.1 Identifying Stakeholders

Who are the people who have a stake in the testing and quality of a system? We can broadly classify them as being either technical stakeholders or business stakeholders. A *technical stakeholder* is someone who understands and participates in the design and implementation of the system. The following people are considered technical stakeholders:

- **Programmers, lead programmers, and development managers.** These people are directly involved in implementing the test items, and so testers and programmers must have a shared understanding of what will be built and delivered. These stakeholders receive defect reports and other test results. In many cases, they need to act on these results (for example, when fixing a defect reported by testers).
- **Database administrators and architects, network architects and administrators, system architects and administrators, and software designers.** These stakeholders are involved in designing the software and the hardware, the database, and network environments in which the software will operate. As with programmers, they receive defect reports and other test results, sometimes based on early static tests such as design reviews. These stakeholders also may need to act on these results.
- **Technical support, customer support, system operators, and help desk staff.** These stakeholders support the software after it goes into production, including working with users and customers to help them realize the benefits of the software. Those benefits come from the features and quality of the software but can be compromised by defects in the software that remained when it was released.

A *business stakeholder* is someone who is not so concerned with the design and implementation details but does have specific needs that the system must fulfill. The following people are considered business stakeholders:

- **Marketing and sales personnel, business analysts, user experience professionals, and requirements engineers.** These stakeholders work with actual or potential users or customers to understand their needs. They then translate that understanding into specifications of the features and quality attributes required in the software.

▪ **Project managers, product managers, and program managers.** These stakeholders have responsibilities to the organization for the overall success of their projects, products, or programs, respectively. Success involves achieving the right balance of quality, schedule, feature, and budget priorities. They often have some level of budget authority or approval responsibility, which means that their support is essential to obtaining the resources required by the test team. They will also often work directly with the test manager throughout the testing activities, reviewing and approving test plans and test control actions.

▪ **Users (direct and indirect) and customers.** Direct users are those who employ the software for work, play, convenience, transportation, entertainment, or some other immediate need, while indirect users are those who enjoy some benefit produced or supported by the software without actually employing it themselves. Customers, who might also be direct or indirect users, are those who pay for the software. They are the ones whose needs, ultimately, are either satisfied or not by the software (though satisfaction is typically more of a spectrum than a binary condition).

These lists are not intended to be exhaustive but to help you start thinking about who your stakeholders are. In addition, in some cases a stakeholder may be simultaneously a business stakeholder and a technical stakeholder. So, don't worry too much about trying to place a particular stakeholder clearly into one category or another.[1]

1.2.2 Understanding the Mission and Objectives

Having identified the stakeholders, the next step is to work directly with each stakeholder, or a qualified representative of that stakeholder group, to understand their testing expectations and objectives. That might sound easy enough, but when you start that process, you'll find that most stakeholders cannot answer a straightforward question such as, "What are your testing expectations?" They simply will not have thought about it before, at least not with any real clarity, so the initial answers will often be something like, "Just make sure the

---

1   For a more thorough discussion of testing and quality stakeholders, you can refer to Chapter 2 of *Beautiful Testing: Leading Professionals Reveal How They Improve Software (Theory in Practice)*, by Tim Riley and Adam Goucher.

system works properly before we ship it." This, of course, is an unachievable objective, due to two fundamental principles of testing: (1) the impossibility of exhaustive testing and (2) testing's ability to find defects but not to demonstrate their absence. You'll need to discuss the individual stakeholder's needs and expectations in terms of quality and then the extent to which testing can realistically help the organization achieve their objectives.

These discussions may initially be hazy and often unrealistic, but ultimately they should coalesce into a crisp, achievable mission and set of objectives. The specific mission and objectives that you and your stakeholders arrive at will vary, so we can't provide a one-size-fits-all list here. However, a typical mission statement might be something along the following lines:

> To help the software development and maintenance teams deliver software that meets or exceeds our customers' and users' expectations of quality.

Notice the word *help* here, which in this context means to assist (i.e., cooperate effectively with) others involved in the software process to achieve some goal. In this case, the goal is the delivery of quality software. You want to avoid mission statements like this one:

> To ensure that our customers and users receive software that meets or exceeds their expectations of quality.

There are two problems with this mission statement. First, it leaves out the software development and maintenance team, making software quality a testing problem entirely. Second, it uses the word *ensure*, which in this context means to guarantee that customers and users are satisfied or even delighted with the quality of the software. Due to the two principles mentioned earlier, both of these flaws are fatal. Testing is an essential part of a broader strategy for quality, but it is only a part of that strategy and can never guarantee quality by itself.

Given a realistic and achievable mission for testing, what objectives might you establish that would support achieving that mission? While your objectives will vary, typically we see one or more of the following:

- **Find critical defects.** Critical defects are those that would significantly compromise the customers' or users' perception that their expectations of quality had been met—that is, defects that could affect customer or user satisfaction. Finding defects also implies gathering the information needed by the people who will fix those defects prior to release. The person assigned to fix a defect can be a programmer (when the defect is in software), a business analyst (when the defect is in a requirements specification), a system architect (when the defect is in design), or some other technical or business stakeholder.

- **Find noncritical defects.** While the main focus of testing should be on critical defects, there is also value in finding defects that are merely annoyances, inconveniences, or efficiency sappers. If not all noncritical defects are fixed, which is often the case, at least many of them can be known. With such defects known—especially if the test team can discover and document workarounds—technical support, customer support, system operators, or help desk staff can more effectively resolve production failures and reduce user frustrations.

- **Manage risks to the quality of the system.** While testing cannot reduce the risk of quality problems to zero, anytime a test is run, the risk of remaining, undiscovered defects is reduced. If we select the tests that relate to the most critical quality risks, we can ensure that the maximum degree of quality risk management is achieved. If those tests are run in risk priority order, the greatest degree of risk reduction is achieved early in the test execution period. Such a risk-based testing strategy allows the project team to achieve a known and acceptable level of quality risk before the software is put into production.

- **Build confidence.** Organizations, especially senior managers in organizations, don't like surprises. At the conclusion of a software development or maintenance project, they want to be confident that the testing has been sufficient, the quality will satisfy customers and users, and the software is ready to release. While it cannot provide 100 percent surety, testing can produce, and test results reporting can deliver, important information that allows the team to have an accurate sense of how confident they should be.

- **Ensure alignment with other project stakeholders.** Testing operates in the context of a larger development and maintenance project and must serve the needs of the project stakeholders. This means working collaboratively with those stakeholders to establish effective and efficient procedures and service-level agreements, especially for processes that involve handoffs between two or more stakeholder teams. When work products are to be delivered to or from testing, then test managers must work with the relevant stakeholders to establish reasonable entry criteria and quality gates for those work products.

At this point in the process, you will have established a clearly defined mission and objectives for testing. What should be done with this important information? The best practice is to document them in a test policy. The test policy can be a standalone document, or it can be a page on a company intranet or wiki.

In addition to the testing mission and objectives, the test policy should talk about how testing fits into the organization's quality policy, if such a policy exists. If no such quality policy exists, it's important to avoid the trap of calling this document or page the "quality assurance policy" because testing by itself cannot assure quality. If your group has the phrase *quality assurance* in its title, and therefore you must call this page the "quality assurance policy," be careful to explain in the policy that testing is not a complete solution to the challenge of delivering high-quality software.

1.2.3 Measuring Achievement

The test policy should not only list the objectives, it should also establish ways to measure the achievement of the objectives. Without some way of measuring achievement, the success or failure of the test group becomes a matter of stakeholder opinion, a kind of dangerous popularity contest. Given the test team's role in pointing out defects in other people's work, the wise test manager does not bet on winning such contests. Instead, establish, in the test policy, clear metrics for each objective.

These metrics should be used to measure effectiveness, efficiency, and stakeholder satisfaction. Effectiveness refers to the extent to which an objective has been achieved. An effectiveness metric will often be expressed as a percentage, with the upper end of the scale (100 percent) indicating complete achievement of the objective. Efficiency refers to the economy with which an objective has been achieved. An efficiency metric can likewise be expressed as a percentage. In some cases an efficiency metric can exceed 100 percent, such as measuring the efficiency of testing using cost of quality analysis (as will be discussed in Chapter 4). In some cases an efficiency metric can indicate success through a lower percentage, such as when the metric is used to measure the degree of waste in a process.

Satisfaction refers to the stakeholders' subjective evaluation of the achievement of an objective. Satisfaction is often measured via surveys, asking stakeholders to react to statements in terms of their agreement or disagreement. A typical scale for measuring this reaction is called a *Likert scale*.[2] In this scale, which is often a five-point scale, a reaction of 1 indicates strong disagreement

---

2   For a more detailed explanation of Likert scales, see en.wikipedia.org/wiki/Likert_scale.

with the statement, while a reaction of 5 indicates strong agreement. The other points on the scale—2, 3, and 4—indicate disagreement, neutrality, and agreement, respectively. While we might seem to be venturing back into the realm of popularity contests by including subjective satisfaction metrics, note that perceptions *are* realities. If objective effectiveness and efficiency metrics show success but at the same time many stakeholders are dissatisfied with your group's work, something is clearly wrong, and your job as a manager is to fix it.

Because this topic of establishing metrics is new to many test managers, even experienced ones, let's look at some examples of effectiveness, efficiency, and stakeholder satisfaction metrics for testing. We'll start with a couple of effectiveness metrics. For the objective of finding defects, we can measure the effectiveness of the overall test process using the defect detection effectiveness (DDE) metric:

$$DDE = \frac{\text{defects found in test}}{\text{defects found in test + production defects}}$$

For the objective of managing risk, we can measure the effectiveness of the test design process by looking at the risk coverage (RC) metric:

$$RC = \frac{\text{quality risks for which tests were designed}}{\text{total quality risks identified during quality risk analysis}}$$

Of course, in the RC metric, we should exclude from the denominator any quality risks that were identified but for which the stakeholders explicitly decided not to design or implement any tests. If you do not exclude those risks, you might end up designing more tests than intended by trying to get to 100 percent risk coverage.

Here are a couple of efficiency metrics. For the objective of finding defects, we can measure the efficiency of the overall test process by using cost of quality analysis to calculate the testing return on investment (Test ROI):

$$\text{Test ROI} = \frac{(\text{average cost of a production defect} \times \text{test defects}) - \text{cost of internal failure}}{\text{cost of detection}}$$

You might notice that you will need to be a bit careful about this metric because it could lead to dysfunctional behavior in the organization. For example, finding large numbers of defects is easy with very buggy software, but you don't want to incentivize people to find more defects in testing than in earlier parts of the software lifecycle. It's also possible to increase Test ROI by reducing the investment made in test planning, analysis, design, and implementation, but that will tend to drive down the team's overall effectiveness at finding defects (as measured by DDE). If we use both DDE and Test ROI as key metrics, with an emphasis on DDE, then we have a balanced pair of metrics.[3]

A major element of confidence for existing systems is having confidence that the existing features will continue to work. This can be done through regression testing, but manual regression testing is expensive and inefficient in many cases. So for the objective of building confidence, we can measure the efficiency of the regression test implementation process by looking at the automated regression tests (ART) metric:

$$ART = \frac{number\ of\ automated\ regression\ test\ cases}{total\ number\ of\ regression\ test\ cases}$$

This is another metric that must be used with care (as indeed must all metrics be). For one thing, while it addresses efficiency, it does not address effectiveness. To provide this balance, we would also need a metric to measure the percentage of existing features covered by regression tests (whether manual or automated). For another thing, we have to make sure the manual regression tests and the automated regression tests are similar in size and scope. The size of the test case can be measured by the number of screens, data records, or test conditions covered by the test. If the manual regression tests are considerably larger than the automated regression tests (e.g., if the manual tests cover an entire use case while the automated tests each cover only a single screen), then adding the number of manual tests and automated tests to calculate the total number of regression tests is meaningless. It's like adding two temperature measurements, one in Celsius and one in Fahrenheit.

Finally, here are a couple of satisfaction metrics. For the objective of ensuring alignment with other stakeholders, we can measure the satisfaction of project stakeholders who have work product handoffs to or from the test group at any point during the test process via a survey. We can ask them to react to the following statement:

The handoff of work products between the test team and our team goes smoothly.

---

3   Capers Jones makes a similar point about the weakness of cost-per-defect metrics in his and Olivier Bonsignour's book *The Economics of Software Quality*, but he acknowledges the usefulness of cost of quality analysis.

For the objective of building confidence, we can measure the satisfaction of all project team stakeholders with the test results reporting process via a survey. We can ask them to react to the following statement:

The test results, as reported to you, help you guide the project to success.

For both surveys, we can use a Likert scale, as described earlier. We can calculate an average score using that scale as well as flag any responses at 3 (neutral) or below for further investigation.

Note that we have defined metrics not only for test execution, but also throughout the test process. During test execution, we need project and product metrics that allow us to measure the completeness of testing and the quality of the software being tested. These metrics allow us to report test results and fulfill the information-delivery objective of testing (see Chapter 6). However, the metrics we need in a test policy are process metrics, which measure the degree to which our team and processes are achieving established objectives.

It's important to remember that the objectives of testing, and the metrics used to measure them, are affected by the level of testing in question. For example, while finding critical defects is a typical objective of testing, it takes different forms in different levels of testing. For unit testing, we want to find defects that would prevent the function or class being written from providing services or capabilities to other functions or classes such that the system, when integrated, would not satisfy customers or users; that is, the objective is narrowly focused on the individual unit of code being tested. In comparison, for system testing we want to find defects that would affect the customers' or users' ability to enjoy the capabilities and functions provided by the entire system; that is, the objective is broadly focused on the entire system in the context of actual usage. As another point of comparison, note that finding defects is typically not an objective for user acceptance testing and that finding critical and/ or numerous defects in this test level is often seen by stakeholders as a sign of failure of early quality assurance and testing activities.

As another example, the objective of confidence building applies to unit testing and is often measured using code coverage metrics.[4] The same objective applies to system testing, but here we should not rely on achieving thorough code coverage because that should have happened in unit testing. We focus in-

---

4   You can find a detailed discussion of code coverage metrics in the book by Jamie Mitchell and Rex Black, *Advanced Software Testing, Volume 3: Guide to the ISTQB Advanced Certification as an Advanced Technical Test Analyst* (2nd edition), as well as in Rex's book *Pragmatic Software Testing: Becoming an Effective and Efficient Test Professional*.

stead on coverage of quality risks, requirements, design-specification elements, supported environments, data and metadata, and similar test basis items. Note that again the focus of the objective and the metrics for that objective is narrow in the case of unit testing and broad in the case of system testing. For user-acceptance testing, confidence building is typically the primary objective and is measured through coverage of requirements, use cases, user stories, supported environments, data, and metadata.

1.2.4   Setting and Meeting Goals

You should set initial goals for the metrics once they're established. By *goals,* we mean target measurements that you want to achieve. You should also establish some rules for when you will measure each metric. For example, some metrics are most appropriately measured on a project-by-project basis, while others can be measured weekly, quarterly, semiannually, or annually across all the project teams.[5]

If you have an existing test process established and operating, you should measure your current capabilities as part of the goal-setting process (i.e., baseline). You should also consult industry averages and experts to understand typical capabilities of other test organizations (i.e., benchmark). If your current capabilities fall short of typical capabilities, then you should introduce test process improvement plans to correct the underlying problems.[6]

With the baselined and benchmarked measurements in hand, you should work with the key stakeholders to set current goals and, if appropriate, longer-term goals that can be achieved once process improvements are made. Key stakeholders must be included in the goal-setting process because only with their concurrence can you achieve a situation in which the test team can, measurably and with data, demonstrate that it is succeeding in its mission and achieving its objectives. The test manager or test director must ensure that key stakeholders reach consensus on actually achievable goals. Where goals are not measurable, or are measurable but not achievable (e.g., a goal of 100 percent DDE), success is ephemeral and transient at best and stakeholder expectations are unlikely to be satisfied.

---

5   You can read more about this topic in Rex Black's e-book *Testing Metrics: Measuring Product, Process and Project Quality.*

6   This topic is discussed in detail in the ISTQB's Improving the Testing Process syllabus and in Rex Black's e-book *Improving the Testing Process: A Value Based Approach to Assessing and Enhancing Testing Maturity.*

With these examples of a typical mission and objectives, goals, and metrics given, keep in mind that the wider context will affect what your objectives are and the goals you set for them. If you are in a highly competitive and fast-moving market or writing software subject to regulatory deadlines for delivery, you might have to compress the test execution period, which will reduce the defect detection percentage you can achieve. If the organization selects a software development lifecycle that reduces the scope of the test effort prior to release, it will result in a higher level of residual quality risk at the end of testing. Basically, to the extent that constraints or priorities limit testing, whether those constraints or priorities come from the business, customers, users, or other realities, the software development lifecycle will reduce what is achievable in terms of the testing goals.

Reducing the achievement of goals does not mean utter failure. Constraints in terms of budget, schedule, resources, and personnel are ubiquitous; no test manager gets everything they want. Priorities in terms of schedule, budget, or feature set always compete with quality; few test managers operate in an environment where quality is the number one priority, and those who do find that such a situation brings with it additional challenges. So, like all managers, the test manager operates within parameters. Those parameters affect the degree to which goals are achieved. That effect shows itself in specific measures for our metrics of effectiveness, efficiency, and satisfaction, which reflect not only the test processes' and test group's capabilities but also the influence of those parameters.

The previous paragraph is not intended to provide an excuse for suboptimal performance and lackadaisical effort. As a manager, you should focus on maximizing the degree to which you satisfy the established test objectives. When establishing the test policy, test strategy, and test plans, test managers must carefully evaluate how those parameters will affect the selected objectives. Goals can be adjusted based on these parameters. During test control, emergent constraints or priorities must also be evaluated and further adjustments potentially made. Executives and senior managers will not be pleased with a test manager or test director who excuses underachievement of goals with a collection of excuses about constraints and priorities when that manager cannot provide evidence that they took steps to achieve the best possible outcome within those parameters.

Another mistake to avoid is writing the test policy in an aspirational fashion or setting so-called stretch goals in it. Understand the parameters and how they will affect your processes' and team's capabilities. The test policy, especially the goals, should reflect what can actually be done. You should plan to measure the effectiveness, efficiency, and satisfaction delivery of your team. When goals are not achieved, you should understand why and take steps to avoid such short-falls in the future. If the team is continuously underachieving, then individual contributors and line managers will perceive the test policy as, at best, irrelevant or, at worst, a cudgel with which they can be beaten regardless of their competency. Either situation is a classic sign of poor leadership.

That said, there is nothing wrong with using the test policy as part of a continuous test process improvement initiative. In fact, you should do so. If during a test retrospective, people note things that went really well, try to determine why and whether that can be instituted as a best practice across subsequent projects. Ask your teams, during test retrospectives and as part of continuous test process improvement projects, to look at the objectives and ask themselves whether new goals can be set or existing goals improved. Should new objectives be added? Are there additional stakeholders who could receive useful services from the test team? A test director or test manager should regularly look for ways to improve the effectiveness and efficiency of their teams and to increase stakeholder satisfaction with their work.

This whole process of identifying stakeholders and working with them to define the test group's mission, objectives, goals, and metrics may sound like a prolonged, political, and painful exercise. Because technical people are often introverts who prefer to focus on the work at hand and their technical abilities to perform that work, rather than the people doing it, we have noticed reticence to engage with the stakeholders in this way. However, make no mistake about it: If you, as a test manager or test director, do not make the effort to align your testing services with the needs of your stakeholders—your internal customers, really—you have chosen the most risky of omissions that we have encountered in our decades of practicing, training, and consulting. Excellent technical capability will not make the test team successful if those capabilities are being deployed in the wrong directions.

1.3   Test Strategies

Learning objectives

LO 2.3.1   (K4) Analyze a given situation and determine which individual strategies, or blended strategies, are most likely to succeed in that situation.

LO 2.3.2   (K4) Analyze a situation in which a given test strategy failed, identifying the likely causes of failure.

LO 2.3.3   (K6) For a given situation, create a test strategy document that contains the important elements, enables success factors, and mitigates causes of failure.

In the previous section, we talked about defining a test policy, which contains the mission and objectives of testing along with metrics and goals associated with the effectiveness, efficiency, and satisfaction with which we achieve those objectives. In short, the policy defines *why* we test. While it might also include some high-level description of the fundamental test process, in general the test policy does not talk about *how* we test.

The document that describes how we test is the test strategy. In the test strategy, the test group explains how the test policy will be implemented. This document should be a general description that spans multiple projects. While the test strategy can describe how testing is done for all projects, organizations might choose to have separate documents for various types of projects. For example, an organization might have a sequential lifecycle test strategy, an Agile test strategy, and a maintenance test strategy.

1.3.1 The Contents of the Test Strategy

Because the test strategy describes how testing proceeds, independent of any particular project, the document can include any information that is not project specific. (While we use the word *document*, the test strategy could be a set of pages on the company intranet or an internal wiki.) For example, the test strategy may include material on the following topics:

- **Test specification techniques.** This material should discuss the process by which the test basis is analyzed and documented and then separated into specific tests. In other words, how does the test team gather information about the project and product, generate a set of test conditions to be covered, generate sufficient tests from those conditions, maintain traceability, and assure the quality of those work products (e.g., with reviews)? It can also include links to various templates used for documenting tests, guidelines on the level of detail required in tests, rules for documenting references to the test basis and test oracle, and procedures for updating tests when the test basis or test oracle change or a defect is detected in a test.

- **Scope and independence of testing.** This material can describe how to coordinate across the different levels of testing, which are typically carried out by different participants who have different degrees of independence. For example, the test strategy may specify that unit testing is performed by developers, integration testing by developers and technical test analysts, system testing by business-oriented test analysts and technical test analysts, and user-acceptance testing by senior users of the application being developed. It may further specify how these different groups coordinate their efforts to eliminate any gaps or overlap that might occur.

- **Test environments.** This material should describe the hardware, software, infrastructure, facilities, networking capabilities, and other equipment needed for testing. To the extent that the test environments differ from the production or customer environments, the test strategy should describe the impact of those differences on the testing results. If, for unavoidable reasons, test environments must be shared across test levels or production hardware used for testing, the test strategy should describe how to coordinate that sharing and how to manage the attendant risks.

- **Test data.** This material should include information on how test data is to be obtained, created, maintained, and managed during testing. If production or actual customer data is to be used, the security of sensitive information should be considered and procedures around both access and use of such data should be put in place.

- **Test automation.** This material should describe the use of automation in the various test levels. In organizations where extensive test automation is used—for example, to automate functional regression tests or unit tests—this section could consist of links to other documents that describe the tools to be used, their acceptable usage, documentation requirements, and so on.

- **Confirmation testing and regression testing.** This material should discuss how to carry out a proper confirmation test, which typically involves at least repeating the steps to reproduce a failure from a defect report and may also involve rerunning the test(s) that previously failed due to the defect. It should also cover how to carry out regression testing for single changes or defect fixes as well as for larger groups of changes; for example, it might discuss how frequently to run a functional regression test or how to perform impact analysis to determine which manual regression tests to run.

- **Nonfunctional testing.** This material should describe how the test organization addresses activities such as security testing, reliability testing, and load and performance testing. This section could include links to other documents that describe tools to be used, corporate or external standards to be followed, and regulatory information, if necessary.

- **Reusability and configuration management.** This material should address which software work products and test work products (i.e., all the testware) can be reused and how these work products should be specified, named, stored, managed, and maintained. It should include a discussion on version and change control for test work products as well as information (or links to information) about how the configuration management tools are used.

- **Test control.** This material should cover the ways in which the test manager monitors progress against the test plan throughout the test process and exercises control actions when needed to redirect efforts when necessary. This includes regular meetings with test team members (e.g., daily test team debriefs during test execution) and other project participants (e.g., weekly project status meetings). This also includes executing risk mitigation and, when necessary, implementing contingency actions.

- **Test measurements, metrics, and reporting.** This material should include detailed information about the various data gathered by the test team during the test process; how that data is used to generate project, product, and process metrics; and how those metrics are used to report status for the project, including product quality and test progress. (Note that the process metrics that measure testing capability were discussed in the test policy.)

- **Defect management.** This material should give test team members and other project participants detailed insight into the essential topic of defect management. It should describe the defect lifecycle, including the various states in the lifecycle, the roles of the various project participants as each defect report goes through its lifecycle, and the expected response time. It should describe the various data and classifications gathered throughout the defect lifecycle, including enough information for project participants to properly and completely document each defect.

- **Tools.** This material should include basic information on the tools used by the testing organization. In addition to general descriptions, links to tool documentation and information on where and how to access the tools should be available in this section as well. This list may include the test case management tool, defect management tool, automation and performance testing tools, database querying tools, proprietary tools, and the test organization's wiki, just to name a few.

- **Standards.** If applicable, this material should explain and reference any mandatory and optional standards that testers should or must adhere to during the test process.
- **Integration procedures.** To the extent that component integration testing and/or system integration testing are applicable, this material should describe how integration proceeds and the way in which appropriate integration tests are created and executed.

You probably noticed that many of the preceding elements refer to coordination across different groups and test levels. Ideally, a single test strategy spans the different test activities across each project to maximize the effectiveness and efficiency of these activities. This requires the author of the test strategy, often a test director or senior test manager in the independent test organization, to work closely with managers in the other groups that participate in testing. This is similar to the interaction required in the definition of the test policy but in this case involves a smaller cadre of people and a focus on the work to be done.

It is a best practice for test organizations to create training material for new testers that covers the test policy and, especially, the test strategy. Simply having these documents available to testers or even assigning new testers the task of reading these documents will generally not ensure adequate compliance. There is no point in spending hours and hours creating test policy and strategy documents if those documents do not guide behavior during testing.

While the test strategy should guide behavior on each project, there is usually a need to provide more specific information for each project. This is either to instantiate a general procedure given in the test strategy or to handle unique properties of the project. These details about the implementation of a test strategy on a particular project are referred to as the test approach and should be captured in the test plan for the project. For example, if the test strategy calls for risk-based testing, the test approach might specify the particular people involved in the risk analysis on a project.

In addition to the content of the test strategy, it's important for the test manager or test director writing a test strategy to understand the common types of test strategies; their benefits, success factors, and risks; and how these

> **ISTQB Glossary**
>
> **analytical test strategy:** Testing based on a systematic analysis of product risks or requirements.
>
> **reactive test strategy:** Testing that dynamically responds to the actual system under test and test results being obtained. Typically, reactive testing has a reduced planning cycle and the design and implementation test phases are not carried out until the test object is received.

types of test strategies relate to key stakeholders. In the following subsections, we'll review these types of test strategies and their associated details. Remember that you can and typically should mix these types of strategies to maximize the benefits while minimizing the risks.

1.3.2 Analytical Strategies

Anytime a test team analyzes the project, the product, and the documents describing the project and the product as a way of determining the test conditions to be tested, they are following an analytical test strategy. The test conditions are then elaborated into tests during test design, using black box, white box, and experience-based test design techniques. During test implementation, the test data and test environment necessary to run the tests are defined and created.

In all analytical test strategies, the analysis takes place before test execution. Often, this analysis can be done early enough so that the design and implementation of the tests can occur before test execution begins. However, because this is not always possible or practical, a test charter may be defined that blends reactive and analytical test strategies, stipulating the analysis to occur prior to test execution while specifying the design and implementation of tests to occur during test execution. Alternatively, logical tests can be written early, with the concrete tests defined during test execution, or concrete tests can be written during test implementation, with the testers given the latitude to respond to observed behavior in a reactive fashion during the execution of these concrete tests.

Two of the most common analytical test strategies are requirements-based testing and risk-based testing. In requirements-based testing, one or more test conditions are identified for each requirement element. In risk-based testing, each quality risk item is a test condition. In either case, one or more tests are elaborated for each test condition. In the case of requirements-based testing, the number of tests is sometimes determined by factors such as the specified priority of the requirement, by the details of the specification itself, and by the test design technique(s) used. In the case of risk-based testing, the number of tests is determined by the level of risk associated with the quality risk item.

An analytical test strategy has a number of benefits:

- **Alignment of testing against a clearly defined test basis.** In analytical strategies, the test basis is well documented. In properly performed analytical test strategies, traceability of the tests back to the test conditions, and from the test conditions to the test basis, is defined and maintained during test design, implementation, and execution.
- **Measurability of testing against the test basis.** During test execution, the traceability of the tests and their results back to the test conditions allows the test team to deliver to the project participants and stakeholders a clear and data-based presentation of what has been tested and what has not been tested, what works and what does not work.
- **Defect prevention through early analysis of the test basis.** The analysis of requirements, risks, and other project documents often results in the discovery of defects and project risks. These defects and risks can then be eliminated or managed early in the project, improving the efficiency of the achievement of quality goals and the overall execution of the project.

Ideally, project and product stakeholders participate in the analysis sessions and define the test conditions to be tested. This has the added benefit of providing these stakeholders with transparency and insight into what is to be tested (including to what depth), what is not to be tested, and the way the testing process will proceed and will help in their understanding of the test results.

To succeed with an analytical strategy, the following factors are required:

- For document-focused analytical strategies such as requirements-based, design-based, or contractual-based testing, the test team must receive the underlying documents prior to test analysis. These documents need not be final because they can undergo revisions or iterations (e.g., based on defects or risks discovered during analysis), but they should be sufficient for the discovery of the test conditions.
- For stakeholder-focused analytical strategies such as risk-based testing, the test team must be able to get the technical and business stakeholders to

> **ISTQB Glossary**
>
> **model-based test strategy:** Testing based on a model of the component or system under test, e.g., reliability growth models, usage models such as operational profiles, or behavioral models such as decision table or state transition diagram.
>
> **operational profile:** The representation of a distinct set of tasks performed by the component or system, possibly based on user behavior when interacting with the component or system, and their probabilities of occurrence. A task is logical rather than physical and can be executed over several machines or be executed in non-contiguous time segments.
>
> **operational profiling:** The process of developing and implementing an operational profile. See also *operational profile*.

participate in the analysis of the project and product to identify the test conditions and the level of risk associated with each condition. The test conditions need not be finalized during this stakeholder-driven analysis.

In either case, while the test conditions will change during test design, implementation, and execution, a significant amount of change in these conditions can reduce the efficiency of testing. Sequential lifecycle models attempt to limit the amount of change over the long time period from analysis to execution. Iterative and especially Agile lifecycle models limit the number of test conditions that will change by limiting the number of test conditions defined for each iteration.

For analytical test strategies to succeed, the following risks must be managed:

- For document-focused analytical strategies, any unmanaged change to the documents used as a test basis will result in incongruity between the tests and the test basis. In addition, this strategy will fail when these test basis or test oracle documents are not delivered or are extremely vague or ambiguous. In this case, the test conditions or test cases will be incomplete or incorrect.
- For stakeholder-focused strategies, if the test team cannot engage the relevant stakeholders in the process of identifying the test conditions (e.g., the quality risk items), the test conditions or test cases will be incomplete or incorrect. Even if the list of risk items is complete, if the assessment process is incorrect due to insufficient stakeholder involvement or a lack of stake-

holder consensus, the depth of testing will be incorrect. Either outcome will reduce the effectiveness and efficiency of the strategy.

Analytical test strategies are well described in a number of books on testing, which makes these strategies one of the best-defined and most common types of test strategies.[7]

1.3.3 Model-Based Strategies

When a test team generates a model of system behavior and then uses that model to design and implement tests, they are following a model-based testing strategy. The model can be mathematical, statistical, graphical, or tabular. The model can include the environment, the inputs processed by the system, the conditions in which the system operates, and the expected behavior of the system under those collective circumstances. The model is often based on some analysis of actual situations or of predicted situations. It can address functional behavior, as when the analysis is based on UML models, or nonfunctional behaviors.

For example, in performance and reliability testing, technical test analysts will examine the proposed or actual production environment and the test environment. Predicted or actual load is analyzed, including the variations of those load conditions over time and background loads constantly or periodically present on the system. This analysis results in a characterization of the system's operating conditions sometimes referred to as an operational profile. For these various operating conditions, maximum allowable response time, maximum acceptable resource utilization, and/or minimum allowable throughput are defined.

During test design and implementation, this model is typically automated using a load testing tool. These automated reliability and/or performance tests are then run during system test and/or system integration test. During this period, however, it is very difficult to resolve the types of fundamental design defects that underlie performance and reliability failure. Therefore, it is a best practice for this model to be developed during system design and implemented using a spreadsheet or an automated performance simulation tool. This allows static performance testing of the system design before any effort or

---

7   For example, for requirements-based testing, see Rick Craig and Stefan P. Jaskiel's book *Systematic Software Testing*. For risk-based testing, see Rex Black's book *Managing the Testing Process: Practical Tools and Techniques for Managing Hardware and Software Testing*.

money is expended on implementing a (possibly flawed) approach to building the system.[8]

A model-based test strategy has the major benefit of realistic testing of the system. The generation of the model focuses on the real-world environment, conditions, inputs, and other usage characteristics of the system. For nonfunctional tests such as performance and reliability testing, this realism of environment, load conditions, and usage is often critical to meaningful results. If the production environment and test environment are not the same (e.g., memory, disk space, load balancing), the model must be adjusted, though the adjustment entails significant risk that the test results will not reflect production results.

As you might expect given the foregoing, one critical success factor for model-based testing is an accurate model of real-world usage. Another factor that applies for many nonfunctional forms of model-based testing is the availability of a tool to support the testing. Most often, we think of load testing tools that automate test execution for performance and reliability testing, and such tools certainly are irreplaceable for those test types. However, performance simulation tools as mentioned earlier can play a critical role too.

For model-based test strategies to succeed, the following risks must be managed:

- The technical test analysts may find, during analysis, that they do not have all the data they need to create an accurate model. This can lead to a scramble to find answers to hard questions such as, "How many concurrent users can we expect during peak system load?" In some cases, these questions remain unanswered even during test execution, resulting in significant erosion in the confidence building aspect of testing.
- Even if the data is available, the model constructed by the analysts can be inaccurate. Even skilled analysts can make such mistakes, and the likelihood of this risk occurring becomes almost certain if inexpert testers are used. For example, the tests for performance and reliability testing are some of the most difficult to create, and unless someone with five or more years' experience is involved in the process, mistakes will probably occur.[9] If the

---

8   Rex has personal, firsthand knowledge of two multiyear, multimillion-dollar, person-century projects that failed during system integration testing due to the discovery of irresolvable performance-related design defects. You can read about the right way to manage performance risks in Rex Black and Barton Layne's article, "The Right Stuff," found at www.rbcs-us.com/images/documents/Risk-Mitigation-and-Performance-Testing.pdf.

9   The five-year figure is quoted in Malcolm Gladwell's book, *Outliers: The Story of Success*, and he cites numerous examples where this rule applies.

> **ISTQB Glossary**
>
> **methodical test strategy:** Testing based on a standard set of tests—e.g., a checklist, a quality standard, or a set of generalized test cases.

model is wrong, the tests will be wrong and severe defects can escape into production.

- Even given an accurate model, model-based testing can still go awry if the wrong tools are selected. A tool can be wrong not only because it is incapable of implementing the model, but also because the testers themselves are unable to use the tool to implement the tests, to execute the tests, or to interpret the results reported by the tool. The most frequent outcome in these situations is a level of false confidence when the tests don't reveal failures or the failures that are revealed are mistaken for correct behavior.

- Another mistake that can endanger model-based testing is a natural tendency to test what the model tells you should happen rather than testing for what should not happen. This preponderance of positive path tests also tends to result in false confidence.

As with analytical risk-based testing, technical test analysts performing model-based testing rely on key test stakeholders, both business and technical. These stakeholders can help provide and explain data for the model, construct the model, and validate the model.[10]

1.3.4 Methodical Strategies

In analytical strategies, analysis produces the test conditions; in model-based strategies, the model determines the test conditions; in methodical strategies, the test team follows a standard set of test conditions. This set of test conditions can come from a variety of sources. Some test teams use a quality standard such as ISO 9126. Other test teams assemble a checklist of test conditions over time, based on their experience. The checklist can arise from the business domain of the system, the characteristics of the system itself, and the type of testing being performed. For example, security testing often relies on checklists of common vulnerabilities.

---

10 For more information on model-based testing, see *Practical Model-Based Testing: A Tools Approach*, by Mark Utting and Bruno Legeard.

Sometimes test managers become confused about the difference between analytical test strategies and methodical test strategies. For example, the result of a risk analysis is a set of risk items and their associated risk levels, which serve as the test conditions, and this can look a lot like a checklist. The difference is that, with analytical strategies, analysis occurs at the beginning of each iteration (for iterative and Agile lifecycles) or at the beginning of each project (for sequential lifecycles), generating a new set of test conditions. In methodical strategies, the set of test conditions does not vary from iteration or project, though periodic updates to the test conditions can occur.

A methodical test strategy has the benefit of consistent testing. Once a particular set of attributes is put on the checklist, we can be sure that those will be tested. For example, if usability characteristics such as learnability, understandability, operability, and attractiveness are placed on the checklist, we can be confident that these behaviors have been evaluated during testing. The checklist is typically defined at a logical level, allowing all stakeholders to evaluate it for completeness.

To succeed with a methodical strategy, the following factors are required:

- The set of test conditions, checklists, or test cases used by the testers must reflect what is required for the system to satisfy customers and users. It must be accurate, complete, and current. Therefore, some periodic maintenance, perhaps as part of the test closure process, must occur.
- Since the maintenance of the test conditions will be retrospective and thus slow moving (as compared to an analytical strategy), methodical test strategies work best when the test object is stable, varying only slowly over time. This is often the case with successful and mature applications in the enterprise, mass-market, and IT context.

The main risk of methodical test strategies, obviously enough, is the possibility that the test conditions, test cases, or system attributes are incomplete, incorrect, or obsolete. Such defects in the checklist will result in significant gaps in test coverage, and therefore testers will likely miss important defects.

In situations where methodical strategies work well, such as very stable, slowly evolving systems, these strategies can be very successful. The use of a standard set of tests makes practical economical approaches such as test technicians or outsourcing to a stable test team. The stakeholders, after helping to define the set of test conditions, are required only to review the periodic updates, making this a lightweight strategy in terms of stakeholder workload.

ISTQB Glossary

process-compliant test strategy: Testing that follows a set of defined processes—e.g., defined by an external party such as a standards committee. See also standard-compliant test strategy.

standard-compliant test strategy: Testing that complies to a set of requirements defined by a standard—e.g., an industry testing standard or a standard for testing safety-critical systems. See also process-compliant test strategy.

1.3.5 Process- or Standard-Compliant Strategies

In methodical strategies, the test team follows a standard set of test conditions; in process- and standard-compliant strategies, the test team follows a set of processes that are defined by people outside the test team. The process typically does not predetermine the conditions, but it does determine the extent and type of test documentation gathered, the way in which the test basis and test oracles are identified and used, and how the test team is organized relative to the other parts of the project team.

For example, in teams following Agile methodologies, there is an emphasis on lightweight documentation, including in testing. Logical test cases rather than concrete test cases are more typical. The tests are derived from user stories, and these user stories and acceptance criteria are the test oracles. Individual testers are embedded in development teams, though the best practice is to matrix these testers into a central test team, with test managers and even a test director, to preserve independence of testing.

The primary benefit of a process- or standard-compliant test strategy is that the test team can take advantage of the skills and experience of the people behind the standard or process. For example, very experienced people were involved in defining the ISTQB syllabi, the IEEE 829 test standard, and the Agile methodologies. If the problems being solved by these processes or standards are similar to the problems facing the test team, the processes or standards provide out-of-the-box solutions, allowing the test team to be more efficient (by not having to generate its own solutions) and more effective (by not having to arrive at good solutions through a painful period of trial and error).

Of course, that requirement for similarity of problems is a critical success factor for these strategies: The processes or standards were created in response to a particular set of problems that the creators regularly faced in their consulting work, dealt with in their employment as practitioners, or studied in their capacity as academics. If those problems are also your problems, then these strategies can work, if you select the right processes or standards. Agile methodologies are very different than the IEEE 829 standard, and you have to select the right one, given your specific context.

For process- and standard-compliant test strategies to succeed, the following risks must be managed:

- If the test team or broader project team does not understand the process or standard they are implementing, they will make mistakes. This risk can be mitigated through good training and proper use of consultants during the implementation process, but this mitigation is imperfect in that many trainers and consultants also have an imperfect understanding of the process or standard they are advocating, promoting, and promulgating and, furthermore, these trainers and consultants often have a vested interest in minimizing the weaknesses and fallibility of the process or standard.

- Even with a good theoretical understanding, a team can make mistakes in implementation of the process or standard. This is especially the case because there is no truly out-of-the-box way to implement a process or standard in an organization; some tailoring is always required. In this tailoring, the team (or the trainers or consultants) can make the mistake of being too compliant with the approach, not modifying those segments that will impede success, or too loose with the approach, modifying or omitting parts of the process or standard that enable its success. We've observed both mistakes with clients, though the most frequent is the dogmatic application of a process in spite of clear warning signs that it won't work. We have seen a number of good testing ideas executed by the three-word firing squad: "That's not Agile."

- Even the perfect understanding and implementation of a process or standard will fail when it is implemented in the wrong situation. For example, it is a best practice to take aspirin at the first signs of a heart attack, but for people who are allergic to aspirin or who are at an extreme risk of stomach bleeding, this can kill rather than cure. If the problems facing your organization are dramatically different than those facing the creators of the process or standard, you will be effectively trying to win a chess game by applying a backgammon strategy.

The degree of stakeholder involvement varies considerably in these strategies. Agile methodologies require daily interaction between the business and technical stakeholders and the test team, though this practice is frequently mini-mized. IEEE 829 standards generally recommend reviews of test work products by stakeholders but not daily meetings.[11]

1.3.6 Reactive Strategies

A test team follows a reactive test strategy when the focus is on reacting to the system or software that is delivered for testing. Reactive test strategies are characterized by the following:

- While test analysis to identify the test conditions (often captured in test charters) may occur prior to test execution, the test design and implementation occur primarily in parallel with test execution.
- The test plan and approach are dynamic, evolving rapidly as the needs of the project change and as the true state of the product being tested becomes clear.
- The test cases are designed and implemented using primarily experience-based and defect-based techniques.
- Aids such as heuristics, software attacks, and defect taxonomies are used during test design and implementation.[12]
- Processes and documentation are lightweight and informal.

Reactive strategies can be used in any lifecycle, including sequential and itera-tive lifecycles.

A reactive test strategy has a number of benefits:

- Finding a complementary set of defects. Reactive strategies tend to find some defects that other strategies would miss (and vice versa).
- Locating defects efficiently. The cost to find a defect is lower because of the lightweight documentation and rapid evolution of the tests.
- Refocusing continuously. Information gained from testing, especially about emerging defect clusters, allows the test team to redirect their efforts on the most productive test areas.

---

11   For more information on process-compliant strategies, see *Agile Testing: A Practical Guide for Testers and Agile Teams*, by Lisa Crispin and Janet Gregory, and Rodger Drabick's book, *Best Practices for the Formal Software Testing Process: A Menu of Testing Tasks*.

12   See, for example, James Whittaker's *How to Break Software: A Practical Guide to Testing W/CD*.

> **ISTQB Glossary**
>
> **consultative test strategy:** Testing driven by the advice and guidance of appropriate experts from outside the test team (e.g., technology experts and/or business domain experts).

- Responding robustly to challenging situations. Unlike some strategies, such as analytical requirements-based testing, reactive test strategies can handle incomplete or even entirely missing test-basis documents.

That said, not all teams that try reactive strategies succeed with them. Success requires highly skilled and experienced testers. These testers must understand the business problem that the application solves and the technologies involved in the solution, and they must be proficient in a wide variety of testing skills and techniques.

For reactive test strategies to succeed, the following risks must be managed:

- If the testers executing have insufficient skills, the tests will be superficial at best and often just plain wrong. Testing will reveal less important defects at the expense of more important ones, and the rate of false positives will be high. Reactive testers, to succeed, must have skills and experience with testing techniques, the business domain of the software under test, and the technology used to implement the software.
- By default, reactive testing does not produce documentation of what was tested or how the expected results of the tests were determined. This means that test coverage is unknown and arguments about test results ensue. Test charters, with traceability back to the test basis and a definition of what test oracles should be used, must be provided to the testers.

To enjoy the benefits of reactive strategies while reducing the risks, the best practice is to use a reactive strategy in combination with other, more formal and systematic strategies. This allows the test team to achieve a high level of measurable coverage while at the same time taking advantage of the skills and experience of the test team to find defects that the other strategies often miss.

1.3.7 Consultative Strategies

A *consultative test strategy* is one where the test team asks a few of the key testing stakeholders to select the test conditions that the test team should cover. The test team will often define the specific tests to cover those conditions—which is what makes the strategy consultative—but test coverage is determined by the stakeholders. This differs from an analytical risk-based strategy in that the test team does not build a consensus about the test conditions but simply responds to the conditions provided by the stakeholders.

Consultative test strategies are also called *directed test strategies*, a name that is particularly appropriate when clients direct testing service providers to perform particular tests. If the stakeholders provide the tests themselves, that is also a consultative strategy, though the name *directed strategy* is probably more appropriate.

When properly executed by the test team, a consultative test strategy has the benefit of providing the consulted stakeholders with the exact test coverage they requested. Proper execution means that the test team designs, implements, and executes the right tests, based on the specified conditions. This assumption actually applies regardless of the test strategy because the failure to test the test conditions identified by the test strategy is a well-known breakdown in testing.

The benefit of consultative testing is realized only when the stakeholders ask for the right areas of test coverage. The accuracy of the stakeholders' requested test conditions is a critical success factor. If the stakeholders do not know what conditions should be tested, the depth of testing required for each condition, and the order in which to cover each condition, the test team may do exactly what was asked but not what is needed.

For consultative test strategies to succeed, the following risks must be managed:

- When two or more stakeholders are consulted, they may have conflicting opinions about what should be tested, in what order, and to what depth. This places the test team in a bind that it will find difficult to resolve, especially since consultative strategies often occur in situations in which the test team is disempowered relative to the stakeholders.
- Even if the stakeholders agree about the test conditions, they might hold conflicting expectations about what testing can accomplish. While not a problem unique to consultative strategies, it is particularly acute in such situations.

> **ISTQB Glossary**
>
> **regression-averse test strategy:** Testing using various techniques to manage the risk of regression—e.g., by designing reusable testware and by extensive automation of testing at one or more test levels.

- As mentioned earlier, if the stakeholders provide an incorrect definition of the test conditions to cover, the test effort will be misdirected. Many implementations of consultative strategies do not include a way of self-checking after the analysis phase (where the test conditions are provided to the test team).
- If some of the key stakeholders are not consulted, the neglected stakeholders might disparage and even disrupt the test effort. Trying to enlist the support of these disgruntled stakeholders after the fact is generally harder than including them beforehand.

To mitigate some of these risks, some test teams blend a consultative strategy with other test strategies. This blending will tend to reduce coverage gaps. However, in the case of testing services providers, it is often difficult to use other strategies.

1.3.8 Regression-Averse and Test Automation Strategies

The last of our list of common test strategies are the regression-averse and test automation strategies. These involve various techniques to mitigate a particular risk to the quality of the system—namely, the possibility that existing features of the system will regress or cease to work as well as they currently do. The most effective and efficient technique for managing regression risk is the extensive automation of existing tests. This automation can and ideally should occur at multiple test levels. Testing through application programming interfaces (APIs) at the unit test and component integration test level often prove easier to create and maintain compared with the system test and system integration test levels. However, many defects cannot be detected at these levels, so some degree of regression risk mitigation at the system and system integration levels is necessary.

Sequential models, such as the V-model, tend to have relatively stable code bases once system testing begins. The regression risks are relatively low and are focused on those features already delivered to customers. However, regression risk management is critical for iterative lifecycles. In such lifecycles, the existing code base, with a stable, tested set of features, is repeatedly modified and new code is added. In Agile lifecycles, there is a need for regression testing that is not only thorough but also very quick. The test team should work closely with developers to ensure the design of testable software and to develop a maintainable, multilevel approach to the automation architecture and the automated test scripts.

If properly carried out, a regression-averse test strategy has the benefit of reducing the risk of regression in key feature areas without excessively impeding the release of new versions of the system or product. Because complete regression risk mitigation is not possible in a finite period of time, proper execution of this test strategy implies reaching an agreement on how much regression risk mitigation is required to make people comfortable.

A critical success factor for regression-averse strategies is successful test automation. Manual regression testing of all but the simplest systems is too time-consuming, tedious, and error prone to be effective and efficient. Successful test automation implementation involves the ability to create, execute, and maintain a large set of automated tests.

For regression-averse test strategies, especially automation-based strategies, to succeed, the following risks must be managed:

- Depending on the interface being tested, the test team might find that suitable automated test execution tools are insufficient or even nonexistent. This is especially true at the system and system integration test levels, when testing using a graphical user interface other than Windows or via a browser.
- In some cases, testers find that tools are available but that automation of tests is not an efficient solution. Wide-ranging system test and system integration test automation through a graphical user interface can prove difficult, particularly if the features and interface are changing rapidly (requiring significant maintenance and revision of existing scripts), if tests require human intervention to keep them running, or if there is no way to automate the comparison of actual and expected results.
- Test automation, the best technique for mitigating regression risk, is a very complex endeavor, in spite of the efforts of the last 20 years to make it simpler. Anecdotal evidence indicates that about half of all test automation efforts fail, often because these efforts are undertaken by people with insufficient skills. We have seen situations in which people with no experience

in testing, not to mention test automation, were placed in senior positions in test automation efforts, resulting in a sad but predictable failure. As with automated performance and reliability testing, mentioned earlier, five or more years of experience with test automation is required to achieve expertise, and at least one person with such expertise should be included in any automated testing effort.

- While regression is a significant risk for software, there are other quality risks to consider. One problem that can occur is that the test team becomes overly fixated on regression testing and automating the regression tests. This results in stable existing features but poorly tested new features. This can be very dangerous for test teams in organizations that rely on aggressive release schedules of highly touted new features because testing will be misaligned with the overall corporate strategy for software.

- If the scope, technology, or features for the product are constantly changing, it is difficult to predict what tests will be needed in the long term. Extensive investments in automated testing for features that are dropped from the project or retired from the application reduce the efficiency of testing, especially when other areas that remain unchanged are not tested. The lack of a clear road map for the product's features or technology is a key reason for test automation failure.

In spite of the risks and challenges, most test teams should consider at least some type of regression-averse test strategy as part of their overall test strategy blend. Test stakeholders will tend to demand that currently working features continue to work in subsequent releases; regression failures are generally seen as unacceptable.[13]

1.3.9 Developing a Workable Test Strategy

In the previous sections, we have surveyed a variety of test strategies. All of these strategies have succeeded in certain test situations, and all have also failed when misapplied. One of the most common test strategy failures occurs when a single strategy is selected, especially under the misapprehension that it and the strategies not selected represent mutually exclusive "schools" of thought.

---

13 Dorothy Graham and Mark Fewster's book *Software Test Automation* is a valuable resource for those trying to design, implement, execute, and maintain automated tests.

Even worse occurs when a single strategy is selected and that strategy is inapt for the testing needs of the test stakeholders and test team. Even the perfect execution of the wrong strategy will result in the failure of the test team. That error is sometimes fatally compounded when the strategy continues to be applied in the face of evidence of its inadequacy. An expert test manager must be able to recognize when a test strategy has failed. Further, he or she must be able to identify reasons a strategy might have failed.

To avoid these failures, the expert test manager must be able to analyze the actual needs of the test team and test stakeholders. They must discard the dogma which says that one must choose between competing schools of testing methodologies and instead remain open to the use of all applicable test strategies, based on a cold-eyed evaluation of the strategies, their benefits, and which ones are most likely to work. The best test strategy is often a blend of two, three, or more of the canonical test strategies discussed earlier. In addition, other, less frequently observed test strategies exist, and the test manager should consider those as well.

Part of selecting the right test strategy involves considering the skills and resources available to the test team specifically and the organization in general. For example, selecting an analytical requirements-based testing strategy in an organization that does not write requirements specifications is a recipe for failure. The level of formality of the test strategy can vary as well, and implementing an overly formal test strategy in an organization that is highly informal is another common cause of test strategy failure. Successful test strategies are aligned not only with the needs of the organization but also with the practical realities.

Having selected test strategies and blended them into a coherent test approach, the test manager must be able to explain the benefits of this strategy to key testing stakeholders. While Bismarck's famous saying that those who enjoy sausage and respect the law should never watch either being made is a clever one, it does not apply to testing. Test stakeholders need not understand all the details of what we do, but they should understand how we select what to test, the general set of activities involved in testing, and most important, how they will benefit.

1.4   Alignment of Test Policy and Test Strategy with the Organization

---

Learning objectives

LO 2.4.1   (K6) Define, describe, evaluate, and improve the test policy and strategy(ies) both long- and short-term for a company, organization and/or a test team, including process and organization of test, people, tools, system, and techniques.

So far in this chapter, we've discussed the use of a test policy to document overall test objectives, metrics, and goals for those metrics and the use of a test strategy to document how the test team will achieve those objectives in measurable fashion. However, producing these documents is not enough. For the test policy and the test strategy to succeed, the policy and strategy must be practical, complete, and consistent. What does this mean?

1.4.1   Practical, Complete, and Consistent Test Policies and Strategies

Practical test policies and strategies are those that can actually be carried out. As mentioned earlier, the documents that describe them are not aspirational documents. If you write these documents and then do not put them into action, or must continuously compromise them to proceed with your testing work, they are not practical. At best, these documents are irrelevant, but in fact, such documents are often worse than irrelevant. Making statements concerning what testing is about and how it should be done but that have no relationship to daily operational realities can distract testers and other stakeholders.

In writing test policies and strategies, do not focus on what *should* happen. Focus on what *can* happen. The gap between *should* and *can* is something to discuss, indeed, but that discussion should happen upward in the organization. If you feel that project realities constrain testing, talk to your managers about that problem. That conversation is best held after you have established a solid record of accomplishing what can be done. For example, if you are achieving your goals, as established in the test policy, and management asks you how to set those goals higher, that provides an ideal opening for the discussion.

It's also important to remember that different strategies can apply to different test levels. You might use a strategy of risk-based testing, requirements-based testing, reactive testing, and model-based performance and reliability testing for system testing while working with the development manager to develop a comprehensive, integrated strategy and technology of test automation that works at both the unit test and the system test level. Know what will actually work in your organization, and focus on achieving the best possible result given those realities.

Complete test policies and strategies address the important elements for such work products. In the preceding sections, we gave general guidelines about the content of both documents. There might be additional elements needed in these documents in your organization, but be careful about incorporating excessive or irrelevant details. You should consider the audience and their information needs.

Completeness also implies that the documents are separate, non-overlapping, and targeted. The test policy is about what testing does. The audience for this document does not necessarily need to know the details of how testing accomplishes the policy. The test strategy is about how testing does that, in a general way that applies across projects. The audience for this document does need to know the details.

Consistent test policy and strategies are described in documents that reinforce and do not contradict each other. You should be able to show the relationship between each activity in the test strategy and each objective defined in the test policy. If you define an objective in the test policy document and yet have no activity in the test strategy document to accomplish that objective, how confident can you be that the objective will be accomplished? Similarly, if you define an activity in the test strategy document that does not relate to an objective in the test policy document, how can you explain why that activity should take place?

Consistency also means that the test policy and strategy make sense in context. Is each objective, metric, and goal in the policy consistent with the objectives established for the project, process, product, and organization? Is each activity in the strategy consistent with the activities that will occur in the project and organization? If the answer is 'no' in either case, you will probably find yourself and your test team in effect swimming against the tide, you and your stakeholders working at cross-purposes.

This issue of cross-functional consistency brings us back to the practicality issue. It is not practical to attempt to implement objectives or activities that will result in conflicts with your colleagues. Not only will your efficiency and effectiveness suffer as you try to do things that don't fit with your colleagues' vision of what should occur, but you and your team will gain a reputation for being difficult and disconnected from project and organizational realities. If you feel that contextual realities pose an obstacle to doing what the test team needs to do, this is again a conversation to have with your managers, and this conversation is best held after you have established a solid record of success, accomplishing what can be done in the context in which you are operating.

1.4.2 Successful Test Policies and Test Strategies

So, what constitutes success? This brings us back to the objectives in the test policy. If the stakeholders tell you what constitutes success and you then achieve those goals, you are a success. The objectives defined in the test policy say what success means to them. The metrics for effectiveness, efficiency, and satisfaction say how you will measure success. The goals for the metrics say what constitutes success. You should be able to evaluate the metrics on a regular basis and, in an appropriate way, demonstrate the value you and your team deliver.

Remember, however, that success is not a static thing. As the saying goes, "What have you done for me lately?," you must maintain a record of success to be seen as a success. Occasionally falling a bit short of a goal is not necessarily a disaster, but you should never assume that a past record of success immunizes you and your team against situations in which you have indeed messed up.

You should also remember that what was good enough yesterday is not necessarily good enough tomorrow. Free-market competition, as Peter Schumpeter famously said, involves creative destruction, which means that businesses advance themselves by creating new ways of doing things better, thus destroying old ways of doing things—or their competitors will destroy them. Even organizations in noncompetitive endeavors, such as government agencies, adopt best practices from industry and hold themselves to standards set by competitive business.[14]

---

14   This is not always a good thing and can create situations in which the expert test manager must educate their managers about differences in context. Rex remembers once being asked by a large US government agency, in all seriousness, how they could "test like Google." Given that this government agency was in the business of storing and processing terabytes of taxpayer data that needed the highest levels of integrity and quality over periods of human lifetimes, the question was not whether they could test like Google but whether Google's test policies and strategies had any applicability to their agency.

So, you need to take your successes and compound them. Look at your objectives and ask yourself, "What else can we accomplish, how else can we deliver value to the organization?" Look at your metrics and ask yourself, "How can we do better?" The policy and strategy should evolve to reflect both the short term and long term. Where do you need to be on the next project? What do you need to do in the next two years? The next five years?

These questions should consider a number of perspectives. For example, where is the software engineering process going, and how are organizational realities changing? Back in the early 2000s, just as the Y2K scramble was winding down, how many of us as test professionals honestly assessed what the trend toward Agile lifecycles (at least in some contexts) would mean for us? As another example, how many of us understood how outsourcing, and its cousins cloud computing and open-source software, would have an impact on testing? Those who did ponder these questions are better positioned to succeed now. The available market of people, with different skills and talents, will continue to evolve. Tools will also evolve. Systems and technologies evolve, often at startling speed. The set of test techniques available to us grows. So to succeed in the long term, our policies and strategies must evolve too.

1.4.3 Achieving Alignment

As explained throughout this chapter, testing policies and strategies need to be determined according to the testing objectives for the key stakeholders, which in turn need to be appropriate for the organization. We have seen policies and strategies work very well for some organizations, while the same policies and strategies work poorly or even not at all in other organizations. Across different organizations, the stakeholders can legitimately have different testing objectives. These differences must lead to different test policies and strategies if the test group is to succeed.

For example, some of our clients are in defense industries, where government agencies rely on defense contractors to develop and deliver systems to support and enable warfighters. While we believe that these contractors have the best interests of the taxpayers and their militaries in mind, it is also the case that the contractors have as a primary objective that of maximizing profits, just as all companies do. This implies a need for independent verification and validation on these projects, where an independent test team—employed by the government rather than the contractor—is asked to check and in some cases reject the system delivered by the contractor. However, in private industry, we have seen situations where test groups, setting themselves up as such "quality cops," made themselves into very unpopular obstacles in the organization, often resulting in the dissolution of the group.

Furthermore, in some cases, even policies and strategies that work well in part of an organization do not work well in other parts of that organization, or even within particular projects. For example, consider an organization that makes complex, regulated, safety-critical systems. For the most part, this organization needs a test policy that ensures the highest levels of quality and rigor throughout the lifecycle, and highly rigorous, formal, auditable strategies must be employed to achieve appropriate objectives for such an organization. However, if the organization uses a corporate website to market these products, the standards need not be so high for the program that develops and maintains that site.

How does the expert test manager deal with this variability? First, as stressed in this chapter, you need to do your homework. Talk to stakeholders. Understand their objectives. Develop solid metrics for effectiveness, efficiency, and elegance. Set realistic goals. Think carefully about the proper mix of strategies to achieve those goals. Then, compare your actual performance against the targets. If you fall short, focus on how to make improvements, and avoid making excuses.

The preceding paragraph is a difficult prescription, but an expert test manager is resolute in following it to success. You might not get it right the first time, but with diligence and perseverance, you'll align your test policy, test strategy, and test team with the needs of the organization. Learn to recognize discrepancies between what is really needed and what you test, how you test, and the skills people bring to testing. Once you recognize these discrepancies, formulate plans for improvement. Understand the realities and constraints of your organization so that you can align the test policy, test strategy, and the organization. The result will be a testing group that minimizes risks and maximizes benefits.[15]

That said, remember Deming's rule that quality is achieved through constancy of purpose.[16] While adapting to the evolving needs of projects, programs, and the organization is a best practice, you are not well served by allowing chaotic diversity in your testing teams or spastic reactivity in your approach.

---

15   You can find more information about this in Chapter 2, written by Rex Black, of *Beautiful Testing: Leading Professionals Reveal How They Improve Software (Theory in Practice)*, as well as the ISTQB's Expert in Improving the Testing Process.

16   See *The Deming Management Method*, by Mary Walton and W. Edwards Deming.

Once you have arrived at a policy and strategy that work well, be conservative in your philosophy of change. Too much change and diversity in your strategy will render your metrics ineffective, and thus it will be impossible to determine whether you are succeeding. Absent truly discontinuous change in the needs and business of the organization, you should strive for consistency and constancy, with a slow evolution over time as needs and realities evolve. Define your test strategy in a way that responds well to such a slow evolution.[17]

1.5   Sample Exam Questions

In the following section, you will find sample questions that cover the learning objectives for this chapter. All K5 and K6 learning objectives are covered with one or more essay questions, while each K2, K3, and K4 learning objective is covered with a single multiple-choice question. This mirrors the organization of the actual ISTQB exam. The number of the covered learning objective(s) is provided for each question, to aid in traceability. The learning objective number will not be provided on the actual exam.

The content of all of your responses to essay questions will be marked in terms of the accuracy, completeness, and relevance of the ideas expressed. The form of your answer will be evaluated in terms of clarity, organization, correct mechanics (spelling, punctuation, grammar, capitalization), and legibility.

Question 1

LO 2.2.1

Assume that you are working for an organization that is maintaining an operating system that supports mission-critical applications on its customers' mainframe computers. The number of new features introduced in a year is small, but the existing feature set is quite large and relied upon by customers to ensure data center reliability. Which of the following mission statements is best for the test team?

---

17   Currently, the ISTQB program and books based on it are the best sources for information about test policies and strategies. There is an upcoming standard, ISO IEC 29119 (part 3), that will discuss processes for defining test policies, the test strategies, and test management. Once released, this standard may be a useful resource, but keep in mind that standards documents do not always do a particularly good job of explaining the contextual subtleties of applying and tailoring a standard in a particular situation.

B. To ensure the removal of any defects that would affect the availability and reliability of our systems.

C. To detect the bugs present in any new release of our software, especially those present in new features of the operating system.

D. To participate in all phases of the software engineering process in order to maximize defect removal prior to release.

E. To help deliver software that continues to operate with high availability and long mean time between failure.

Question 2

LO 2.2.3

Assume that a major objective of testing is to detect defects, especially important defects that will affect customer satisfaction. Consider the following statements.

Which THREE of the following options is true?

A. You can measure efficiency for this objective by calculating the cost per requirement covered by testing.

B. You can measure efficiency for this objective by calculating the cost of quality associated with internal and external failure.

C. You can measure effectiveness for this objective by calculating the cost of quality associated with internal and external failure.

D. You can measure effectiveness for this objective by calculating the percentage of customer-impacting defects found by testing.

E. You can measure satisfaction for this objective by surveying stakeholders about their confidence in test coverage prior to release.

F. You can measure efficiency for this objective by calculating the percentage of regression tests that are automated.

G. You can measure effectiveness for this objective by calculating the percentage of defects found by testing.

Question 3

LO 2.3.1

Assume you are working as a test manager on a small project without written requirements specification but with generous access to business and technical stakeholders. You have some testers on your team who have experience with the business problem to be solved by the software as well as some testers with experience with the technology of implementation.

Consider the following test strategies:

I. Risk-based testing
II. Requirements-based testing
III. Reactive testing
IV. Directed testing
V. Model-based testing
VI. Automated testing

Based solely on the information given above, which of the following statements is true?

A. Strategies I and III will be effective on this project.
B. All these strategies will be effective on this project.
C. Strategies II and VI will be effective on this project.
D. Strategies IV and V will be effective on this project.

Question 4

LO 2.3.2

Assume you are working as a test manager on a program to build an e-commerce system that sells clothing. The business analysts have defined business requirements by working with the marketing team. These requirements are delivered to the test team, and the business analysts and marketing staff are available to the test team. The project follows an iterative lifecycle model. The developers list the test conditions they believe the testers should test in each iteration. Due to time constraints, your team follows a blended reactive and directed test strategy (following the developers' test conditions). After the first major release of the system into production, customers find an unacceptably large number of defects that were not detected during testing.

Based entirely on information given above, which of the following statements best identifies the cause of this breakdown in the test strategy?

A. The test conditions given by the developers were incorrect.
B. The test strategy was not executed by competent testers.
C. The test strategy did not include analytical elements.
D. An iterative lifecycle inherently leads to poor-quality software.

Scenario 1: The Job Has Its Ups and Downs

You accept a job as the software test director for an organization that makes escalators and elevators. Consider the following excerpt from the Test Objectives section of the existing test policy document:

Testing has the following objectives:

1. Detect software and integrated hardware/software defects, especially those defects that would affect customer safety.
2. Reduce risks to system quality to an acceptable level prior to release.

The test group measures the effectiveness and efficiency with which it achieves these objectives, works with executive management to set goals for these measures, and receives merit raises based on meeting or exceeding those goals.

Assume that this organization is subject to external audits for both hardware and software elements of the system. Hardware testing is performed by another group in your organization, but your group performs hardware-software integration testing on the systems.

Question 5

LO 2.2.2, LO 2.3.3, and LO 2.4.1

Consider the scenario given above. Answer the following questions:

Part 1. Which test strategies, listed in the Expert Test Manager syllabus, are relevant to the test objectives given? Explain why.
Part 2. Evaluate the given test objectives and the remuneration policy. Are these objectives adequate given the organization's business? Consider long-term effects.
Part 3. If you consider the test objectives and remuneration policy inadequate, describe the additional objectives that should be present and how company remuneration policies can best incentivize the achievement of those objectives?

2 Managing the Test Team

Keywords: Myers-Briggs Type Indicator (MBTI), RACI matrix, SMART goal methodology, test architect

2.1 Introduction

Learning objectives

No learning objectives for this section.

In the previous chapter, we talked about defining what you are trying to accomplish (test objectives), how you will go about it (test strategy), and how you will measure success (test metrics and goals). In this chapter, we turn to an essential ingredient in successful testing: managing the people doing the testing work.

To be successful as a test manager, you must be able to build a test group, develop the skills of the people in that group, and lead it toward the objectives. You may have a single group of individual testers or a collection of two or more test teams, each run by a test lead or test manager who reports to you. The group may consist of people working at a single office, people working at multiple locations, or people working many miles and time zones away. There are many variations in the way test groups are organized, and an expert test manager should be able to manage any of those approaches.

In some organizations—especially larger ones—you might have a human resources (HR) department or personnel office dedicated to supporting staffing issues. Such a department would typically handle employment agreements and benefits packages. It might also provide support for employees and managers in terms of interviewing, conflict mediation, and when necessary, employee lay-offs and termination. In some cases, there is not an actual department but just one or two people who handle these tasks.

In this chapter, we'll assume that such a department does exist and that you will work with them on many of the activities covered here. If there is no department or person responsible for this role in your organization, then in some cases, you'll need to work with your management colleagues and company legal staff (if applicable). In other cases, you'll be on your own, though we hope you have some senior managers and some precedents to guide you.

2.2   Building the Test Team

Learning objectives

LO 3.2.1 (K5) For a given job opening, evaluate a set of résumés, and determine the best candidate.

LO 3.2.2 (K6) For a given job opening, devise an appropriate and effective approach to interviewing candidates, and conduct the interview.

LO 3.2.3 (K3) Outline the major points of a training program for new people.

LO 3.2.4 (K2) List considerations that must be made when terminating an employee or contractor.

It is a management aphorism that smart managers surround themselves with a team that consists of people smarter than they are. The "smarter than they are" part might be an exaggeration, but it is certainly true that only bad managers deliberately hire sycophants and underachievers so that they can enjoy flattery and look good by comparison. Smart managers know that hiring mistakes such as these—hiring the toady, the incompetent, the hostile, the lazy, and the downright evil—will damage the productivity and morale of your group. In some cases, such a mistake can cost the organization a lot of money, as companies have discovered when employees abuse their position to steal, avenge themselves on coworkers, or throw a monkey wrench into the organization itself.[1]

So, we can state an ironclad rule for managers here: Hire the right people. While the hiring process should involve multiple people, if you are a test manager hiring a tester or another test manager, the decision ultimately comes down to you. The decision whether to hire someone is among the

---

1   We could give references to a few news stories or articles here, but you can certainly find ample recent references by scanning the news. This kind of behavior occurs regularly.

most important decisions you will make as a manager. Make every effort to do it right.

Hiring the right people involves the following steps:

- Have a good process for evaluating and hiring candidates.
- Clearly define the position for which you're hiring.
- Understand the skills a person will need to have to fill that position.
- Together with other people, carry out effective interviews that definitively sort candidates from least qualified to best qualified.

If your human resources department offers training or support for hiring and interviewing, you should take advantage of that.[2]

In many organizations, strict rules exist about how the hiring process must work. These rules are usually there for a good reason—e.g., obeying the law, avoiding a lawsuit for discrimination, etc.—and so you should study them carefully and adhere scrupulously, if they apply. Check with your human resources staff. Ask them to explain the rules and process thoroughly, including whatever documentation is required throughout the process. These rules are perhaps most commonly violated in the résumé selection and interview processes, so be careful.

Building the right test group doesn't end with hiring the right people. The new people must be assimilated into the group and melded together with the existing staff into an effective team. People also leave teams, in some cases because of contractual reasons. In other unfortunate cases, some of the staff—hopefully people you inherited rather than hired—must be terminated. An expert test manager must be able to handle all of these activities, and we'll discuss these activities further as this chapter continues.

---

2   Other good resources are Johanna Rothman and Gerald M. Weinberg's book *Hiring The Best Knowledge Workers, Techies & Nerds* and Judy McKay's book *Managing the Test People: A Guide to Practical Technical Management.*

2.2.1 Job Descriptions

A job description, obviously enough, is a document (or web page or wiki page or some other human-readable item) that describes the job and, by implication, the ideal person to do it. It should address the following questions:

- What tasks and responsibilities will the successful candidate have?
- What kind of experience, and how much experience, is required?
- What specific skills will the successful candidate need to have?
- What additional skills would be preferable for a candidate to have?
- What is the salary range for the position, including base salary and bonuses if applicable?
- Are there specific training, education, certification, security clearances, or licenses required?

The best job descriptions often include other relevant details, such as the work hours; the dress code; a polite notice that background checks or drug tests apply (if they do); what perks like telecommuting, a company gym, or other benefits the job brings; whether travel is required and, if so, how frequently; what the career path is for the position; when should the candidate plan to start and, if applicable, whether the position has a predefined end date (e.g., when program funding will end). If you have an HR department, there is probably a template and guidelines for job descriptions, and you should comply with those. You can find examples of good (and bad) job descriptions on Internet recruiting sites such as Dice.com and Monster.com.

If you're writing your first job description, spend some time to study the art form before slapping together a bad one. You'll miss out on good applicants and probably have to sort through a lot of bad applicants if your job description is poorly done.

The job description should be concise, clear, and free from jargon because the people soliciting candidates and screening their résumés may be unfamiliar with testing. That said, be sure to be sufficiently specific and precise so that you and the candidates can determine whether a fit exists. The job description should not dissuade the qualified from applying, nor should it encourage the unqualified to apply. This also means that you should be clear about which qualifications are required (a candidate without these qualifications will not even be considered) and which qualifications are desirable (a candidate with these qualifications has an edge in the hiring decision).

Depending on the size of the test group and the way in which it's organized, you might have specialized test positions, each with its own job description. We'll return to this topic of team specialization a bit later in this chapter.

Some job descriptions fit into a sequence, as someone moves up their career path. For example, someone might join as an entry-level tester and, after some time, apply for a promotion when a senior position opens up in the testing team. You should consider this as you write your job descriptions. You don't want to create a situation in which promotion from the inside is difficult or impossible because the senior positions have requirements that junior people would be unlikely to gain during their work in your group. One example would be requiring only a high school degree for entry-level positions but then requiring a college degree in computer science to advance to any testing position beyond the entry level. You might be better off simply requiring the college degree from everyone, even the junior testers, to avoid situations in which people get stuck.

All too many companies take the job description for another position and use it as the basis for the tester job description, but this is a worst practice we recommend you avoid. For example, it's common for software sales technology companies to use the entry-level programmer job description and glue on some language about testing. IT organizations (which build software used inside their company or agency) often make a similar mistake, which is taking a technical support, business analyst, or senior user job description and gluing language about testing on it. While technology and business domain knowledge is important for testers, a tester is more than a modified programmer, analyst, or user.

Please note that when we're talking about job descriptions here, we are not referring to the typical job postings you'd find in a newspaper or in a technology magazine. Most of these are too terse, due to the limitations of space, to serve as a good model for a job description. Frequently, those job postings are distilled from the large job description. If someone other than you does that distilling, make sure you review the job posting before it gets posted. If key points are missed (or mangled), you will again face a situation in which you don't attract candidates that you want and, possibly, do attract candidates that you don't want.

Once the job description is written, the job posting should be properly distilled and submitted to the appropriate locations. This would include job bulletin boards and Internet recruiting sites, corporate employment sites, newspapers or industry magazines, and other appropriate media. The idea is to attract qualified candidates to start the hiring process.

2.2.2 Résumés

Given that you wrote the job description and posting properly—and depending on the local job market—the result will be an incoming stream of résumés or curricula vitae (CVs), most of which will be from qualified candidates. In some organizations, the human resources staff filters these incoming résumés, eliminating people who are clearly unqualified. Of course, there are limits to how well they can do this, given that they are not subject-matter experts. You should expect to receive some number of unqualified candidate résumés because otherwise the human resources staff would be filtering out qualified candidates. If there is no human resources assistance available, you will need to filter the résumés yourself or delegate that task to someone on your staff.

So, how should you review résumés? What do you look for? Here are some ideas:

- Does the candidate have the required skills and experience? You should match these against the job description and eliminate candidates that don't match. People tend to embellish their skills and experience, so be sure to note, on any résumés you retain, which skills and experience areas you want to check in the interview.
- If applicable, does the candidate have the required or preferred education and certifications, such as a college degree or the ISTQB Certified Tester Foundation Level certification? If they do claim such educational degrees or certifications, ask the candidate to provide proof prior to the interview process. For some reason, lying about these types of qualifications is amazingly common.
- Is the candidate's salary history and requirements consistent with what you can offer? Asking someone to take a huge pay cut, even if they have been out of work for a while, is a source of eventual disgruntlement.
- Is the résumé organized and easy to read? Remember, testing typically involves a lot of written communication, and the candidate's written communication skills are on display in their résumé.
- Are there spelling or grammar errors on the résumé? Testing also involves attention to detail. Not rereading the résumé, forgetting to use built-in spell and grammar checkers, or worse yet, ignoring unsolicited warnings from

the word processor indicates a level of sloppiness that you might want to avoid associating with your test team. It's not unusual for the test manager to eliminate candidates with such mistakes on their résumés for exactly this reason.

Remember to retain résumés for those who meet the required credentials. If you have desirable but not required credentials included in the job posting, those should not be used to eliminate candidates. The additional credentials should be used to create an "A-list" of people you want to interview first.

2.2.3 Interviewing

A good interview process is much the same whether you are hiring a tester, business analyst, or developer. It has the following attributes:

- **Multiple rounds of interviews.** A candidate should not be interviewed by a single person, who then decides without any input from others. Instead, the candidate should go through a multistage interview process.
- **A mixed interview team.** A candidate should be interviewed by people at different levels in the organization and by people outside of testing who are testing stakeholders.
- **An understood interview process.** The process progresses clearly through a set of steps, each step designed to efficiently remove those candidates who would not be suitable hires, until the final candidates are the best fit for the position.

During the interview, the interviewer should explore whether the candidate displays the appropriate strengths for a testing position:

- **Good problem-solving skills.** Given a typical problem that the candidate would face daily, can they solve it?
- **Critical thinking skills.** Given a realistic work scenario, can the candidate recognize the essential elements, analyze them, select useful paths forward, reject dead ends, and be able to explain the entire path of thinking that lead to their conclusions?
- **Good written and verbal communication skills.** As mentioned, the ability to explain facts, observations, and directions in written and verbal form is essential for testers. Can the candidate be easily understood in the interview? Can they write acceptable defect reports and test cases?

- **A strong ability to work within a team.** Hiring someone who is otherwise perfectly qualified but disrupts morale and cohesion within your test group is a disastrous mistake. Does the candidate seem like a person who will enjoy working with your existing team, and will your existing team enjoy working with the candidate?
- **A curious nature.** Does the candidate show signs that they would investigate anomalous situations and use good judgment in how far to take those investigations?
- **Technical and business domain knowledge.** Does the candidate know enough about the underlying technology behind the system under test, given the type of testing they will do? Does the candidate know enough about the business problem solved by the system under test, given the type of testing they will do?
- **The appropriate testing skills.** Does the candidate have appropriate test design skills, test automation skills, test management skills, and so on, given the position they are interviewing for?
- **The experience and background needed for the position.** Beyond these specific qualifications, are there other qualifications identified in the job description that the candidate must have, and does the candidate have them?

The exploration of the candidate's strengths and weakness through the interview consists, naturally enough, of asking the candidate questions, considering their responses, and perhaps pursuing a line of questioning related to their responses before moving on to the next topic. Also, remember that the candidate is also interviewing you and your organization, so make certain to show your best self and be cordial, respectful, and prepared.

The ISTQB Expert Test Manager syllabus includes a number of very useful questions to keep in mind as you explore these strengths and weaknesses. The questions will help you assess the interviewees' statements during the interview. They fall into various categories, and various interview questions can address these categories. In Table 2-1, we have taken this material, categorized and reformatted it, and provided sample interview questions.

Table 2-1 Considerations for Interviewing Testers

Category	Example Interview Question(s)	Key Response Considerations
Attitude	What do you enjoy about working as a tester?	Does this person have the right attitude for the job and for the organization? Will the person be a good fit for the group? Will the person be effective in the job? Does (s)he take the role of testing seriously? Will (s)he maintain a positive attitude even when schedules get tough?
Presentation	For a recent bug report that you filed and had to discuss with others on the project team, what information did you include and how did you explain the report to people?	Does this person present themselves as a confident and knowledgeable individual without overstating their capabilities? Will the person know when to stand up for their work? Will the person be able to admit when they are wrong and handle the situation in a mature manner? If needed, can this person be sent to a project meeting to represent the interests of the test team?
Organization	How do you decide how much time to spend writing a test case or researching a bug before reporting it? How do you keep track of the different tasks you have to do as a tester, including when you are interrupted during a task?	Does this person have the organizational skills required for the job? Can the person work in an environment that has frequent interruptions? If interrupted, will the person be able to return to their original tasks with minimal downtime? If they find a defect, will they remember to return to the test they were running and complete it?
Interpersonal	When was the last time your test results caused controversy on a project? How did you handle it, including working with developers and other project team members to explain the results?	Does the person exhibit the maturity needed in the role? Do they have the leadership potential the position requires? Can they deal effectively with interpersonal issues that may arise? Does the person have the capacity to deal with others empathetically? Can they present a defect to a developer without causing offense? Can they see both sides of an argument? When prioritizing a defect, can they weigh multiple factors that affect the priority rating?

Table 2-1 is not an exhaustive list, but it should help you start creating interview questions as you plan your interview process.[3]

---

3   Other good sources for interview questions include Judy McKay's book *Managing the Testing People: A Guide to Practical Technical Management* and Rex Black's book *Managing the Testing Process: Practical Tools and Techniques for Managing Hardware and Software Testing.*

Your planning should also include the use of different types of interviews. In Table 2-2, we've organized the types listed in the syllabus and the pros, cons, and our own opinions for each type.

Table 2-2   *Interview Types*

Type	Description	Pros, Cons, and Our Opinion
Telephone screens	One or more of the other interview types discussed in this table, but over the phone.	Pros: A quick first interview, which allows a check of verbal skills. A cheap way to screen out unqualified candidates, especially if you might be considering flying people in for interviews. Cons: The nonverbal cues that interviewees give are not visible over the phone. Our opinion: It's an essential first step but should almost never be used as the only step.
Group and panel interviews	Multiple people interviewing the candidate at one time.	Pros: Given the stressful nature of such an interview, it shows how the candidate responds to tricky situations such as the delivery of bad test results to the project team. Cons: Some people aren't very good at thinking on their feet, and the position you're hiring for might not require this skill. Our opinion: Use this for test leads and test managers, but skip it for hiring individual testers unless you are using a matrix organization—e.g., where testers work embedded in Agile teams.
Behavioral questions	Asking about how candidates have behaved in past circumstances.	Pros: When done properly, such questions give you a good feel for what it will be like to work with someone. Cons: A clever raconteur or charming incompetent can sometimes outfox you on these questions, so be wary of attempts to steer you away from painful realities. Our opinion: These are an essential part of your interview process and will help you avoid dreadful hiring mistakes.
Situational questions	Giving the candidate a real example of a project situation, then asking them how they would have handled it.	Pros: Helps you evaluate how effective the person will be in your test group. Cons: As with behavioral questions, the glib-tongued interviewee might slip through if you're not careful. Our opinion: These are useful as part of a larger set of questions.

Type	Description	Pros, Cons, and Our Opinion
Technical questions	Asking the candidate about test design techniques, coding, scripting, or other technical skills they will need.	Pros: Allows you to explore, at a detailed level, whether the person has the technical qualifications for the job. Cons: Such questions may focus on "book learning" and not take practical application into consideration. Sometimes people ask testers technical questions that draw on skills they won't use in their role, which can result in dropping perfectly qualified candidates from consideration. Our opinion: These are also essential types of questions, but they must be asked by someone with more technical skill than the position requires (otherwise the interview won't go deeply enough into the candidate's skills).
Puzzle solving	Presenting the candidate with a brainteaser puzzle to evaluate their problem-solving skills and ability to think quickly.	Pros: Helpful in assessing critical thinking skills and creativity. By watching and listening to a candidate think through a problem or puzzle, you may gain insight into how they will handle new and different testing challenges. Cons: Some candidates may not perform well under the pressure of an interview situation. Therefore, even if they have strong problem-solving skills, these traits may not be demonstrated fully. It's also possible that some people who do really well on these types of interview questions (which are basically IQ tests) will make significant mistakes in other areas, so there is a real risk in overweighting these questions. Our opinion: Rex feels that there usually is very little demonstrable connection between these puzzles and the work someone will do on a daily basis, so he is reluctant to use them. Some people, however, find that how a candidate handles a puzzle or problem scenario may be indicative of how they may think through and handle difficult or unfamiliar situations on the job.

Type	Description	Pros, Cons, and Our Opinion
Specialized questions	Asking questions about the specific business domain, the type of testing to be done, or the underlying technology.	Pros: Checks for knowledge the tester will need to do experience-based testing of the application, based on the industry. Cons: Excessively applied when people overestimate the unique elements of their situation (the "we're different" mindset). Our opinion: If parochialism is avoided, these can be essential for software security testers, highly regulated industries, and other situations in which it would take too long for someone to learn on the job.
Team dynamics	Asking questions to explore how the candidate would fit and will work with the rest of the test team. Also, allowing the test team to participate in the interview.	Pros: Very helpful to avoid hiring mistakes where the candidate cannot work effectively with some people on the test team, especially the "team participation" elements. For example, if the test manager is a man, he might not detect sexist attitudes that women in the test group would. Cons: If you have one or more people on the team who are relentlessly negative about new or different ideas, overemphasis on team dynamics can effectively shut down pollination of new ideas from differently minded outsiders that you might hire. Our opinion: A very important part of the test manager's job is preserving the morale and cohesion of the group, so team dynamics must be a consideration.
Exams	Checking technical knowledge, self-organization capabilities, and the ability to structure a problem. Can also evaluate written communication skills if essay-style questions are included or a verbal exam (question and answer form) is used.	Pros: If the company allows a standardized exam to be given to all candidates for a specific position, it can provide consistent and fair evaluation of candidate skills, assuming the exam is a valid one.[4] Cons: If the exam is invalid, includes areas irrelevant to the person's daily work, is not approved by the organization's human resources department, or somehow gets into legally protected areas, it could create significant problems. Our opinion: Based on our experience with the ISTQB program, while some people complain about exams, we have not encountered any fairer or more objective way to measure certain types of knowledge.

---

4   The question of exam validity is a complex one. Do an Internet search on "psychometrics" to see all the statistical and other issues involved.

While interviews are useful, it's always good to see someone in action, doing what they will actually do in their daily work. This is the idea behind audition interviews, which are called assessments in the Expert Test Manager syllabus. These could take a number of forms, depending on the position for which the candidate has applied:

- **Junior or senior tester:** Provide the candidate with a typical, existing test, written at the same level of detail as the tests the candidate will execute if hired. Have the candidate run the test against the actual system, record their results, and log any anomalies noted. You can make this more challenging by picking a test with subtle anomalies.
- **Junior or senior tester:** Provide the candidate with one or more test conditions. Have the candidate create tests that adequately cover the test conditions.
- **Senior tester:** Provide the candidate with an actual requirements specification or user story from a current or previous project. Have them identify test conditions. Depending on the requirement, have them create a flow chart, state transition diagram, or decision table.
- **Senior tester, test lead, or test manager:** Have the candidate present a topic to the test team (and perhaps to non-testers as well) or discuss some topic with that group. For example, provide the candidate with a typical or challenging test status report, and ask them to role-play presenting that information as the test lead to the project team.

These are just some examples; you can apply this technique to any pertinent and demonstrable skills. After the audition is complete, the work product produced by the candidate, and the way the work product was produced, should be assessed by one or more members of the test team, perhaps in consultation with other staff members who are qualified to judge such work. This should often include a discussion with the candidate to ask them why they decided to approach the work the way they did. Just as we have not encountered any fairer way to measure certain types of knowledge than exams, audition interviews are the fairest way to evaluate certain types of skills.

2.2.4 Selecting the People to Hire

Once you have finished interviewing the candidates, you can make your decision on whom to hire (and whom not to hire). This decision involves evaluating the results of the interviews, of course, as well as any other organizational hiring processes:

- **Reference checks:** This can involve speaking with (or at least emailing) past employers, managers, and colleagues. You have to be careful about these reference checks because you can get into trouble by asking the wrong things. Your HR department should have some tips on how to check references and might even require you to allow them to carry out all reference checks.
- **Background checks:** In cases where past criminal history matters, you might need to do a background check. Again, be careful; there could be legal consequences if background checks are conducted improperly. As with reference checks, the HR department might be able or required to help.
- **Credit checks:** These are similar to background checks and applicable in certain situations. Consult with HR before carrying these out.
- **Verification of legal work status:** This can take the form of getting standard identification information from the candidate and possibly making copies of these documents. Consult with HR.
- **Verification of, or request for, security clearance:** Where applicable, you or the HR department might need to verify someone's security clearance or start the process of applying for a security clearance. Obviously, this latter action would apply only to candidates that you were confident would qualify and had already decided to hire (pending their obtaining a security clearance).

Of course, you might decide to hire none of the candidates. If none of the candidates met the minimum qualifications, then this can be a smarter decision than hiring someone who is unqualified. You can consider using a contractor to fill the need or, if applicable, a testing service provider (see Chapter 3). However, you should remember—during the interviewing process and when selecting the new hires—that your goal is to build and maintain a cohesive and effective team. Are you setting the minimum qualifications too high? Are you looking for the perfect person when what you need are people who will fit into your team in terms of personality and who have the potential to grow into strong contributors? Even if individuals are not perfect, you might have the perfect test team for the job. Different types and levels of experience and knowledge, along with varied viewpoints, can create a team whose whole is greater than the sum of its parts.

2.2.5 Bringing People Into the Team

Even when a new hire is amazingly well qualified, there are sure to be parts of the job he/she doesn't already know. Processes, procedures, tools, and methodologies used to create and manage tests, defect reports, and other work products tend to vary from one organization to another. While immediate immersion is one approach to ramping up new hires (also called "sink or swim"), it's certainly not the best practice.

The best practice is for the test manager to create and deliver some sort of standard training for new hires. At a minimum, this training should cover the following topics:

- Processes and procedures for the test group as well as the larger organization (with the latter elements often provided by the human resources department)
- Tools that the new hire will use within the test department and on the project
- Examples of and standards for work products the new hire will create, such as tests and defect reports

In addition to explanation of these topics, the training should include hands-on demonstrations, discussions with existing test team members, and exercises on selected topics. If multiple people are hired at the same time, they can attend this training together as team-building as well as skills-building exercises.

Consider assigning the test team the task of creating and delivering the new-hire training program. This will promote uniformity in practice and approach across the test team, allow the test team members to share their knowledge with each other, reduce the possibility of deliberate or inadvertent information hoarding by test team members, and motivate the test team by making them key players in defining and promulgating the "way things are done around here." If your organization tends to hire a lot of testers, it might make sense to create (or to have created) an e-learning course that can be used (often supplemented by some live training elements).

The new-hire training need not—indeed, should not—occur all at once. A two-, three-, or even four-day training course that starts the day the new hires arrive is likely to leave them feeling overwhelmed. Not only can this be demotivating (e.g., the confused new hires start to doubt their ability to master all the necessary skills), it is generally ineffective because people start to have minimal retention once they have hit a limit. Instead, break the training into consistent modules, with each module, say, three or fewer hours long. Not only will this make it easier for experienced test team members to deliver the training, it will also result in new hires acquiring new skills and immediately applying those skills after the training. Immediate application of skills aids retention and training effectiveness.

For example, you might use a schedule such as the following, where each training session is a half-day or less:

- First week: HR trains the new hires on organization policies and procedures on the first day. That same day, the new hires are given their workstations and set up for access. The second day they are trained on the basic processes and procedures for the test group, such as the organization of the project information repositories. They are assigned some tasks, such as reviewing project documentation, that are within their current capabilities.
- Second week: The new hires are trained on more advanced processes, such as defect reporting, defect management, test creation, and test management, possibly over a sequence of days. Again, the new hires are assigned tasks that are within their current capabilities.
- Third week: The new hires are trained in any additional tools they'll use within the test department and on the project. For example, if the new hires will be involved in test automation, the existing test automation team might give the new hires a walk-through of the existing test scripts, the standards about how the scripts are created and maintained, and so forth.

While the test manager might not deliver all of these training sessions, they should make sure new hires do indeed attend all appropriate training events. For particularly critical training elements, it is a best practice to develop an exam to check the new hires' knowledge after the training, or alternatively, after returning to work for a few days.

It's also a good practice to assign a mentor to each new employee, someone who can answer the employee's questions as needed for the first few months. For example, a tester might ask a mentor about the right way to handle a defect report when the confirmation test fails. Without a mentor, new employees must either ask their manager (who might not be available when needed), figure out the answer on their own (which might result in the wrong answer), or simply be stuck (which is both demotivating for the individual and inefficient for the team).

So far, we've talked about forging the team from people you've hired. Of course, you might not always have the luxury of hiring your entire team. You might take over a test management position where the team already exists. Perhaps you were promoted from within the team to replace a departing or promoted test manager. Perhaps you are integrating two or more existing test teams, such as, for example, after a merger or acquisition. Any number of situations can result in your managing people who were hired by someone else. Regardless of how the people on your team came to be on your team, you must make sure it's effective. This topic will be addressed further in later sections of this chapter.

2.2.6 Termination of Employment

Sooner or later in your tenure as a manager, you'll have to terminate someone's employment. Even when the person being terminated deserves the termination, you are unlikely—unless you have no empathy—to find doing so a pleasant experience. For this reason, some managers go to great lengths to avoid the task. This can result in inappropriate people remaining on the team or inappropriate approaches to removal being taken.

What are the situations in which trimming the test team is necessary? There are three typical triggers for terminating an employee:

- **Poor individual performance.** A person might display inappropriate attitudes or behaviors at work. Alternatively, the person might be unable to carry out the essential roles of their job. Unless the behavior is so egregious as to require immediate termination (e.g., sexual harassment, threatening coworkers, actual violence in the workplace, etc.), you should avoid a knee-jerk reaction in these situations. There was some reason the person was hired, and you should try to help

Rex's Tales from the Termination Dark Side

On a test team I was managing early in my career, one of the test leads—a person I had hired—turned out to be a bad fit. It wasn't a matter of skills but rather of attitude. He encouraged the people on his team to openly criticize other people in the organization, including in the test team. I tried to deal with the situation with humor and with gentle one-on-one comments to this fellow. The problem persisted, and his behavior damaged the credibility of the entire test team. Ultimately, I believe that my failure to terminate this individual contributed to a larger layoff that occurred and disproportionately affected the test team.

On another occasion, I was managing a test team in an organization that was clearly not headed in a good direction business-wise. I started to hear rumors about the test team being eliminated and the testing function given to the technical support staff. I asked the president of the company—who was my manager's manager—whether there was any truth to the rumor. He replied that there certainly was not and that he was happy with the work my team was doing. Three months later, the entire test team was laid off. The worst part of it was that the president took that day off. He was there the day before, and friends within the company later told me he was there the day after.

the person get back on track. If, after attempts at remediation on your part, the problems cannot be resolved, then termination is the best course of action. You are doing yourself, the rest of the test team, and probably even the poor performer a disservice by avoiding termination. Of course, there is a possibility in this situation that a bad hiring decision occurred; you should see if there are lessons you can learn.

- **A change in business focus or process.** In some cases, businesses find that they must redefine themselves to succeed or even just survive. For example, the adoption of cloud computing proved to be such an event for one of our enterprise software clients, and it was quite a successful move for the organization. However, this did change the skills needed in its test teams. Similarly, it is often the case that teams adopting Agile methodologies require a higher level of technical skill in their testers. If it's not possible to retrain the testers affected by these changes, you might find yourself forced to pick winners and losers and terminate some of your team members.

- **Reduction in force (or layoff).** Businesses that lose their way or that fail to keep up with evolving consumer and business tastes—and these trends can move lightning fast in high tech—might impose across-the-board reductions in force or layoffs. These layoffs can fall disproportionately on test teams. I've seen and heard of situations where 20 percent reductions in programmers were coupled with 50 percent or more reductions in test staff. Unlike the "change in focus" situation mentioned earlier, there will be no way to soften the blow by trying to find other homes in the organization for displaced testers. You must pick winners and losers, and there might even be more losers than winners.

In all of these situations, HR may have defined policies and procedures. You should certainly comply with these strictly. Failure to do so could trigger a wrongful termination lawsuit, with you as the star witness. It could also constitute a violation of applicable union regulations, state or national labor laws, or employment agreements.

In the "change in focus" or "reduction in force" situations, you must pick the testers you will keep in a clear-eyed fashion. You should consider the kinds of skills you'll need for the team in the future rather than favoring your personal friends on the test team. Yes, we realize that this advice is much easier to give than to take. However, in both of these situations, the entire organization—and especially the test group—is in a perilous, high-risk position. You will need the strongest possible test group to increase your own likelihood, and your organization's likelihood, of success.

In the case of termination for poor performance, company policies and plain old fairness often require that you document the problems before starting a termination procedure. If you, as a manager, find someone's performance unacceptable, you should talk to the human resources department. You need to understand the proper steps to take to try to remediate the problems (sometimes called *performance improvement plans*) and the plan for terminating someone should they not improve.

When someone must be terminated, you must consider skills transfer, knowledge transfer, and intellectual property retention. Outgoing testers might know undocumented configuration steps, passwords, data locations, and more. This knowledge will be needed by the person taking over for the terminated employee. If you discover that you must bring back a terminated employee as a consultant because they have unique knowledge and skills, they might not be gentle in their rate negotiations if they feel ill-used by the termination. Of course, the about-to-be-terminated employee might not feel motivated to complete the knowledge transfer, especially given that a failure of the knowledge transfer may enable the very consulting engagement you would prefer to avoid. Therefore, the smart thing is to use cross-training, throughout the employment period, for everyone. If no single person knows something that no one else knows, you have minimized the risk of someone leaving with critical, unique, irreplaceable knowledge.

2.2.7 Ending Contractual Relationships

Not everyone who works on a project or team is an employee. A number of organizations use individual contractors and outsource testing service providers to provide temporary help on projects. This can be driven by a need to fill skills gaps or to quickly increase the pool of available, qualified resources. The contractual options exist for testing as well as for other parties in the software development lifecycle, as will be discussed in the next chapter.

The best practice in the use of individual or outsource contractors is to have a contract with a predefined end date. This allows clear visibility into when resources and perhaps specialized skills will leave the organization. The test manager should make sure that they have planned for that moment, with resources identified to take over recurring tasks (if any) once owned by the contractors and a knowledge transfer plan in place for essential skills (if any) currently held by the contractors.

As with individual employees, it's also possible for contractors or outsource test firms to fail to meet expectations. In this case, you might need to terminate the contract early. You'll want to be sure, when the contracts are initially signed, that you can do so. Some organizations are good at winning contracts, not so good at fulfilling those contracts, and yet very good at avoiding being held accountable for their failures. As is the case with terminating an employee, you should plan to work with the human resources department when terminating a contractor or outsource services group. You might also have to involve the legal and procurement departments. If someone other than you made the engagement decision with the contractor or service provider, you'll have to work especially hard to document the reasons for the termination because this termination might reflect badly on the business acumen of the individual who engaged the failed contractor or service provider.

2.3 Developing the Test Team

Learning objectives

LO 3.3.1 (K2) Discuss the purpose for creating development plans and stating goals and objectives for individual testers.

LO 3.3.2 (K4) Review a set of SMART goals for an individual tester to determine if the goals are appropriate based on the tester's résumé and the organization's test strategy.

LO 3.3.3 (K2) Explain the importance of an individual understanding their role and responsibilities within a test team.

LO 3.3.4 (K2) Explain how a particular Myers-Briggs Type Indicator profile might determine the role assignment for an individual.

LO 3.3.5 (K3) Identify areas where a tester should monitor and develop their skills, and select appropriate learning options including training and mentoring.

LO 3.3.6 (K5) Conduct a performance review that is targeted to encourage growth in a high-performing individual as well as to acknowledge and reward their accomplishments.

LO 3.3.7 (K5) Conduct a performance review that is targeted to redirect the efforts of a poor performer to improve performance and to set achievable short-term and long-term goals.

An old management cliché says that managers are only as good as their teams. Like many clichés, it's founded on truth. We may seem to be contradicting something we said in a previous section, that hiring managers should not look for a perfect candidate but rather a capable one who can grow. The key to resolving that apparent contradiction is in the last three words, "who can grow." You might not be able to hire the perfect test team, and you probably won't inherit a perfect test team either, but you can take a group of capable people with a thirst for new knowledge and turn those people into one remarkably good test team.

So, how do you accomplish this amazing transformation? There are three essential elements in developing a great team:

- Giving each member of the team an opportunity to acquire new skills in a way that complements the strengths and offsets the weakness of the existing skill set (e.g., cross-training)
- Arranging work assignments so that each member of the team can use those new skills and their existing skills to carry out their duties
- Ensuring that you, as the manager, support the development of each person on the team and of the team as a whole, inspire their best work, and never get in the way

While each of these three elements is important, perhaps the most challenging one for managers is the last. Because it's so challenging, we'll spend an entire section on effective leadership later in this chapter. In the following sections, we will focus on the first two elements.[5] Let's see what we need to do to develop a strong test team.

2.3.1 Developing Individuals

Just as the strength of a manager derives from his/her team, the strength of the team derives from the individuals on it. Other than in silly movies, collections of misfits and losers typically do not accomplish amazing things. So, to the extent that your team is not perfect to begin with—and it won't be—you need to develop the people on the team. This is not only good for your organization and test team, it's also good for their individual careers.

However, you need to ensure that the individual development complements the needs of the test team as a whole. This complementary nature of skills development typically means that you as a manager must identify and then fill skills gaps within the team. This allows you to do well by your team and the organization while at the same time doing good for the individuals on the team.

Just as throwing a box of toothpicks on the floor is unlikely to result in a miniature model log cabin, you should not expect that ad hoc and reactionary approaches to skills development will result in a balanced team with strong

---

5   In addition to the material discussed in this section and the next, we recommend Tom DeMarco and Tim Lister's book, *Peopleware: Productive Projects and Teams,* and Steve McConnell's *Software Project Survival Guide (Developer Best Practices).*

individuals. As a manager, you should work with your team to create a development plan. (Indeed, your company might require you to do so.) This plan should identify current skills gaps and a road map for resolving them.

In terms of identification of skills gaps, the best practice in this area is to use a task analysis to identify the important tasks done by your team and the skills required for those tasks. The result of that analysis is then used to perform a skills inventory for your existing team. This process will clearly identify where your team is strong and where skills gaps exist. You can then use an awareness of those gaps to put together training plans for the people on your team. These training plans collectively make up the road map for filling the gaps.

What types of activities should you include in this road map? Here are some essential tasks:

- Send people to training courses that are aligned with the skills gaps in your organization (more on this topic in the section "Skills Development, Training Opportunities, and Mentoring" later in this chapter).
- Have individuals or groups use books, webinars, and other resources to self-study specific, relevant topics.
- As part of training or self-study, recommend that people work toward a testing certification or other certification that relates to the skills gaps in your organization.
- Encourage people to start or continue work toward a college degree (at least to the extent that this degree makes sense given the skills gaps in your team).
- As individuals gain new skills, assign them to take on new roles or tasks that require those skills.

As mentioned, individual development is good for the individual but also essential for the test team. Therefore, as a test manager, you should not just support individuals in their skills growth but actually require it. A common way to do that is to tie successful completion of skills developmental tasks to each person's periodic objectives or goals (see the next section).

Of course, many of these training activities require money. Part of your development plan should include a budget for the training your team needs. Being able to show a clear connection between the work your team does (via the task analysis) and the skills needed and currently lacking (via the skills inventory) will help you justify this budget to management. We will address the process for performing a task analysis and creating a skills inventory later in this chapter in the section "Defining Clear Roles and Responsibilities."

2.3.2 Setting Goals and Objectives

One key role in managing people is guiding them to achieve their best possible work. One element of this role involves defining goals and objectives for each person on the team and then periodically evaluating their performance toward those goals and objectives. This is typically done as a part of regular performance reviews, which often occur annually.

In some organizations, companies tie employee achievement of their goals and objectives to their salary increases, bonuses, or other incentives. This is sometimes referred to as *management by objectives* (MBOs). In any case, but particularly when financial motivations are involved, it's critically important that the goals and objectives be defined in a way that is fair to each employee and to the company as a whole. While this approach can be a rational and impartial way to evaluate employees, it can prove quite problematic when done poorly (or with ill intent).[6]

One approach to defining these goals and objectives is to use the SMART goal methodology. This approach says that each goal and objective should have five properties:

- **Specific.** Exactly what is expected, what will be true or accomplished if the goal is met? A general goal for a tester might be "Increase testing skills," while a specific goal might be, "Take an ISTQB Foundation training course and apply techniques learned in the course to regular project work."
- **Measurable.** How will you measure progress toward the goals? To make our specific goal measurable, we might rephrase it to say, "Take an ISTQB Foundation training course, pass the Foundation exam with a score of 95 percent or better, and apply at least ten techniques learned in the course to regular project work."
- **Attainable.** Is the goal something that can be achieved and also something that goes beyond simply typical performance? To make our goal attainable, the manager must assure that there is budget available for the training and the certification exam and that the tester will be able to attend the training (through adjustments to their workload, for example).

---

6   Rex actually saw a situation where the CEO of a company manipulated the personnel evaluation process to reduce people's merit increases to cover up some financial mistakes made by the CFO (who happened to be his girlfriend). It was a particularly ugly situation made even uglier when someone in management decided to forward the memo where the CEO made his plan clear. The company was out of business within 12 months.

> **ISTQB Glossary**
>
> **SMART goal methodology:** A methodology whereby objectives are defined very specifically rather than generically. SMART is an acronym derived from the attributes of the objective to be defined: Specific, Measurable, Attainable, Relevant, and Timely.

- **Realistic.** Given all of the constraints and realities extant in the projects (both underway and coming in the future) and in the organization as a whole, would achieving this goal be something that would make sense for the individual, the test group, and the organization? To make our goal more realistic, suppose a review of the syllabus and a discussion with people previously taking the exam leads us to conclude that few people score 95 percent or better and that there are really six techniques that apply for most testers. We might rephrase the goal to read, "Take an ISTQB Foundation training course, pass the Foundation exam with a score of 85 percent or better, and apply six core techniques learned in the course (risk-based testing, equivalence partitioning, boundary value analysis, decision tables, state-based testing, and use case testing) to regular project work."
- **Timely.** When should the goal be completed, and if milestones along the way exist, when should those milestones be reached? To make our specific goal timely, we might rephrase it to say, "Take an ISTQB Foundation training course and pass the Foundation exam with a score of 85 percent or better in the next three months. Apply six core techniques learned in the course (risk-based testing, equivalence partitioning, boundary value analysis, decision tables, state-based testing, and use case testing) to regular project work starting with the project immediately following the training."

By using this approach, the managers can establish goals and objectives that not only provide fair standards for performance reviews but also provide employees with a meaningful framework for improving themselves.

Unfortunately, managers (and not just test managers) tend to make a number of mistakes when setting goals. One common mistake is to set goals that are unachievable, either because the goal is beyond the current capabilities of the employee or because organizational and project realities will pose insurmountable obstacles. For example, a manager sets a goal of ISTQB Foundation certification for all testers on their team, but does not have a sufficient training budget or the possibility of getting people away from work long enough to prepare for the exam. Another common mistake is to set goals that are so simple that achieving them really is no achievement at all and should rather be seen as a basic condition of remaining employed. For example, a manager sets a goal of attending all mandatory meetings. Yet another common mistake is to set goals that are so vague as to be meaningless. For example, a manager sets a goal like the "Increase testing skills" example given earlier.

It is not the case that managers make mistakes in setting goals because they are stupid or lazy or uncaring. These mistakes occur because setting good goals is hard. Sometimes tasks are hard to measure, or using easier tasks is not actually a fair way to measure employees. For example, setting a goal for testers of completing all their assigned test cases within the allotted time might not be a realistic goal if the time assigned to the tests is too short or poor-quality software is delivered for testing. Neither of these factors is within the control of the testers. When a factor that influences the achievement of a goal is not within the control of the person being evaluated, that goal is unfair and the person being evaluated will perceive it as unfair.[7]

If you look closely at many of the metrics we use in testing—metrics such as the number of defects found, the percentage of test cases passed, the number of defects found in production, and so forth—you will see that they are not controlled by the individual tester. That's because most of those metrics are concerned with measuring the project, product, or process, as discussed in Chapter 1, Chapter 6, and Chapter 8. What we are talking about here are people metrics, and that's a different matter. If you use process, project, and product metrics as people metrics, you must take care that doing so does not encourage bad behavior or penalize good behavior.

For example, incentivizing testers based on the number of defects they report—a common enough test manager mistake—generally leads to a higher number of low-quality defect reports as well as testers being rewarded for disproportionately reporting inconsequential, low-priority failures, which are often easier to isolate and report than complex, high-priority failures. This incentive will result in overall process metrics trending downward for the test

---

7   The classic demonstration of this problem is Deming's red-bead experiment. In that experiment, management provides the tools to be used to separate a mixed container of different-colored beads into two containers of same-colored beads. Management also defines the process and the timeline for separating the beads. Individuals are then rewarded and punished based on their speed and error rate, even though the differences are due entirely to natural variation in the process as defined. Video clips and explanations of the experiment are available on the Internet, and Amazon even sells a red-bead experiment kit, should you want to try it yourself.

team and in behaviors that are disconnected with desirable project and product outcomes. Thus we can say that goals and metrics must be properly aligned in terms of process, project, product, and people.

The best practice is for the manager to work with each employee, as part of their regular performance review, to set their goals and objectives for the upcoming evaluation period. These should be individual goals, with measurable deliverables produced by the employee. Note that individual goals are distinct from group goals, such as an initiative to improve defect detection effectiveness for the test team.

This is not to say that you shouldn't establish group goals. These goals could apply to the entire test team or to specific people within the test team. In addition to setting individual goals for test team members, you can establish group goals for the test team at large or for specific roles within the test team. Suppose that three people support test automation within a larger test group. You might set the following group goal for them: "Using best practices in test tool selection, choose an open-source tool that supports GUI test automation for browser-based applications within the next three months. Acquire that tool and install it in the test environment within one month after selection. Identify a pilot project, train the test staff on that project in the use of the tool, and complete the pilot project within six months. Deliver a cost-benefit analysis on the pilot within one month of the completion of the pilot."

One last point about defining goals. In addition to using the SMART methodology, and avoiding goals that lead to incorrect behaviors (through misalignment of process, project, product, and people goals), you want alignment of the people goals vertically. To continue the example given earlier, if we have set a goal for a team to introduce automation of testing, that should support a goal for the test director; for example, the test director might have as a goal reducing the cost of regression testing by 20 percent over the next year without increasing regression risk.

With the goals and objectives defined, the manager should not forget about an employee's progress until the next performance review. Good managers will often meet regularly, in some cases weekly, with their direct reports. In addition to discussing the employee's current workload and status in those meetings, the wise manager will spend time discussing progress toward the goals and objectives. That way, the manager can praise and encourage progress made and, if necessary, make adjustments to ensure that progress *is* made.

For example, suppose the director of a testing group has defined a goal of attaining ISTQB Advanced Test Manager certification for the four test managers who report to them. Due to heavy project loads, sending all four managers to external training is impractical, as is having in-house training in any given week. So, the director has decided to use a blended e-learning approach to training the test managers, with two months of e-learning access and four two-hour facilitation sessions with a trainer via a webinar-style interface.

In this example, the test director would be prudent to ask the test managers, in their weekly one-on-one meetings, how things are going with the training. Suppose that three of the test managers report making great progress. The director would encourage the managers to continue their hard work and focus not only on passing the exam, but also on learning skills they can apply to their projects. Suppose that one of the test managers says, "You know, this current program has some real challenges, and I find I have to spend a lot of time with the testers on each project team to keep them going. That's preventing me from spending time on the e-learning course or attending the facilitation sessions." This would be the time for the test director to brainstorm ways to redirect some of the manager's time and energy toward the course, perhaps by identifying and resolving some of the problems facing the program.

2.3.3 Defining Clear Roles and Responsibilities

This discussion of goals and objectives for individuals is strongly related to and parallels the discussion of mission, objectives, and goals for the test group as a whole, covered in the first part of Chapter 1. The goals and objectives for individuals must be aligned with the mission, objectives, and goals for the test group as a whole, as mentioned earlier. The individuals must understand the mission, objectives, and goals for the test group so that they consistently act in a way that supports them.

Furthermore, the objectives and goals for individuals must be aligned with their individual roles and responsibilities. As with the derivation of metrics and goals for the test group from the mission and objectives, the roles and responsibilities of teams and individuals within the test group must clearly relate to the team and individual goals and objectives. You must clearly define the roles and responsibilities of teams and individuals within the test group and ensure that these roles and responsibilities are clearly understood by everyone in the test group. Otherwise, the manager cannot properly or fairly evaluate individual or team performance.

There are two models for organizing the roles and responsibilities for individual contributors within a test group. One model is the generalized test

ISTQB Glossary

test architect: (1) A person who provides guidance and strategic direction for a test organization and for its relationship with other disciplines. (2) A person who defines the way testing is structured for a given system, including topics such as test tools and test data management.

group, where all testers have a consistent skill set. Any testing task that comes along can be done by almost any of the testers. The opposite model is the specialized test group, where small teams of two or more testers are specialized in certain skills. As testing tasks come along that require a certain skill, testers are assigned based on their particular specialty.

The generalized model favors efficiency. At least in the idealized case, because any tester can do any task that needs to be done, test managers can maintain almost perfectly even utilization of each human resource. However, effectiveness can be reduced because the testers will not tend to be experts in any particular area.[8] In addition, there will be certain types of tasks—e.g., test automation—that cannot be handled by a purely generalized team because these tasks require a high degree of specialization and experience.

The specialized model favors effectiveness. The tester assigned a task is exactly the right person for that task, based on their skills and experience. However, efficiency can be reduced because different skill sets might be required at different points of time, resulting in some people being overallocated while at the same time other people are underallocated. If you take the specialized model to extremes, where a single tester has unique skills, this creates the problem mentioned earlier in the context of unavailability or termination and also can create bottlenecks with tasks that require unique skills.

Specialization is also a function of the size of the test group. It's very difficult for a small test group to be highly specialized because there are too few people to dedicate to a small set of capabilities. In these situations, the test group may need to use outsourcing or insourcing—which we'll discuss in the next chapter—to fill roles that require highly developed skills in particular areas.

---

8   This variance in effectiveness can be significant. As DeMarco and Lister cite in *Peopleware*, for any given task, the difference in effectiveness between the most qualified and least qualified person can be an order of magnitude—e.g., a ten-times capability difference.

Assuming that you do want to have some degree of specialization in your test group, what options exist? This depends on the skills you need, but here are some examples:

- **Black box tester:** Someone with business domain expertise as well as expertise in sophisticated black box test design techniques. This person follows the test analyst career path in the ISTQB program.
- **White box tester:** Someone focused on the technical details of system implementation as well as having expertise in sophisticated white box test design techniques. This person follows the technical test analyst career path in the ISTQB program.
- **Performance test engineer:** Someone focused on technical details of the system, but especially the design of the system. Not only are sophisticated white box and black box test design techniques required, but some understanding of modeling of system behaviors is necessary. This person also follows the technical test analyst career path in the ISTQB program, but with additional expertise in performance.
- **Test environment and data administrator:** Someone with the skills required to implement and maintain production environments and databases but applying those skills to the test environment. This person's testing skills might be limited, or they might have the ability to run certain tests when demand requires.
- **Tools developer:** Someone with a strong background in programming and in test automation. Depending on the sophistication of the tools being developed, this person might follow the technical test analyst career path in the ISTQB program.
- **Test lead and test manager:** Someone focused on organizing and leading the individual testers. This person follows the test manager career path in the ISTQB program.
- **Test architect:** Someone with skills similar to those of a tools developer but with a strong understanding of testing on both the test analyst and technical test analyst side.
- **Test automation specialist:** Someone with a strong background in programming and in test automation. This person differs from the tools developer in that their focus is on using existing tools rather creating new tools. This person also follows the technical test analyst career path in the ISTQB program and should have at least five years of test automation experience.
- **Security test engineer:** Someone with a broad technical background who understands programming, system administration, and database adminis-

tration as well as sophisticated black box and white box test design techniques. This person also follows the technical test analyst career path in the ISTQB program.

Now, as with any models, these are simplifications of reality. Furthermore, these models exist on the extreme ends of a spectrum. Most test groups tend to use a mixture of these models, with some elements of generalization (perhaps limited to some members of the test group) and some elements of specialization (again, perhaps limited to some members of the test group). For example, a test group may choose to have specialized business domain experts that create tests and execute experience-based tests, specialized technical experts that create test automation frameworks, specialized test leads and managers that organize and lead the testing efforts, and generalized testers who carry out all the other tasks that do not require specialized expertise. In addition, there may be some mobility in the sense that the generalized testers over time advance into specialized roles.

Whether you follow a specialized or generalized skills model, you will need a way to track and manage the skills of your team. One way to do so is via what is called a *skills inventory*. To create a skills inventory, you first perform a *task analysis*. A task analysis involves reviewing the tasks undertaken by your testers as part of their projects and their other regular operations. In this review, you analyze each task to identify the skills required to perform it competently.

These skills can typically be grouped into four categories: general professional qualifications, technical skills, business domain skills, and testing skills. If you haven't identified skills in one or more of these categories, you probably haven't analyzed the tasks thoroughly enough.

For example, suppose your test team is responsible for testing a web-based application that allows people to find, contact, and review businesses and attractions in their current location. It runs on all browsers and operating systems and supports mobile devices as well. Here are some of the skills you might need for testers, grouped by category:

- **General professional qualifications:** Oral and written communication, education (e.g., college degree), and testing certification
- **Technical skills:** Browsers, operating systems, mobile devices, programming, and Internet
- **Business domain skills:** Cartography and guidebook creation
- **Testing skills:** Black box, white box, and experience-based testing; test planning and estimation; functional test automation; performance and reliability test automation; and test status reporting

Once the skills are identified, you can organize your skills inventory. One method is to list the skills, grouped by category, in the left side of a spreadsheet. Then list the test team members across the top of the spreadsheet. At this point, evaluate each test team member's level of skill for each identified skill. You can use a simple scale for this evaluation:

0   (No Knowledge): The person cannot perform any tasks that require this skill.

1   (Some Knowledge): Given someone available to answer questions, this person can perform simple to moderate tasks that require this skill.

2   (Knowledgeable): This person can perform simple to moderate tasks that require this skill, can answer simple to moderate questions about this skill, and can perform complex tasks that require this skill, given someone available to answer questions.

3   (Expert Knowledge): This person can perform all tasks that require this skill and can answer simple to complex questions about this skill.

It's important to ensure objective and meaningful evaluations of these skill levels across the team.

With the skills inventory in place, you can identify areas of individual and team weakness based on these ratings. These areas of weakness should be addressed through training, mentoring, and other forms of skills development.

You can also use this skills inventory to create job descriptions. The skills required for a position should be consistent with the skills identified for that position in your inventory. You should also use recruitment as an opportunity to fill skills gaps in your team, by hiring people who are strongest where your current team is weakest.

Finally, you should also consider the skills inventory when making task assignments. Keep in mind that sometimes you will want to assign people to tasks for which they are not currently quite qualified. When you do, assign them a mentor. They can consult the mentor if they have questions, and the mentor can review their results and deliverables. This way, cross-training can be accomplished as part of people's regular work.[9]

---

9   Further information on skills inventories and their use in creating job descriptions can be found in Rex's book *Managing the Testing Process, 3e*. You can find examples of skills inventories in the Basic and Advanced Libraries on www.rbcs-us.com.

> **ISTQB Glossary**
>
> **RACI matrix:** A matrix describing the participation by various roles in completing tasks or deliverables for a project or process. It is especially useful in clarifying roles and responsibilities. RACI is an acronym derived from the four key responsibilities most typically used: Responsible, Accountable, Consulted, and Informed.

Another useful tool for task assignments and to identify roles and responsibilities is a RACI matrix. RACI matrices define four types of participation for any given task:

- **Responsible:** Doing the work involved in the task, and creating any work products the task should deliver. Typically, only one role is assigned responsibility, though it's important to note that a role is not the same as a single individual, as explained later. A variant of the RACI matrix, the RASCI matrix, adds a supporting role, which involves assisting the responsible individual(s).
- **Accountable:** Being answerable (to the various project, product, or program stakeholders) for the proper, thorough completion of the task and its associated work products. There should be a single individual accountable for a task, but it's not unusual to see organizations breaking this rule. In some cases, the accountable person approves the work done by the responsible person(s). In other cases, the accountable and responsible roles are the same.
- **Consulted:** This role involves advising, discussing, and reviewing solution options with the people in responsible and accountable roles. The communication is inherently two-way. Multiple roles can be assigned consultative participation.
- **Informed:** This role involves receiving information about the progress of the task from the accountable and responsible roles. This information may come periodically or perhaps only at the completion of the task. The communication is primarily one-way, though typically a person in an informed role could ask questions about information or even initiate a flow of information on request, such as, for example, by requesting a status update.

Other than the possibility of the same role being responsible and accountable, the best practice is for each role to have a single participation type for a given task. If a role has multiple participation types, that can indicate some confusion about who is doing what on the task.

A typical RACI (or RASCI) matrix has a list of tasks or deliverables on the left-hand side, with roles shown across the top of the columns in the matrix. The assigned participation type for any given task/role deliverable—i.e., R, A, C, I, and possibly S—is shown in the appropriate cell of the table.

As alluded to earlier, it's important to distinguish between roles and individuals. A role arises from some group of activities, and multiple people can play a given role. For example, you can have a role of automated test engineer, which involves creating automated testing frameworks using open source and commercial off-the-shelf (COTS) testing tools. The role could be played by a developer who is building an automated unit testing and continuous integration harness. The role could also be played by a tester who is building a framework for functional regression tests.

Not only can multiple people play one role, but one person can play multiple roles. For example, the developer mentioned in the preceding paragraph is playing a programmer role when writing code and is playing a system analyst role when designing a system's architecture. The tester mentioned is playing a test lead role when guiding a group of automated test engineers in the creation of a new, large, and complex framework.

Not only does the RACI matrix help test managers assign tasks, but for testers, it should clarify their specific roles and responsibilities. The RACI matrix may also be circulated outside of the test team, to help test stakeholders understand who does what within the team.

2.3.4 Individual Personalities and Roles Within Teams

As a test manager, you must understand how each tester can best contribute to the test team. In part this is a matter of skills and qualifications and can be determined from the skills inventory discussed earlier. Even if the goal is to have a generalized team organization, you will find that there is no factory in the world that produces fully substitutable, equivalent testers; variations in skills and experience will create differences in testers that will affect what roles they can play.

The variations are not only in skills and experience. As you have noticed already, people have different personalities. In personal interactions, including those between managers and their testers, those personality traits have a strong influence. If managers do not skillfully handle their interactions with their

ISTQB Glossary

Myers-Briggs Type Indicator (MBTI): An indicator of psychological preference representing the different personalities and communication styles of people.

testers, that can lead to a number of negative outcomes. One such outcome is a personal misunderstanding on one or both sides, where a difference of opinion or interpretation becomes a personal or relationship problem. Another such outcome is a loss of trust by the tester, resulting in the tester withholding information or providing information that is incorrect or false (perhaps because the tester fears the consequences of telling the truth). There are a number of psychological aspects of management, especially test management, that a good test manager should understand.[10]

One way to gain insight to these personality differences is personality profiling. Personality profiling is not something that an amateur should undertake. The Myers-Briggs Type Indicator (MBTI) is one of the most popular profiling tests used in business. MBTI tests can place people into 16 compound personality types, based on four classifications:

Extrovert (E) or Introvert (I): A person who focuses on the world around them, and especially the people in it, is extroverted. A person who is more inward focused is introverted.

Sensing (S) or Intuition (N): A person who focuses on facts and data is sensing. A person who is likely to interpret and draw conclusions from their observations is intuitive.

Thinking (T) or Feeling (F): A person who makes decisions on facts, logic, consistency, and coherence is thinking. A person who makes decisions based on people and is more comfortable to making exceptions to rules based on special circumstances is feeling.

Judging (J) or Perceiving (P): A person who wants to have clear plans and decisions, which are then followed closely with variation occurring only when clearly necessary, is judging. A person who prefers to take in new information and evaluate new options, perhaps in a continuous fashion, is perceiving.

---

10   For general psychological issues of management, it's hard to top the gold standard set by DeMarco and Lister in *Peopleware, 2e*. Some of the psychological issues specific to test management are covered in Rex's book *Managing the Testing Process, 3e*, and Judy McKay's book *Managing the Testing People*. You can also listen to Rex's webinar The Psychopolitics of Test Management, found at www.rbcs-us.com/software-testing-resources/library/digital-library.

These four classifications are combined to give the compound personality type. For example, someone on your team might be an ENFP, and that person would tend to be gregarious, sensitive to people's feelings, and happy to proceed in situations where plans and roles are not clearly defined. Such a person would be a good fit to work as a tester on an Agile team. Another person might be an ISTJ, and that person would tend to be more thoughtful and reflective, fact-focused and logical, and decisive. Such a person would be a great fit to lead a team charged with selecting a new automated testing tool and creating and implementing an automated testing framework and strategy.

Another use of these personality types is to be aware of, and insightfully responsive to, potential personality conflicts within your team. For example, suppose you have a senior test engineer who has a judging personality type and is working on a testing project and reporting to a test lead; the test lead is more perceiving. On the one hand, the test engineer might become frustrated with the test lead because the senior test engineer might see the test lead as wishy-washy, unreliable, and providing weak leadership. On the other hand, the test lead might become irritated by what they perceive as rigidity and perhaps resistance from the test engineer. (Rex notes that he has personally been in exactly this situation, being more comfortable with setting and following plans in most cases.) The use of the MBTI can help you predict and ameliorate (sometimes in advance) such conflicts.

Classifying into personality types is a form of modeling, as was discussed in the Foundation and Advanced levels. This particular model is based on work done by psychologist Carl Jung in the 1920s and thus reflects his own philosophies and beliefs about human psychology. As with any model, to paraphrase W. E. Deming, the model is wrong (in that it is a simplification that captures only certain elements of the whole), but potentially useful (in that it aids understanding of the relevant elements of the whole). These MBTI types simplify the infinite nuances of human personality. Be informed, but not dominated, by the model.[11]

Not only must the test manager understand the testers, but each member of the test team must understand their own position and relate effectively with the others. Do people understand their own roles and capabilities? Do people understand their colleagues' roles and capabilities? Do people understand and respect their colleagues' skills? Do people understand that colleagues with different skills are complementary to them, not incompetent and unqualified?

---

11   You can find more information on the MBTI test at www.myersbriggs.org.

If the answer to any of these questions is 'no,' then you as a manager have some work to do. At the very least, you should take steps to help people understand these things. In addition, you might want to consider having a professional evaluation of your team, such as the MBTI test mentioned earlier. Such a test can help you better understand the dynamics of the test team. It can also help the individuals understand their own behavior and their colleagues' behavior.

In addition to skills and personality types, there are other ways in which people are unique. People learn differently, which we'll discuss in the following section.

Another important difference is how people deal with stress and where their stress thresholds are. The most extreme example comes from the military, in the form of combat stress reaction. (This is not to be confused with post-traumatic stress disorder, or PTSD, which is a permanent problem that can be caused by both physical and psychological factors but for which combat stress can be an initiating or aggravating factor.) Under stress, whether it is the stress of combat or the less potentially lethal but often quite stressful project gone wrong, people tend to become chronically fatigued and demotivated (often referred to as burnout). They don't react as quickly as they once did because they have difficulty reaching a conclusion about the right thing to do next. They can lose track of important details or lose focus (often referred to as spacing out or in Internet parlance, 404). They can become angry, aggressive, bullying, or even violent (often referred to as snapping). Other factors may contribute to these behaviors, such as underlying psychological problems or chronic substance abuse issues, which are exacerbated by the stress.

A stress reaction can happen to anyone, but many important differences exist between people in terms of stress reactions. Some people find certain factors are particularly stressful, such as excessive overtime or concern about job stability. Different people have different levels of stress they can handle before a stress reaction occurs. Different people find that different activities can help them cope with and relieve stress. And different people have different tendencies to try to relieve stress in a functional rather than dysfunctional way.

Rex once worked with a project manager who treated his stress reaction with truly astounding rations of alcohol, including during the workday. He was moderate in his use of alcohol, and a very inspiring leader, until he suffered this stress reaction as the large, complex, and expensive project they were working on started plummeting toward destruction. As the day went on, his decision-making become more clouded by the alcohol, and his mood more erratic, irascible, and unpredictable. Rex started avoiding him, because as the test manager, he frequently had only bad news to tell him, and he did not react well when intoxicated.

It can help to keep stress in perspective and help your staff do so too. Rex remembers complaining on one project, after what he found to be a stressful meeting with the project management team, to one of his test leads. The test lead had been a noncommissioned officer in Iraq. He responded respectfully but with a Socratic smile, "So, did someone shoot at you down there?" Rex laughed, but he also learned something about himself and his need to keep things in perspective. (And he's thankful to Amos for that insight.) While you need to manage your team, remember that you will learn a lot about management, and about yourself, from doing so. Ultimately, every test team is nothing but a collection of human beings: disappointingly fallible, yes; infinitely variable, yes; and yet often capable of amazing things.

2.3.5 Skills Development, Training Opportunities, and Mentoring

In a previous section, we talked about skills inventories and using them to identify skills gaps in individuals and the team as a whole. Okay, let's assume you have gaps in your team. We all do. As managers, we want our teams to be better and the people on our teams to be better. What can we do about it?

First, a manager should encourage their team members to improve their skills. In fact, we would suggest that continuing education—relevant education, of course—be part of the performance reviews mentioned earlier and discussed further later in this chapter. Relevant education would include the areas of tools, general areas of testing such as the ISTQB certification career paths, technology, methodologies and their effect on testing (e.g., Scrum), technical testing areas such as test automation or white box testing, business domain knowledge, and soft skills such as communication and leadership.

So, how can we improve people's skills? As mentioned earlier, one approach is training. Training can take many forms:

- Training can be informal, where the materials and the training are delivered by other test team members. The advantage of such training is the direct relevance to your immediate needs. The disadvantages are the lack of training professionalism and the potential loss of exposure to externally recognized best practices.

■ Training can be on the job, where the testers learn from mentors and colleagues while doing the actual work. The advantages of such training are not only the direct relevance of the training but also the fact that the knowledge transfer, from conceptual to applied, occurs immediately during the training. The disadvantages are the same as those for informal training but in addition, the fact that time pressures can lead the mentor or colleague to reduce the amount or scope of the training or to simply take over the job.

■ Training can be professionally delivered by an instructor from outside the test team. The advantages of such training are a higher quality of materials and teaching (if you select the right training company) and the importation of externally recognized best practices. The disadvantages are the need for the attendees to figure out how to translate the lessons learned in training into actions in their daily work, though good, realistic exercises in the professional training can help with this problem. Cost is sometimes seen as a disadvantage for professional training, but careful selection of the training course and training company will result in a positive return on investment for the training.

Professional training can be delivered in three main modes. The first mode is instructor-led training, where an instructor comes to the client's site, or members of the test team travel to a public training event, or a webinar-style interface is used to deliver the training. The second mode is pure asynchronous training, where trainees use an e-learning system to access training at their leisure. The third mode blends the first and second modes, where instructor facilitation and question-and-answer sessions accompany e-learning.

What if your training budget is limited and your organization small? You can always use cross-training by colleagues and mentors, as mentioned, to help fill skills gaps and increase the skill levels of your test team. What do people within your team know? You can use the answer to this question to try to generalize the skills within your test team. And don't forget about reaching out to other groups such as development or marketing. The cross-training can involve technical skills, testing skills, or business domain skills.

There are various models for how people learn, wherein the models explore these different types of learning. For example, Neil Fleming's VAK model says that people can learn through visual, auditory, or kinesthetic experiences. While most people will be able to learn through all three types of experiences, Fleming suggested that people tend to have one mode of learning that allows them to learn most quickly. A visual learner is someone who likes to see pictures or text; such a person would do particularly well in an interactive, live instructor-led course. An auditory learner is someone who prefers listening; while such a person can do well in a live training course, they are also well suited to take purely asynchronous e-learning courses where they listen to lectures. A kinesthetic (or tactile) learner is someone who prefers to apply new concepts immediately while learning them; such a person will do best when their training includes a lot of immediate sample questions, discussion points, and realistic exercises. When setting up less-structured training opportunities for people, such as brown-bag lunches and cross-training, you should take care to address people's learning mode preferences.

Even if you are pursuing a specialized model of test team organization, there are likely some skills that you feel are required across the entire team. And, in specialized models, it's a best practice to have more than one person with expertise in each critical skill so that you can handle situations in which one person is unavailable or leaves the company. Of course, in generalized teams, the need to ensure that all team members have an appropriate level of expertise is critical, so you should use cross-training aggressively to spread organization-specific skills.

Another variant of cross-training within the team is the use of mentors. Are there people within the test team who are particularly suited to help another within the test team move to the next level of skill? Is there someone on the cusp of becoming an expert in some critical skills area who could cross that boundary with the help of a current expert? Are there people entering the testing profession who need one or more experts to set an example for them and get them started in the right direction?

Mentors do not need to be from within the test team. You should consider what people outside the test team but within the organization know. These people can include developers, database administrators, and business analysts, among other people within the organization. Cross-training by such fellow professionals can be a good approach in any situation but especially in specialized teams where people need to learn particular skills that relate to the business domain or technology of system implementation.

Another excellent way to spread business domain or technical knowledge is through formal or informal job rotation. If a programmer or business analyst works in the test team for a few weeks, or maybe even months, imagine the knowledge transfer that can occur. Imagine the relationships that can be built on all sides and the informal problem solving that can occur through such relationships. This exchange of personnel can go both ways, of course, and testers can work within technical and business stakeholder groups as part of job rotation. You could assign a technical test analyst to work with programmers to help build an automated unit testing framework. You could assign a test lead to work with a programming or business analysis team to learn more technical, business domain, or management skills.[12]

2.3.6 Performance Reviews and Feedback

Earlier in this chapter, we mentioned setting goals and objectives for employees and evaluating performance against those goals and objectives. It is important that this happen periodically, at least annually, and many organizations hold managers accountable for such reviews. Your human resources (HR) department might have specific requirements, forms, and so forth that relate to this process, so be sure to contact them before you start.

If you dread this periodic responsibility, you might be making mistakes in your management style. For one thing, if the periodic performance evaluations are a carnival of pain, perhaps your employees are not getting regular feedback on their work in a way that allows them to course-correct prior to the review? For another thing, don't people deserve the attention and care inherent in their manager's thoughtful consideration of their employees' work products and deliverables, and the quality of that work, at least once in a while, away from the daily torrent of tasks and urgent issues? For yet another thing, part of your job as a manager is to inspire people to do their best possible work, so what could be a better avenue for doing so than such a discussion?

Of course, doing a good job does not just mean "doing a good job in my manager's opinion." Just as the test team has a number of stakeholders, each member of the test team has a number of stakeholders. Three-hundred-sixty-degree reviews allow the test manager to incorporate the opinions of those stakeholders in the review process. A first step, naturally, is identifying those people who have worked with or received work products from the person under review. (For those unfamiliar with the term, a "three-hundred-sixty-degree review" refers to a review that involves input from a person's manager, their peer managers, and their direct reports.)

---

12   Rex had a number of clients tell him that they use job rotation in one form or another for cross-training. And don't underestimate the power and value of informal problem-solving either. In many business cultures, including North American cultures, the ability to work with someone you know outside of your immediate working sphere to solve a problem will, as you move up, have a greater and greater influence on your ability to move up the organizational ladder. Tom DeMarco makes a number of related points in his book *Slack*.

The next step of such a review is coming up with a questionnaire about the employee. This should include specific and open-ended questions about the employee. What work products have they delivered to the stakeholders in question? What is the quality of their work products? These questions should be both objective and subjective. Whether subjective or objective, the answers should be supported by facts and examples.

Of course, some managers dread performance reviews for good reason. Dreadful performance evaluations indeed can occur when employees have unrealistic expectations. These expectations can have to do with what their job is or how quickly they can advance in that job. So, when giving someone a performance evaluation you expect them to be unhappy with, be sure to explain the requirements of the job (which should already be clear from the job description), the employee's demonstrated capabilities (backed up with data and facts), and the difference between those two. It's great to have employees with aspirations, but when aspirations and reality diverge, your job as a manager is to bring those back into alignment, clearly and factually explaining the difference. Of course, it would be best not to wait until once a year to do this.

2.4 Leading the Test Team

Learning objectives

LO 3.4.1 (K5) For a given situation, evaluate the information and guidance needed by the test team and determine the most effective method of communication.

LO 3.4.2 (K3) Brainstorm on various team-building activities that will help to foster loyalty and trust within the team.

LO 3.4.3 (K2) Explain the challenges of motivating a test team, both short-term and long-term.

LO 3.4.4 (K4) Create a plan for team-building activities that includes offshore teams and helps improve communication.

In many ways, leading a test team is like leading any other team. After all, people are people, no matter what work they do or where they live. Of course, there are some aspects that are specific to managing technical teams. And there are a few aspects that are specific to managing a test team. This will be the focus here in these final sections of Chapter 2. Given a good team, which you've developed carefully, how can you get the best work from them and keep them engaged and motivated?[13]

2.4.1 Information Sharing and Communication

In Chapter 1, we discussed the importance of clearly defining the mission, objectives, and goals of the test group as well as how those goals are to be achieved and how to ensure that they are aligned with the needs of the organization. We also discussed the importance of defining the skills, roles, and responsibilities of people in the test group. Those are all necessary activities, but they are not sufficient. The test manager must ensure that the test group understands their role in the organization so that they can fulfill that role.

In addition to this general information about the role of the test group and each person within the group, the manager of a test group must ensure that each tester, test lead, and test manager understands how they fit into the project or program they are working on and how they fit with the stakeholders they are working with. Part of leadership is making sure that you obtain, and share with your staff, correct, current, and relevant information. So, not only do *you* need to be in the loop, you need to keep *your people* in the loop. Without obtaining and sharing the necessary information, your team cannot effectively and efficiently fulfill the goals discussed in Chapter 1.

While this may sound simple, there is a balance you must achieve. As a manager, you have to decide what information people need versus what information is irrelevant or distracting. We know of a company that had a stated policy of overcommunication. Everyone in the company received hundreds of emails and instant messages a day. Even the most effective and efficient employees spent inordinate amounts of time sifting through irrelevant and often inscrutable dross, trying to figure out whether any useful or actionable information existed therein. The less fortunate among them essentially drowned in a sea of trivia and irrelevancies, losing so much time and becoming so distracted that their effective productivity fell to zero. This was not a

---

13   More on management of technical workers can be found in Tom DeMarco et al.'s book *Adrenaline Junkies and Template Zombies: Understanding Patterns of Project Behavior*. For discussions that are specific to managing testers, see Rex Black's book *Managing the Testing Process: Practical Tools and Techniques for Managing Hardware and Software Testing/Edition 3*, Chapter 8, and Rick Craig's book, *Systematic Software Testing*, Chapter 10.

problem specific to the testing group because everyone suffered from this disease, but certainly the test director did not do anything to help the team rise above it.

We have also seen the opposite problem occur. We have known test managers and directors who adopted such strict need-to-know communication styles that people within their teams often found themselves lacking essential information. The most effective and efficient employees would often realize their dilemma and seek the information they needed from their managers and colleagues. This resulted in delays, of course, and sometimes incorrect actions when they received wrong information in spite of their best efforts. The less fortunate employees would simply become stuck, not knowing where to go for information or what to do in the absence of information.[14]

So, how to resolve this bind? One of the first things to accept is that you will not do a perfect job of resolving it. All managers—indeed, all employees—do an imperfect job of communicating within the organization. Every manager at some point or another communicates some irrelevancy to their staff, and every manager at some point fails to communicate some relevant fact or information to their staff. Be aware that you will have communication breakdowns, and deliberately choose which type of breakdown you want to have more frequently.

We prefer to lean toward liberally sharing information with our staff. This is because we have, as a manager, what Tom Peters referred to as bias toward action, and we want our teams to share that bias toward action. This means that we try to ensure that the pool of information available to each person is as complete as possible. It also means that we cannot punish or berate people for taking actions that were well-intentioned and well-informed but that did not turn out well. If someone on our team makes a mistake, our first assumption is

---

14   For readers not familiar with the term, *need to know* is an intelligence term that refers to classification of information in such a way that only those with a demonstrable and preapproved need to know some piece of information—i.e., as part of their current duties—receive that information. While this may sound reasonable, it presumes that everyone's superior and those driving the classification system have a perfect understanding of what each person in the organization needs to know. That's impossible. The most significant failure of this sort of policy of information hiding occurred in the events leading up to and upon September 11, 2001, when various intelligence and law enforcement agencies in the United States did not "connect the dots" and thus missed numerous indicators of the impending attack. The few individuals who did connect some of the dots were unable to overcome the information-siloing that was built in to the overall system. You can read more about this failure to use intelligence intelligently in *The 9/11 Commission Report*.

that they did the best they could, acting on the information they had, and we work with them to find a way to avoid that mistake in the future.[15]

We have arrived at this preference for reasons we consider good. However, for various reasons, including the issue of organizational alignment discussed in Chapter 1, you might arrive at a different conclusion about how to strike the balance. We're not trying to be prescriptive about what balance you should strike but rather trying to call your attention to the fact that you will strike a balance in this regard. That balance needs to be consistent with the way you choose to manage your team and your personal management style.

You should also remember that your staff will tend to mirror your own communication style. In other words, information-sharing and communication is a two-way street. If you are open in your communication style, then your staff will probably be open with you about information they have—provided you don't create disincentives for them to do so. If you adopt a communication style that is too strict in holding information back, don't be surprised when someday you *are* surprised by some pertinent fact that someone on your team already knew but didn't tell you.

Within the parameters of your communication style, you will communicate with your team. How should that communication occur? There is a plethora of options, but typically one (or more) of the following methods is used:

- **One-on-one meetings.** These are private meetings between the manager and a direct report. Ideally, each person who works directly for the manager would have a chance to have such a meeting. The meetings should happen regularly rather than only in response to a crisis or mistake on the employee's part. We think this is an excellent practice, especially when the manager adopts a policy of egalitarianism within the team because that encourages open communication.
- **Weekly status reports.** These reports should include discussions of current tasks, the progress on those tasks, and any obstacles or risks confronting the team member. Status reports can be individual and can then be aggregated into a group status report. We have used these, especially when information needs could be clearly defined. We have also used daily team status reports, especially during test execution when status evolved rapidly and information needed to be shared widely across the team.

---

15 See Tom Peter and Robert H. Waterman Jr.'s classic management book *In Search of Excellence: Lessons from America's Best Run Companies.*

▓ **Informal communications.** These can include emails, casual conversations, and social events with the team. Many managers adopt an open-door policy to encourage informal communication. Another practice is called "management by walking around," where managers mix with their staff, often at all levels, to gather information. Of course, if you expect this to work, you must never punish or otherwise disincentivize people for sharing information with you. People who expect or fear negative consequences for sharing information will withhold information and probably look for ways to plausibly deny they knew about it or make it look like someone else had the responsibility of communicating it to you.

These communication channels need to go beyond simply the day-to-day tactical issues that arise in moving projects and programs forward. For example, on one of Rex's teams, a personal dispute arose between two testers that did not—at least at first—directly affect project progress. The test leads became aware of the dispute but did not escalate it to Rex because they felt they did not need to distract him with it. (Rex accepted some responsibility for this error because he admits he was unconsciously sending a message of unavailability by being too absorbed in the moment-by-moment tactical realities of a project that was, indeed, barely staying within control.) By the time this problem reached the point where one person was accusing the other of harassment and accusing the test leads and Rex of unintentionally allowing a hostile work environment to arise, it posed a crisis to the progress of the project. Alcohol and gender were factors, which further complicated the situation. Your job as a manager is not just to manage the project and program work but to manage your people too.

Effective communication, especially verbal communication, is a matter of receiving information as much as transmitting it. If you send the message that you are not paying attention, or that you are exasperated, bored, or uninterested, that will come through to your staff, and they will stop communicating. Some managers are very good at communicating *to* their teams but not very good a communicating *with* their teams, which results in those managers not having important information when they need it.

When you are talking to someone, be an active listener. Look the person in the eyes. Reflect back to them what you understand from their communications, and give them an opportunity to confirm or clarify. Don't allow yourself to be distracted by text messages, instant messages, Twitter or Facebook posts, incoming emails, and so forth. If your phone rings, use caller ID to decide whether to interrupt the discussion, and if you must, apologize before so doing and ask your communicant to hold their thought because you want to get back to the discussion as soon as you can complete the urgent call. You owe it to your staff to be open, present, and responsive during communications with them.

In addition to these communication channels, you should have test management tools that track project status information. That information should be available to test team members. Another approach to make information readily available is to use what are called "information radiators"—walls or whiteboards of reports and status information visible to all who walk past. Of course, this information must not only be available but also understandable. We'll discuss test results reporting further in Chapter 6.

2.4.2 Fostering Loyalty and Trust

According to Rex, the highest compliment he received as a manager occurred when a test lead on his test team told him, "You know, this project is really badly managed, and I can't see how it can succeed. I've thought many times about quitting because there are so many things going on that bother me, but I know that quitting would leave you in a bad position. I guess I'd walk across fire to avoid creating a problem for you."

A lot of the good luck Rex has had promoting loyalty and trust within his test teams arises from following the golden rule in terms of not doing to your employees what you wouldn't want done to you. If you do have to ask people to do something you don't want to do—e.g., working overtime or weekend hours—then make sure you share the pain with them. Stand by your staff members, and protect them from outside interference, innuendo, or intrigue. Supporting your team is a sign of respect, and you should, of course, respect your team. After all, if you've followed the steps outlined in this chapter, you built the team.

People also tend to respect managers who are open and honest with them. This goes back to the point made earlier on sharing of information. If you hide information from your team and then that creates a problem, people will be less motivated to help you resolve that problem than they would if you allowed them to see the problem coming. Of course, you can be put into a real bind here if you are told something by your managers and told not to disclose it to your employees, which we have seen happen during decisions about layoffs and outsourcing. When the information does come out, be sure that you explain to the team your reasons for withholding it, and do so in a way that does not come across as a weasel-worded attempt to evade your responsibility for keeping your team informed.

In addition, your staff should feel safe and valued. When people feel safe, they use their best judgment and efforts to advance the mission, objectives, and goals of the test team. When they feel valued, they trust their judgments and insights. They feel free, and indeed compelled, to tell their colleagues and managers what they need to know—in a respectful way—even when that is bad news. As a manager, if you want loyalty and trust, you should reward and never punish team members who do what is right, respectfully tell the truth, and act with good intentions and prudence, even when the outcomes are not always desirable. Feelings of safety and value promote excellence from your team.

Some people, when feeling threatened, will focus on doing exactly as they are told, nothing more. They will be sure to gather evidence, a paper trail, to prove that they are beyond reproach in their actions. They will waste time on petty intrigues against each other, and possibly against you. It's very difficult to get excellence from a team that operates under conditions of fear, especially if it is you that they fear.

2.4.3 Team Building

It is not enough that the team trust and be loyal to you. Another essential element of obtaining excellence from your test team is team cohesion, trust, and loyalty between each member. Even when people worship their manager, if the team is riven with disputes and enmity, it will prove a distraction at best. Even the most competent team, with the best manager, can be rendered ineffectual by internal disputes. If those arise, you must as a manager quickly extinguish them, but it's far preferable to avoid discord in the first place.

Creating and fostering a sense of shared mission, of "teamliness," if you will, is a complex thing. However, there are at least three important factors to consider. The first is open communication: We discussed this earlier in the section "Information Sharing and Communication." A team feels more like a team when people feel that communication channels are open between you, as a manager, and them, as testers and test leads. A team feels more like a team when people feel safe communicating openly with each other within the team. You should avoid a situation in which all information has to flow up to you as a manager before flowing out across the team. We know of an organization in which such strict hierarchical information channels significantly stifle teamwork, and it is particularly frustrating to people that the manager of this organization, who had created this dynamic, keeps stressing collaboration and blaming individuals for not communicating openly with each other. You should also avoid a situation in which people on the team feel free to communicate with each other but not with you as a manager or with other members of the management team. When you create open communication channels within a team, people will tend to feel included. Closed or hierarchical communication channels make people feel isolated at best and at worst, embattled.

The second important factor in creating a team is respectful behavior between team members. While you want people to have open communication, we believe it is best to ensure that communications are respectful. Being encouraged to communicate openly does not mean being free to say whatever you want to your colleagues. However, this belief is not universally shared. Steve Jobs, the late head of Apple Computer, had a very blunt communication style and would openly and sharply criticize people when he felt disappointed or unhappy with their work.[16]

It's also true that courtesy of communication lies on a spectrum, and each manager must establish, within the broader corporate culture, what the proper balance is between politeness (which can interfere with openness if it is excessive) and directness (which can feel disrespectful if it is excessive). That said, disrespectful behavior goes beyond communication, and teamwork is always degraded when people feel devalued or, worse yet, fearful and threatened. Such disrespectful behavior is especially unacceptable if it has cultural, gender, or sexual overtones. You lose credibility as a manager, and expose yourself and your company to legal risk, if you tolerate such a hostile work environment.

The third important factor is creating a shared understanding of the roles and responsibilities of the group, which we touched on in the section "Defining Clear Roles and Responsibilities." Simply defining those clear roles and responsibilities is not enough. As a manager, you need to make sure people understand their own roles and responsibilities and those of their team members.

So, given these factors, how can you build a team and create positive team dynamics? As the cliché goes, you must talk the talk and walk the walk. When you say that open communication is important, you must be as open as you can with your team. When you say that respectful behavior is important, you must treat everyone on your team with respect. When you say that a shared sense of roles and responsibilities is important, you must share with people the entire team's set of roles and responsibilities.

---

16   See, among numerous other sources and Internet mythology, Walter Isaacson's book *Steve Jobs*.

There are a number of team-building activities that can help you encourage a sense of team as well:

- **Group meals.** You can have lunches brought in, especially during hectic periods or at major project milestones. You can organize an event where an individual member brings in a special dish, which can be especially fun when you have a multicultural team. You can have group dinners from time to time too, but be sensitive to the situation of people with families.

- **Celebratory parties.** When a project is completed or other major milestones occur, you might consider marking the occasion. The party can be as simple as a quick break for cake or something more elaborate such as an off-site party. Party favors such as special shirts or coffee mugs (with a project logo or slogan, for example) can help people remember the event later. In certain company and local cultures, having alcoholic drinks available can be appropriate too, but you should remain sensitive to the problems and risks that excessive alcohol consumption can create.

- **Sharing special events.** When a team member has a major life event, such as a birthday, wedding, or new baby, it's appropriate to notice that and in many cases organize a simple team celebration. This can be overdone, so take care that you do not mark these events in a way that makes people feel uncomfortable. When the major event is negative—such as a death in the family or a major illness—then sincere, thoughtful, and supportive actions are in order.

- **Team newsletters or intranets.** Having an internal newsletter, web page, or wiki page that provides opportunities for further communication can also help the team feel more connected.

- **Educational sessions.** We referred to "brown-bag" sessions earlier, where, over lunch, test team members can present new concepts to each other. These new concepts can include new test tools, interesting articles on testing, and a test technique that others can benefit from, among other ideas.

- **Professional help.** There are a number of companies that offer services to help build teams. For example, some companies arrange "ropes courses" where people and teams are challenged to do various rope-walking activities or simulated rock climbing. These can be appropriate for adventurous teams and can result in a feeling of energy, trust, and unleashed potential when people find that individually and together they can overcome self-imposed limitations and irrational fears. Other companies arrange more introspective types of activities, including human potential and group encounter events. You must use your judgment on how to implement these activities though; the situations used to build a team must be physically, emotionally, and psychologically safe for the participants if they are to result in actual team building rather than injury to the team spirit if not physical injury to the team members.

When you set up team-building activities, try to be as inclusive as possible. It can be hard to work around everyone's schedule, but simply scheduling events without considering individuals' personal situations, holidays, and other constraints tends to defeat the purpose. In the current distributed approach to working, scheduling inclusive team-building activities is made more complicated by the fact that teams are often not colocated. If you can't get everyone into a single activity, then consider multiple activities.

Team-building activities need not be limited to building the test team only. Testing groups work within larger software organizations, which include other groups such as business analysts, programmers, technical publications, and so forth. Organizations of any kind work more effectively and efficiently when people understand each other's roles and responsibilities, as mentioned earlier. Consider organizing a cross-functional event or series of events (such as an on-site lunch) where all the major groups within the organization give quick presentations about what their group does, what major inputs they need to receive, what major outputs they deliver, and how their work benefits the organization. Not only will such events make the organization more effective and efficient, they will build a stronger sense of teamwork across the organization.

2.4.4 Motivating and Challenging the Test Team

Most adults are not inherently lazy and do not require constant pressure and micromanagement from their superiors to stay on task. Most adults are relatively self-motivated. They want to work and enjoy the feeling of accomplishment that comes from a job well done. They like to overcome challenges and learn new things in their jobs. They look forward to the next project or assignment. People are motivated by a salary that they consider fair. So, much of motivating a team consists of simply letting these natural human motivations work.[17]

---

17   See, for example, Daniel Pink's book *Drive: The Surprising Truth About What Motivates Us.*

That said, motivation is a matter of degree, and part of your job as a manager is to create a team that is highly motivated to succeed. Major elements of motivation have to do with skills growth and team building, which we've already discussed in this chapter. What are some other ways we can produce highly motivated teams?

Open communication is one part of motivation. When people understand the status of their projects, the organization, and the company as a whole, that tends to improve motivation. As a consultant, Rex sometimes hears line managers and individual contributors say, "This company practices the mushroom management style: We're all kept in the dark and fed lots of steer manure [to use a polite term]." The people saying this are generally not motivated employees.

This also includes evaluating your team-members' work. When their work is good, you can give the feedback publicly, and many times you should. It's important that public praise be given in a way that is sincere and specific rather than phony and vacuous. Simply walking up to someone's desk, apropos of nothing, and saying, "Great job, Janet; I really like your work lately," only makes you look like a clueless management dork—someone straight out of a television parody of office life—while leaving the praised employee entirely nonplussed and possibly a little embarrassed.

When their work is not acceptable, the feedback should be one-on-one. Criticizing people's work in public, especially if it's accompanied with personal put-downs, is never acceptable and is demotivating to the individual and to everyone who witnesses it. It's important that, in private sessions where you criticize someone's performance, you start with a clear statement of the problem, including an objective presentation of the facts, and then honestly and supportively work with the person to guide them toward doing a better job. This includes listening to and considering their side of the story, because it's possible that significant external factors contributed to the problem. Simply calling someone into your office, yelling at them about their lousy performance lately, and sending them along their way is less likely to produce the desired result than an honest discussion that includes specific guidance toward better work products and behaviors.

Most people are perfectly willing to work hard but find it difficult to do work that might be easy but is tedious or boring. The human brain is wired to seek out and enjoy activities that result in acquiring new information, new abilities, new challenges. You can take advantage of this evolutionary reality by giving people opportunities to do new and different work. Assign work in a way that challenges and stimulates people, considering their abilities and experience. Job rotations, training, and other ways of making people's work life diverse and novel can all help maintain motivation.

We discussed team development and your need to build a team that is well aligned with the organization's needs earlier in this chapter. There's a motivational opportunity in this area too, which you can and should use. When you identify areas where the team needs to improve, ask the test team members which of those areas are of interest to them. You can then simultaneously promote and positively take advantage of an individual's motivation by having them grow their own skills in that area.

One important benefit of leading an engaged and motivated team is that of retention. People who are happy in their work are generally less likely to "jump ship." In fact, the positive feedback loop of a motivated team may entice others to try to join your team because working there is such a positive experience.

2.4.5 Managing Distributed Teams

In the next chapter, we'll take a look at some of the important "hard" factors associated with managing distributed and outsourced testing work, but there are also "soft" factors—human issues—to consider. The colocated project team, for all its manifold benefits and advantages, is a rare luxury these days. For many, indeed most, test managers, managing testing teams that are distributed throughout the building, around the city, across the country or even the world is a fact of life now. What are some of the challenges to consider, and what are the management questions raised thereby?

One of the challenges can be time-zone differences. Obviously, when members of a group work in different time zones, they are not all working at the same time. In extreme cases, such as overseas outsourcing, the number of common work hours—the window of time when everyone on the team can be assumed to be at work—may be limited or even nonexistent. This can create numerous communication challenges that you should be aware of and actively manage. This lack of overlapping hours can also affect the team-building activities discussed earlier, and you should look for creative ways to overcome this challenge to ensure that local and remote teams feel equally engaged.

Another challenge relates to cultural differences. People are people, it is true, but cultural differences can obscure that. For example, cultural differences can lead to problems when people misunderstand each other's verbal and non-verbal communication. What we have found helpful is encouraging people on each side of the cultural divide to instead see cultural differences as a paid opportunity to learn about different cultures without having to spend a single vacation day or fly around the world packed into the economy end of an airplane.

Often concurrent with cultural differences are language differences. Language differences may seem to be the ultimate barrier to communication, but in fact, because these differences are so obvious and so clearly require direct action, they have the advantage of being managed in just about every instance where we've seen them arise. In fact, it's the situations in which people spoke different dialects of the same language—e.g., US English versus UK English versus Indian English—where we've seen the most frequent language-related communication and other problems arise.

Language differences, cultural differences, and time-zone differences all directly affect communication. You should plan, in advance, how you intend to manage communication between the distributed elements of your team. Regularly scheduled conference calls or video meetings are useful. Internet telephony and webcams have made it possible for people to have sophisticated communications from around the world, and perhaps even from their homes, which can reduce the need for people to be in their offices at odd hours when you're trying to coordinate a conference call across three far-flung time zones. For example, try to find a common work hour between New Zealand, United States, and Europe.

While no country has a monopoly on intelligence, it is true that skill levels tend to vary depending on whether a country's IT economy is fully developed (e.g., North America, Europe, and Japan), just emerging (e.g., Vietnam and the Philippines), or somewhere in between (e.g., India, Brazil, and China). As a test manager, you must manage the impact of the relative skill levels of the testers available in a given locale. For example, outsourcing highly complex and interactive activities such as performance testing to a team of smart but utterly inexperienced testers in an emerging economy will not turn out well.

Finally, we have discussed in this chapter and the previous chapter the importance of alignment of expectations. That is a particular issue for distributed teams. When people are working with inconsistent expectations or objectives in a colocated situation, those misalignments become obvious in a relatively short order. The manager need not be especially observant to see them. However, in distributed situations, such issues can lurk, undiscovered, for quite some time. You will need to actively work to ensure that expectations and objectives are consistent and that there is an understanding and acknowledgement of these expectations across the team.

A common theme throughout this discussion of distributed teams is that of communication. Your goal, as a test manager in charge of a distributed test group, is to attain the same level of clarity, timeliness, and effectiveness of communication that you would have with a colocated team. Similarly, your goal is to attain the same level of alignment of expectations and objectives that you would have with a colocated team. While these goals may be a challenge to realize, you should aspire to this end, and you should remain aware that, to the extent that your distributed team falls short, the benefits of distributed work are reduced while the risks associated with distributed work increase.

2.5   Sample Exam Questions

In the following section, you will find sample questions that cover the learning objectives for this chapter. All K5 and K6 learning objectives are covered with one or more essay questions, while each K2, K3, and K4 learning objective is covered with a single multiple-choice question. This mirrors the organization of the actual ISTQB exam. The number of the covered learning objective(s) is provided for each question, to aid in traceability. The learning objective number will not be provided on the actual exam.

The content of all of your responses to essay questions will be marked in terms of the accuracy, completeness, and relevance of the ideas expressed. The form of your answer will be evaluated in terms of clarity, organization, correct mechanics (spelling, punctuation, grammar, capitalization), and legibility.

Scenario 2: Social Gamer

Assume that you have accepted a new job as director of testing for an organization that develops games for social media applications such as Facebook. The existing test team has experience with games testing, for social media application games as well as for gaming platforms such as PlayStation. Games testing experience is considered essential for members of the test team. Other than their experience with games testing, the test team members come from diverse backgrounds. Some of the testers have strong technical skills while others do not. Some of the testers have been trained in software testing, with about one-third having ISTQB certifications and one-third having other test-related training; the remaining third has no test training. The testers have, on average, been working with the company for a little over a year, but due to rapid growth, a substantial number are new to the company.

An analysis of the test process and its current capabilities shows that the most significant skills-related problems occur due to differences within the test team in understanding how to approach test analysis, design, implementation, and execution.

After evaluating the situation with the test team and assessing their skills, one of your goals is to build a test team that has a more consistent and generalized set of skills. Another goal is to standardize the team's testing skills and approach on the ISTQB program.

Question 1

LO 3.2.3

Consider Scenario 2. Evaluate the following options:

I.   Training in the application business domain for all staff.
II. Training in the application business domain for some staff.
III. Training in the application technology for all staff.
IV. Training in the application technology for some staff.
V.   Training and certification in the ISTQB program for all staff.
VI. Training and certification in the ISTQB program for some staff.

Which of the following training programs best meets your needs and puts the options in the proper sequence?

First IV, then VI.
First V, then III.
First II, then VI.
First VI, then IV.

Question 2

LO 3.2.1 and LO 3.2.2

Assume that you are going to hire a new tester. You have résumés from three candidates, which can be summarized as follows:

▪ Candidate A's résumé indicates a strong background in testing financial applications and nongame consumer electronics, strong technical skills, excellent testing skills, and ISTQB certifications.
▪ Candidate B's résumé indicates some experience in testing games, limited technical skills, good testing skills, and ISTQB certifications.
▪ Candidate C's résumé indicates a strong background in game testing, limited technical skills, and no structured testing skills or certifications.

▨   Candidate D's résumé indicates some background in game testing, strong technical skills, five years of testing experience, and a desire to avoid ISTQB certification.

The question consists of two parts:

I.   Explain which of the four candidates you consider the best candidate(s) and why.
II. Describe, using the interviewing concepts listed in the syllabus, how you will interview the candidate(s).

Answer each part succinctly but fully.

Question 3

LO 3.2.4

Consider the following options:

A. Frequent personal conflicts involving a particular employee.
B. Personal relationships between you and individual testers.
C. Cross-training the people who will replace the terminated employee.
D. Test execution effort exceeding planned effort on a project.
E. Ways to internally reassign the terminated testers.
F. A mismatch between an employee's skills and the new product line.
G. Percentage of defects found by each tester.

Select three considerations that are always important when terminating an employee.

Question 4

LO 3.3.1

As a test manager, you have a development plan that covers all the individual testers on your team and addresses the existing skills gaps. This plan is aligned with the needs of individual testers, the test team, and the wider organization. The tester's annual performance goals include making progress toward skills development planned for them in that year, and these goals conform to the SMART guidelines. You regularly review progress toward these goals with each of the individual testers.

Based only on the information given, which of the following statements is true?

A. This plan will gradually increase the capabilities of your team.
B. Using the goals is not a fair way to measure employees.
C. You now should do a task analysis and then a skills inventory.
D. This plan replaces any need for formal training.

Question 5

LO 3.3.2 and LO 3.3.5

Assume that you are working with an individual tester to set skills-development goals for that person in the coming year, working within the situation described in Scenario 2. Assume that risk-based testing is the primary test strategy for your group. The tester's résumé indicates some experience in testing games, limited technical skills, good testing skills, and an ISTQB Foundation certification.

Which of the following goals is consistent with the team development plan outlined in Scenario 2 and fits the guidelines for a SMART goal?

A. Take a course on technologies used in developing social media games, identify ways to apply those technical skills on your next project, and develop and execute appropriate technical tests assigned by your test manager.
B. Take the in-house e-learning Advanced Test Analyst course, participate in quality risk analysis on your next project, and develop and execute tests consistent with the quality risk items assigned by your test manager.
C. Attend a lunchtime brown-bag session on risk-based testing, participate in quality risk analysis on your next project, and develop and execute tests consistent with the quality risk items assigned by your test manager.
D. Take the in-house e-learning Advanced Test Manager course, participate in quality risk analysis on your next project, and develop and execute tests consistent with the quality risk items assigned by your test manager.

Question 6

LO 3.3.3

Assuming that the test manager has aligned each tester's roles and responsibilities with the goals and objectives for testing, which of the following answers best captures the reasons individuals should understand their roles and responsibilities in the test team?

A. To define a generalized model for organizing the test team.
B. To ensure that the test manager derives proper metrics for each tester.
C. To help them align their actions with the mission of the test group.
D. To support termination of testers that do not meet performance expectations.

Question 7

LO 3.3.4

Assume you are working on a project and most of the test development and execution will be done by an offshore team. The offshore team has clearly defined service-level agreements (SLAs) for their work and templates for their work products. If you need to assign a senior tester to review this team's work products and advise them on how to improve those work products, which of the following statements is correct?

A. A thinking individual is not suited to review the work products from the offshore team.
B. A feeling individual is best suited to review the work products from the offshore team.
C. A judging individual is not suited to advise the offshore team.
D. An extroverted individual will tend to engage well with the people on the offshore team.

Question 8

LO 3.4.3

Assume you are managing a test team and significant regression testing is required and most testing is currently done manually. Which of the following approaches best manages the challenges of motivating this test team?

A. Build a regression-testing framework and train testers to build automated regression tests.
B. Publicly praise testers for finding regression defects with manual tests.
C. Publicly criticize testers when they fail to find regression defects with manual tests.
D. Outsource the manual regression testing to an offshore team.

Question 9

LO 3.3.6 and LO 3.3.7

Consider Scenario 2. Assume that you are doing annual performance reviews for two people on your team:

- The first person is a high performer. She has high skills in terms of testing generally, games testing specifically, and games technology. She has ISTQB Foundation and Advanced Test Analyst certifications.
- The second person is a poor performer. He is perfectly pleasant to work with and fits well with the rest of the team in terms of personality. However, he lacks general testing skills and is not ISTQB certified.

Describe the main elements of each of the two performance reviews you will write.

Question 10

LO 3.4.1

Assume that you are managing a team of testers that performs maintenance testing on monthly releases of bug fixes and patches for a commercially success-ful mass-market application. The testing process for these releases is routine, including regression testing using an automated functional and performance regression test set along with manual tests of new functionality. Work is pro-ceeding smoothly, and your testers are able to work independently without regular course correction from you. Each tester has their own area of responsibility, but they also need to be aware of each other's work. Your manager expects you deliver a regular report on the status of your testing.

Which of the following is the most effective communication method in this situation?

A. Have informal communications with your team toward the end of each week, and then aggregate the information from that meeting into a group status report that you deliver to your manager but not the test team.
B. Obtain weekly status reports from your testers, and aggregate that information into a group status report that is delivered to your manager but not the test team.
C. Hold one-on-one meetings with your team each day throughout the week, and aggregate the information from that meeting into a group status report that you deliver to your manager and the test team.
D. Obtain weekly status reports from your testers, and aggregate that information into a group status report that you deliver to your manager and the test team.

Question 11

LO 3.4.2 and LO 3.4.4

Consider scenario 2. Assume further that an analysis shows that miscommunication and failure to communicate within and between test teams was responsible for the largest number of incidents that reduced overall effectiveness or efficiency and that these communication breakdowns arose mostly from a lack of trust between individuals.

You have decided to address this problem in an urgent fashion because some of the incidents that have occurred are quite significant in their impact and embarrassing to the test team. Which of the following is the best team-building activity to help resolve the problem?

A. Team newsletter.
B. Professional help.
C. Group meal.
D. Celebratory party.

3 Managing External Relationships

Keywords: None for this chapter

3.1 Introduction

Learning objectives

No learning objectives for this section.

There was a time, ages ago in Internet time but within living memory of grizzled software veterans such as your humble narrators, when everyone on a software project worked in the same building. Rex's first experience writing software—and also testing his own software, which was how most testing was done when he started in the software business—was with a team of people in West Los Angeles who all sat within 50 feet of each other on the same floor of the same office building, most of them working in product teams in open spaces together.

Of course, even then, in the early 1980s, plenty of projects involved third parties, outsourcing, and other forms of distributed work. Rex and his colleagues created a customized version of the company's portfolio management and accounting system for a client on the East Coast, Goldman Sachs. Conference calls, letters, and on-site visits were used (as this was BE—before email) to communicate project status, change requests, and the like.

However, it's certainly true now that a test manager is much more likely—indeed, probably certain—to be involved in projects where a third party is involved. In this chapter, we'll focus on situations in which this third party is a vendor or another group in a different part of the organization. We'll assume that this third party is creating, testing, or delivering some or all of the product. We'll discuss the specifics of this third-party relationship—which can be complicated—in the next section.

As a test manager, you need to ensure that the vendors deliver the proper level of quality. Working with third-party vendors affects the schedule, the test approach, the documentation, the communication channels and styles, and more. Facilitating smooth delivery of a quality product in these situations is a special challenge to the test manager.[1]

3.2 Types of External Relationships

Learning objectives

LLO 4.2.1 (K3) For a given contract, define the third-party relationship regarding testing responsibilities.

Let's start by examining the various types of external relationships that can exist and affect your job as a test manager.

The first type of external relationship is where a third party delivers a completed software product or system. This is sometimes referred to as *turnkey* development. This can run the spectrum from the purchase of commercial off-the-shelf (COTS) software to custom development based on the customer's specification. In addition, the system itself can run the spectrum from being used in a purely standalone fashion to being tightly integrated with other systems in the customer's data center. Examples of this type of relationship include purchase of a custom-developed loan origination package or an enterprise virus-protection package.

The second type of external relationship is where a third party does only the software development, with the testing left to the customer or recipient. In our experience, even when the relationship is supposedly a turnkey one, developing organizations often perform inadequate testing. So, this type of relationship explicitly allows for the deliberate detection of defects by the recipient, with (one would hope) some mechanisms for defect repair, confirmation testing, and regression testing. An example of this type of relationship is an organization having an e-commerce site custom developed.

The third type of external relationship is where a third party develops a subsystem or module that the customer will integrate into an overall system. The difference between this type and the first type is that, in the first type, a complete system is delivered, where in this type, the delivered component must be integrated into a larger system. An example of this type of relationship is an

---

1   Rex has written about distributed testing in various books and articles, but most especially in *Managing the Testing Process: Practical Tools and Techniques for Managing Hardware and Software Testing/ Edition 3*, Chapter 10.

organization purchasing a business-card scanning subsystem to include in its sales management application.

The fourth type of external relationship is where a third party will handle the testing of a product that has been developed internally. This typically would include the higher levels of testing and less frequently might include unit or component integration testing. An example of this type of relationship can occur when a start-up company—or just a few smart programmers—creates a software product but has no testing staff, environment, or capabilities, so it hires an outsource testing service provider to perform all the testing.

The fifth type of external relationship is where a third party and an internal test team each do some of the testing of internally developed software. As with the fourth type of relationship, the work done by the third party typically involves higher levels of testing. This might seem like a variant of the fourth type, but it tends to be more complex (at least when done well) due to the need for coordination between the groups doing the testing. We'll discuss the issues associated with integrating test strategies across multiple organizations in a subsequent section.

On any given project, more than one of these types of external relationships might exist. In addition, external relationships might exist that contain elements of more than one type. The purpose of presenting these relationship types is not to provide a way for you to perform a clean, one-to-one classification of actual business relationships on a project but rather to help you think about these various types, and, in subsequent sections, how the properties of these relationship types affect testing.

The type of external relationships that exist will strongly influence the test work on the received product and the organization of that work. Obviously, each additional party involved in a project increases the importance of good communication, proper documentation, and appropriate means of coordination between the parties. We'll discuss these issues further later in this chapter, but first let's look at how contractual matters affect these external relationships.

3.3   Contractual Issues

Learning objectives

LO 4.3.1   (K4) For a given project with an external vendor,
            define suitable SLAs.

Regardless of the relationship type, in most circumstances we've seen, working with an external entity involved a contract. In the best case, you as the test manager will have input into the drafting of the contract, at least on those elements of the contract that involve testing. In this fortunate circumstance, you will be consulted on the implications for the testing process and be able to contribute to certain technical and methodological aspects that will affect testing and quality. In most cases, though, the legal department or senior management will handle the contract. In some cases, we have seen management completely surprise the test team with the external relationship, with predictable results on morale and trust.

Regardless of whether you are involved in the contract negotiations up front or only become aware of the contract afterward, you will need to be aware of certain relevant details in it. As mentioned, elements of the contract often have implications for testing, which you need to understand. In addition, you need to at least be aware of, and plan for, those technical and methodological clauses that will affect testing and quality.

While there is no industry-standard contract for these relationships, there are some typical test-related elements of these contracts that you should be aware of and plan to handle. The first of these involve service-level agreements (SLAs). When the third party is developing all or some of the software product, the SLAs may include turnaround time for defect fixes, which can vary depending on the severity or priority. When the third party is testing all or some of the software product, turnaround time might relate to confirmation testing of defect fixes. In all cases, contracts should specify response time for questions or requests for information. (Requests for proposals relating to additional work usually don't require an SLA, but we have seen situations in which the customer had to chase the provider around, waving money at them, to get a quote, which is usually a sign that you picked the wrong service provider!) Support staff should be named for the various kinds of questions and information flows that will occur, and methods of contact should be specified. Ideally, there should also be a process that can be used to escalate a question, concern, or problem to senior vendor management if the use of normal channels does not result in timely resolution.

Another important test-related element of these contracts concerns the deliverables. Whichever party does the testing, a clear understanding is needed of what is to be delivered; which of those deliverables are to be tested by the delivering party, the receiving party, or both parties; whether aids to testing such as test data, test cases, test tools, and testing frameworks are deliverables; what information about the deliverables will be provided along with the deliverables—and in what format; and the schedule for those deliverables. Deliverables can include documentation such as user guides, help files, and specifications. Especially if your team is to do the testing, you'll need test release or test build schedules. Information about deliverables should include a list of any known defects along with release notes that indicate what areas of the system might not be ready for testing yet. Test aids should be thoroughly described, and if test data is to be provided, the requirements for removal of sensitive information (e.g., via anonymization) must be described. The schedule for deliverables should be part of the SLAs, especially for builds that resolve defects.

You might be tempted, or be told by others on the project, to relax and assume problems will work themselves out. But ambiguity in these details about deliverables can be the source of grief on many projects and contracts. It's hard to be precise in these details, so it's a common mistake to assume that the fuzzy spots will resolve during the term of the contract. Yes, those fuzzy spots will resolve, but they usually don't resolve in a way that makes sense or meets the needs of both parties. Our rule of thumb: Be prepared to be precise about deliverables, or be prepared to be disappointed by deliverables.

Yet another important test-related element of these contracts is the quality process used to assure the quality level of the deliverables, which we consider important enough to break out from the deliverables themselves. It's not enough for the contract to state that deliverables will be of the highest quality. We have seen such vague statements in contracts, in some cases contracts involving millions of dollars. Ideally, the contract should specify expectations for the following quality assurance activities: code reviews; static testing of code and other deliverables; code coverage during unit testing; the approach to unit testing, component integration testing, system testing, and system integration testing and how the test results for those test levels will reported; what constitutes acceptable testing for those test levels, including the additional measures of coverage applicable to each test level (e.g., requirements coverage instead of or in addition to code coverage); and how many residual defects, blocked or unexecuted test cases, and uncovered areas may remain when a deliverable is considered done. Service-level agreements should address many of these areas as well. For example, it's not enough to say that each unit must be unit tested, with 100 percent statement and decision coverage achieved, if you don't also say that this must occur *before* the unit is delivered.

Are we being picky to call out so many expectations about quality and the quality process? You bet. Why are we so picky? Because in most of these contracts there is what's called *producer's risk* and *consumer's risk*. The producer's risk is that the consumer might reject a deliverable that should have been accepted. The consumer's risk is that the consumer might accept a deliverable that should have been rejected. Without clear expectations about what is acceptable, these risks become unmanageable for both parties. The situation becomes one of politics, a matter of relationships, presentation, and persuasion, rather than of facts.

In addition to the items mentioned in the syllabus, we have an additional suggestion, based on our own experiences with external resources (on both sides of the relationship). We recommend that you look for the contract to include named resources, including human resources with specific skills, each subject to being interviewed and accepted prior to involvement on the project. This clause is not unusual in such contracts, but it is often forgotten. This means that the clients who forget to include this clause will get whichever resources are left over. In the case of loss, delay, or turnover of resources, include a clause about clawbacks, which means that the external party must replace the lost resource in such a way that ramp-up costs or other associated inefficiencies are absorbed by the external party.

Will you be likely to see contracts that address all these elements? Our experience is that you will not. You can work to improve the contracts if you are involved before the contract is signed. You can bring up the questions and problems if you are involved after the contract is signed. The most likely situation is that not all of these elements have been addressed. These unaddressed elements are project risks, and some of these risks affect testing. You should be sure to manage these risks in your test effort if they remain.

Furthermore, depending on the contract, the industry, the product being developed, and the relationship with the third-party, additional items may be required. For example, a third-party that is contracting to produce a medical device probably will be required to obtain levels of government approvals as well (e.g., the FDA in the United States). Similarly, a third-party testing organization that has an existing relationship with the contracting company may require less definition of the SLAs and deliverables, assuming that everyone is happy and comfortable with the established vendor practices and further assuming that those vendor practices are consistently followed.

If you are involved in the vendor selection process, you can use the preceding information to review and contribute to the contract. Check for coverage of each of these items. If you see the contract only after it's signed, then, as mentioned earlier, be sure to manage the relevant project risks. In addition, gather metrics on how problems with the contract affect testing. You might have been left out of the discussion about the current contract, but such metrics can help you make the argument that you should be involved in discussions about future contracts. Armed with such metrics, you should be able to help the organization improve future contracts. You should also be able to participate in a fair evaluation of whether a given third-party should be used again.

3.4 Communication Strategies

Learning objectives

LO 4.4.1   (K2) Discuss potential communication strategies for
a given third-party engagement.

As mentioned, communication is one of the main challenges that arises when organizations involve external parties in software projects. Proper communication requires an appropriate approach on a number of dimensions, appropriate tool support, and appropriate attention to other relevant considerations. Let's examine these issues.

3.4.1 Dimensions of Information Strategies

First, the appropriate amount of information needs to be communicated. Each party needs enough information to determine the current status and the appropriate control actions to take (if any). However, there should not be so much information that one side or both cannot process the information provided. Overcommunication can create a feeling of being overwhelmed, while undercommunication can create a feeling of being in the dark. Either way, one party (or both) may find themselves surprised by sudden developments or problems, even though the information was available to foresee the situation. If there is consistently too much or not enough information, there may simply be a failure to understand the information needs of the recipients. However, withholding information or providing too much is a tactic sometimes used to obfuscate troublesome situations, so expect problems if a sudden change into overcommunication or undercommunication from the external party occurs, especially if attempts to resolve the problem are met with irrelevant, nonresponsive, or absent replies.

Second, not only is the volume of information important, but level of detail is too. For individual contributors and line managers, insufficient detail can leave the recipients unable to determine status and to decide what to do next. For senior managers and executives, too much detail, without a clear summary, can lead to the wrong conclusions being drawn and the wrong control actions selected. As with the amount of information, problems here can reflect either an intentional obfuscation or simply an inability to understand what the recipients need.

Third, and closely related to the problems with the amount or detail of information, is the frequency of communication. Think of it this way: If you check your watch every second, are you better informed of the current time or distracted from acting on that information? Each party needs information often enough to understand what has happened, what is happening, and what should happen next, but they also need a break in the communication that allows the analysis of that information to translate into insight, decisions, and action.[2]

Finally, consider the proper style, format, and formality of communication. In some cases, a quick informal email to various members of the project is perfectly acceptable, such as a status update that shows work that is on track to meet the current schedule. In other cases—e.g., missing a major project deadline or failing to provide a key deliverable—such a mode of communication would be seen (at best) as flippant and inappropriate. When troublesome information that requires discussion and tact must be communicated, an in-person meeting or at least a conference call is much more appropriate than an email or voicemail. Regardless of the type of news—good or bad—project status information should almost never be communicated in public (e.g., via Twitter, Face-

---

2   For a timely discussion about how excessive, continuous distraction has become a problem for everyone, not just those of us in technology, see Nicholas Carr's interesting book *The Shallows: What the Internet Is Doing to Our Brains*. Ironically, Rex downloaded this book over the Internet from Amazon.com and read it on his Kindle, but at least he didn't stop reading every other paragraph to check his email.

book, Google+, or on a publicly accessible wiki), except as part of a deliberate, appropriately managed public relations press release. In addition, the manner of communicating with project colleagues is often less formal than the manner of communicating with the other party's corporate counsel.

The appropriate fashion for handling these various dimensions cannot be uniformly prescribed. The nature of the product will influence communication. For example, in the case of regulated software such as medical or financial software, laws and standards can specify certain communications that must occur and indeed the exact format and style of these communications.

Communication is also affected by the third party involved. Some third parties will have sophisticated existing communication facilities, such as online meeting capabilities, intranets, videoconferencing, or even telepresence systems. Other third parties will tend to rely on simpler systems such as teleconferences, FTP servers, and email. Some third parties will automatically name primary contacts as part of the engagement, while others might have multiple contacts defined based on the particular subject being addressed. Your organization may choose to accept the default way in which the third party wants to communicate or may want to customize the approach.

You need to consider the locations of the various parties involved too. When common time zones and team languages exist, it's easier to have frequent spontaneous and scheduled communications. If work is proceeding in a number of different locations, this can be difficult. When only designated points of contact within the third party speak the other organization's project language, the pathways for communication are more limited.

The criticality and complexity of the project influences the communication. Generally, as project criticality or complexity increases, the project team needs to increase the frequency of communications, the number of prearranged contingency communication channels (in case of problems), and the precision, reliability, and alacrity of the escalation processes. For simple projects, especially when the third party's deliverables are not on the critical path for the project, you can rely on regular status reporting and deliveries, often via email or other simple channels.

Finally, any previous working relationships with the third party and the points of contact will influence communication. Established ways of communicating will often be continued, simply because it's simpler. Rex recalls that in one project, he had an informal—and sometimes confidential—communication channel with a vendor's test manager. He would give Rex frank appraisals of quality and warn him when problems were arising.

The test manager must be aware of each of these factors before defining the communication strategy for the project. For example, if the project involves having the development and unit testing done by an offshore facility, it might make sense to require weekly detailed status reports, daily defect reports, semi-weekly conference calls, and perhaps even an agreement on the language to be used in written communication.

Ideally, routine communication should be addressed in the contract. However, exceptional situations—which, in our experience, tend to occur more than once on a project—are not easily codified in a contract. The way a party in such an exceptional situation chooses to communicate with the other party speaks volumes. There is an aphorism that says that one's character is defined by their actions when no one else is looking. That is true, but it's equally true that one's character is defined by their actions, and their communications, when everyone is looking, and looking very hard. Certainly, when problems arise—and don't they always?—we respect people who act and communicate plainly, honestly, transparently, and with an eye toward the ultimate success of the larger goals, especially if they step forward to take responsibility for whatever problems have occurred.

3.4.2 Communication Tools

In our experience on projects that involve third parties, testing—whichever party is doing the testing—goes much more smoothly when appropriate tools are used for defect management and test management. By *appropriate* we mean two things:

- The tools were actually designed for the purposes of defect management and test management, respectively. We have yet to find a client that was fully successful in forcing a tool to manage defects, tests, and/or coverage when the tool wasn't designed for that purpose.
- The tools represent the best of breed in terms of tools designed for these purposes. The tools can be commercial or open source—we have clients successfully using both types of tools—but the tools should be carefully selected according to best practices for tool selection.

It is said that the craftsman is known by his (or her) tools. Indeed, you can drive nails in the wall by banging on them with the handle of a screwdriver, but it's certainly not the right way to do so. The use of the right tools will facilitate effective, efficient, and consistent communication between the various parties as well as gathering project, process, and product metrics. (We'll discuss metrics further in Chapters 6 and 8.)

Not only must we have the right tools, but we must have a single set of tools across the project or program. Trust us on this: We have tried to integrate test results data from across disparate repositories. It's a nightmare, and the resulting information is considerably less reliable than it would be with a unified set of tools. Yes, establishing appropriate access, and especially support, for these tools can be hard work. However, remember that the deliverables of testing are forms of information, and these tools are the conduits by which that information is transferred between the parties.

It's not just enough to give everyone access to these information tools. There are two other important factors: motivation and education. The contract should be defined such that the third party is motivated to provide accurate, timely, and credible information using these tools. That motivation should flow from the managers who signed contracts to the individual contributors, but it won't always do so. Be sure the contract includes penalties for bad data in these tracking systems, and don't be shy about escalating data problems when they occur.

In terms of education, there should be at least usage guidelines for the various narrative and classification fields in the tools. The best practice is to have mandatory training that ensures that each party agrees on the proper use of such tools. This includes tactical information such as severity and priority classifications as well as more strategic information such as where defects are introduced, detected, and removed. One of our clients learned this lesson the hard way when they discovered that some 10 to 25 percent of their technology budget was being wasted on excess costs of failure. Worse yet, their defect information was so full of improper classifications that they could not determine the best way to attack that waste.

3.4.3 Other Communication Considerations

While we've been focused on communications between testers and developers in this discussion of tools, there are other external stakeholders who have communication needs. You might find that you need to communicate with end users, regulatory authorities, and other stakeholders. These stakeholders probably don't want to be embroiled in the daily tactical details, but they might need to understand the test basis (i.e., the test conditions to be covered) and the high-level test results. Some of our clients open these communication channels by using a risk-based testing strategy and including these stakeholders in the risk identification and assessment processes.

Some of the communication can be done via tools, but not all of it. Meetings happen, and often meetings (or just plain phone calls between two people) are the most efficient and rapid way to resolve open issues. When these meetings must occur across time zones, as they often will when third parties are involved, the best practice is to establish regular time slots that accommodate the different parties. It's not just considerate to take people's schedules into account, but you can hardly expect someone's best work from them if they must be in a meeting at midnight or worse yet 3 a.m.

Another topic relevant to communication is that of holiday and vacation schedules. In most cases, people will be highly resistant to having to engage in anything but emergency communications while on a holiday or vacation. This consideration is especially important when you have teams working in distributed sites, often in different countries, sometimes with very different holidays, religions, and cultures. You might also find, if you are from North America and East Asia, that the work culture in other parts of the world can be less intense and fast-paced than you have come to expect. You might find a more relaxed pace refreshing or frustrating, but either way the holiday and vacation schedules are generally not subject to negotiation or override-by-dictate, so you must accommodate.

If you are working in an organization following an Agile approach, there should be daily meetings between the members of the projects. These are sometimes called "stand up" meetings (because they are supposed to be kept brief by keeping people standing). When the work is distributed across time zones, they might be sprint handoff meetings. Whatever the name and whenever they happen, Agile methodologies require frequent and regular communication, due to the reduced amount of documentation available. Everyone, including participants distributed around the world, must be able to participate in these meetings.

3.5 Integrating from External Sources

Learning objectives

LO 4.5.1   (K4) Analyze a given project scenario to determine
the appropriate level of testing required by the
internal test team for a product that has employed a
third party for some portion of the development or
testing.

It's not unusual for a project to involve integrating components or even entire systems from external parties. There is some amount of testing required by the recipient party under any circumstances, but the exact amount of testing, and the levels of testing, can vary. Let's look at various situations that can exist here.

At one end of the spectrum, a third party or multiple third parties deliver a fully developed and tested product. This is sometimes called a turnkey project. In this case, the developing party (or parties) should have completely tested the product. Your test team should plan and execute an acceptance test. The basis of the acceptance test should be the predefined acceptance criteria from the contract, from requirements specifications, and from other sources of information about what the vendor was obligated to do. The objectives of this testing should not include detecting defects because the third party should have sufficiently tested the product prior to delivery. That said, it's not unusual for third parties to deliver products that were clearly not sufficiently tested. Contracts should be structured so that the third party pays a substantial penalty for defects detected during acceptance testing.

It's often the case that these externally developed systems must be integrated into a larger set of systems. A number of our clients sell enterprise software that must work in data centers with many other systems, some externally developed and some internally developed. Another similar situation arises when a product is integrated with other products and then released as a complete package. Either way, system integration testing is a key part of completing these deliveries. Unlike with acceptance testing, it's not always possible to anticipate the various test conditions that will arise, so some number of defects will typically be found. Testing should be planned to accommodate those defects, but at the same time the contract should reflect what a reasonable number of such integration defects would be.

Moving along the spectrum of possible test involvement, we come to the situation where the third party delivers a component they have developed and unit tested. The wise test manager will request proof of testing, including code coverage metrics, the unit tests themselves (ideally automated and executable), and the test results. Assuming that the test manager is satisfied with the testing, acceptance testing of the component should occur, possibly using (in part) the unit tests provided by the third party. (As mentioned earlier, the contract should clearly specify what is required in terms of acceptance.) Following successful acceptance of the component, the test team should proceed to component integration testing, system testing, and perhaps system integration testing. This component could be integrated with other externally developed components, where each of the components would follow the same process specified in this paragraph, or with components developed internally. Acceptance testing often does not occur for internally developed components—though it does on properly run Agile projects—and doing so, regardless of lifecycle, is a good software engineering practice.

A related situation occurs when the third party delivers a developed product but cannot prove that it was tested or frankly admits that it was not tested sufficiently or even at all. Just to state the obvious, this situation really should never happen, and the contract should absolutely prohibit the possibility. However, sadly, this is not uncommon and in fact might be the most common situation. What to do? In the ideal case—well, the ideal recovery case, because this situation is far, far from ideal—your team would be able to conduct the unit tests. That typically involves technical capabilities that your team might not have, so you might have to proceed with component integration, system, and system integration testing. If there's any way for your team to perform an acceptance test of the component, by all means do so, but it might not be independently testable by your team and the developers might well have better things to do. If you must proceed with higher levels of testing without any sort of proof of testing or acceptance testing, you should carefully track the costs of poor quality associated with this situation. Also, if there are contractual penalties based on code quality and defects found, you should also carefully document test escapes.

At the entire other end of the spectrum, what of the situation in which a third party tests an internally developed product—that is, when some or perhaps all of the testing is outsourced for a project that was developed internally? Here, the test team is not necessarily involved, but the test manager should be. The test manager should be able to define, or at least accept, the test strategy to be used. The best practice would be for the test manager to meet with their counterpart in the third party to review and agree on the test approach, the test documentation, the test tools, the test automation (if any), and the tracking of the test results. The requirements for delivering these items should also be discussed. Furthermore, after this discussion, the best practice is that the test manager remains engaged with their counterpart in the third party to monitor the status of testing as it proceeds.

While considering these various types of external party situations, also consider the level of integration and handoff documentation required. For example, if you are going to perform component integration and/or system integration testing, you'll need to know how things fit together. As another example, when we mentioned earlier that you should ask for "proof of testing," well, what exactly would constitute adequate proof, sufficient for you? What requirements exist for your project? What are the various milestones that will occur, and how can you measure adequacy of testing and quality at those milestones?

As important as testing and quality metrics are in any situation (as discussed in Chapters 6 and 8), in situations with external parties, they are even more important. Ideally, these metrics are part of how the external party's effectiveness and efficiency are measured, and the test manager is involved in defining and monitoring the metrics. The metrics should include test escapes, defects trends, unit test coverage, and so forth.

As mentioned in the section on contractual issues, the best practice is that issues such as the ones discussed in this section are firmly defined in, and enforceable through, the contract. Without the contract behind you, no matter how egregious the violation of testing or quality best practices, you will often find that there's little you can do to solve the problem for the current project. However, that doesn't mean you can't change future projects. These metrics can drive such changes.

3.6 Merging Test Strategies

Learning objectives

LO 4.6.1 (K2) Summarize the items that must be considered when merging test strategies with a third-party organization.

As you might have gathered from this chapter so far, the involvement of third parties poses a number of challenges for test management. It's especially true when some or all of the testing is done by the third party. That might seem counterintuitive, but it's often the case that test managers or test directors retain ultimate accountability for the testing, even when that work is not done by their team. The test manager must assemble a coherent picture of testing and quality from across multiple locations, multiple organizations, or multiple internal or external groups.

It can feel like trying to assemble a realistic Goya painting such as *The Duchess of Alba* from a cubist Picasso painting such as *Dora Maar au Chat*. After all, both are portraits, paintings of an individual person with a pet. Each painting is of a woman, indeed of attractive women of the same approximate age, and each woman has the same general Western European features, so how hard could it be? However, go online, look at these two paintings, and figure out how to manage it. Cutting the Picasso painting into pieces and trying to make the Goya painting from those pieces will clearly not work. The answer is to try to paint a coherent Goya from the beginning.

Let's look at the various ways in which third parties can complicate the situation and how those complications can be resolved. One of the first avenues of complication is the merging of disparate defect and test management information into a single tool. The potential problems here are myriad, and some were mentioned previously. It's difficult to ensure consistent classification and narrative information across disparate tools unless strenuous and ongoing efforts are taken to harmonize the various fields and the way they are used. One example of this type of inconsistency is when one party prioritizes defects on a scale from 1 to 5 (where 1 is the highest priority and 5 is the lowest) but the other party's scale is reversed (5 is highest priority and 1 is the lowest). Even after all parties agree on a prioritization scheme, care must be taken to make sure there is no confusion in how to report defects going forward and how to manage the defects that are already in the systems. The lack of consistency, especially in the classifications, inserts noise into the test results, making it difficult to understand the process, product, and project implications. Avoid this situation if at all possible. If disparate defect and test management tools must be used, invest the effort to harmonize the information gathered. Simply because the immediate tactical needs of the project are met doesn't mean that you can obtain adequate process information in the long term.

Beyond information management tools, there are other test automation strategies and tools involved. For example, if the third party creates automated tests using Selenium and your team uses Rational Functional Tester, you will have problems integrating the automated tests and even making sense of the results across the set of tests. When there is no common definition of a test—e.g., how many conditions are covered, how many inputs are submitted, how many outputs are confirmed, etc.—it's not possible to aggregate test counts to report test status. If your third-party partner sends you tests implemented with J-Test and you are using an open source tool like J-Unit, you will have trouble using those tests.

And this leaves open the wider question of whether the automation strategies are the same. If your strategy is to automate regression tests only and your partner's strategy is to automate reliability, performance, and regression tests, then your organizations are not aligned in terms of strategy. If you want automated functional regression tests at the graphical user interface for every feature before that feature is released but your partner intends to deliver regression tests at the application programming interface (API) only, then your organizations are not aligned in terms of strategy.

Another area of wide variance between test organizations is the definition of test levels. While the ISTQB program has clear definitions for unit, component integration, system, system integration, and acceptance test levels, these definitions are not universally accepted or followed. If you can standardize with your partner on these levels of testing—or any other mutually agreed-upon set of levels—then you can proceed to define clear responsibilities for each level. Otherwise, gaps and overlap in test coverage will tend to arise and persist.

In addition to defining the test levels and ownership of those levels, we need to make sure that commonly accepted entry and exit criteria exist across those levels. What does it mean for us to be ready to start one level? What does it mean for us to be ready to declare another level complete? Are the definitions of entry and exit criteria consistent between adjacent levels of testing? Without clarity on these questions, testing activities cannot be coordinated across teams.

With clearly defined levels, ownership, and touch points between each team, we can identify a clear plan for who does what testing, when and how they do it, and with what deliverables. The idea is that we have clearly defined activities, with overlap only where we want it. A lack of defined activities can lead to gaps in our coverage, which means less testing and lower quality, while excessive overlap means efficiency is reduced and the meaning of the test results is confused.

In the Abrahamic religions, there is a story of the Tower of Babel. In this story, people set out to build a tower to Heaven so that they could discuss the whys and wherefores of the human condition with God. God frustrates their plan by telling the angels to "confuse their tongues," causing them to speak different languages. As often occurs when people cannot communicate on a project, the tower project failed. Whether you are building a tower (or just a stairway) to Heaven or a banking application, you will need a common glossary of project terminology. This should cover both technical and testing terms.

With mutually defined test levels, responsibilities, criteria for those levels, and terminology, the next step is to define shared testing and quality objectives. How is coverage to be measured at each test level, and what constitutes adequate coverage? What quality metrics should be used, and what constitutes adequate quality for release? With consistent objectives, you can define metrics and reporting frequencies for each team involved in the project. Only with consistent answers for these questions, across all the partners, can the quality of a release be managed in a truly meaningful and informed fashion.

As discussed in Chapter 1, there are various test strategies that can be used. It's not necessary—or even ideal—for every partner involved in testing to use the same strategy. Strategies can complement each other. Ideally, a conversation occurs where the various parties involved in testing discuss the different test strategies and arrive at a common understanding of which party will employ which strategy and when. The overall result of testing should meet the needs of the project through a blend of test strategies across the various partners. The test manager for the procuring organization (i.e., the client) should be able to ensure that the disparate test strategies align with their organization's overall test strategy.

When the test strategy includes risk-based testing, then the risk analysis should be comprehensive, across all the partners involved. The partners might or might not be involved in doing the risk analysis, but they should certainly be aware of the results and how their testing addresses the identified and assessed risks. This provides a centripetal force that aligns the testing effort across the various partners.

When merging test efforts with third parties, test managers should not expect the complications discussed in this section to resolve themselves. They won't. Instead, as the project progresses, the damage created by these complications will increase. So, before the project starts, the test manager should spend some time planning and coordinating these areas. Even if the project manager—and perhaps you—forgot to include this work in the estimate, you should do it anyway. The cost of not doing it will exceed the cost of doing it, and the cost of not doing it will certainly not fit within the project estimate.

This caveat applies to the division of test work in general. You need to agree on these arrangements before the project starts or problems will occur. But what if the project starts and your testing counterparts are not available for planning work? In that case, it will be difficult (or maybe impossible?) to resolve the issues mentioned in this chapter. Ideally, the contract requires that all the appropriate parties are involved in the planning of the testing work before the project begins.

3.7 Verifying Quality

Learning objectives

LO 4.7.1 (K6) Create a set of entrance and exit criteria for a specified third-party project scenario.

Suppose you went to a restaurant for dinner, sat down, and told the waiter, "Bring me dinner and a drink." You didn't provide any further details, though you had something specific in mind. What are the chances that you'll get the dinner and drink you expected? While no one would ever do this in a restaurant, it happens sometimes on projects that involve third parties.

If we have certain expectations and requirements for an engagement with a third party, those should be defined and clearly communicated between the parties. The best practice is to have that definition and communication before the project starts and to put the agreed-upon terms into the contract. If the third party is delivering software, then these requirements should include quality targets, including measurements of those targets. The measurements should be objective and not subject to distortions, as discussed in Chapter 8.

In addition to defining the requirements, the point at which those requirements must be met should be defined. This can be done by defining entry and exit criteria that establish quality gates for deliverables. Because these quality gates will control the start and end of project phases, they should be synchronized with the phases of the project and aligned with project schedule milestones.

The Expert Test Manager syllabus provides a number of examples of entry and exit criteria for various test levels. We reformatted them into Table 3-1 below and provided our comments and suggestions on implementation or improvement of each criterion.

Table 3-1 *Annotated Entry and Exit Criteria*

Type	Level	Syllabus Criterion	Comment/Suggestion
Exit	Unit	Statement coverage meets or exceeds 85 percent.	We prefer to see a standard of 100 percent statement and decision coverage for all new or changed lines of code. We also recommend that automated unit tests, implemented with a specified tool, be deliverables for each unit of code.
Entry	Component integration	Code static analysis complete, no outstanding errors.	We would make static analysis of units an exit criterion for unit testing for all new or changed modules. For entry into component integration testing, we would require two or more communicating units that had exited from unit testing. We would also require an approved integration and integration test plan.
Exit	Component integration	All components of functional areas integrated (interfaces verified to be working correctly).	If you can make this happen, another excellent criterion is to have automated integration tests, built with the same tool as the automated unit tests, be deliverables of integration testing. Together with the automated unit tests, you will have a powerful and maintainable regression risk mitigation tool.
Entry	System	No outstanding blocking defects.	This works, but it does require that earlier levels of testing have some type of defect tracking process. Otherwise, a special sanity or smoke test must be run prior to entering system test, with the results of that smoke test determining whether the product is ready for testing.
Entry	System	All known defects documented.	As with the previous criterion, this requires that sufficient information be collected during the earlier levels of testing. Otherwise, the smoke test can be used to establish the known defects, but that really doesn't address the spirit of this criterion.
Exit	System	All performance requirements met.	We would suggest that, in addition to performance requirements (i.e., resource utilization, response time, and throughput), all functional and nonfunctional requirements should be met. If any requirement is not met, then a cross-functional team including product and project management should be allowed to accept the problem as a known limitation.

Type	Level	Syllabus Criterion	Comment/Suggestion
Entry	System integration	No outstanding high-priority or severity defects open.	Assuming this test level is preceded by system test, it's reasonable to assume that defects are tracked. However, if different groups are involved, integrating and making sense of the information can be an issue if you didn't or couldn't address the issues discussed in the previous sections on communication and merging test efforts.
Entry	Acceptance	All planned testing by the test group(s) has been completed and the testing results meet the specified criteria.	Of course, the "specified criteria" mentioned in the syllabus must actually be written, measurable, and relevant for this to work. Also, you should be careful to define what "completed" means in terms of testing. Ideally, completed testing has the connotation that all important coverage items were tested, all of the tests pass (or known failures have been officially accepted as limitations), and there are no known defects (other than these accepted limitations).
Exit	Acceptance	Sign-off by the accepting parties.	We suggest that the sign-off occur after a management review where the results and completeness of the acceptance test are evaluated, discussed, and approved.

It's important to note that Table 3-1 provides only a small sample of the criteria you would include. On an actual project, you should have a large and thorough set of criteria, addressing various issues that affect the testing work on the project, the test results, and the quality of the software being tested.

As mentioned in the Foundation syllabus, typical entry criteria for test levels should address issues such as the availability, readiness, completeness, and quality of the test environment; the availability, readiness, completeness, and quality of the test tools, including their installation in the test environment as needed; the availability, readiness, completeness, and quality of test items being delivered for test execution; and the availability, readiness, completeness, and quality of the test data. As mentioned in the Advanced syllabus, entry criteria should also address whether the tests are complete and ready to run; whether the tools are available to support test management, defect tracking, and (if applicable) automated test execution; and whether defined approaches for test results logging and tracking, defect reporting, and test metrics analysis exist and are understood by all the testers.

As mentioned in the Foundation syllabus, typical exit criteria for test levels should address issues such as the level of coverage achieved, in terms of code, functionality, requirements, or risks; predicted numbers of defects remaining, defect density, mean time between failure, or availability; cost of continuing versus ending testing; the residual level of quality risk (in terms of known defects, known failed tests, or gaps in test coverage); and schedule targets.

The stringency and formality of the criteria will vary. The product and application domain influences the criteria; for example, safety-critical systems need tougher criteria than a company's promotional web page. The past experience—good or bad—with the third party influences the criteria; for example, if a vendor provided poorly tested software in the past, the rigor of the entry criteria should be increased. The requirements for the system being built and those in the contract or agreement influence the criteria; for example, if usability is central to the value of the software, usability testing and its results should be in the criteria.

In addition to criteria to measure the status of the product, there should be well-defined, objective, measurable project milestones that allow test managers, project managers, and product managers to track the testing and the project against a schedule. To make a milestone measurable, it is imperative to have clearly defined deliverables, with a linkage to the entry criteria for those deliverables. While project or product managers should track the overall schedule, test managers should track milestones, or at least participate in the tracking of milestones, that relate to testing work and the quality of the system under test.

As important as these entry criteria, exit criteria, and milestones are for a single colocated team on a project, when other parties are involved, they become essential bulwarks against chaos and disorder. Therefore, it's important to spend the time to carefully craft the proper criteria and milestones. Not only do all important issues need to be addressed, but the criteria and milestones must be measurable in a way that all sides will agree is objective and conclusive.

It's frustrating to have criteria and milestones that are contested and relitigated by a third party once problems arise with its deliverables. It's also frustrating to find that a third party is trying to find gaps or ambiguities in criteria. However, those situations can happen. For you to deal with these situations, the criteria and milestones must be complete, measurable, objective, and—here comes the tricky part—enforceable. To be enforceable, the criteria and milestones must be clearly traceable to some clause in the contract, if not actually directly in the contract (which is the better practice). There needs to be a defined process that allows the test manager to work with the third party to resolve a violated criteria or missed milestone and, if resolution proves impossible, a defined process to escalate the problem.

During that period of resolution and, if necessary, escalation, the test manager should have clear direction on how to proceed. If testing is not to start or conclude unless certain entry or exit criteria, respectively, are met, then the test manager must have the authority to effectively stop the project, and the test manager must—absolutely must—be insulated from any negative consequences associated with such an action. Be very careful here; we have seen entire testing groups shipwreck themselves—literally put themselves in such a bad way with their colleagues that the test group ended up being dissolved—by allowing themselves to be dragooned into a process cop role, with rigorous entry and exit criteria that they had to enforce on very unhappy coworkers. We feel the best practice is for the test manager to report the status of the criteria to project and product managers and have them make the decision about whether to enforce or waive the criteria.

3.8 Sample Exam Questions

In the following section, you will find sample questions that cover the learning objectives for this chapter. All K5 and K6 learning objectives are covered with one or more essay questions, while each K2, K3, and K4 learning objective is covered with a single multiple-choice question. This mirrors the organization of the actual ISTQB exam. The number of the covered learning objective(s) is provided for each question, to aid in traceability. The learning objective number will not be provided on the actual exam.

The content of all of your responses to essay questions will be marked in terms of the accuracy, completeness, and relevance of the ideas expressed. The form of your answer will be evaluated in terms of clarity, organization, correct mechanics (spelling, punctuation, grammar, capitalization), and legibility.

Question 1

LO 4.6.1

Assume you are managing a testing project for an e-commerce website. A third-party testing service provider, using its own test environments, will handle the performance testing of the site during system testing. You will deliver the test object (i.e., test items used to install the website in its test environment) to the testing service provider once system testing has started. Which of the following is the most important element in aligning test strategies in this situation?

A. Performing a comprehensive assessment of the testing service provider.
B. Defining a unified, compatible set of test tools.
C. Agreeing on the system test exit criteria with the provider.
D. Defining testing and product performance goals.

Scenario 2 (continued): Social Gamer

Assume that you are the director of testing for an organization that develops games for social media applications such as Facebook. You have a competent test team that you have successfully grown over the past year in terms of staff size and skills. For an upcoming project, your company will be outsourcing some of the project work to third parties.

Question 2

LO 4.3.1 and LO 4.4.1

Consider Scenario 2. Further assume that you have determined that it is most economical to use an outsource testing service provider to perform compatibility testing with various mobile devices, browsers, operating systems, and other platform factors that affect the way in which your games work. Management has asked you to locate a competent provider to carry out this work.

You plan to have the provider do the compatibility testing as part of the system test level. Your team will continue to manage the system testing and carry out the rest of the functional and non-functional testing.

Which of the following statements best summarizes an element of effective, timely communication of test results by the vendor that you should include in the request for proposals (RFP) you will use to locate and select your testing service provider?

A. Require the testing service provider to send daily test results reports via its existing tools to a designated point of contact in your team.
B. Require the testing service provider to report its test results, once all testing is completed, directly into your test and defect management systems.
C. Require the testing service provider to report its test results immediately and directly into your test and defect management systems.
D. Do not include any requirements on test results reporting in the RFP because too many qualified vendors will be excluded from bidding.

Question 3

LO 4.2.1 and LO 4.5.1

Consider Scenario 2. Further assume that your company is considering an out-source development vendor with which no current or past business relationship exists—that is, it will be a new vendor to your company. Your company's objective is to outsource development of a complete product that will complement the existing line of games but is not considered essential to the business. The managers negotiating with the vendor want your input on planning the testing and putting the proper test-related clauses in the contract.

Which of the following statements best summarizes the advice you should give management in terms of planning the testing responsibilities and contractual arrangements in this third-party relationship?

A. Plan a cursory acceptance test of the delivered product, and contractually require that the vendor's testers have ISTQB Foundation and Advanced certifications.
B. Plan a thorough system test of the delivered product against clearly defined contractual requirements, with contractual rewards and penalties based on the results of this system test.
C. Plan a thorough acceptance test of the delivered product, but also plan to audit, and if necessary, manage the vendor's unit test, integration test, and system test process and results throughout the project.
D. Plan a thorough acceptance test of the delivered product against clearly defined contractual requirements, with contractual rewards and penalties based on the results of this acceptance test.

Scenario 1 (continued): The Job Has Its Ups and Downs

You are the director of software testing for an organization that makes escalators and elevators. Due to the safety-critical nature of these systems, this organization is subject to external audits of its testing.

A new model of the elevator will include a video display that is used primarily to display news or entertainment content in the elevator as people are riding between floors. However, it also connects via wireless networking to the building's security system. This allows two-way communication with elevator occupants in case of emergency and access to real-time information for firefighters when it's switched into the appropriate mode.

This video display system is being created and delivered by a third-party vendor. Your team will be responsible for performing an acceptance test on the system when it's delivered and then a system integration test of the video system with the other systems in the elevator.

Question 4

LO 4.7.1

Consider Scenario 1.

Part 1: Create a set of entrance criteria for the acceptance test.
Part 2: Create a set of exit criteria for the acceptance test.

4 Managing Across the Organization

Keywords: None

4.1 Introduction

Learning objectives
No learning objectives for this section.

No matter what type of organization you work in, or what your management reporting structure is, there will be managers across the organization that you must work with. No matter how effectively you do all the other tasks of test management, you will not be seen as successfully managing testing unless you work effectively with your fellow managers outside of the test team. This is often referred to as *outward management* or as Peter Drucker put it, *managing your managers*. Even if you are quantitatively effective and efficient in terms of the metrics discussed in Chapter 1, other managers' perceptions of your capabilities are also an important measure of your capabilities.

These managers include your peers and colleagues in development, release engineering, technical support, and business analysis. They also include your direct supervisors, senior business and technical management, and executive management. Testing involves inputs from other groups, and these needs must be communicated effectively to the managers in order for you to obtain the inputs in a way that supports testing. Testing generates information that must be shared with other managers in order to deliver the value of testing to the organization.

In this chapter, we'll examine important considerations related to managing across the organization.

4.2   Types of External Relationships

Learning objectives

LO 5.2.1   (K4) Define appropriate steps to take to promote or advocate the test team.

LO 5.2.2   (K6) For a given situation, define the quantitative and qualitative benefits of testing, and communicate those benefits effectively to project stakeholders.

LO 5.2.3   (K3) Give examples of situations in which the test manager would need to defend the test team.

In every case in which we have assessed test groups and their value to the organizations they serve, and in our own personal experiences as test managers, we have found that testing saves far more money and effort than it costs. Much of this savings is due to the escalating costs associated with customers and users finding defects compared to the relatively cheap cost of finding and removing defects in testing. Sadly, it is often true that this value is not fully understood by the others in the organization. Therefore, the test manager's job includes promoting the test team and its value across the organization.

In addition, in most of our assessments, and in our personal experiences as test managers, we have found that test groups can increase the value they deliver to their organizations. This often involves finding ways to get more closely integrated and involved with the entire development process, especially in early testing activities such as requirements reviews. However, this is often perceived as an extra cost and sometimes even as a pesky interference. Therefore, the test manager's job includes advocating the test team's role—and the expansion of it.

Finally, in most of our assessments, and our personal experiences as test managers, we have found that testing is often a controversial activity. In some cases, this is due to an unfortunate and erroneous perception that testing is an adversarial activity, one that targets the developers to make them look bad. Even when this dynamic does not exist in an organization, it can be controversial to say that some feature or characteristics of the system under test does not work properly. People might become upset at the testers involved in the testing when such defects are reported. In these situations, the test manager must defend the test group. The test manager must always look for ways to position testing as constructive and valuable.

4.2.1 Promoting and Advocating the Test Organization

Part of any manager's job is marketing their team within the organization, because no manager—at least none that we've ever met—had the power to approve their own budget. Managers must sell the value of their group's work to the people who fund it and to the people who receive that value. With test management it's no different, but the job is a little tougher because testers don't produce saleable products. What we do produce is information: assessments of the quality of the test items, measurements of our progress in testing, surrogate measures of how confident the organization should be in the software. We'll discuss this information, and how to deliver it, further in Chapter 6.

Information can be miscommunicated. Information can be misunderstood. Information can be taken for granted. Information can be frustrating when it confounds plans. Information is intangible. Our products and their values are more subtle than those of many other groups in the organization, who deal in saleable software products. You must identify the value of testing and the people who receive that value. We'll talk more about how to do that in the next section.

However, before we get into the specifics, let's talk in general about promoting and advocating a test group, or really any group. Here are four important elements in marketing and selling a test service, whether to your colleagues down the hall or to clients around the world.

Demonstrating the benefits: Be sure you capture the quantitative and qualitative benefits of testing, as we will discuss in the next section. Identify the recipients of these benefits and discuss the benefits with them. If you have saved the company 1,000 person-hours in terms of avoided costs of field failures, the technical support manager, managers of teams that use or sell the software, and your own managers should know that. Notice that we are talking about external recipients of these benefits. If your group does something that benefits your group internally but has only indirect benefits to external groups—e.g., having monthly team-building lunches to build esprit de corps—these activities are not your best candidates for promoting your group. Also, be careful to be honest, unpretentious, and realistic about the benefits you promote. Making bloated and ridiculous claims about the benefits testing is delivering will undermine your credibility and the cause of the test group.

Emphasizing the successes: In addition to the ongoing benefits, when your test group accomplishes something worthwhile or achieves a major milestone, make sure to let the appropriate people know. If your automation team finishes a complete set of regression tests in place for a major software system produced by your organization, tell the managers in charge of that system and those who either use it or sell it to customers. Be sure to explain this accomplishment in terms of the benefits it offers to the organization. You can tell people, "We have 7,547 automated regression tests for the BusyWhack system," and that's likely to be received with a polite smile or maybe a more pointed, "So what?" Instead, tell people, "We have on average 25 automated regression tests for every functional requirement for the BusyWhack system and can now, in a weekend of automated testing, reduce regression risk to the same low level that used to require four weeks of five testers doing manual testing." And again, remember to be realistic about the benefits you claim for these successes.

Publicizing upcoming improvements: When your team is working on a major improvement, inform the people who will benefit from it. If you are introducing a new test management system that will provide better and faster test results reporting and make the results accessible to all project stakeholders, talk to people who work on projects and can benefit from the improved reporting. Make it a conversation too—not just an announcement. What do people want to see in the way of test results reporting? How can your new system better serve people's information needs? If you haven't tried it, you might be surprised how helpful it is to ask stakeholders, "Here's what we're currently doing to improve this part of our test process. What improvements would you like to see?"

When necessary, admitting to and fixing mistakes: No one is perfect. Mistakes happen. Remember, the whole reason your group is there is because of the mistakes made by business analysts, system designers, database administrators, programmers, and other people engaged in creating the systems you test! So, when people in your group make mistakes, find the root cause of the mistake and fix it, if you can. If you need help from people outside your group to fix the root cause, approach them forthrightly and ask for their help. If people outside your group notice the mistake—or are impacted by the mistake—take responsibility and explain how you have fixed it—or have a plan to fix it. Trying to hide the mistake, or laying the blame elsewhere, will often do more harm than good to your reputation and the reputation of the test group.

Now, marketing and selling a service are good and important, but you also must be able to perform the service. This means that part of advocating the test group includes advocating to your direct managers and upper management the need to maintain a *capable* test group, one that can deliver the benefits, achieve the successes, continuously improve, and fix mistakes when they happen. Here are five important elements in maintaining a capable test group:

Adequately staffed: We discussed test objectives and test goals, and test strategies to achieve those goals, in Chapter 1. Having a strategy for success is important, but you will need enough people to carry out the test strategy. We'll discuss how to estimate the number of people needed in Chapter 5. Understaffed test groups simply bounce around from one project to the next, and often one crisis to the next, perhaps sufficient to do some testing and make some incremental difference, but such a group cannot be—or be seen as—an important, strategic part of the organization's quality strategy. Relevant to the topic of this chapter, you will not be able to credibly promote such a group as central to achieving quality; you will need to start by advocating sufficient staffing to your managers.

> **Rex Sees a Vendor Make It Right**
>
> I recently had an experience where I was flying Delta Airlines across the United States. There was a flight delay that caused me some inconvenience and concern about missing a connection along the way. It turned out that I did make the connection, and so did my checked bag. I felt reasonably satisfied with the way things had turned out and did not make any complaints at the airport. I arrived at my hotel, downloaded my email, and received a certificate from Delta for a bunch of bonus frequent flyer points as a way of apologizing for my inconvenience. The positive feelings engendered by that unprompted and substantial apology far outweigh the negative feelings I had about the delay. Therefore, the folks at Delta managed, by the way they handled their mistake, to make me a more satisfied customer, and one more likely to choose their service in the future.

Well-trained: Not only do you need *enough* people, you need *competent* people. As was discussed in Chapter 2, a strong contributor can be 10 times more capable than a weak contributor. You might say, "I don't have a team of strong contributors, but they're about average for their roles, so what's the problem?" Well, a strong contributor is about two and a half times more capable than an average contributor, which means you can effectively double the capability of your test group by focusing on increasing skills.[1] Part of that skills increase involves training, and getting training funding is a key part of making that happen. So you need to advocate adequate funding to build a strong test group.

Properly resourced: Even an adequate, trained test group can do little without the proper resources. Test environments, test tools, test management systems,

---

1   For the source of this data, see Tom DeMarco and Tim Lister's book, *Peopleware: Productive Projects and Teams* (3rd Edition).

defect tracking tools, workstations, reliable and fast Internet access, and good communication facilities are among some of the resources needed to do the job of testing. The resources required for testing are often expensive, so once again effective advocacy and promotion of the test group, and its successes and benefits, by the test manager is often necessary to secure these resources.

Well-informed: As we've mentioned before, testing produces information. For that information to be timely, credible, and useful, the people producing it must have the information they need to do their job. Testers need adequate test bases and test oracles to create and execute tests. Testers need to understand the intended production or customer environments to set up test environments. Testers need to be up-to-date on current project developments to respond currently to changing circumstances. If the requirements change during testing, testers must know that.

Respected: This final element is deeply intertwined with the other four. When a test group is respected, all four of the other elements will either follow directly or at least be more easily obtained by the test manager. When a test group is not respected, all will be more difficult to obtain. Respect is not given; it is earned. Part of earning respect is dealing respectfully with others; the test manager and all members of the test group must do so. In addition, the test manager must look for opportunities to advance the test team and its capabilities through the elements discussed in this list and the one preceding it. The test manager should continuously evaluate ways to improve the test group (e.g., through skills growth as discussed in Chapter 2) and look for ways in which the test group can contribute more to the organization.

These elements of marketing and selling a capable test team need not be a matter of persuasion and politicking. Fortunately, it is possible to objectively quantify the value of testing and to put forward solid, direct, qualitative benefits too. These values can be used both statically, to define the value currently delivered, and dynamically, to forecast the value that can be delivered. These forecasts can be based on proposed process improvements and possible paths forward for current projects. This predictive power is yet another value of testing.

Let's see how the test manager can accomplish these goals in the next section.

4.2.2 Selling the Value of Testing

As you just saw, part of the role of the test manager is effectively communicating and selling the value of testing. As the president of a global test consulting company, this marketing and selling role is something Rex has become quite familiar with, but he's also learned that test managers within an organization must be no less adept at this skill.

As discussed in the Advanced and Expert syllabi, values of testing are both quantitative and qualitative. They can be delivered to the organization as a whole, to projects, or to ongoing operations. Let's look at some of these values.

Finding defects: Since the cost of repairing a defect tends to increase the longer it persists through the software lifecycle, this value of testing can be quantified. Later in this section, we'll look at an established technique, cost of quality, that can allow you to do so. This can apply both to defects found during dynamic testing, such as system test or system integration test, and to defects found during static testing, such as requirements and design reviews. For defects found and removed by static testing, the effect is magnified because these defects are prevented from amplifying their cost and number by escaping into the coding process.

Reducing risk by running tests: This value can be quantified through a calculation of the likelihood of certain types of failures along with the financial impact those failures would have if they occurred in production. Because of the difficulty of obtaining reliable numbers for likelihood and impact, this value is typically discussed in more abstract and qualitative terms. It is important to remember that the level of quality risk cannot be reduced to zero through testing, due to two principles discussed at the Foundation level: the impossibility of exhaustive testing and the ability of testing to demonstrate the presence of defects but not to prove the absence of defects.

Delivering information: The test process delivers—or at least should deliver—information about project, process, and product status that leads to better decisions. Given the high percentage of projects that fail, and the fact that these failures often result from bad decisions, this value can be quantified by looking at the percentage of similar projects that fail and the potential loss if this particular project failed. As with risk reduction, it is usually difficult to obtain precise numbers for likelihood and impact, so this value is typically quantified with a rough estimate or simply discussed in abstract and qualitative terms.

Building and increasing confidence: The more thoroughly tested a product is, the more confidence we can have that fewer undiscovered bugs remain. This value can be somewhat quantified through various coverage measures, such as risk coverage, requirements coverage, configuration coverage, interface coverage, data coverage, code coverage, and other relevant coverage measures. If such quantification is attempted, three caveats are important. First, different relevant measures apply to different products and test levels, so carefully select the coverage dimensions used as a surrogate metric for confidence. Second, similar with risk reduction and for the same reasons, do not let people believe that 100 percent coverage means 100 percent confidence that no undiscovered bugs remain. Third, due to another testing principle, the absence of errors fallacy, a high level of confidence in the quality of the product does not mean people should expect automatic success of the product in the market or with users.

Improved reputation for quality: Organizations that have experienced quality problems on past projects, especially when quality problems affect customers and users, often institute or improve testing groups in a desire to improve their quality and thus their reputation. Indeed, this is practically the mother of all testing values, in the sense that very few organizations would bother with testing if they didn't feel that testing had some ability to improve quality. This value also has the potential to be enormous and wide-ranging. Higher-quality products enjoy improved customer satisfaction, and those customers have increased goodwill toward the producer. This leads not only to avoidance of lost sales due to quality problems, but also to increased sales due to positive word of mouth. A reputation for poor quality has the opposite effect, of course, and has been known to create serious, even existential problems for products. Be careful not to oversell this value, though, because so many other parts of the software engineering process affect the quality of the product. The best testing group in the world cannot save a fatally flawed product. This value is best sold as a qualitative value because it is unlikely that there is any meaningful way to quantify it.

Smoother and more-predictable releases: Similar to the value of improved quality, organizations that have seen quality problems affect their release plans and schedules, especially defects discovered late in a project, may institute or improve testing groups. Indeed, testing can help in this regard. Risk-based testing can result in important tests being run earlier in test cycles. Early testing activities (another principle mentioned in the Foundation syllabus) can reduce the number of defects that need to be found in later testing activities. However, as with improving quality, there are limits to what you, as a test manager, can do to deliver this value if other parts of the software engineering process are not arranged in a supportive way. This value also is best sold as a qualitative value because, again, it is unlikely that there is any meaningful way to quantify it.

Protection from legal liability (compliance with regulations, standards, and contracts): This value is a variant of one or both of the previous two values that applies when an organization has a legal responsibility for the quality of its products. Two common examples are regulated products, such as medical devices, and custom development for a client, at least a client that has been smart enough to include appropriate wording in its outsourcing contracts. This is an interesting value in that 100 percent coverage of specified requirements, along with complete adherence to other applicable contractual agreements or standards, can be sufficient to provide almost bulletproof protection. (We say "almost" because situations that result in death or serious injury will usually result in legal complications. As the lawyers' aphorism puts it so well, you might beat the rap, but you won't beat the ride, and that ride can be very expensive.) Our clients that work in regulated environments have very little difficulty in selling the value of testing. However, custom development—at least at this time—still suffers from a bad reputation for quality, so you can combine this value with the previously mentioned one when selling testing.

Reducing risk of loss of whole missions or even lives: If you work on weapons systems, there is significant risk that, if such systems malfunction, so-called friendly-fire incidents or other mishaps could result in the death of the warfighters trying to use those systems to military advantage. Alternatively, the malfunction could cause enemy warfighters to escape demise and thus live to effect death or injury on friendly troops. Even when the results of failure are not so dramatic, there are plenty of mission-critical systems in banks, insurance companies, investment companies, government agencies, electrical power companies, oil refineries, telecommunications and Internet infrastructure, and other socially critical entities. If these systems fail, the lives of users and other members of society can be significantly affected. It is often—but not always—the case that the necessity of testing of these critical military and nonmilitary systems is obvious to most stakeholders, but the wise test manager is ready to make the case. Be careful not to overplay this value, though, because it's a fine line between accurately stating the potential consequences of insufficient testing and verging into melodrama.

This list is not necessarily complete. Different stakeholders will have different values that they receive from testing. When you're communicating about the value of testing, you must take into account the stakeholders' perceptions of those values. Telling a stakeholder about values they care about will motivate them to respect and support the test team, while talking about values they find irrelevant to their needs will have the opposite effect. You should ask the various test stakeholders about the objectives they have for testing, as discussed in Chapter 1, as part of deciding which of these values to discuss with them.

Let's look more closely at how to use cost-of-quality analysis to quantify the benefits of testing. These benefits can be quantified either in terms of money saved or time saved. Cost of quality says that, anytime we plan, build, deliver, and support a product, we have costs associated with doing so. If the revenues associated with the product exceed the costs, then we have a profitable product, but we can increase the profitability of a product by reducing the costs. Some of these product costs are unrelated to quality, and cost of quality ignores those costs. Cost of quality says that there are two general categories of costs that relate to quality:

cost of quality = cost of conformance + cost of nonconformance

The cost of conformance is money (or effort) spent to deliver a quality product. There are two categories of cost of conformance:

cost of conformance = cost of prevention + cost of detection

Cost of prevention includes various quality assurance costs, such as training and process improvement, which the organization spends to try to reduce the number of defects introduced into the product. Cost of detection includes those costs of testing that we would spend even if we didn't find any defects, such as test planning, test analysis, design, and implementation and the first time we execute a test.

The cost of nonconformance is money (or effort) spent on quality problems with the product. There are two categories of cost of nonconformance:

cost of nonconformance = cost of internal failure + cost of external failure

Cost of nonconformance includes both direct costs for defects and indirect process costs (e.g., schedule delays and test downtime due to bad test releases). The defects and their process repercussions result in rework, repairs, delays in schedules, idle time while waiting for resolution of problems, and so forth. If the defects are found and fixed prior to release, these costs are classified under internal failure; if the defects are delivered in the product, these costs are classified under external failure.

When defects are found and fixed prior to release, that's a good thing, of course. However, the test group must isolate and report the defect. The defect review committee must review and prioritize the defect. If appropriate, the development group must fix the defect and unit-test the fix. The release engineering team must deliver a repaired build. The test group must then repeat one or more tests to confirmation-test the fix as well as run some (or maybe even all) of the previously run tests for regression testing. While this is better than delivering a low-quality product to the customers—for a number of reasons, one of which will be seen in a moment—this effort is classified as rework, which is a form of inefficiency for the software engineering process. Depending on the quality of the incoming software, anywhere from 25 to 75 percent of the test budget is cost of detection, while the remainder is cost of internal failure. Similarly, as much as 75 percent of the development budget can be cost of internal failure.

When the defects escape to production and plague our customers or users, then we have cost of external failure. These expenditures often include half or more of the technical support costs, along with 100 percent of the expenses incurred when creating, testing, and deploying field fixes, product recalls and refunds, liability costs, and lost sales due to quality problems. Worse yet, the average cost of an external failure is always much greater than the cost of internal failure. We have seen the average cost of external failure range from 200 to 5,000 percent higher than the average cost of internal failure, on a per-defect basis.

This means that, expensive as testing can seem when viewed without the context of the alternative of failures in production, it typically saves many, many times more money (or effort) than it costs. This is why, as we wrote in Chapter 1, we can calculate the return on the testing investment as follows:

Test ROI

$$= \frac{(\text{average cost of a production defect} \times \text{test defects}) - \text{cost of internal failure}}{\text{cost of detection}}$$

Cost of quality is a very well-established technique, with over a half-century of published results across many industries. It is a technique you can apply easily because the math behind it is simple.[2]

As described earlier, you can discuss the value of testing both in static terms and in dynamic terms. Statically, you can capture benefits such as cost of quality and even the qualitative benefits to talk about the value of testing that has been delivered to current and past projects. We refer to this as static in the sense that the decisions have already been made, the actions already taken, the value already delivered. Discussions of static value allow you to promote the test process and team as currently working and constituted.

Dynamically, though, you can talk about values that can be delivered in the future. For example, you can talk about increasing the return on the testing investment by increasing defect detection effectiveness, phase containment, and other potential improvements. Discussions of dynamic value allow you to make forecasts of how improvements to the test process or test team could deliver even more value. Alternatively, you can talk about how proposed decisions in terms of future project or process activities might reduce the value delivered by testing. This ability to forecast, the ability to make solid predictions about what certain decisions mean in terms of testing and quality, deliver more value to the organization.

Let us conclude this discussion on selling the benefits of testing with some general observations. In addition to the needs and objectives of the stakeholders influencing the test benefits they care about, the industry and the organization influence the relative value of these benefits. For example, mass-market software vendors will tend to highly value the benefits of smooth, predictable releases and reputation for quality, while safety-critical system makers tend to highly value the benefits of regulatory compliance and reduced risk of loss of life. Be sure to take these considerations into account when preparing your marketing pitch for your stakeholders.

---

2   The original reference is J. M. Juran's *Quality Control Handbook*, a magisterial (and weighty in many ways) book first published in 1951. Rex's own books *Managing the Testing Process Practical Tools and Techniques for Managing Hardware and Software Testing*/ Edition 3, *Advanced Software Testing - Vol. 2, 2nd Edition: Guide to the ISTQB Advanced Certification as an Advanced Test Manager*, and *Critical Testing Processes: Plan, Prepare, Perform, Perfect* include discussions of applying the technique to software and systems development. You can find an online explanation of the technique on the RBCS website at www.rbcs-us.com/software-testing-resources/library/basic-library in the article called "Testing ROI." You can find a spreadsheet that will help you calculate testing ROI using that technique at www.rbcs-us.com/blog/2010/09/09/free-tool-for-calculating-software-testing-roi.

In addition, remember that your stakeholders are not testers. This means you need to communicate in terms that they can understand and appreciate. Whenever you are trying to convince a stakeholder that some particular testing activity is valuable to them, first ask yourself the question, "What's in it for them, and how will they see it?" For example, if you are talking to a business analyst manager about the importance of traceable requirements and coverage analysis, don't say, "We need traceable requirements so we can cover the requirements." Instead, say, "If we have traceable requirements, we can make sure that our tests cover those requirements. That way, we can help you have confidence about which requirements are satisfied while also letting you know which requirements are not satisfied and what defects exists for those requirements."

Last, remember that your stakeholders are smart. Just because they don't understand testing doesn't mean that they can't see through an inflated business case or value. When you're talking to fellow managers about how testing will benefit them, be accurate and, if anything, undersell a bit. As Tom DeMarco wrote, a good manager has a nose for lies and exaggeration.[3] At the same time, don't hedge and waffle, because that will damage your credibility.

The secret here, which is no secret at all but practiced by many successful test managers around the world, is this: In plain terms that they can understand, tell stakeholders how testing will benefit them, make solid commitments about the value of testing, and then keep (or exceed) those commitments. Doing so will allow you to get the resources you need for your current projects and programs. As your credibility grows through promises made and promises kept, you'll be able to spend that political capital to get more resources for testing, to motivate earlier and deeper involvement for your test group, and to attract support for test process improvements and scope expansion.

This political capital will also help you in the darker hours, when you have to defend the test group under difficult circumstances. That is the topic of our next two sections.

4.2.3 Creating a Defensible Team

It's great when projects go perfectly, exactly according to plan. It does happen, especially with smaller, simpler projects. However, as the size and complexity of projects increase, so does the likelihood of significant unexpected events.

---

3   Actually, DeMarco used a more frank and pungent US English word for lies and exaggeration, which we'll avoid to retain a general audience rating for this book. This memorable quote on management, and other good ones, can be found in his book *The Deadline*.

Capers Jones
Shares Notes from the Field

Capers Jones shared some observations on selling the value of testing, based on some work he did with a company that was spending about $750,000,000 per year on software bug repairs and related costs:

1) The company had 10,000 software people and was increasing staff at 5 percent per year. With better quality, the company could stop growing and reach a steady state of only 9,000. Better quality would free up almost 1,000 developers and 2,000 maintenance people.

2) Its major products were late to market by about 15 months, primarily due to delays in testing. With better quality up front and better test methods, it could chop more than one year off development schedules. This translated into more revenue dollars since the applications were being marketed commercially.

3) For the past five years the company was spending roughly 50 cents out of every dollar spent on software finding and fixing bugs. With better defect prevention, pretest removal, and better testing, it could cut those costs below 15 cents out of every dollar. This would translate into savings of 35 cents out of every dollar spent on software.

From a risk point of view, we can say that the larger and more complex the project, the greater the number of project risks, the greater the likelihood that some of those risks will become outcomes that must be dealt with, and the greater the impact some of those risks can have. Ideally, the project management team would have all of these risks cataloged and managed, but even in that case, serious project consequences can ensue. In the real world, on many projects there are unforeseen risks that suddenly blossom into project crises.[4]

So, the expert test manager will prepare to handle these risks. For the foreseen risks, mitigation and contingency plans for each test-related risk should be part of the test plan. For the unforeseen risks, the test manager and the test group must be prepared to react nimbly. Whenever a risk becomes an outcome, the best managers respond, first and foremost, by taking prompt (but not rash) and efficient (but not penurious) actions that will minimize the consequences that most directly threaten project objectives.

To take the correct action, it's often important to understand exactly what has happened. For example, if you have a fire in your house, throwing water on that fire might be a good idea, but not if the fire originates from an electrical short or a deep fryer full of burning oil. Similarly, if the project is in trouble because of an enormous defect report backlog, having testers spend more time running tests and finding further failures will probably be less helpful than having testers support the developers in the location and removal of the underlying defects. When a crisis arises, take the advice of Rudyard Kipling: Keep your head when all around you are losing theirs. Objectively, and as calmly as possible, try to determine what has gone wrong so that effective measures may be taken. The focus should be on the effective measures, not on evading culpability. The word *excuse* shares many letters in common with the word *success*, but no one mistakes an excuse for success.

---

4   For two interesting perspectives on projects gone awry and why, see Ed Yourdon's book *Death March* or, for a quality-focused perspective, Capers Jones and Olivier Bonsignour's book *The Economics of Software Quality*.

Regrettably, when things go wrong, some people will not seek first the actions that must be taken. Instead, they will look for causes to blame. Even worse, this search for causes is often focused on mistakes people have made rather than processes that failed. In some cases, the test process or the test group will be where the failure lies, while in other cases testing will simply be a convenient or simple explanation for why the project is in trouble. As a test manager, if your team is being blamed, you need to defend the test group against unfair accusations while at the same time forthrightly and honestly holding yourself accountable for your contribution to the problems that have occurred.

As the saying goes, the best defense is a good offense. In this situation, that aphorism means that you should act, before crises happen, in a way that helps avoid the crises and, when crises do happen, respond effectively to them. Here are three up-front actions you can take, before the project starts and throughout the project, to make your team less likely to be blamed for project disasters.

Open communication: In Chapter 2, we gave our opinion about why open communication within the test team is helpful in terms of building a strong, loyal team. Open communication within the team also helps when the project gets into trouble, because matters are clearer to all participants in testing about what is going on, why it happened, and what is going to happen next. Open communication with managers outside the test team has similar effects. If external project and product stakeholders and participants have been kept informed throughout the project, they are less likely to make false assumptions about the culpability of the test team and test process.

Open communication also means that, after the project gets into trouble, you, as the test manager, admit your group's role in the problem, if any. At the same time, resist any temptation to blame particular people within your group. As the manager, you are accountable for your group; it is the mark of the cowardly manager to attempt to shift blame onto those who work in their group. To the extent that you need to coach or, if necessary, discipline someone within your team for the problem, it should never, ever be done in public. Further, open communication means that, whether the test group is responsible for the problem or not, you should communicate with your fellow managers and stakeholders about how the test group intends to help the project recover.

Good documentation: It's not possible for people to remember exactly how the project got into trouble. Eyewitness testimony, often relied upon in trials, is in fact one of the least reliable forms of evidence. People will forget key facts, or may simply never have been aware of them, no matter how much you strive

**Rex Shares a Story About
Stepping Up to Responsibility**

In a recent assessment, talking to a client's program manager, he told me how refreshed he was when a test manager took responsibility for an error and then immediately told him how he intended to fix the problem. He said, "I have made it a point to have that test manager work on every one of my projects since then." As much as the natural instinct can be to avoid blame, you may find that accepting blame that is yours will help to defend the test team and build your credibility.

for open communication. In the regrettable case that you are called upon to prove that your group should not be blamed, good documentation can be priceless. For example, email trails that show how decisions were made about testing by groups of stakeholders rather than by the test group alone can explain why things were done. Test logs that show how external factors affecting testing can provide a similar role. There is a fine line between documenting what happened and working proactively to have ready excuses, though, so be careful here.

Strong processes: When there are clear, accepted test processes, then the reason why events transpired in a particular way will be more clear to people. Making sure stakeholders understand why and how the test group works the way it does is not just a matter of defending against blame. It's also about building consensus about the right way to go about testing in a particular situation. When this consensus exists, it's much harder for people to credibly second-guess what testing did. Instead, this shared understanding of the test process builds confidence in the test group and helps the test manager manage stakeholder expectations.

Open communication, good documentation, and strong processes should all work to effect a broad understanding, across the organization as a whole and within the project stakeholder team, of what the role of the test group is, why it does what it does, how it manages project risks, and how it responds to project crises. This point goes back to topics covered in Chapters 1 and 2: Establish clear expectations about the objectives and responsibilities of testing and what testing will do within any given project. The definition of roles and responsibilities discussed in Chapter 2 helps make this clear. A clear test strategy, as discussed in Chapter 1, and good test plans, as discussed in the Foundation and Advanced syllabi, help make clear the approach followed and the reasons for it.

You might be thinking, "Okay, I've fostered open communication in my test team, but I'm not sure how to go about putting in place good documentation and strong processes." Fortunately, you don't need to create these from scratch. The ISTQB Fundamental Test Process, from the Foundation and Advanced syllabi, can give you a good starting point for process, and those syllabi also contain a number of ideas about how to document properly and incorporate good feedback mechanisms.

Good documentation and open communication have implications in terms of test status reporting. In Chapter 6, we'll discuss the importance of good test results reporting dashboards. Such dashboards provide appropriate, timely, credible, and useful visibility into not only the status of the product, but also the workings of the test process. Status reports, test execution progress, coverage, and defect information should provide stakeholders with what they need to make smart decisions and to see trouble coming in the project when it does. To some extent, if stakeholders are surprised by product quality problems or test process breakdowns that have been brewing for days or weeks, it is quite likely that you need to revisit your test results reporting practices.

We should point out that, like everything else in testing, context matters. The product, the project, the organizational structure, and the software development lifecycle influence the way and degree to which a test team needs defending. For example, in Agile projects, it is often the case that one or more testers are embedded in each team. This close collaboration with the developers and with the business can help to prevent scapegoating of the testers when a sprint or even an entire project goes awry, though testers may bear the brunt of Agile disasters in some cases. The solution here is to ensure that the Agile principles of efficient, effective communication; close collaboration; and good teamwork replace any effort to blame one or another participant for what's gone wrong.

4.2.4 Protecting and Supporting the Team

Nobody likes to be told how to do their job. Winston Churchill said, "I am always ready to learn, but I don't always enjoy being taught." However, as a test manager, you have probably noticed the plethora of people who are happy—or sometimes unhappy—to interfere with your test group and your management of it. In some cases the intention is good (as when the instant expert on testing wants to dictate what actions they would like to see your group take), and in other cases the intention is bad (as when the individual wants you to simply get the heck out of the way). Either way, any situation in which a nontester is telling you or your group, which should be composed of professional testers, how to do your job, is a problem sign.

By the way, we want to clearly distinguish between unreasonable interference and reasonable interactions with a service organization. The former occurs when someone tells you *how* to do the job, insults the *way* you do the job, or creates *obstacles* to doing the job, while the latter occurs when someone tells you *what* they need from you. If it wasn't obvious from Chapter 1 and earlier in this chapter, we consider the testing group to be a service organization in most circumstances. Talking to stakeholders about what objectives they want you to achieve and the benefits they need from your group is a conversation you should initiate yourself, and if it's initiated by one of your stakeholders, you should welcome it. Having stakeholders telling you how to achieve those objectives, or telling you that the objectives are being incompetently achieved, or telling you that you are in the way, well, these things indicate some sort of problem.

What's the Problem?

This is one of the obvious questions: Okay, it's a problem, but is it your problem or theirs? There are two answers to this question. One answer is that it could be either your problem or theirs. You need to understand why the problem is happening, so that you can address it. The second answer is, either way, it *is* your problem. If one of your stakeholders feels that your group is not doing their work properly and feels strongly enough about that to behave in an aggressive or socially inept manner, then there's at least one dissatisfied testing stakeholder out there. So, let's start with the question of why the interference is happening, and then we can address ways to deal with it.

Misunderstood and underestimated: It's often the case that stakeholders outside of the test team do not see that the test process includes activities before and after test execution. "Why do you need to see the requirements specification," the business analyst may ask, "since you won't need to test that function for a few months?" This is your opportunity to explain the value of early testing. Make sure, when you do so, to explain how early testing benefits the business analysis team. Moving beyond this specific example, you, as an expert test manager, need to be able to explain the entire test process *and* how that process benefits the organization.

Undervalued testing: If you don't do a good job of marketing and selling testing, as discussed earlier, stakeholders might (and often do) see your group as a low-value-add. That's likely to result in interference with your group whenever your group's behavior is anything other than obsequious. Some test groups respond to this situation by getting their backs up and asking for management "to support them in enforcing" the test process, test entry or exit criteria, or other similar rules. This is referred to this as the "process cop" model of testing, which leads to the problem of "testing seen as obstructing progress" discussed later. Instead, refer to the material discussed earlier and in Chapter 1 about how to make sure your group delivers value to your stakeholders and your stakeholders see that.

Undervalued testers: There is a subtle difference between this item and the preceding one. In undervalued testing, the stakeholder belief is that testing itself is of limited value. In undervalued testers, the stakeholder belief is that testing itself is valuable but the current team is not very valuable. Alternatively, the belief can be that testing is valuable but it does not require any special skills, so anyone can test. If you are managing the skills of your team as discussed in Chapter 2, you should be able to demonstrate, in great detail, the skills required from your testers, how they deliver those skills, and the wide extent of the skills required.

Right tester, wrong place or right testing services, wrong test group: The impression here is that someone in the testing group would be better in another role or that your approach to organizing the test group is wrong (e.g., recall the specialized versus generalized discussion in Chapter 2). Okay, this is a tricky one. There were probably good reasons why you assigned people to different roles and why you organized the group the way you did. That said, such reasons are always trade-offs. Be ready to reevaluate the trade-offs. If the stakeholder is simply suboptimizing (i.e., valuing their own needs over the wider needs of the project, product, process, or organization), then you have made the right decision. However, be open to the possibility that you can do better in this regard. It's one of the hardest trade-offs to get right as a test manager, so if someone tells you that you are doing it wrong, listen and think. Reflecting on the test groups we have set up, we are certain that there are many decisions about role assignment and organization we would do somewhat differently if we had a chance to do those over again.

Ineffectively utilized testers: This is a broader variant of the problem mentioned earlier—not only one or two testers are misplaced, but they're all misplaced. Or more exactly, their roles are not well defined. The assertion here is that your team organization model needs to be rethought completely. As earlier, this can be a matter of the individual seeing their own tree and not the whole forest, but it could be that circumstances have changed and your organization should as well.

Testing seen as obstructing progress: This is a very dangerous situation, and one that should be addressed immediately if it comes up. Developers will become frustrated with the testing obstructions and start agitating to have testing responsibility put in the development team. On more than one occasion, Rex has seen entire test groups disbanded, test managers fired, and testing outsourced once this impression became widely held, in some cases even when the test team was enforcing processes at the request of executive management. If you are trying to rigidly enforce entry and exit criteria, trying to force developers to document unit tests and unit test defects, trying to block releases, and otherwise trying to put the brakes on the project in the name of more testing and higher quality, you are in danger of building this impression. In some organizations, nontest stakeholders want and value process cops and quality cops who play such a role, but usually it's a losing game. Instead of chasing this path, refer back to the discussion in Chapter 1 about how to identify the proper objectives for testing from your stakeholders.

Test management seen as obstructing progress: This is a special case of the preceding problem, where the test team in general is seen as a positive force in the project but one or more of the managers are seen as obstructive, uncooperative, inefficient, or just plain unpleasant to deal with. Frankly, we do have a problem, as professional testers, in that some people seem to have come to the conclusion that being personally obnoxious is part of having integrity and independence, and that reputation has stuck to our profession to an unfortunate degree. In our experience, a leading indicator of the unsuccessful test manager is someone who feels that being a test manager is a license to tell everyone on a project exactly how they feel about the quality of the software, the quality of their work, and how everyone should be doing their work. Again, going back to the ideas mentioned in Chapter 1, the successful test manager is usually one that focuses on how to provide useful testing services to project, product, and program stakeholders.

Role clarity problems: In the absence of a clearly defined set of responsibilities, objectives, and goals, the role of testing is often very fuzzy, especially for stakeholders who've never been involved in testing. The best practice, again as discussed in Chapter 1, is to have a clearly defined test policy that makes these things plain. If you already have such a policy in place and you are still finding that people don't understand testing, then the problem is one of sales and marketing for the test role, as discussed earlier in this chapter.

The wise test manager works proactively to address these underlying preconditions of interference. If such a condition comes to the test manager's attention, in spite of efforts to address them in advance, then the test manager moves quickly to resolve the problem. When these conditions persist, they will often lead to various resource and respect issues that can be very dangerous to the test team and at the very least undermine your attempts to sell and market testing.

Let's look at some of these resource and respect issues that can arise in these circumstances.

External Interference

On big holidays like Thanksgiving, at big family gatherings, or at occasional parties, Rex is often the cook. He enjoys it, in part because it's like a mini-management challenge. There's planning, preparation, execution, and closure (the meal), all within a few hours. The few times he hasn't enjoyed doing it came when people decided to hang around in the kitchen while he cooked to tell him what to do. He doesn't mind people hanging around and helping, of course, but telling someone what they're supposed to do next is usually not helpful, and neither is preemptively taking over some tasks already underway without someone asking for help.

It's irritating when someone decides to interfere with something you are managing. This sometimes happens in testing, when other project or product stakeholders decide to try to manage the testing work or even take some of it over. For example, if the development team feels that testing has become a bottleneck for release, they might try to dictate a reduction in testing scope based on what they feel should be covered and what should be left out. While many test strategies, including risk-based testing, do involve developers in discussions about test scope, only directed test strategies allow outside parties to completely determine it. If you are not following a directed test strategy, then such input would constitute unwarranted external interference.

While trying to change scope or curtail the testing schedule is perhaps the most common form of external interference, it's not the only form. Outside stakeholders might try to determine the way in which test cases will be formatted and documented, especially if they are involved in reviewing those cases. Outside stakeholders might offer unsolicited advice or even inputs to your test automation programs. They might also provide unsolicited critiques or even modifications to templates, test documentation standards, and other testing work products.

As discussed, the reasons for this kind of interference can vary considerably. You need to understand why this is happening, if it does. You also need to be receptive to input from project stakeholders and interfacing organizations because a brusque response to these inputs can trigger (or reinforce) the "testing/test managers are obstructive" problem mentioned earlier. However, the test organization is supposed to focus on quality, and this external interference is usually not focused on quality. So you need to politely but firmly maintain a focus on your mission.

If external interference happens, remember that it is a symptom of a larger problem. A bad manager just reacts to symptoms, thrashing inefficiently in the face of crises like a badly operated marionette. A good manager resolves the underlying problems and thus spends a lot less time reacting to symptoms. Remember that, in cost of quality terms, any time spent reacting to a problem that has created a crisis is a cost of internal failure—and thus a form of inefficiency.

Micromanagement

Micromanagement is similar but more severe than external interference. External interference usually happens only when outside stakeholders come to a conclusion that they need to direct testing so that it better serves their objectives or institute constant monitoring of the test work being done so that they can stop anything they don't like. Micromanagement usually happens when a testing stakeholder—usually one in a senior or peer management position— has lost trust in the test management team's ability to do their job. This can be because the test manager and the team have not done a good job in selling and marketing the mission and strategy of testing, or perhaps the mission and strategy are not clearly defined to begin with.

Here are some classic symptoms of micromanagement:

- The test team is the only team required to account for their hours, perhaps in hourly or even 15-minute increments, while the other teams are not.
- The test results are closely scrutinized for inconsistencies and minor flaws, with more attention given to the mistakes of the test team than to the meaning of their results.
- Members of other teams demand and receive the right to change the status of tests and defects and use this capability frequently to modify the test results.

⬛ Managers of other teams demand and receive the right to redirect test resources, including testers, to assist with nontest tasks, perhaps without any need to consult or even inform the test manager.

If you see symptoms of micromanagement—or even attempts at micromanagement—you need to act. While you might be tempted to react by saying, "Oh, well, that's just Joe [or whoever's being the micromanager]; it'll be easier to just go along with this nonsense than to fight it," the chances are good that, in the long run, it won't be easier. If you have all the responsibility and none of the authority, how long do you suppose it will be before someone else's bad decision comes around to nail you and your team?

When we say that you must act, we don't mean that you should simply put your foot down and refuse to allow it. First, you need to understand why the problem is occurring. If multiple parties are involved in micromanagement, keep in mind that each party might have its own reasons for doing so, even though the behavior is the same.

In addition to the reasons previously discussed, there are two other reasons micromanagement occurs that we have seen in our careers. One cause is when people get appointed to a management role but they simply cannot get out of the habit of being in a lead role as a subject-matter expert. A subject-matter expert or technical lead is supposed to advise their colleagues on how to do some elements of their work, and some leads (not the good ones) get a real thrill from being the smartest guy (or woman) in the classroom rather than being an effective teacher, if you follow the analogy. Once promoted to management, they simply can't get out of the habit or in fact don't even understand the difference between a lead and a manager. If a former test manager or director with these kinds of predilections is appointed to a project or program management role, they might feel an overwhelming temptation to micromanage their test successor.

This is a tricky problem to handle because you are dealing with what could best be called a mild personality disorder (keep in mind that none of us is a psychologist, so we are not diagnosing here). Our practice with these kinds of managers is simply to avoid giving them opportunities to micromanage. We look for every possible way to ensure that, by the time they become aware of a problem, our teams have already solved it or are well on the way to solving it. By working "around" the micromanager, engaging with other colleagues and fellow managers, you can often minimize the impact. You are probably not the only person to have developed a healthy dislike for this individual; no one likes a smarty-pants.

Another reason for micromanagement is when a manager has had a long, unpleasant experience of managing incompetent or dishonest employees. This can lead to a habit of having to micromanage employees because otherwise nothing (or at least nothing good) gets done. This is actually a simpler problem to solve because it's merely a matter of winning trust through constant, stunning excellence on the part of you and your team. Notice that we said "simpler problem to solve," not "easy problem to solve." It's not easy to be really good all the time, but if you can raise your game to that level, you can earn your way out of the micromanager's basilisk glare.

As with external interference, the first step is to understand why the micromanagement is happening, and the next step is to address the cause(s). In addition, you should work to reduce contributing factors through the following actions:

- Get involved in the overall planning and estimation for the project or program. If you don't know how to participate effectively in such exercises, then you need to sharpen your project management skills (see Chapter 5).

- Make sure that you are clear in your communications during these planning and estimation activities. Explain the test strategy, the test plan, and the estimate to the stakeholders. Have reviews and sign-offs, yes, but also make sure people really understand *why* you intend to do things and *how* those things will benefit the organization.

- As project work continues, continue that habit of clear communication about your progress. Keep people apprised of where you and your team are. If things go badly, develop a good way to solve the problem, and then communicate the solution. (Our experience is that simply coming to managers with a problem, without offering any solution, is a great way to trigger any latent micromanager tendencies among those managers.)

- When you are asked to provide additional information about test results, test status, test progress, or test activities, respond forthrightly and without delay. If a request for information is based on an honest desire to better understand, then you risk alienating a friendly stakeholder with irresponsiveness. If a request is a symptom of micromanagement, you will accomplish very little by resisting the request directly because it simply feeds the narrative that you and your team have something to hide.

In general, micromanagerial tendencies will be exacerbated or perhaps even triggered by feelings of uncertainty about testing work and surprise at the testing results. Working to increase transparency and understanding of what the test team is doing, is planning to do, and might have to do should certain project risks eventuate can help to reduce the likelihood of micromanagement.

Three final notes about micromanagement: First, if the micromanager is your boss, be very careful about how you handle the situation. Every manager who succeeds over the long term learns how to work successfully with their managers, accommodating their work habits and personalities; we cannot think of an exception to this rule. Second, remember that micromanagement is not a problem because it offends your pride. Micromanagement is a problem because outside micromanagement by underinformed individuals cannot be as effective as competent management by competent test managers. Third, don't confuse situations that have offended your pride with micromanagement. If you make a mistake and your manager gives you sharp and clear direction about how to avoid that mistake in the future, that's not micromanagement, it's intervention. If you don't like the way the intervention was delivered, please refer back to our first note, at the beginning of this paragraph.

Disrespect

For years now, Rex has been writing about the "second-class citizen" problem with testing, and he wasn't the first to do so.[5] We'd love to be able say that this problem was solved, but unfortunately it's not. We still see situations with clients where the test team is seen as inferior and treated with disrespect.

As a manager of any team, including a test team, you cannot tolerate such a situation. It's bad enough for people outside a team to direct disrespect at that team, but should the manager acquiesce, any remnants of morale will be destroyed. What signs of disrespect should you watch for? While not a comprehensive list, here's a start:

- Sarcastic, unfriendly comments about the test team's capabilities, the skills of the testers, or their value. Just as every dog knows the difference between being tripped over and being kicked, you should know the difference between this and good-natured repartee.
- Openly insulting comments. Here, no subtlety is involved. If someone says something like, "Another typical stupid status report from the test team," right in the middle of a project meeting, guess what? You're disrespected.

---

5   You can see Boris Beizer's book *Software Testing Techniques* for the first mention of this problem we're aware of. Rex wrote about it first in the first edition of *Managing the Testing Process: Practical Tools and Techniques for Managing Hardware and Software Testing*, and that material remains, revised to some extent, in the third edition.

- Working assignments that have nothing to do with testing. While this can be a form of micromanagement, a failure to understand what testing does, repeated actions in this regard in spite of attempts to resolve the confusion, will often be a sign of disrespect.
- Insufficient time and resources for testing. Again, this could be a failure to understand what testing does, but it could also be a way of saying, "We don't think you're competent to manage this effort, so we're going to give you limited resources."
- Insufficient training. This can be a symptom of the "how hard can be it, just make sure it works" opinion about testing. However, it can also be a way of saying, "Those testers are hopeless; no amount of training could make them valuable team members."
- Information hiding or barriers to information access. Usually these situations come down to a severe lack of trust or an opinion that you and your team can't handle information because you'd make bad decisions with it.

When we've encountered respect issues, the typical (but not universal) cause is a failure to understand the value of testing and the ways the test team contributes to success. As with the other situations mentioned, know the cause first, then address the cause.

A special case in this category is disrespect due to sexism or racism. When test teams comprise disproportionately people of one gender—and I'm sorry to say we've only seen or heard of cases where the gender was female—then sometimes the disrespect is gender bias. When testing is outsourced, we've seen situations where racial elements enter into the disrespect. With that nasty possibility acknowledged, we would encourage you to look for every other way to deal with the problem of disrespect before attributing it to sexism or racism. Certainly, if you hear sexist, racist, or other comments that create a hostile work environment directed at your team, you have an absolute duty to act, immediately, both as a human being and as someone with a responsibility for protecting the interests of your employer. However, if you call out to management, "Help, help, we're being oppressed," in response to every slight, you will damage your team's credibility.

Reorganization and Resource Reallocation

Finally, there is one last topic to address with respect to defending the test team. In the absence of clearly defined testing tasks and testing value, reorganizations and reallocation of test resources can lead to significant reductions in the testing resources available. We have seen this involve test hardware, test networks, and testers. These situations often affect test teams disproportionately. We have seen test teams cut by 50 percent when their development colleagues lost only 10 percent of their staff. Worse yet, in some cases after the resources were withdrawn, the expectation was that the committed testing work would nonetheless be done.

This situation can occur when the rest of the organization doesn't understand the testing tasks or they underestimate the work to be done. A typical exacerbating factor is that people don't understand the value of testing, especially in situations where the test manager has not bothered to measure the value. Remember, the value of development is clear—no developers means no software—while the value of testing, both quantified and qualitative, is less obvious. This is another reason why defining and communicating the value of testing, as mentioned earlier, is so important.

Note that this problem is not the same as outright disrespect, because the underlying message is not "testing has no value." Typically, the underlying message is "testing has value, but we're not sure how much of that value we need." In the absence of clearly defined value for testing, half of the value is just as good as all of the value. However, going back to the dog's perception of the difference between being tripped over and being kicked, the understanding of a lack of malice must be cold comfort to the dog with a bruise on its back. Similarly, if half of your test team is fired, you are unlikely to be mollified by an executive who says, "We really respect the valuable testing work your team does, but we have to focus resources on development and other high-ROI activities." The worst part of that situation could be realizing that better communication about the value of testing might have prevented it.

4.3   Placement of the Test Team

Learning objectives

LO 5.3.1   (K5) Evaluate an organization's structure, missions, products, customers, and users, and priorities, in order to determine the options for proper placement of the test team within the organization, assess the implications of those options, and create an analysis for upper management of those options.

We have worked with test teams around the world, within various organizations from small to large, in a wide variety of industries. There is considerable variation in organizational structure. There is also considerable variation in how test teams are organized and how those teams relate to the organization as a whole.

We've also seen situations where the structure and relationships of the test team changed for each project, and often in those situations the larger organization was restructured to suit the needs of each project. For example, a testing services provider will need to form teams for a client's specific project or program. Mass-market and enterprise software development organizations often form special teams to work on particular releases.

In some cases, the structure and relationships with the wider organization work well, and in other cases, the structure and relationships are a source of friction. The same approach that works in one situation may fail in another. A given structure may be perfect for a specific project, program, or organization, but there is no single structure that is perfect for all projects, programs, and organizations.

As is the case elsewhere in testing, though, just because context matters doesn't mean there are no best practices. We have observed many common characteristics in testing teams where the structure and relationships with the wider organization worked well. In the following sections, we'll examine some of those characteristics.

4.3.1   Independence and Reporting Structure

Most testing exists within the wider context of some endeavor such as a project, program, or operation to deliver or utilize some set of features, and usually there are schedule and budget targets for that endeavor. It's seldom realistic for test teams to expect that those targets must be subservient to quality targets. Perfect software is not possible within the constraints and realities of most systems and organizations. The proper balance of schedule, budget, features, and quality will vary from system to system and from organization to organization.

The test team's role in achieving that balance is to focus on quality. This usually does not mean being a quality cop, someone who enforces a certain level of quality, but rather it means assessing the quality of the product or system. That assessment must be accurate, timely, and credible. It then must be reported honestly. For these things to happen, it is necessary that the test group receive adequate resources and time. It is also necessary that the testers and test managers be able to speak the truth, as they understand it, about the quality of the software without having to worry about negative consequences for themselves or the group.

This privilege—indeed, an essential duty for testers—to speak the truth is often accomplished by independent test groups. Independence means that the reporting chain of the testers leads to senior or executive management rather than to product, project, program, or operational managers. The reasoning is that if testers report to managers that are incented primarily by schedule, budget, and feature targets, those managers will censor the testing assessment before passing it along, and testers will learn to self-censor. If testers report to managers who have the broader perspective of the organization in mind, there will be no incentive for the testers to withhold the facts, and those managers will be able to make a balanced judgment.

For example, one of our clients has a structure where system-integration testing is performed by a separate organization, which provides services to the various programs that are underway. Each program has an assigned test manager. The test managers report to a director of testing. He in turn reports to a vice president in IT, whose other direct reports are not program managers or their directors. The vice president reports to the CIO.

As another example, one of our clients is following an Agile approach to software development. Most of their testers are assigned, with a dotted-line reporting structure, to work within Agile teams. (Other testers who are working on support activities such as test automation frameworks are in separate teams, not within the Agile teams.) However, they report directly to test managers, based on product line. Those test managers report to a director of testing, and he reports to the CIO.

Given a proper reporting structure, the test group should deliver honest, unfiltered assessments of quality, with no fear of retribution. The test management team must ensure that the reporting structure is such. However, the test managers must also remember that all communication is a two-way street. This duty to deliver a frank assessment must not be taken as a license to offend or obstruct, though. Not only will such a communication style produce significant long-term damage in many cases, it will also interfere with the receipt of the message by the very people you are trying to inform. The entire test team must instill and practice a style of communication that is honest and at the same time respectful, relevant, and helpful.

4.3.2 Access to Information

Independence of the test team is important, but it can be in tension with another important issue related to organizational placement of the test team: access to information. Some organizations that go too far in insulating their test teams find that those test teams can't get the information they need to do their testing. We've seen this happen with certain outsource testing services providers as well.

What information do the testers need? In short, they need information about the product, project, and process. Product information includes requirements and design specifications, among other test bases and test oracles. Project information includes project plans and project status reports. Process information includes defect trends, defect clusters, and other process capability indicators.

Not all of the information comes in the form of documents. Informal communication such as email, hallway and lunchroom conversations, whiteboard sessions, and phone calls are often essential channels of information for the tester. This is another reason testers must communicate in a way that is respectful, relevant, and helpful. By doing so, testers encourage bidirectional communication and are much more likely to receive the information they need.

We've seen examples where the test managers did not work to ensure this kind of good, mutually supportive communication, with disastrous results. Testers were given minimal information and left out of the information conversations entirely. When the test managers complained that they didn't have the information needed to do their job, the development managers countered that the entire test group was merely demonstrating its irrelevance and inability to operate within the context of the organization. In one case, the end result was the dissolution of the test group and outsourcing of all the testing.

4.3.3 Skills

We discussed skills for testers extensively in Chapter 2. It's an important topic and has various effects on the placement of the test group and the way it operates. A group with the perfect skills for one situation may be exactly wrong in another. An individual tester or test leader with the right or wrong skills can make a difference in the way the entire test group is perceived. These are two more reasons the task analysis, skills inventory, and skills management discussed in Chapter 2 are so critical.

Rex's company has clients that work in highly complex business domains, such as oil and gas exploration and industrial control systems. As the director of testing explained to Rex when he was asked why he hired only domain experts for his test team, "I can teach them what they need to know about technology and testing. I hire smart geologists and petroleum engineers, people with experience in the oil and gas industry. Those people can learn technology and testing. What I can't teach someone without domain expertise quickly enough is how the system works, the problems it actually solves. The learning curve is simply too long, and by the time those people are useful testers, they'll have made too many mistakes that have damaged the test team's credibility."

Rex has clients and vendors that work with his clients who really need skilled testers. For example, if you are managing a test group that provides outsourced testing services to your clients, your company is selling expertise in testing, plain and simple. The ability to bring that expertise to bear for your clients is paramount. If you are hiring a testing services provider to help your team, a gap in testing expertise is often what you need to fill. If you are a director of testing, as some of Rex's clients are, and using outsourced testing services providers, you need to focus on the testing skills those service providers bring.

He has yet other clients who work with extremely advanced, leading-edge technologies. These companies often see technology as a key competitive advantage, and their focus is on using that advantage to win in highly competitive markets. For example, he has clients that make and sell enterprise software, providing or enabling the benefits of cloud computing, virtualization, and so forth. Testers in those situations must have deep knowledge of system configuration, networking, and similar technical skills.

Be aware of the fact that the proper skills mix might not be uniform across the organization. In some cases, the specific needs on a particular program or project could differ significantly from one program or project to another. This is especially important if you are the director or vice president of testing for a large organization, providing services to various software development, maintenance, and operational groups that build, maintain, and support disparate software products. We have seen this situation even in smaller organizations, where different groups are involved with very different kinds of products or following different software lifecycles.

For example, some of Rex's clients use both Agile and sequential lifecycles, usually for very good reasons. Some of their products are best produced in the quick, iterative manner Agile delivers, while other products require longer lifecycles. For their Agile testers, these people work embedded within development teams, as described earlier. Because of the close work within development teams, stronger technical skills are often required. These testers often need a broader level of experience, too, because the Agile teams are supposed to operate in a self-organizing fashion.

Finally, don't expect that this consideration of skills is a "once and done" activity. The skills management approach described in Chapter 2 could be misconstrued as meaning that, having determined the critical skills for your group, you simply continue on a linear path toward that ideal group skill level. Nope, it doesn't work that way. The requirements of the job will change as the technologies, testing techniques, and business domains themselves evolve.

For example, Rex has a client in the retail space. Its IT organization builds software and systems that support everything from the retail sales operations on the store floor all the way to the analysis of big data. Technological advances, and their applicability to retail businesses, have absolutely rocked that business to its foundations in the last ten years, and show every sign of continuing to do so. If the organization's director of testing was continuing to build the right test group for retail IT in the year 2000, he would be building a hopelessly outdated group at this point.

Internal and external stakeholder expectations will evolve too. For example, if you are the incoming director of testing for a group that has underachieved for years, the stakeholders will be thrilled to see you work through the process, described in Chapter 1, of aligning the testing with their needs. They will be thrilled to see you align the test group's skills with those required to execute the strategy, as described in Chapter 2. Remember to keep them thrilled. Keep asking yourself, and asking the stakeholders, "What's next for us as a testing group? How can we continue to get better?"

We have mentioned before in this book that test teams should have a service-oriented attitude and work to provide good services to their stakeholders. You simply must have the right skills to be able to make good on this promise.

Both the attitude and the skills are essential. If you and your group apply the right skills and attitude to the mission, objectives, and strategies that fit your organization, you are highly likely to succeed. Testing stakeholders will see your group as the right people to do the job. That means that you and your group are highly likely to attract the respect, receive the information, and have access to the resources necessary to carry out the mission, achieve the objectives, and execute the strategies.

4.4   Stakeholder Communication

Learning objectives

LO 5.4.1   (K3) Communicate effectively with testing stakeholders, including nontest staff, about critical issues related to testing.

So, you have a service-oriented test group that has access to the information it needs and the skills necessary to execute the test strategy. Good enough, right? Well, there's another important element here. Since a key objective for testing is to be a credible, understandable, timely, accurate source of information, it's also essential to deliver the information stakeholders need when they need it. We'll discuss specific types of information you can deliver in Chapters 6 and 8, but because we are talking about how test groups relate to stakeholders in this chapter, let's look at the issue of communicating that information to stakeholders here.

Here are some types of stakeholder information communications that can be useful and for each, the questions that good communication can answer.

- **The testing project:** Stakeholders, especially project stakeholders such as development managers and project managers, often need to understand where the test team stands in terms of testing. Are the test cases ready? Is the test environment ready? How many of the tests have been run? What requirements, risks, configurations, and other essential test basis elements have been covered? How many defects have been found? Where do we stand on the exit criteria? The answers to these questions help project stakeholders better understand the state of the project.
- **Trending information:** In addition to understanding the state of the project, stakeholders, especially project stakeholders but also product stakeholders

(who include program managers, product managers, and business analysts, among others), need to understand the trajectory of the project and the product. Will we complete the tests, achieve adequate coverage, and satisfy the exit criteria on schedule? If not, how far off will we be and what can be done to get closer to done by the scheduled date? The answers to these questions help stakeholders see possible paths to the most successful outcomes for the project.

■ **Specific test status and defect status:** Project stakeholders and product stakeholders, including individual contributors such as developers and users, often need to understand what works, what doesn't work, and what is not yet known. Which tests have been run, and which have passed and which have failed? Which defects have been found, which remain to be fixed, and which are resolved? What test-basis elements are associated with these tests and defects? What specific risks and functional limitations are inherent in the current test status? The answers to these questions help stakeholders understand the current quality of the product and make smart decisions about how to manage the quality of the product.

■ **Test process effectiveness and efficiency indicators:** Process stakeholders who are accountable for testing—or who have an interest in knowing how well it is working—often need to understand the capability of the test process. What percentage of defects does testing find? What are the current costs of quality? What percentage of the test basis is covered by testing, and what is the average cost per test-basis element covered? This information can also be useful for project and program estimation.

This is not a comprehensive list, and other metrics will be covered and illustrated in detail in Chapters 6 and 8. The main point of this list is to see some examples of the relationship between particular stakeholders, types of information available from testing, and how that information satisfies stakeholder needs.

Testing information is often ephemeral in its value, especially project and product information. Information that is old may at best be useless and at worst lead to bad decision-making. So good information communication to stakeholders requires working with those stakeholders to ensure that timely, regular delivery of information occurs. This is necessary to support smart, effective decisions. Any test information that is greeted with a chorus of "Oh, cripes, if we'd known that we would have done something differently two weeks ago" was delivered too late.

Test process information is often measured in longer intervals and has more lasting value, at least if the test process is stable. Delivering daily reports on defect detection effectiveness, for example, is likely to swamp the recipient in a sea of transient noise. The signal emerges in the longer term. Even so, establishing timetables for communicating process information is also important.

Just as with the speed of sound, there is an upper limit on the speed and precision with which certain types of information can be generated. Delivering inaccurate information quickly is just as bad as delivering accurate information too late. Part of the job of working effectively across the organization is working with stakeholders to identify their information needs, how testing can support those needs, when that information can be provided, and how to balance speed and accuracy.

This is, of course, a two-way communication. Just as stakeholders need information from the test group, the testers need information from other stakeholder groups. These groups have the same challenges in terms of speed and accuracy. The volume and mode of information delivery is another part of this puzzle. What information do people need, how should it be delivered, and when? Successful test managers work effectively with their colleagues to find the right answer to this question.

We really should say, though, that they work effectively together to find the right answers to these questions, because the answers to the "how" and "when" questions depend on what information is being delivered. An urgent problem that has the potential to delay or even derail a project must be communicated quickly, even if the information might be incomplete. Routine information, such as a weekly status report about testing that shows normal progress, can be communicated in a regularly scheduled meeting or even via an intranet page. As you can see from these examples, the answer to the "when to communicate" question depends on what's being communicated.

A similar situation exists with the "how to communicate" question. If you publish the same set of test project reports on a weekly basis and everyone knows how to read and interpret those reports, then successful communication can occur via email, intranet pages, and other asynchronous channels. However, if you have found a problem, and performed some analysis to understand the cause of that problem, simply sending a couple of trend charts and a scatterplot or Pareto chart via email will probably not lead to clear understanding by the recipients. A meeting, online presentation, or phone call allows synchronous communication—yes, a conversation—where the test manager can explain the problem and why they think they have found an explanation for it. This is especially critical when the explanation might be politically explosive, such as blocking issues found during system testing that could have been detected during unit testing.

Here's another important point about effective communication across the organization. There's an aphorism in public relations that says when interviewed, the person should answer the question they wanted to be asked, not the question they were asked. If you watch reporters interview astute manipulators of public opinion, you will often see this aphorism in action.

This aphorism absolutely does not apply to test managers. Smart stakeholders will see through any attempt to manipulate them, and they will not appreciate it. This attempt will, at least in the long run and often in the short run, damage your credibility. Earlier in this chapter we wrote about the testers' duty to report honestly, and that duty is not served by trying to manipulate stakeholders with selective and biased information communication.

Instead, answer the questions that the stakeholders need answered. Each piece of information gathered, interpreted, and reported should add value for the recipients of that information. Unnecessary or irrelevant information, even if accurate, is frustrating to the recipients and often distracts them from the information they really need, even if you do ultimately deliver that information as well. You are not only wasting the stakeholders' time, you are wasting your own time and, as we said, draining your precious reservoir of credibility.

Now, when we say that you should provide information that stakeholders need, that's not the same as saying you should provide information that stakeholders want to hear. Often, test managers are in the difficult position of providing information that is not pleasing to the recipient. Understand what you are trying to accomplish with the communication and what kind of management decision, support, or commitment you are trying to achieve. If you are explaining a problem and a path to solving that problem, be clear about the costs of the problem and the solution, the benefits of the solution, and what will be required to implement the solution. And above all else, be objective.

At the risk of dating ourselves by teasing meanings out of old popular music from the late 1960s, we're reminded of a refrain that goes, "I'm just a soul whose intentions are good/Oh Lord, please don't let me be misunderstood." If your intentions are good—a desire to effectively meet the information objectives for testing—you will be pointed in the right direction when you communicate with stakeholders. However, when you communicate, not only must your intentions be good, you also need to ensure that the message you intended to send was the message that the recipient received and understood.

In some cases, it's not enough for the recipient to receive and understand your information. If you are trying to propose a particular course of action, effective communication also means that the proposed action is understood. Now, the recipient might or might not act in the way you propose. However, if you are an effective communicator, the recipient will at least understand what you want to see happen, why you want that action taken, and your reasoning behind that proposal.

4.5   Creating and Building Relationships

Learning objectives

LO 5.5.1   (K3) For a given situation, demonstrate how to create and build relationships with other managers and teams.

LO 5.5.2   (K3) Explain and give examples of important relationships a test manager needs to create in a complex project environment.

When Rex does assessments for clients, he talks to a lot of people, both inside and outside the testing group. In the opening moments of each interview, he tries to engage in a friendly exchange, where he breaks the ice between the interviewee and himself. Not only is it more pleasant to have a friendly conversation than a tense one, but people are more open and honest with someone with whom they have some kind of positive relationship, compared to a complete stranger—or someone they see as hostile, cold, or inscrutable. Most of the time, Rex succeeds, and he gets to spend an interesting hour or so with someone who gives him the benefit of their insights and opinions.

The same is true, on a much larger and longer scale, for test managers. As we've stressed throughout this book, testing is a matter of providing useful services to stakeholders. If those stakeholders have a good relationship with you and the other test managers in your test group, information will flow more smoothly in both directions. The job of the test group will become easier because it has better access to information it needs. The test group will also become more valuable because the information the group produces will flow more smoothly to the recipients of that information. It's just human nature: We listen to and value the communications we receive from people we are comfortable with, and we are happy to reciprocate that flow of information.

It's not that you must be a personal friend to every stakeholder with whom you work, but a good professional relationship with those stakeholders is a major factor in the success of a test manager. How well you and the other managers in the test group initiate, cultivate, and sustain these relationships will strongly influence the flow of information, as well as the support, you obtain from your colleagues.

A relationship is necessarily a two-way affair. You and the test group can't be the only beneficiaries from a relationship, at least not a good one. Once, a person with whom Rex worked on a project described the CEO of one vendor as follows: "Every time I meet with that guy, I want to take a shower afterward," meaning that he felt soiled just by being in the same room. Later in the project, when Rex's colleague legitimately but accidentally came into possession of a memo that was certainly not in the vendor's interests to disclose to its client, he felt no compunction about copying the document before returning it in a way that did not disclose that he had seen it. The relationship had become two-way, but not in a good way.

As a contrast, Rex had an excellent relationship with this same vendor's test manager. Across a significant cultural difference—the same difference his colleague and the CEO had not bridged—he and Rex forged a relationship of honesty and trust. Rex felt he could tell him the truth about what was happening on their side of the project, and he felt the same. They shared information to advance their mutual goals of a successful project and high-quality deliverable while at the same time respecting the limits on communication imposed by their different positions in terms of who their employers were. Even when the relationship between the two companies became testy, he and Rex were always able to communicate as friends with a good relationship of mutual respect.

Rex notes that this anecdote (see callout on the left) does not represent an isolated incident but rather a truth that has become plain to him throughout his career in testing. The successful test manager, perhaps more than any other managers in the software business, must cultivate strong relationships with stakeholders, continuously reinforce those relationships with mutual benefits, and maintain the relationships through good times and bad. In the next few subsections, let's look more closely at how.

4.5.1   Random Relationships

While going to work and going to college are very different experiences, a workplace is not terribly different than schools or universities in one interesting way: You will be placed in a communal setting with people, some of whom you probably didn't know before, in an almost random fashion. In either situation, you get to choose how you approach the relationships you build and maintain, whether in college or at work.

Here's where there's an important difference: In college, you don't have to build a relationship with anyone and you can still succeed. You could choose to go to your classes, spend all your free time studying, skip the parties and the games and the social events, talk only to your professors and teaching assistants about the material you are studying, and be a phenomenal success (at least academically). While this could be a sad but feasible path toward straight A's in college, such an asocial approach to any form of management, but especially test management, will simply not work. You don't have to drink beers and go to football games with your coworkers to get ahead, but you need to make these random relationships mutually beneficial. You won't succeed at that task if you approach it like some heartless cyborg or, worse yet, like a selfish manipulator.[6]

Why are these relationships so essential? Consider the following example. You are working as a test manager on a project to develop a new piece of software. That software will be built by a development team, so you need to communicate regularly and honestly with the development manager about the project. You'll want to ask about the status of the development and where the team stands in terms of the lifecycle. You'll want to discuss what level of quality the team can deliver to you, what level of quality the organization needs to deliver to customers, and how testing can help meet that goal. The development manager will want to know what kind of metrics and reports your team can provide. You'll each want to know about deliverables you'll exchange, along with details like how and when those deliverables will arrive, what should be done if there are problems with the deliverables, and so forth. You and the manager have a lot to talk about, and those communications will be much more pleasant and effective if your relationships are good.

As the anecdote about the vendor's slimy CEO illustrated, this need for relationships is not just a within-the-organization thing. You need a good relationship with your vendors too. Of course, this is complicated by the fact that contracts proscribe limits on communication and also the fact that some testing service providers and other vendors are very good at putting glib and charming people in client-facing positions. It may take a while to learn how to juggle this balance, but it is possible to be professional, to fulfill your obligations to your employer and client, and at the same time have positive and enjoyable relationships with vendor representatives. And, if you are on the vendor side of the relationship, be a professional: Treat the client personnel you interact with exactly the same way you'd like to be treated, and don't try to exploit the relationship.

Relationships—good or bad—are built through interaction. A major element of interaction in professional settings is communication. Some of the communications that will occur are formal communications, such as test results reporting. However, you should not rely on these formal communica-

---

6   One of our reviewers, Capers Jones, wrote, "I've seen projects canceled because high-level managers did not like each other and would not cooperate."

tions alone to build strong relationships because people might see these as the test group simply doing their job. The best relationship builders are events that show you as a person willing to go beyond your obligations, to make a special effort to connect with your colleagues.

What are good ways to connect with colleagues as people? We have worked with clients and colleagues around the world and can attest to the fact that the right answer to this question differs culturally, organizationally, and individually. Here are some ideas.

Share a meal: This one sounds simple, but in fact, it is a very human way to make a connection. Many animal, even herbivorous animals, will tend to fight over food. Humans are, if not unique, certainly special in their ability to make meals a social activity where friendships are formed rather than a contest. You can choose to make the conversation social or about business, as the situation requires, but we have found that, in most cultures, setting aside business to talk socially with your colleagues will make a deeper connection. After all, you can talk about business in a meeting. However, if your colleague decides—at the beginning of the meal or at some later point—to talk about business, it's a good idea to follow that lead. In some cultures, a shared meal, followed by business talk, is a major vehicle for problem-solving.

Share a drink: This is a somewhat weaker, but easier, variant of the previous technique. As before, our experience is that a social conversation is a stronger relationship builder than talking about business, so follow your colleague's lead on topics but don't jump directly to business unless you've agreed to do so. What you drink depends on the culture and the company, of course. In the United States, coffee, tea, or other nonalcoholic drinks will often be the only option during normal working hours, but it is not uncommon to have beer or wine with colleagues in Europe and Asia in the middle of a workday, usually with lunch. Drinking alcoholic beverages after work is an established tradition in some cultures, and in some cultures it's almost essential to relationship building, while other cultures and individuals frown on drinking alcohol for religious or personal reasons. Remember that your objective in this situation is to build a relationship: If your personal habits include knocking back a couple of whiskeys at the end of the work day, when out for a social hour with a colleague who doesn't drink, be careful about engaging in behavior that will actually damage your colleague's opinion of you.

Inviting stakeholders to testing meetings: One of the risks associated with independent test teams is the possibility of isolation and even alienation. As we stress throughout this book, most test groups should see themselves as providing valuable testing services to their stakeholders, which goes a long way to managing this risk. However, it can also help to make sure that stakeholders feel welcome to contribute and participate in the way testing is done. For example, if you are introducing a new technique such as risk-based testing, why not invite stakeholders to a brief discussion on how the technique works? Obviously, you need to consider whether the invitee will find the topic interesting; issuing invitations to every testing meeting to every testing stakeholder will send a message of disrespect for their time, not relationship-building.

Celebrate the successes: Project and program teams often have events such as post-project parties, retrospectives, dinners, and other similar events on major milestones. You and the test group should attend. These can be good opportunities to set aside any negative baggage that accumulated during a tough project, provided you and your group are positive contributors in these events.

There are many other ways to approach relationship-building, but these four—breaking bread together, relaxing together, being open with each other, and celebrating together—are keystones of human society that go back to the dawn of human history. Relationship-building is a matter of social networking, and that goes beyond Facebook friending and Twitter following. Indeed, trying to establish such "social networks" without first doing the groundwork of building a real human relationship, via these types of techniques, will often come across as insincere and exploitative.

Relationship-building is an ongoing activity, not a one-time activity. Those of you who are extroverts may cheer to hear that, while introverts may groan. It is indeed the special challenge of the introverted manager to learn how to enjoy this obligation, but it will pay benefits to you, not only at work but also in your personal life. You should maintain and grow your relationships with stakeholders as the organization changes, as people change positions, and as roles and missions change. Having strong relationships is essential to being a successful test manager. Without such relationships, your team will be less respected than it deserves to be (based on its contributions) and less productive than it could be (based on its intrinsic capabilities).

It's an interesting irony of our business that relationships are so important, isn't it? After all, computers can communicate with each other on an entirely factual basis, and—other than in *Star Wars* movies—there is no need for politeness in the "protocol 'droid." In software, one program that refused to interact with another program based on a bad relationship—say because the other program hogged the CPU or memory—would be considered buggy. However, as long as software engineering remains a human endeavor, "courtesy...the lubricant of human relations," and indeed relationships themselves, remain essential to its working.[7]

4.5.2 Who You (Should) Know

So you need to have good relationships to succeed as a test manager. But with whom? If you are in any organization larger than a small start-up, you can't know everyone personally. From a purely Machiavellian perspective, even if you could, you probably don't need to know everyone. Who should you know, and how well? The answer to this question will depend on the organization, but here are some thoughts.

Development and other peer managers: These people are the managers that you interact with on a regular, perhaps daily, basis. Development managers, of course, deliver the software you need for testing (possibly indirectly, through a release manager), and your group will be passing an evaluation of that software to the development managers, their developers, and other project stakeholders. Other peer managers on the project may also work closely with you and your group. These managers are probably also the people who are most influential in terms of the organization's perception of you and your group's effectiveness, which, as we've remarked elsewhere in this book, is a reality that you need to manage. It would make sense to get to know these people well and build strong relationships with them.

Technical documentation: It's easy to forget about these people, but in organizations where technical documentation teams exist, they are key stakeholders for testing, with test-related interests similar to development managers.

Program and project managers: These people are often peer managers included in the first element in this list. However, if they are not, you should treat them as if they were, within the constraints mentioned earlier about upper

---

7   We had heard this aphorism that "courtesy is the lubricant of social relations" many times before, without knowing the source. Quoting it here required that we determine where it first appeared, and someone found it in *The Management of Men*, by Edward L. Munson. Of course, we would suggest that courtesy is important whether managing men, or women, or both.

management if applicable in your organization. Rex recently did an assessment where every program manager and project manager he interviewed had words of praise for one particular test manager in the test organization. After delivering the assessment report, he went to lunch at a Japanese restaurant on the way back to his hotel. Lo and behold, he meet her there—having lunch with a key project manager!

Sales and marketing: If you work in an organization that builds and sells software or software-based services, the people are very much interested in—and affected by—the quality of the software. They will have strong opinions about what you should test and how well your group is doing your job. (If your organization builds software for internal use, business analysts have a similar interest in testing.) As with peer managers and project managers, a strong relationship with key people and managers within these groups is essential.

Technical support: These people and the sales and marketing folks have a very similar interest in testing. They want to be sure that software is well tested, and they want to know the quality of the software before it goes to customers or end users. Rex has often found a strong relationship with technical support managers to be essential and very useful. He once managed to get the test scope expanded, and additional resources to do the testing, based on strong lobbying by a technical support manager.

Upper management: These are the people who approve your budgets, who write your performance evaluations, and who ultimately measure the success of your team. You definitely need a good relationship with upper management, but you must approach the task sensitively. An overly forward attempt to win over your superiors through meals or drinks will almost certainly come across badly with your peers, undoing any relationship-building you've done there, and will probably not work with the manager either. However, by celebrating successes with upper management, and assiduously ensuring positive and friendly professional interactions with all upper managers with whom you interact, you can establish a reputation as a valuable member of the team.

Vendors: In some cases, you may be testing software or systems provided by vendors. If so, strong relationships with vendor managers—especially test managers, development managers, and program or project managers—are essential. As illustrated in the opening anecdote of this section, a strong relationship with vendor counterparts can provide you with invaluable insights.

Key individual contributors: These are senior individual contributors, such as developers, system designers, business analysts, support staff, and even sales or marketing staff, who work regularly with you or your testers. Many IT organizations are egalitarian meritocracies, and the organizational structure and job titles do not completely reflect how power is distributed. People who have earned respect through doughty hard work and intellectual prowess will have a lot of influence on opinions, including opinions about you and your test team. These are also people to have good relationships with. Inviting them to participate in testing meetings will probably be a better approach than the "meals or drinks" approach because it fits better with their perceived thought leadership in the organization.

Key stakeholder representatives and other stakeholders: As discussed in Chapter 1, there are potentially many other stakeholders for a testing group. You should consider other people (whether managers or key individual contributors) who contribute to or influence testing or your group's test results and quality assessments. If you went through the exercise discussed in Chapter 1, where stakeholders were identified, you should know who the test representatives or points of contact are for you. You should cultivate a relationship with these people as well, based on their importance to the actual and perceived effectiveness of the testing group.

Contrary to what you might expect, this job of relationship-building becomes more challenging as you move up the organizational structure. This is due to the fact that the individual test manager, working on a single project, will know and can build relationships with all of their coworkers on that project. However, as you move up into director or vice president positions, it will become difficult to know all the members of all the various project teams, and it would indeed probably come across as phony if you tried to do so. So from the broad menu given earlier, you must select the right people to build relationships with. Certainly that should include the peer managers and key individual contributors from that list. In addition, if there are people who have information that your test group needs or who control access to resources you test group needs, you need relationships with them as well.

In addition, you should not confine your thinking about whom you should know to those within your organization. Think about external relationships too. While the approach will often be different, and certainly influenced by various niceties of the business relationship, you should be just as careful to cultivate people outside your organization who are all the same important. If you ever catch yourself thinking, "Who cares what that person thinks about me; he's just a vendor employee," stop yourself immediately. Dehumanizing people not only is a moral issue, but also creates barriers to communication with people you need information from. Furthermore, it can undermine your other relationship-building efforts when people see how you behave toward others when you think nothing is at stake. As American humorist Dave Barry put it, "A person who is nice to you but rude to the waiter is not a nice person."

You will probably find it easier to build relationships with some people than with others. Your social antennae may well push you toward going for the easy wins in terms of relationship-building and ignoring the others. Don't let this impulse convince you to skip the harder cases, for two reasons.

First, there is a management cliché that says, " 'I like you' often means 'I'm like you.' " In other words, people often tend to prefer friendships with people who are similar to them in outlooks, personality type, and so forth. (Unfortunately, that can extend to gender and race, which has broad implications for test managers, including in hiring.) Since you manage a test group, which is a recipient and a source of information, you should be sure to avoid any sort of confirmation bias that could occur by building relationships only with those predisposed to agree.

Second, it's no great feat to make a friend of someone who is already inclined to be your friend. Making a friend of a skeptic or an enemy, now that's an accomplishment. Converting a skeptic or enemy not only makes your life easier by changing a negative to a positive in your political balance sheet, it also makes the organization *as a whole* more effective and efficient. In Rex's years of doing assessments for clients, he has seen few things more generally corrosive to organizational success than negative personal relationships between key participants. He has become so convinced of this truism—mutual respect enables organizational success, and vice versa—that this dynamic is one of the first things he examines when he does assessments, and keep in mind that Rex has a degree in engineering, not psychology.

In case it's not obvious by this point, your objective in this relationship-building and -maintaining exercise is not about assembling a coterie of drinking buddies or personal friends. It's not about manipulating people. You want to make sure you and your test group are visible contributors to the organization. As a senior test manager, you must represent the test group in a way that wins respect and shows you as a strong, able, and emotionally intelligent leader.

We want to close this subsection by making an important point. Good relationships are important. Good relationships will make it easier for you and

Rex on Why Relationships Matter

You will find, as you advance in your management career and see your scope increase, that building relationships, along with other politics and stakeholder management tasks, takes more and more of your time and becomes more and more central to how you enable the success of your team. In the consulting work my associates and I do, we find that test groups with good relationships with their colleagues have the best results, both qualitatively and quantitatively. The best test managers have soft skills every bit as strong as their technical, testing, and business skills.

As we wind down this section of this chapter, I want to stress something I think is important. Remember the quote at the beginning of this section from my colleague about "wanting to take a shower" after meeting with someone he disliked? You might feel the same way right now, after my frank discussion about how to benefit from your relationships. Are you thinking, "Gee, Rex, is this all about how to make friends with people so I can take advantage of their friendship?" No, it's not a one-way street, nor is it manipulative.

If you are a manager, you must understand that your job is to get work done through other people, to paraphrase my wise colleague Johanna Rothman. You'll be a lot more effective at working with other people when you have a good relationship with them, as I've said before, and your effectiveness is to their benefit as well as yours. In addition, you may well find that a friendship that starts as purely professional grows into something much more personally meaningful to both of you over time. Almost every personal friend I have made since graduating from UCLA I made through working relationships. Far from being a cold and inhuman thing that I am suggesting here, I am in fact suggesting that you be fully human in your work as a test manager, and not only for the sake of better organizational effectiveness.

your team to do your job, and to do it better. Good relationships will also, frankly, buy you some political cover if there's a big witch hunt for a scapegoat (pardon the mixed metaphor) after some particular disastrous quality issue during testing or in production. However, good relationships are no substitute for competence. If your intention is to cloak your inabilities with sycophancy and false friendships, that is unlikely to work in the long term. As Abraham Lincoln put it, "You can fool some of the people all of the time, and all of the people some of the time, but you can't fool all of the people all of the time."

4.5.3   A Real Social Network

As a manager of a test group, you cannot—and should not—be the only networker. Key people in your group should also form relationships across the organization, and you should be aware of those relationships. That way, members of the test team can act as your emissary. Effectively, you are delegating some of your relationship building to your team. This not only frees you up for other duties, it also teaches key people within your team the importance of this key management task, thus aiding them on their career path. In large organizations, or organizations doing distributed work, this "one degree of separation" approach to relationship-building can be not just a good idea but also necessary.

4.6 Advocating Quality Activities Across the Organization

Learning objectives

LO 5.6.1   (K2) Identify other groups within the organization who are also involved in quality-related activities.

One problem we see in a few organizations is the "throw it over the fence and let the test group find all the bugs" attitude toward quality. In other words, developers and other project participants assume that one level of testing, right at the end of development, is sufficient to achieve quality. Of course, testing and quality tasks should be pervasive, spanning different groups and the entire software lifecycle. Part of managing across the organization is working with testing and quality stakeholders to make sure they understand the role other groups play in testing and quality when they define, create, and support software.

The specific roles these other groups play will vary from one organization to another. The lifecycle being followed matters too. So does the way in which the organization uses outside vendors and service providers, if any. However, here are some common examples to consider.

Reviews: Industry studies show that a substantial percentage of defects are introduced in precursor work products such as requirements specification, user stories, software design, database design, architecture specifications, acceptance criteria, and user documentation.[8] Defects can also be introduced in test documentation. As explained in the Foundation and Advanced syllabi, and as borne out by numerous time-and-motion studies, the effort required to remove these defects is minimized when these defects are found and removed as close as possible to the moment of their introduction. Therefore, project stakeholders should participate, as appropriate, in reviews of these work products before they are used as the basis for subsequent project work.

Developer testing: There aren't a lot of categorical statements that can be made about software testing and quality, given the highly contextual nature of software development, but there are few practitioners who would contest the assertion that developers should unit-test their own code before they call their code

---

8   See, for example, any number of Capers Jones's books, including *Estimating Software Costs: Bringing Realism to Estimating* and *The Economics of Software Quality*.

ready for a wider audience. Rex's personal opinion is that this testing should achieve at least statement and branch coverage as well as covering whatever unit-specific risks the developer is aware of. In a number of organizations, developers are also responsible for component integration test. Ideally, testers (with a sufficiently technical background) would also participate in this level of testing. He has also seen a number of situations in which developers were able to contribute significantly to automated testing frameworks and even automated tests that were useful for system test and system integration test.

Validation, user acceptance testing, and operational acceptance testing: No matter how good the reviews are, no matter how good the developer testing, and no matter how good the testing your group does, some risk remains that the software built is not quite what the user needs. In addition, even if the software is what the user needs, the level of user confidence might not be what it should be at the end of the development process. To address these issues, business analysis, marketing teams, or others who understand the needs of the customer might need to do some validation testing during the system test or system integration test levels. Users, customers, or their representatives should be involved in user acceptance testing for IT software. Operators, such as system administrators, network administrators, and database administrators, should be involved in operational acceptance testing. When you're building software that will be sold to a wide audience, such as mass-market and enterprise software, alpha testing and beta testing are ways to carry out this acceptance testing.

For optimal effectiveness and efficiency, the test manager should be—at the very least—aware of these other activities and what they will cover. This awareness allows the test manager to avoid retesting areas already adequately tested by others as well as to ensure that areas not tested by others are tested by their group. The best practice—which is far from the common practice — is for the test manager to work with the managers of other project participants to plan which testing tasks are best done at which points in the lifecycle. This determination allows the proper people to carry out these tasks, thus maximizing effectiveness, as well as to remove defects at the optimal point, thus maximizing efficiency.

In addition, the test manager should be provided with the results of these other testing and quality activities as they proceed. A comprehensive understanding of these activities, including the effectiveness of the testing done by the test group itself, will allow the test manager to understand and present stakeholders with an entire testing and quality picture. Suppose you are working with a client to develop a test strategy that includes a comprehensive test coverage plan and test results reporting process. While it's not trivial to implement, the business case for doing so is immense. In engagements where we've examined the costs associated with suboptimal defect removal, we've found as much as 25 percent of the software development budget was wasted due to avoidable costs.

When this understanding reveals breakdowns in the total process for testing and quality, the test manager should be ready to analyze the causes, explain those causes, and present ways to fix the problem. For example, defects discovered late in the process, such as during user acceptance testing, could indicate inadequate reviews, gaps in the system test or system integration test, or problems with test environments of data. Human psychology and brain structure leads us to jump to conclusions when presented with problems, but the wise test manager knows that proper root cause analysis should be done carefully and with data. To paraphrase Jerry Weinberg's Rule of Three, if you haven't thought of at least three different ways in which a process breakdown could have occurred, you probably haven't thought enough.[9]

The analysis of other groups' testing work can be complicated by differences in record keeping. Independent test groups, composed of professional testers, tend to have detailed documentation and rigorous processes for managing test work products and results such as tests, test basis traceability, and, especially, defects. Other groups involved in testing are typically much less detailed. In the ideal case, the management of all testing work products and results would occur in the same test management tools, but that is seldom the case. At the very least, if a consolidated view of testing is needed, the test manager must work with other groups to define what information must be captured by each group and how that information can be collated.

It is by no means unusual for other groups to commit to perform testing tasks but to perform them poorly or not at all. We regularly hear testers and developers talk about unit testing that is not performed, or is performed by some developers but not by all developers, or that is performed by developers who don't understand the fundamental concepts of unit testing. For example, many developers do not have a good understanding of code coverage.[10]

---

9   This rule appears in Gerald Weinberg and Virginia Satir's book *The Secrets of Consulting: A Guide to Giving and Getting Advice Successfully*.

10   You or others who want to know more about code coverage, or should know more about code coverage, can listen to Rex's webinar Advanced Software Testing: Code Coverage, available at www.rbcs-us.com/software-testing-resources/library/digital-library.

It is typically not the test manager's job to enforce adherence to software engineering best practices. In addition, it's usually not the case that these other groups have omitted or short-changed these testing tasks because they are pathological liars who enjoy telling people they will do things and then shamelessly blowing off those commitments. Tight schedules, scope creep, and resource issues often mean that project pressures limit what these groups can do. Further, if testing tasks are seen as low priority, or perhaps not so critical because after all a test group exists, they'll be the first tasks dropped under pressure.

In some cases, especially when the problem is not omission of the testing tasks but rather incompleteness, the underlying problem is a lack of know-how. As mentioned previously, many developers don't know the basics of code coverage, so their unit testing will not tend to achieve even 100 percent statement coverage. Sometimes the problem is one of motivation, especially when people are being asked to do testing tasks they have not done previously. In fact, we have seen cases of outright demotivation by managers, where perverse incentives result in testing tasks not being done or test results not being recorded.

Whatever the cause, it is important that the test manager knows what has and has not actually been tested. This assessment should be done through proper verification of the work. For example, it is not enough simply to ask the development manager, "Did your programmers unit-test their code?" The answer to that question will almost always be yes, but that answer is not always connected to reality.

Assuming you find that certain tests have not occurred, what can you do? In the long term, the answer is to work with your fellow managers, and with executives, to solve the underlying cause. If management knows to what extent constraints, prioritization, lack of knowledge, and lack of motivation are resulting in the testing gaps, a plan can be formulated to resolve those issues and enable better testing across all the participants. How this plan is created, and who does what to implement the plan, will vary across organizations. Some of our clients have found that Agile lifecycles in particular enable test managers to effectively advocate pervasive quality activities.

In the immediate term, if you discover that some planned set of test activities did not occur, you need to make the best of a bad situation. If you discover the gap early, prior to the start of your own group's test execution role, you have more options. You can, perhaps, work with the team that is experiencing difficulty completing their test tasks in an attempt to salvage the work. While this might have the effect of diverting your resources and reducing your group's effectiveness and efficiency, it could be that, for the overall effectiveness and efficiency of the organization, this is the best course of action. If you discover the gap after your test execution has started, you can try to obtain more resources and/or time for testing. As you make the choice about how to respond, remember that the proper balance of quality, schedule, budget, and feature choices must be optimized on an organization-wide basis.

4.7 Integrating Tools Across the Organization

Learning objectives

LO 5.7.1 (K2) Define the issues that should be considered when dealing with multiuse tools.

LO 5.7.2 (K4) Analyze a proposed change to a multiuse tool and assess the impact on the test organization.

LO 5.7.3 (K6) Create a plan for rolling out a new multiuse tool considering all phases of the tool lifecycle.

In the previous section, we mentioned the advisability of sharing test management tools across groups involved in testing as a way to enable better coordination of testing and reporting of test results. This is but one example of how tools can be—and frequently are—shared across organizations. While sharing tools has obvious appeal, great care and planning is required for this sharing to work.

For example, we've seen a number of situations in which organizations are using the same tool to track defects, development tasks, and requirements. This tool is often one best suited to tracking tasks or user support incidents, thus making the out-of-box defect and requirement tracking abilities limited. This is not to say that the tool cannot be made to work, but a number of modifications will be necessary. For one thing, it's necessary to distinguish between the three quite-different types of data being managed in the tool. It's also necessary to gather different types of classification information depending on the type of data in question. This will allow analysis and reporting of defects to occur in a meaningful fashion.

This type of well-structured multiuse tool implementation cannot happen by accident, and it is much harder to put the structure in place after habits of usage have been established and, often, significant repositories of dirty and confusing data have been accumulated. When tools are bought (or downloaded for free) and then turned loose in the organization, their usage can grow like a weed, with no documentation. It's difficult to maintain, support, and update such tools. Furthermore, if there is a need to convert data to or from such a tool or to migrate tools, the opacity surrounding the tool makes such conversions and migrations inefficient and error prone. Instead, the best practice is to acquire, implement, and use these tools according to a predefined (though often evolving) plan. Let's examine what we need to plan for across the tool lifecycle.

4.7.1 Purchasing, Selecting, and Acquiring the Multiuse Tool

Think back to the last time you went to lunch or dinner with a group of friends or your family. In this situation, it would be unusual for one person to order for everyone, and if they did, some of the diners would probably not be satisfied with their meal. Instead, people choose for themselves. In some workplace cases, there might be constraints, such as limits on what could be purchased (e.g., alcohol may be precluded in a company lunch) or what the total amount for the meal could be. In a sense, the diners are a selection committee.

In the case of a multiuse tool, you also need a selection committee. Just as every diner must participate in the selection of the meal, every stakeholder in the purchase, use, and maintenance of the tool must be involved in the committee. However, there are many more requirements, constraints, and risks to consider. At least in this selection committee, unlike on a family trip to a restaurant, you probably won't have to tell your five-year-old to stop putting carrots up their nose!

Part of the job of the selection committee is identifying the requirements, constraints, and risks associated with the tool. Each of the stakeholders on the committee has insight into some of these items, but people outside the committee might need to have input as well. The well-led committee is careful to understand these requirements, constraints, and risks before taking any further steps.

Some of these requirements, constraints, and risks involve integration, in terms of both integration with other tools and integration with the processes. Each point of integration must be defined. All of the data to be captured and shared must be clearly identified and defined, as must the ways in which this data is to be stored, received, and transferred. If there are any customizations required, especially custom programming or database schemas, they must also be identified and defined, including the responsibility for implementing and maintaining the customizations.

Of course, the multiuse tool must be used by people in various roles. What different user groups exist, and what will they use the tool to do? What administrator roles exist, and what must they do to enable secure, reliable, recoverable use of the tool? How will the users be managed? Are there license issues associated with the users? The selection committee must find answers to these questions.

Another critical area of consideration is ownership and responsibility. For example, if the tool is a commercial one, it must be paid for. That money must come from someone's budget, and the purchase must be approved. Even open source tools have approval issues, because the agreements under which they are distributed (such as the GNU General Public License and the Creative Commons license) often impose responsibilities on the organization. As the committee plans for the implementation project and the long-term maintenance of the tool, clear responsibilities must be assigned. Ideally, as with any project, a project manager is assigned for the implementation work.

4.7.2 Updating, Maintaining, and Supporting the Multiuse Tool

Once the implementation work is underway, there can be a considerable amount of programming and testing involved, depending on the degree of customization and integration required. Many of the best testing tools available these days are multiuse tools or can be integrated with other tools to create a multiuse tool. As such, planning and performing this implementation work often requires significant tool project management and technical expertise that might or might not be present in the organization. Rex and his associates have worked on a number of engagements with clients where RBCS associates provide this expertise.

Software engineering tools, including testing tools, are all forms of software, which makes them changeable. As every test manager knows, this malleability of software is not without risk and must be managed. A clear change management process for multiuse tools is critical because otherwise, each stakeholder group's needs and desires will often create centrifugal forces that degrade the overall usefulness of the tool. At the same time, the change management process must not make change too difficult because in that case changing needs cannot be accommodated.

For some tools, it is possible to make localized customizations that affect only certain user groups. Theoretically, these localized changes do not have the same centrifugal tendencies that overall changes do, but that's not always the case. If, for example, developers decide to modify the classification fields for tasks to include a priority field, that can be confusing if the defined levels of priority differ from those used for defects. For all changes, it's important that impact analysis be done to identify whose use cases will be affected and how.

As mentioned earlier, multiuse tools have a disparate base of users, each with their own particular use cases and abilities. A common mistake is to fail to provide support for these users. Simply providing a tool, even if the tool is perfect, is not enough. People must be trained and supported in the use of the tool. Since, in many cases, these multiuse tools support critical team activities, there must be well-defined service-level agreements (SLAs) in place. For example, if the defect tracking tool were inaccessible or just highly unreliable during test execution for three days, that would likely disrupt the test group considerably. On one project where developers selected the defect tracking tool without input from the test group, the test group suffered from unreliable access to that tool for months, resulting in persistent inefficiencies.

During or after the implementation, it might be necessary to migrate data into the tool. This could include defect reports from a previous tool, tests documented in spreadsheets, or even unstructured data. This must be done with utmost care. It is often the case that production data is riddled with errors, so you should plan to deal with records that contain such data quality issues, especially those having to do with referential integrity. For example, if each test must be related to one or more test basis elements (e.g., a requirements specification element or quality risk item), the process of importing tests from spreadsheets must include some way of establishing this relationship.

For many tools, large quantities of data will be managed over a long period of time. Data related to defects, tests, test results, and test coverage form the raw material from which project, product, and process metrics are derived (see Chapters 6 and 8). Therefore, an additional data quality concern is that of recoverability. In the event of a disaster, ranging from a disk failure all the way up to the loss of a data center, it must be possible to restore the data. This entails clear requirements and responsibilities for backing up, restoring testing, and actually restoring data (if the need ever arises).

4.7.3 Converting and Retiring Tools

When Rex started as a tester in an independent test lab, the state of the art in defect tracking and test management in his organization was a Lotus Notes database. He and his colleagues captured all their test results in that repository and used it to produce reports for clients. Later, they added a Lotus 1-2-3 spreadsheet as a way of summarizing test status in a single consolidated view. Rex thought he had a pretty good set of tools and processes for test management, and it did serve his organization's needs.

The best practice now, of course, is miles beyond such homespun tools. Of course, as sophisticated as test tools are today, there's every reason to think that the evolution of tools will continue. Business needs evolve. Some tools vendors thrive while some vendors fail. Sometimes external factors prevail, such as when a client insists that a testing service provider use their tools on their projects. So don't get too attached to any given tool because conversions will happen.

These conversions are never as simple as flipping a switch. Consider whether some data must be migrated from the incumbent tool to the new tool and, if so, how that will be done. Users staying on the incumbent tool (if any) will need to retain access to it without any interruption. The users migrating to the new tool should see minimal disruption of their service and consistent data, before and after the migration. It's highly desirable that the conversion be to a tool that is at least as usable, reliable, and functional as the incumbent tool.

If all users are to be moved off the incumbent tool, then the tool may well be retired. Retirement of a tool should not occur unless a new tool is fully available to all the users, unless there were no users of the retired tool. The key is that any decision to convert or retire tools should allow (ideally seamless) continuous availability of the relevant business function for all users.

In some cases, a tool or some portion of it must be retained for ongoing access to the original data, though it's typically preferable to migrate the data to the new tool and access it there. However, it might be desirable to retain a utility that can secure and access archived data without putting it into the live dataset of the replacement tool. For example, if the amount of archived data is very large, it might create performance issues to load it.

4.7.4 The Manager Role with Multiuse Tools

What is the test manager's role with multiuse tools? It depends, often more on accidents of organizational history than any deliberate or rational choice. As a test manager, you should be prepared to act as the owner of the tool or as one of the stakeholders. Either way, you and your team need reliable access to the tool, and accurate test-related data in the tool, while at the same time so do the other stakeholders.

If you are the owner of the tool, your job includes understanding and accommodating the needs of the other stakeholders. The implementation of the tool should accommodate all stakeholders and avoid forcing trade-offs where improving the utility of the tool for one group degrades the utility for another group. This imperative to support diverse needs and users in multiuse tools creates complicated issues beyond those associated with single-use tools used only by testers.

Given the complications, there is a considerable time and effort associated with owning these tools. As was explained in the preceding sections, there are many issues that must be addressed with careful forethought in planning for the implementation, use, and support of such tools. Because the plan must span multiple stakeholder groups, the owner of multiuse tools must be adept in organization politics and have a diplomatic approach to the tools' stakeholders. The owner must be ready to negotiate and compromise to obtain support. However, these compromises can have negative side effects for some of the stakeholders, so creativity is often required to avoid that.

In some organizations, the potential conflict of interest associated with a stakeholder group's ownership of multiuse tools is avoided by forming a separate tools group. This group is truly a service organization and must act like one. It should define usage guidelines that reliably enable the key business functions supported by the tool while preserving security, recoverability, and data quality.

4.8   Handling Ethical Issues

Learning objectives

LO 5.8.1   (K5) Evaluate a given set of behaviors under a given set of circumstances to identify possible ethical issues.

In an earlier section, "Creating and Building Relationships," you read about a fellow so ethically challenged that one of his colleagues felt the need for a shower after meeting with him. Now, clearly this fellow lay toward the extreme end of the ethical spectrum, but not one of us can claim to be perfectly ethical. In some cases, we lapse ethically due to ignorance or momentary weakness. In other cases, a herd mentality exists, where we see unethical behavior around us go unpunished—or worse yet get rewarded—and so we adopt an "everyone is doing it" attitude.

As a manager, you are responsible not only for your own ethics, but also for those of your team. If people on your team are behaving badly, you must not tolerate it. Further, you must set an example of ethical behavior for your team. Challenges to ethical behavior can arise in many different contexts within a project and an organization, so you should always be on your guard.

4.8.1 Managing the Team's Ethics

The ISTQB code of ethics is defined in the Foundation syllabus. For ease of reference, we've included it here.

Public: Certified software testers shall act consistently with the public interest.

Client and employer: Certified software testers shall act in a manner that is in the best interests of their client and employer, consistent with the public interest.

Product: Certified software testers shall ensure that the deliverables they provide (on the products and systems they test) meet the highest professional standards possible.

Judgment: Certified software testers shall maintain integrity and independence in their professional judgment.

Management: Certified software test managers and leaders shall subscribe to and promote an ethical approach to the management of software testing.

Profession: Certified software testers shall advance the integrity and reputation of the profession consistent with the public interest.

Colleagues: Certified software testers shall be fair to and supportive of their colleagues, and promote cooperation with software developers.

Self: Certified software testers shall participate in lifelong learning regarding the practice of their profession and shall promote an ethical approach to the practice of the profession.

These ethics apply to any interactions made by you or the test group, including people inside and outside the organization. As mentioned earlier, you need to hold your group to those ethics, but remember that this must be done fairly.

People should be trained in the application of the code of ethics. Make sure the ethics are clearly stated to the team and that each person understands that they are individually accountable to them. Tell them, and show them, that the herd mentality will never be tolerated as an excuse in your group, regardless of what others are doing.

Reinforcing ethics is an ongoing activity. As you carry out annual performance evaluations, be sure to note and reward ethical behavior and conversely to censure unethical behavior. When you find a situation that has interesting ethical implications, use that as a case study for your group, examining and discussing acceptable and unacceptable courses of action.

Ethics are important for all managers, but especially test managers. Because testers are often the bearers of bad news, conflicts can occur, sometimes unexpectedly. This requires testers to keep their professionalism and their cool, regardless of the behavior and comments from those around them. A single outburst, ill-considered email, or ethical lapse in the wrong situation can undo much of the relationship-building that has been a core concern of this chapter.

4.8.2 Interacting with Test Stakeholders and Reporting Test Results

In your interactions with the various test stakeholders, you and your group must behave professionally, keeping personal interests and emotions contained. Tell the facts as well as you know them, accurately and objectively, while also communicating effectively. Consider the code of ethics, particularly those having to do with client and employer, product, judgment, management, and colleagues. People tend to trust and respect others when they respect not only the ends they achieve but also the means by which they achieve those ends.

As a test manager, you'll typically produce numerous reports, metrics, charts, and presentations for testing stakeholders. Remember that the ethics statements relating to product mean that the data and the analysis you've done on the data are accurate. That also means that you should present test results clearly and correctly, because information is not successfully transmitted until it is successfully received. Further, the ethics statements relating to your colleagues mean that reports should not target anyone. A classic mistake test managers make in this regard is producing reports that show the number of defects introduced by each developer or name the developers who own the defect reports that have been languishing the longest in an assigned and unresolved state. Classifications and reporting can be done by any number of impersonal groupings, such as features, quality characteristics, or modules, and using these groupings, you can often achieve the same informational result without making someone feel targeted.

These ethical considerations do not apply only to management-level communications. Defect reports, status reports, email, hallway conversations, instant messages, and indeed any form of written or verbal communication must be ethical. This means that the information is conveyed objectively and fairly, without malice or hidden agendas. If some recipients might misunderstand the information conveyed, providing context and background is required.

Because huge quantities of information come out of test groups and from every level of the test group, consistent application and promulgation of ethical standards are critical. Everyone's communications either support or degrade the credibility and perceived value of test team. We have seen the damage done when one intemperate email, one stupidly expressed defect report, or one angry instant message found its way into the wrong hands, and thence brought to the attention of management.

Containing emotions is often a difficult standard to achieve. Test status and test results can be controversial, and people sometimes react defensively. Testing can be squeezed by project schedules, and it can seem like unfair micromanagement when other managers suggest throwing tests (and thus quality goals) overboard to hit a deadline. It can be particularly galling when you, as the test manager, always thought the deadline was a completely unrealistic fiction to begin with.

It's important to remember that, as a general rule, the more you let anger and frustration enter into your communication, the less effectively you'll communicate. Your emotional state becomes the main information received, distracting people from the objective realities of your testing. Instead, while preserving the integrity of your message, try to understand how each stakeholder will relate and react to it. If it's going to be unpopular, so be it, but be prepared to handle the negative response you'll receive.

4.8.3 Test Management Ethics

As a test manager, you have ethical concerns that are specific to being a test manager, but you also have ethical concerns that are general to all managers. As a manager, you are entrusted with the care of those people in your group. You must behave professionally and ethically at all times. While time and space preclude a complete discussion of the implications, here are some highlights to keep in mind.

Personal issues: It is fairly common for managers to find that their direct reports share certain personal details of their life. For example, someone may tell you that they will be late for work or working from home due to a sick child or that they will need to take a leave of absence for a couple weeks to deal with a parent's terminal illness. Depending on your personality type, your organization's culture, and the people in your group, this can occur frequently or infrequently, but some level of personal communication will inevitably occur. Who else you share this information with, and how, is an ethical question. In the case of someone working from home due to a sick child, you might mention that to coworkers to explain their absence. However, in the case of the death of a close relative, you should ask the employee first before sharing that information. Ask yourself, "How would I want this information to be treated if I were in my employee's place?" That question will usually guide you toward the right ethical behavior.

Individual performance issues: If someone in your group is not meeting the expectations for their work or is behaving in a way that is disruptive, you have an obligation to your organization and to your test group to work with the person to resolve the underlying problem. This must be done in a way that is both fair to the individual who is underperforming and expeditious in returning overall test group performance to expected levels. You should handle the discussion of the performance issues with the individual discreetly, frankly, and with an honest intention to do the best thing for the individual and for the organization. Of course, gossiping about the individual's performance issues is inappropriate, but you might need to discuss the situation with other managers who have observed or been affected by the substandard performance. Often, an organization's human resources department will have rules about how to deal with troublesome employees, and you should follow those rules closely.

Intragroup interpersonal issues: This is a special case, and an especially difficult case, of disruptive behavior in your group. It occurs when two or more individuals in your test group develop a negative or distracting relationship. People don't have to be friends to work together, but they do need to cooperate and behave in a professional, productive way in the workplace. This category of issues can also include the office romance, if organizational rules preclude it or if the romance spills over into open displays of emotion at work. You need to work with the individuals involved to resolve the interpersonal issues that exist or at least to get the individuals to agree to keep the issues from affecting their work performance and behavior. As with the previous item, discuss the matter only with other managers or HR staff who have a legitimate need to know and to be involved.

Legal issues: The apex of all regrettable ethical issues is achieved when those issues rise to the level of civil or criminal legal action—or potential action. Examples include harassment, retaliatory behavior, or discrimination based on gender, sexuality, race, or other protected class. The way you handle this as a manager will prove a true test of your ethical character. (Obviously, if you are the harasser, you have already failed that test.) If someone in your group approaches you and complains of harassment by someone else in your group, that is a situation you must act on, but you must act on it properly, not impulsively. First, get the details (in private, of course), acknowledging the report and assuring the person that action will be taken. Next, contact your human resources department, your organization's legal department (if any), and your manager. If the behavior being reported is of a criminal nature—e.g., brandishing a handgun in the course of an argument—then you might have an obligation to involve the police, but you should be cautious about escalating to the police unless you are absolutely sure it is necessary. Now, you must remember that people have a right to a presumption of innocence, and all sides of the story should be heard. As you work with your manager and the human resources department and proceed through the resolution of a difficult issue, remember to be fair toward all parties, extremely discreet in your discussions of the matter, and sober and serious in your demeanor about the situation. Rex once observed the head of an organization making jokes, in a public setting, about a series of disturbing and abusive emails that were broadcast within the organization to all of the members. Rex didn't have much respect for this person going into that situation, and with this display of utterly unethical behavior, which was a true window into his character, Rex lost all respect for him that remained.

The complexity of handling these ethically charged issues is complicated by the other stresses of your workload. While it's never a good time to deal with the kind of issues mentioned, there are typically a score of schedule, budget, quality, and technical issues vying for your attention when these challenges arise. Nevertheless, you must have the ability to multitask as a manager. The kinds of personnel issues mentioned here rarely resolve themselves on their own, and even if they might, it is highly unethical for a manager to ignore such problems. As much as it is human nature to avoid difficult or distasteful situations, it is your job to handle them, promptly, professionally, and fairly.

In some cases, these issues become further complicated by the fact that the problem involves another manager's employees. For example, if there is a developer who is writing code that causes lots of problems in testing, you might become aware of that individual's performance issues before their manager does. We have seen other examples, such as hostility or aggression toward testers by people in other groups. These situations are the moments where all the relationship building discussed in this chapter will come into play. You'll need to approach the other manager, discreetly and in private, to discuss the problem. If you are dealing with a situation where someone in the test group is being mistreated by someone outside the test group, be ready to spend some of the relationship and political capital you have accumulated on resolving that situation.

Dealing with human and relationship issues is an inherent part of a manager's job. There's no formula for simple resolution of these issues. When in the midst of resolving such issues, remember that you have spent a lot of time building relationships and your reputation as an ethical manager. Incompetent or callous handling of delicate situations can do immense damage to those relationships and your reputation. Carefully assess the situation before you act, and think carefully before you speak.

4.9   Sample Exam Questions

In the following section, you will find sample questions that cover the learning objectives for this chapter. All K5 and K6 learning objectives are covered with one or more essay questions, while each K2, K3, and K4 learning objective is covered with a single multiple-choice question. This mirrors the organization of the actual ISTQB exam. The number of the covered learning objective(s) is provided for each question, to aid in traceability. The learning objective number will not be provided on the actual exam.

The content of all of your responses to essay questions will be marked in terms of the accuracy, completeness, and relevance of the ideas expressed. The form of your answer will be evaluated in terms of clarity, organization, correct mechanics (spelling, punctuation, grammar, capitalization), and legibility.

Question 1

LO 5.2.1

You are the test manager of a small but highly effective testing group. In a discussion with the owner of the company, she tells you that the size of the programming team will double over the next year. She then asks you whether you can continue to operate with the current test team staffing level and still improve efficiency of testing.

Which of the following statements demonstrates how best to advocate the test team in this situation?

A. Use metrics to show the owner the likely reduced effectiveness of testing and thus increased cost of quality.
B. Tell the owner that this plan should be possible if sufficient investments are made in training the test team.
C. Be forthright in admitting the mistakes the test group has made, and explain how you intend to correct them.
D. Explain to the owner that preserving an industry-standard tester-to-developer ratio is essential to the organization's success.

Scenario 1 (continued): The Job Has Its Ups and Downs

You have been hired as the director of software testing for an organization that makes escalators and elevators. Due to the safety-critical nature of these systems, this organization is subject to external audits of its testing.

Management has asked you to propose a reorganization of the current approach to testing, which involves having testers report directly to development managers within each functional area team. Management wants your group, which is called the testing services group, to take responsibility for all levels of testing following unit testing and prior to beta testing.

Question 2

LO 5.2.2 and LO 5.3.1

Refer to Scenario 1. Explain how you would propose to organize your testing group, and connect the proposed organizational approach to specific values that this approach would promote.

Question 3

Consider Scenario 1.

LO 5.6.1

Which of the following statements lists other groups you would expect to be involved in testing, in their order of involvement in the project?

A. Requirements engineers, developers, testing services group, executive management, selected customers.
B. System architects, requirements engineers, developers, testing services group, selected customers.
C. Developers, testing services group, selected customers.
D. Requirements engineers, system architects, developers, testing services group, selected customers.

Question 4

LO 5.2.3

Consider the following situations:

A. Project leadership asks for an analysis of why the number of bugs found exceeds the estimate.
B. People use cost-of-quality metrics to determine the efficiency of the test team.
C. The number of testers assigned to the test team is reduced after test execution starts.
D. Testing stakeholders give the test team input on what should be tested.
E. Testing stakeholders ask to participate in a quality risk analysis session during test design.
F. The development manager says testing is taking too long because too many bugs are being found.
G. Executive management expects to receive regular updates on defect detection effectiveness.
H. A project manager tells the test manager which testers should be assigned to a project.

Select three of the above situations where a test manager would need to defend the test team.

Question 5

LO 5.4.1

Consider the following list of testing work products:

A. Detailed defect reports
B. Test summary reports
C. Test process metrics
D. Requirements coverage report

Consider the following list of testing stakeholders:

I.   Business analysts
II.   Programmers
III. Project managers
IV.   Executive managers
V.   Technical support staff
VI.   UAT manager

Select the answer that correctly matches stakeholders with the testing work products that need to be communicated to them.

A. A: II, V; B: III, IV, VI; C: IV; D: I, III, VI.
B. A: II; B: III, IV, VI; C: IV; D: I, III, V, VI.
C. A: II, V; B: I, II, VI; C: IV; D: I, III, VI.
D. A: II, V; B: III, IV; C: III, IV, VI; D: I, III, VI.

Question 6

LO 5.7.3 and LO 5.7.2

Consider Scenario 1.

Assume that senior managers have directed you to implement a defect tracking tool that will provide better visibility into defect introduction, detection, and removal in the software engineering process. This will involve having a single tool that will be used to track defects at all stages of the lifecycle, including support defects. An existing tool is used to track requirements (in the form of user stories), development tasks, and defects found during development, and this tool has a large repository of historical defect data. You have determined that this tool will not meet the needs of the organization.

Outline a plan for selecting, acquiring, and implementing this new approach to defect tracking.

Assume that senior managers have directed you to implement a defect tracking tool that will provide better visibility into defect introduction, detection, and removal in the software engineering process. This will involve having a single tool that will be used to track defects at all stages of the lifecycle, including support defects. An existing tool is used to track requirements (in the form of user stories), development tasks, and defects found during development, and this tool has a large repository of historical defect data. You have determined that this tool will not meet the needs of the organization.

Outline a plan for selecting, acquiring, and implementing this new approach to defect tracking.

Question 7

LO 5.8.1 and LO 5.5.2

Consider Scenario 1. Assume that you have now implemented the unified defect tracking system described in question 6. During test execution, one of your senior testers tells you that a programmer asked her not to report three critical, potentially safety-related defects that she had located. The programmer told her that his annual performance evaluation would be affected by the defect reports because development management had set maximum defect limits for each programmer after the new defect tracking system was put in place.

The question consists of two parts:

1. Describe the ethical issues associated with this situation.
2. Outline a resolution that results in minimal damage to existing relationships between testers, programmers, test managers, and development managers.

Question 8

LO 5.5.1

Assume that you have recently been hired as a test manager in a growing software-as-a-service vendor. This organization has not previously had a testing organization but rather has relied entirely on programmers testing their own code and limited beta testing managed by the technical support team.

Which of the following is a good first step to start creating relationships in this situation?

A. Ask the programmers to participate in a brown-bag lunch session with the new testers to explain to the testers how they unit-test their code.
B. Schedule a meeting with executive managers, and give a presentation for them on how much more effective independent test groups are at finding defects.
C. Have lunch with the development manager and technical support manager, letting them know you're looking forward to coordinating testing efforts with them.
D. Have drinks with the technical support manager, and ask him if he can help you understand what the developers are currently missing in their unit testing.

Question 9

LO 5.7.1

Assume that a company's test management tool loses some of the classification attributes (e.g., priority) associated with a requirement when importing new and updated requirements from the requirements management tool. Which of the following options is a multiuse tool issue that should have been considered during the purchasing, selection, and acquisition of the test management tool, to help avoid such a problem?

A. Integration of data types
B. Ownership of the tool
C. Defined change management process
D. Continuation of service on tool retirement

5   Project Management Essentials

Keywords: confidence intervals, planning poker

5.1   Introduction

Learning objectives

No learning objectives for this section.

Project management is practically in everything we do. We like to use the simple example of summer vacations to illustrate this point. First, we decide to take a much-needed vacation. We may consider the feasibility of taking a trip, at a very high level considering time (is time off from work available?), cost (the vacation must be within budget), scope (what do we enjoy doing that fits in the budget and time away from work?), benefits (spending uninterrupted fun time with our families, recharging batteries), and even some idea of risk (bungee jumping is *not* our idea of a fun vacation). After these high-level considerations, we begin planning the vacation, including where we want to go, what we want to do, how long we can afford to be away, and so on. After answers to general planning questions, we need to dig into the details and do more specific, in-depth vacation planning of what we need to do to get ready. When the big day arrives, we get into the car and start the vacation, doing all the things and seeing all the sights we so eagerly planned some time before. Finally, we return home exhausted yet refreshed, but the vacation doesn't truly end as memories remain. This is also the time to reflect and consider:

- Did we overall enjoy our vacation time, achieving the benefits we planned?
- Did we stay within our planned vacation budget (or will the upcoming bills wipe us out)?
- Did we spend too long or not enough time on vacation (sometimes, while absence makes the heart grow fonder, familiarity breeds contempt)?
- Is there anything different we would do if we could do it all again (like bungee jumping was worth the risk and is more fun than we thought)?

ISTQB Glossary

consultative test strategy: Testing driven by the advice and guidance of appropriate experts from outside the test team (e.g., technology experts and/or business domain experts).

planning poker: A consensus-based estimation technique, mostly used to estimate effort or relative size of user stories in Agile software development. It is a variation of the Wideband Delphi method using a deck of cards with values representing the units in which the team estimates.

There is considerable overlap and involvement in what test managers and project managers do on projects. While the project manager has direct ownership, accountability, and responsibility in many areas, the successful test manager will be actively involved in many project management tasks, including the development and overall management of test-related tasks on the schedule, risks, reviews, assessments, and proper documentation.

In this chapter, we'll cover common project topics of estimation, scheduling, budgeting, risk management, and quality management, distinguishing between areas and topics within the domain of the project manager and the test manager.

5.2 Project Management Tasks

Learning objectives

LO 6.2.1 (K6) For a given project, estimate the test effort using at least two of the prescribed estimation methods.

LO 6.2.2 (K6) Use historical data from similar projects to create a model for estimating the number of defects that will be discovered, resolved, and delivered on the current project.

LO 6.2.3 (K5) During the project, evaluate current conditions as part of test control to manage, track, and adjust the test effort over time, including identifying any deviations from the plan and proposing effective measures to resolve those deviations.

LO 6.2.4 (K5) Evaluate the impact of project-wide changes (e.g., in scope, budget, goals, or schedule), and identify the effect of those changes on the test estimate.

LO 6.2.5 (K6) Using historical information from past projects and priorities communicated by project stakeholders, determine the appropriate trade-offs between quality, schedule, budget, and features available on a project.

LO 6.2.6 (K2) Define the role of the test manager in the change management process.

While the test manager primarily manages the testing phase, testing activities, and test team on a project, she must also be a participant in the overall project management aspects of the project. This includes task estimation, scheduling, budget, and resource allocation and management, dealing effectively with project trade-offs, change management, risk management, and overall quality management. Each of these areas will be considered in greater depth below. It is key that the test manager, as should other functional area managers such as the development manager, business/systems analysis manager, training manager, etc., not treat her specific areas separately from the overall project, which would be greatly detrimental to the success of the project and its outcomes. Rather, the test manager should collaborate and work closely with the project manager and other functional area managers as all areas are interdependent and rely on each other to build a quality product and influence the success of the project.

5.2.1 Test Estimation

Each functional area must consider the work its team members must do to contribute to the overall success of the project. Since the testing team is one of several functional areas responsible for deliverables, the team must consider estimating the time and effort involved to complete all tasks related both to the test process and in support of other functional areas. One company Jim worked for required that each functional area lead review, contribute, and sign off on all applicable project and software development lifecycle (SDLC) documentation. This meant that he, as the project manager on the team, needed to review, comment on, and approve the requirements, design, test, and supporting documentation such as user manuals and training material. While to some this may seem overly rigorous, the benefits extended to the product, project, and team members. This collaboration promoted not only an understanding of the overall product, familiarizing the team members with the requisite format and content of the project deliverables, but also contributed to building strong working relationships with the other team members. On one specific team that used this rigorous approach, after they delivered a successful project, management rewarded them with a ferry ride across the Hudson River where Jim played the role of Mr. Rock and Roll in the on-boat fun and festivities (he has the pictures somewhere to prove it!).

So, estimation of applicable necessary tasks by each functional area is necessary to develop an overall project schedule. In particular, the test team needs to assess all of its main test tasks and determine the time and effort necessary to satisfactorily complete these tasks properly. The complexity and quality of the software will influence the test task estimates, dependent on the quality of the software and documentation delivered to the test team.

Estimation, like predicting the weather, can sometimes be more of an art than a science (no offense to meteorologists intended). However, here is a list of techniques that can be used to determine the time and effort requirements especially relevant for test implementation and execution efforts:

Brainstorming. This is a popular technique to help a team collaborate, generate ideas, and build on others' ideas. There are various ways to implement brainstorming, each with pros and cons. These vary from freeform, where participants freely express ideas when they think of them, to round robin, where the facilitator calls on each person in line to contribute ideas. Brainstorming can be extended beyond idea generation to a collaborative session on developing task estimates using an Agile technique known as *planning poker*.

- **Test case iterations.** The test team can estimate the time required to execute each test case once and then multiply that number by the number of estimated iterations for each test case. This assumes that the time to rerun the test case again is the same with each iteration. This technique can take into account the expected number of test case failures. Prior history of test failures per runs of test cases on similar projects can help with this estimate.

- **Quality risk analysis.** Risk is generally the product of impact if the risk occurs and the likelihood of the risk occurring. Based on a risk analysis, those higher risk items require additional effort in testing. The test

Planning Using Planning Poker

Jim had the opportunity to work on an Agile project where Planning Poker was used to estimate user stories.

For those history buffs, Planning Poker has its roots in the Delphic methods of estimation. More specifically, the original Delphic method (the term *Delphic* is based on the oracles of ancient Greece, meaning to give advice or prophecy, similar to forecasting the future) debuted in the 1960s. It consisted of asking experts in a particular field to individually and privately (no sharing allowed) develop estimates. One drawback to this approach is that, since the experts could not communicate or collaborate on their estimates, they were free to make their own assumptions necessary to develop their estimates. Thus, as assumptions varied, the estimates lacked a strong foundation and estimations could not always prove reliable. The Wideband Delphi approach improved upon its predecessor by (1) defining a repeatable and consistent series of estimation process steps and, perhaps even more importantly, (2) allowing collaboration among the estimators to discuss and modify estimates which they originally developed independently. Enter Planning Poker, which is founded upon a tradition of these Delphic estimation techniques.[1]

The Planner Poker estimation technique is consensus-based and those with the most experience in the specific area covered by the user story/requirements or those with the most compelling case can influence the overall team estimates to reach agreement. Each team member, such as developers, testers, and support staff, has a deck of playing cards with one of the following numbers appearing on the card face: 0, 1, 2, 3, 5, 8, 13, 20, 40, and 100. Several of the initial numbers in the sequence follow a Fibonacci sequence (for example, the second and third items sum to the fourth item (1 + 2 = 3); the third and fourth items sum to the fifth item (2 + 3 = 5)). For simplicity, the higher numbers, such as 20, 40, and 100, break this sequence and are used to represent relative sizes (akin to medium, big, very big effort). The product owner or user representative reads each user story, which is a short statement of the requirement. The team may ask clarifying questions of the product owner to better understand the effort involved. Then, each team member makes an individual judgment of effort represented by a numbered card, throws her choice card on the table, and the team notes the similarities of and differences between the choices. If all estimations are the same, that is the estimate for that work item. If, however, there are differences in the estimates, the team members discuss their reasoning and try to convince the others in order to reach a consensus estimate. Particularly those who selected very high or very low numbers are encouraged to share their reasoning. The team then re-estimates, and this process is continued until consensus is reached or the item is deferred until more information is obtained to help build consensus.

---

1   Thanks to Klaus Nielsen, "Software Estimation using a Combination of Techniques," PMI Virtual Library, 2013, https://www.projectmanagement.com/articles/283931/Software-Estimation-using-a-Combination-of-Techniques for some brief history and background on the Delphic estimation techniques.

team would then estimate the number of tests needed for these high technical and/or business risk items, determine the average time needed to create or maintain each test case, and calculate the time necessary to execute each test case. Building on the previous estimating technique, it may be necessary to factor in several iterations of test case execution where the risk of failure is higher. Obviously, lower risk items require fewer test cases.

▨ **Function point analysis (FPA).** FPA is a way to measure software by quantifying the functionality that is developed and provided to users. For example, the team can decide that 50 lines of code necessary to produce some functionality equates to one function point. From the test perspective, based on all of the function points included in the project, the test team can then determine the estimated number of test cases necessary to support the application and then determine the time necessary to create and execute those test cases.

▨ **Developer-to-tester-hours ratio.** This estimation technique, as its name implies, attempts to derive a ratio of the number of developer hours to tester hours required on a project. Using historical data for similar projects in the same or similar organizations can help. However, this technique can be very subjective, and depends on things such as the relative abilities of both the developer and tester (e.g., using a highly capable developer's hours against an average tester would not be reliable).

▨ **Test point analysis (TPA).** TPA is an estimating technique useful for black box testing, or testing functionality without necessarily knowing the internal specifics of the functionality, and can be used in system and acceptance testing. TPA estimates take into account the following:

  ● The size of the system, as determined by function points, including complexity (number of conditions in a function), interfacing (number of data sets used by a function), and uniformity (the extent to which the system contains similarly structured functions)

  ● Test strategy (selection of quality characteristics for each function and the degree of coverage)

  ● Productivity (the relationship between the number of hours necessary for a task and the number of associated function points)[2]

---

2   Doctors Erik P.W.M. van Veenendaal and Ton Dekkers, "Testpointanalysis: a method for test estimation", published in Project Control for Software Quality, Kusters R., A. Cowderoy, F. Heemstra and E. van Veenendaal (eds), Shaker Publishing BV, Maastricht, The Netherlands, 1999, http://www.erikvanveenendaal.nl/NL/files/Testpointanalysis%20a%20method%20for%20test%20estimation.pdf.

■   **Historical heuristic.** The past is often a good predictor of the future. When project managers conduct a project retrospective at the end of a project (or, ideally, at the end of each Agile sprint or Waterfall stage), the findings can be very helpful in influencing future, similar projects. Since a simple definition of "heuristic" is using experience to learn and improve, lessons learned over time can contribute to providing more solid estimates on future projects. For example, if a common theme is that the test team underestimates the number of iterations of each test case or the number of defects discovered, the test team can perhaps use other estimation techniques based on this information to more accurately predict test case iterations and expected defects on future projects.

■   **Project management techniques.** Bottom-up estimation techniques begin with detailed information and work up to higher levels of abstraction. The product breakdown structure (PBS) lists the desired outputs or products defined within the project. The requirements document in particular can help with this exercise. Once the products are identified, the work breakdown structure (WBS) is used to identify the tasks and activities necessary to deliver those outputs or products. The PBS defines where you want to go, while the WBS tells you how to get there.[3]

Once one or more techniques are selected and used, it's a good idea to ensure that all test estimates include the following:

■   Planning and preparation work, such as time to develop the test documentation including the test plan, test cases, etc. as well as possibly time to review the test policy and test strategy at the organization level.

■   Time to acquire or create test data, whether manually, through data generators, via the use of production data, or some mix of all three sources. Data security considerations could make it mandatory to create anonymous test data and the effort for that would need to be factored into the test estimates.

■   Time to create and configure the necessary testing environments, test systems, and tooling (when necessary), allowing the proper exposure of defects through normal test conditions, the capability to operate normally when failures are not occurring, and the ability to replicate the appropriate environment (e.g., production) as necessary.

---

3   For a good comparison between the PBS and WBS and how they can both be used successfully on projects, see Patrick Weaver, "Product versus work breakdown structure", projectmanager.com.au, projectmanager.com.au/product-versus-work-breakdown-structure, August 13, 2015.

- Adequate time to prepare test cases (e.g., preconditions, postconditions), execute test cases, analyze results (e.g., pass, fail), and record results.
- Sufficient time to gather and report test execution information. Note that some test tools can help gather this data for reporting purposes or can be customized to facilitate this.

Aside from general, productive time spent devoted to test activities, the test manager and test team should be aware of other project time considerations, which in fact affect each functional area. This includes time allocated to nonproductive work, such as administrative overhead (e.g., completing time sheets), planned vacations and holidays, and training (although this contributes to both the skill set and thus value of testers and their contributions to future projects). Additionally, time devoted to team meetings, although productive, can be classified here as not contributing to real test task completion. These considerations must be taken into account when test team estimates are developed and, from the broader project perspective, the project manager considers this input from all functional areas. One area Jim has personally witnessed involved project leaders noting that work didn't get done as planned since key resources were on vacation. The point here is that, when the team estimates were developed, neither the project leader nor the individual team members thought to adjust the schedule with planned time off.

After factoring in these various time considerations, it may be helpful to clearly state the number of test hours available to the team. This helps provide a straightforward variance analysis over time, where estimates can easily be compared to the actual time spent completing test tasks.

There are even more factors to consider when estimating test activities. These include:

- **An estimation of the quality of the software delivered to the testing team.** This is based on the level of unit testing performed by developers; the quality of reviews, such as requirements or user story reviews, design reviews, code reviews and pair programming; and the results of static code analysis or running the code in an unexecuted manner to find potential defects.
- **Change control and configuration management processing.** This includes the level of change or churn accompanying the software; more change usually translates to more testing.
- **Testing process maturity.** More mature testing processes generally require less testing effort and smaller test estimates due to process efficiencies.

▨ **Project team maturity.** A seasoned list of senior team members who have worked together before on other projects may result in smaller test estimates.

▨ **Software development methodology.** This includes methodology choices such as traditional (e.g., Waterfall), Agile (e.g., Scrum), spiral, prototyping, and so on. If a chosen methodology is new to the team, such as a Waterfall shop using Agile methods on a project, time for learning and making "rookie" mistakes should be factored into the estimates.

▨ **Subsequent quality of defect fixes.** This depends on the reliability and quality of the defect fixes; those defects which are not corrected the first time but require one or more iterations until the defect is fixed would influence the overall test case estimate.

▨ **Test environments.** Limited support resources to build and maintain test environments influence testing estimates.

▨ **Business resources.** The cost of business resources and their overall availability to resolve questions on requirements or participate in user acceptance testing can affect testing estimates.

▨ **Documentation and training.** The availability of current, accurate documentation and trained personnel compared with no or poorly written documentation and untrained staff will significantly affect testing estimates. These areas can too often be neglected when developing valid estimates.

▨ **Reliability.** The reliability of the test systems, test data, and the availability of a test oracle all contribute to the ability of the test team to perform efficiently and should be considered when developing test estimates. For example, if it's suspected that test data from the production environment cannot properly be obtained or will need to be modified significantly for appropriate use in the test environment, testing estimates should reflect this additional work. Also, if the test oracle, or source used to determine how the software should function, for instance, from requirements or design models such as data transition diagrams or object models, are unavailable, ambiguous, or of poor overall quality, the additional work by the test team to understand expected functionality and process flows by whatever means necessary likewise must be factored in when developing testing estimates.

Aside from estimates concerning the effort to conduct or execute test cases, the test manager must also consider the time involved in identifying defects; retesting in terms of regression testing and confirmation testing, used to ensure that defects have been properly fixed by the development team; documenting defect information; and tracking defects for reporting reasons. Depending on the complexity of the functionality, risk ratings of the requirements, or relative importance of the functionality, the test manager may assign varying estimates to ensure proper coverage, anticipating defect work. The test manager can also anticipate defects accordingly based on the size of the software being created, considering the number of developer hours, lines of code, or function point analysis, where, for example, there is a 1:5 ratio of defects per function point, or one defect for every five function points of code. These numbers can be derived from ratio analysis based on similar, past projects, prior working team relationships (developers and testers working together), and similar industry averages. To better understand the quality of the software, estimating defect work separately from test development and execution tasks allows a more flexible approach and can show if the defects are more or less than anticipated. If a standard estimate per defect is generated, this allows flexibility when comparing actual number of defects versus the anticipated number of defects indicating the quality of the software and/or the estimation of number of defects per software functionality and complexity. Estimating defect effort separately from the overall test development, execution, analysis, and documentation tasks allows a more reliable gauge of software quality since defect estimates and actual defect information are not buried in the overall testing effort estimates.

Although Planning Poker (previously explained) is often associated with Agile, in truth from a purist perspective, they are separate and unrelated. However, in practice, the Agile approach often does use Planning Poker and other estimating techniques with a focus on estimating only a smaller effort, specifically the user stories associated with a recent story workshop. It is generally more difficult to estimate and assess risk on a full set of project requirements. Agile has the team focus estimation and risk assessment efforts on only those user stories planned for the next few sprints, efforts that are more manageable by the team. Additionally, the risks on the scope within a short iteration will either be realized or discarded by the end of the sprint, and the next sprint can be planned accordingly.

After the various testing estimates are derived, it is important that, as the project moves forward, the project manager track the actual performance against the planned estimates; the test manager likewise performs a variance analysis between actual time and effort compared with estimates. Depending on thresholds set by the organization (that is, what are and are not acceptable variances), if testing or any other functional area within the project is beyond set boundaries, measures need to be taken to help bring the project back on track, including adjustments to resources, compromised changes to scope and functionality, and/or timeframes adjusted in order to produce a quality product and a successful project.

5.2.2 Defining the Testing Schedule

Generally, once all task estimates are known, the project schedule can be built, as a schedule is nothing more than a way to track who does what when and in what order. While there is an overall project schedule, defining necessary tasks according to the SDLC for software projects, the test manager can work with her team to develop the schedule concerning testing tasks during the various testing phases of the project. Since the testing team, as any functional area within the project, is dependent on other functional areas for delivering work products and meeting milestones, it is important that the testing schedule include these various touch points and highlight deliverables from other areas. The clearer the expectations in terms of the deliverables handed to the testing team, with objectively verifiable criteria to ensure that there is no ambiguity concerning the quality of those deliverables, the smoother the hand-off may be. With clear expectations, the testing team can compare the quality of the deliverables against the objective standards set, thereby either rejecting receiving deliverables if the quality is just not there or assessing the impact to both the testing team and the overall project due to poor quality deliverables. For example, if not all unit tests have been satisfactorily performed by the development team, the decision can be made, given enough schedule and resource availability, to have the development team invest additional time to complete the unit testing before handing the code to the testing team. Alternatively, the testing team can accept the incompletely unit-tested code and conduct additional tests or at least be aware that there will invariably be a higher number of defects discovered since the quality of the code was not to the level expected at the time of hand-off. Additionally, as schedules permit, testers can help developers with unit testing, affording testers greater knowledge of the software while allowing developers insight into test design techniques. Obviously, this also builds stronger working relationships and helps to break down functional area barriers that could otherwise be divisive.

There are many commercial project management tools that are used to develop project schedules, build tasks with assigned resources, track task completion, identify the critical path (that sequence of tasks which must be completed in order for the project to complete on time), and display Gantt charts that illustrate task start and end dates across time. These tools also clearly show task dependencies and the overall effect of a delay of an independent task on the task dependent on it. In fact, in one place where Jim worked, the project manager director ensured that all project schedules developed by her project managers had each and every task, other than the lead task, dependent on another task in the schedule; there were no orphaned tasks but each was inter-connected. This ensured that any change in an early task would have the necessary ripple effect on subsequent, dependent tasks. Jim has carried this process with him and consider it a best practice.

Additionally, dependencies between functional areas may exist where there aren't necessarily any formal deliveries. For example, there may be expectations and deliverables to the usability team such as functional software with complete features along with a usability analysis and then deliverables from the usability team such as defect reports and usability suggestions. This should all be clearly documented in the project schedule.

It is almost a given that, especially on large projects, the schedule will invariably change. Normally, project managers take a baseline, similar to software developers freezing code to prevent any changes through software builds. A baselined schedule allows the project manager and project team to easily assess the changes to the baselined schedule as the project moves forward, as tasks complete and unfinished tasks may move out or even move in with respect to their planned end dates. A baseline acts as a reference point, a fixed schedule, allowing deviations and changes from the planned schedule to be measured. Each organization is different in terms of how much deviation is allowed. At one place Jim worked, a 15 percent variance of the actual end date either later or, less likely, earlier than the planned end date would still be considered a successful project, of which bonuses depended. Of course, if the project manager believes that there will be schedule variance beyond accepted thresholds, she should consult the project sponsor and perhaps petition for additional project time if there are valid reasons for the delay (e.g., increased scope, key resource unavailability, and so on).

The Agile methodology welcomes change, especially to the test schedule based on what is planned for each iteration. It is good practice to freeze the requirements or user stories or items introduced into a timeboxed iteration or sprint based on the velocity of the team, which is a measure of how much work (often measured in story points or person-hours) or how many user stories the team can complete in each sprint. Testing work estimates of course factor into the work planned for each sprint. This ensures that, at least within the sprint, the work is planned, understood, implemented, and tested. Any items not completely working (that is, tested satisfactorily) in the current sprint are deferred to a future sprint and the team does not receive credit for that work item. Of course, especially based on the software functionality demonstrated to the product owner (user representative) at the end of a sprint, new user stories for new or changed functionality can be added to the backlog or list of work to do and the team, especially the test manager and testing team, need to remain flexible to change. However, as previously mentioned, it is a good practice to freeze the scope of work to which the team commits at the beginning of a sprint.

5.2.3 Budgeting and Resource Allocation

Project budgets and resource assignment and allocation to projects are different between projects and between organizations. A test manager typically has a constraint given the number of test team resources she has at her disposal. With this constraint in mind, her project budgeting exercises would be limited to the scope of work assigned to her testing resources. Thus, the scope of work that her team can manage will significantly affect project test schedules. She must adequately plan and manage her test resources across all planned and current projects in order to contribute to the success of each project yet not overwhelm her team.

Regarding specific budget needs, the test manager must consider:

- **Costs of regular, internal test team staff.** This includes the staff's salaries, periodic salary increases (often driven by annual performance goals and results), benefits, vacation allocations (especially important when planning project resource allocations and availability of staff to work on projects during seasonal vacation times of the year), and investing in the future for current staff, including training costs in line with continuing education, travel and entertainment expenses (e.g., to attend testing symposiums and training), books, trade magazine subscriptions, membership fees, and costs associated with achieving certification (e.g., the ISTQB's Certified Tester Foundation Level) and/or maintaining certification.
- **Costs of additional test team staff.** This could include costs to procure staff through staff augmentation, such as external or contingent staff aimed at project-specific work. This could also include external resources in key areas where the test team may not have sufficient competency (e.g., installing, configuring, and using a test automation tool). External resources

could be local or offshore. In the case of offshore workers, specific care must be taken to accommodate differences in work styles, communication styles, and culture, especially across countries and time zones.

- **Costs of facilities.** This can include costs associated with building, maintaining, and configuring test labs.
- **Costs of equipment.** This can include both the costs of the equipment itself to be tested and the costs associated with test equipment used on projects, such as servers, networks, printers, and the like.
- **Costs of software.** This can include the costs of various software used in testing, such as operating systems, interface software, and databases storing test data. This can also include costs of software tools such as database tools, reporting tools, analysis tools, defect tracking tools, test case management tools, and test automation tools. Commercial tools in these categories usually require licensing and maintenance and support costs of which the test manager needs to be aware.
- **Costs in investments in long-term efficiency improvements.** One example is the investment in a test case automation tool. The benefits of this investment include conversion of some number of manual test cases (especially those test cases in the regression test suite) to automated test cases, and improving efficiency (quicker execution of routine test cases with results) as well as team satisfaction (test team members do not need to run mundane tests again and again manually but can focus on more interesting and challenging test activities). The costs of test case automation, however, should not be underestimated, as it takes some time and planning to acquire a tool and use it wisely, often allocating development resources, either internally or externally through contractors, to properly program the tool for best use.

Expanding on the first two staffing items above, the test manager must consider both the composition (including part-time and full-time permanent internal staff and contractors, as well as the mix of on-premises, offshore, and outsourced team members) and capability (skill levels and experience from junior to senior) of the team. In one organization where Jim worked, when performing pre-project estimates of work, we used a simple template with each functional area's specialty noted as columns with corresponding rows denoting seniority level, with each level assigned a fully loaded rate (standard rate of pay with overhead costs and allocations included). When a high-level estimate of work was developed, each functional area manager noted the number of estimated hours of a resource at each specific seniority level. This provided a view as to the number of hours and dollars associated with each functional area for the work involved. This served as a first cut when developing project estimates, of course, until a full work breakdown structure was developed where refinements would undoubtedly be made. The test manager should know her team and be aware of which resources can best meet the needs of each feature or each project. The feature estimates can be taken in isolation but, if combined into a project, each functional area manager must consider the resource capacities of their team members to ensure adequate coverage for the features in the project in addition to other concurrent projects and non-project (e.g., ongoing, maintenance) work. This can be a trivial or involved process depending on the dynamics and size of the test organization as well as the number and size of concurrent projects. At times, resources (human and otherwise) may be shared from other functional areas. The team should assess whether this sharing is beneficial or detrimental to the project. Jim was a software developer shared for a time by a test team, and at the time this arrangement helped the overall project. However, there are times where the sharing of the same system or environment between the development and test teams should not be leveraged, as this shared environment could adversely affect the quality of the overall system.

One thing that the test manager and in fact all functional area managers should remember is that budgeting and resource allocation is not a static exercise but often an ongoing endeavor. Project priority needs which require shifting resources, quitting staff members, and late-added requirements necessitating additional external resources all contribute to the flexibility, adaptability, and dynamicity required of test managers. Test managers must remain vigilant in tracking their budgetary expenditures so that any significant variances can be reported and resolved immediately.

The project manager must work closely with each functional area's manager in monitoring the project budget. While the budgetary estimates provided by the test manager and the quality of the test work provided by the test team are invaluable, the test team, similar to other functional areas such as software development, systems engineering, business/systems analysis, systems architecture, customer help desk support, documentation, and training, provides initial time-and-effort estimates to the project manager, who then combines, assesses, challenges, but ultimately manages the budget for the project from the project's beginning to end. While the managers of each functional area, including the test manager, are responsible for their respective area's budget, the project manager is responsible for overseeing the overall project budget to reduce or eliminate variances from plan as much as possible.

5.2.4 Managing and Tracking a Project

"Failing to plan is planning to fail," as the old adage goes. In order for a project manager to manage and track a project, there obviously needs to be a plan developed and put into place with the proper metrics and mechanisms to assess at various points whether the project is on or off course. Without a schedule and a focus on the test team's tasks, how would the test manager know if her team is on track, ahead, or behind? If your family is taking a trip within driving distance of your home, would you plan the trip from home and not consult a map (either hardcopy or electronic)? Even with a map, as you inevitably make a wrong turn, you need the map to note the variance to help bring you back on course. If there is no map for your journey or schedule to guide the project, how would you know if you are on track or derailed?

To Jim, a schedule or plan is perhaps the most important deliverable on a project. Although definition of requirements (so the team knows what is expected at the beginning) and success criteria (so the team knows if the project was successful at the end) are extremely important, it is the plan that describes who does what when for how long in what order and how the team will know when it is done.

- **Who:** The project stakeholders (e.g., sponsor, working team, management) each contribute to some degree to the project work. These human resources should be clearly identified in the schedule so team members understand what they are to do.
- **What:** These are the applicable tasks at the appropriate level of detail necessary to complete the project. Tasks (*the what*) are done by people (*the who*).
- **When:** Each task is assigned a start and end date either based on calendar dates or as offsets from other tasks.
- **How long:** Each task has a duration or how long it will take to complete from start to finish. Depending on the project, while it may not add value to track tasks at the individual hourly level, it may be helpful to identify tasks at the daily level (e.g., number of days to complete each task).
- **What order:** Tasks follow other tasks on which they are dependent in real time.
- **How to know when done:** In one sense, the project is done when the last task in the schedule has completed. In the Agile Scrum methodology, the definition of done is an important concept and looks beyond simple task completion to truly determining if all the tasks to satisfy users' requirements are done and the software is ready to ship.

A well-managed project then has a well-developed schedule with relevant tasks and clear task ownership. The test team is no exception to this and must have its tasks clearly defined and assigned so the team knows what is expected of them and when it should be done. Specifically for testers, this could include knowing exactly which tests to perform, when to start and complete each test, and the applicable metrics to be produced as a result of that testing. Typically, after the project manager works with each functional area to determine applicable tasks and durations (or estimates), he conducts a kick-off meeting with the project stakeholders. Among other things, this is an opportunity for the highlights and expectations of the project to be communicated to the entire team. After the kick-off, the project manager monitors the project schedule and works closely with the team members through the end of the project, updating and adjusting the schedule of tasks to project (and thus task) completion. The test manager works with the project manager to define the necessary quality goals and to track progress toward those goals. Some trade-offs inevitably occur, such as accepting a feature later than planned, risking incomplete or inadequate test coverage. The test manager needs to understand the risks in this late delivery and adequately communicate that to the project team, especially the project sponsor, so the correct decision can be made.

It is important not only to establish a workable project schedule built from estimates, but likewise to actively manage and monitor it in order to note any variances or deviations from the plan. Variance analysis can apply to budget and cost as well as schedule and timeline variance, and even to scope variance as a measure of scope creep. For example, standard PC tools can be used to establish a baseline schedule, track actual task completion with completion dates, and then compare the actual results against the baselined, planned results. In the case of test tasks, if completion of test cases is taking longer than anticipated, the test manager must determine why. There are various reasons, including unexpected or poorly estimated test case execution duration and tester inexperience. There also may be a greater number of defects discovered than planned in a particular area or module. This could indicate that the requirements were not clearly understood by the development team, the code wasn't properly unit tested before delivery to the test team, etc. Even if the test team wasn't responsible for the variance, bringing the variance to the team's attention can help uncover process issues and the need to create new or improve existing processes. The point is that without a scheduled plan and periodic checks of actual information against that plan, the team would be unable to determine success or would realize issues later than necessary, when it may be too late to course-correct.

In Scrum projects, where many variances are due to circumstances within the team, the Scrum master is tasked with helping to remove obstacles that prevent the team from moving forward. Often, these obstacles are raised during the course of daily Scrum meetings, in which each team member briefly discusses the daily accomplishments, plans for the next day, and current obstacles or impediments. The Scrum master then works outside of these meetings to help resolve these obstacles.

There are various test metrics that can be useful for project tracking:

- **Test case design completion percentage.** This is simply the percentage of test case designs that are completed. This is used to help gauge the additional work required to complete designing the entire suite of test cases.
- **Cost of quality.** This measures the value and efficiency of testing by classifying project costs as the costs of prevention, detection, internal failure, and external failure.
  - **Prevention costs** are those that prevent or avoid quality problems and may include creation and maintenance of a quality system, as well as training.
  - **Detection costs (also called appraisal costs)** are costs involved with measuring and monitoring activities related to quality such as verification testing and performance of quality audits.
  - **Internal failure costs** are costs incurred before delivery to the customer and may include costs of rework to fix defective material and waste such as performing unnecessary work.
  - **External failure costs** are those incurred to fix defects that customers have discovered, such as repairs, servicing, and returns.
- **Defect detection percentage.** This is the number of defects found by testing divided by the total number of known defects. If the percentage here is high, this indicates that the test team has found most of the defects and the customers or users found the remaining defects once in production.
- **Defects found versus defects expected.** This indicates how many defects have actually been discovered compared with those defects expected to be found. If the ratio is too high, this could indicate quality issues where more defects than planned were actually found or there is an improper estimate of the overall expected defects by the test team.
- **Test case execution results.** This reports on the progress of testing by providing the percentage of test cases executed in each of the following statuses: pass, fail, or blocked result.

Developer metrics include:

- **Defect removal effectiveness.** This is the ability to remove defects from where they are discovered, including requirements, design, development, and once in production. It is more effective to remove defects in the same stage as the uncovered defects; for example, it is greatly more effective if a requirements review identifies a defect in the requirements phase and the analyst resolves that defect while still in this requirements phase than if propagated to the design or development phase where it is eventually resolved; basically, the earlier a defect is found and fixed, the better.
- **Feature completion.** This simply relates the number of features considered completed versus the number of features remaining as a gauge of overall project completion.
- **Unit test coverage.** This is an indicator of how much code is covered via developers' unit tests.

5.2.5 Dealing with Trade-Offs

Perfect projects are rare; actually, they don't exist. Most projects require a trade-off between quality, schedule, budget, and features. This is best depicted in the project management triangle noted below.

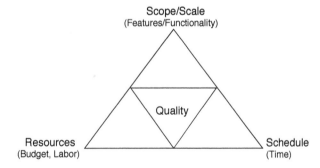

Figure 5-1   *Project management triangle*

Although variations of this triangle exist, let's go with this basic model. Every project has constraints, such as limited time, limited cost, and limited scope. The project management triangle depicts this, with time or schedule on one vertex, cost or budget on another vertex, and scope or features on the final vertex. We like one variant of the triangle, as shown in Figure 5-1, which includes quality within the triangle, showing that quality is dependent on the three constraints as well as depicting the effect on quality based on changes to the constraints.

- The time or schedule constraint refers to the amount of time necessary to complete the project based on project members' estimates of the work required. This, of course, is heavily dependent on the scope of the project.
- The cost or budget constraint is the budgeted amount for the project. This includes both internal costs, such as labor for existing human resources doing actual work on the project, and external costs, such as staff augmentation (e.g., hiring contractors on a temporary basis to complete tasks associated with the project), hardware and infrastructure costs related to the project, and software costs, such as necessary licenses for tool usage.
- The scope or feature constraint refers to the actual features and functionality required by the user that must be implemented via the project.

All three project constraints influence the overall quality of the software product. Affecting any one constraint has an effect on the other two dependent constraints and could affect the overall quality of the product. For example:

- **Time.** If the project sponsor requires that the project complete earlier than planned, thereby reducing the time constraint, this will invariably affect the cost (increased cost by perhaps paying human resources additional evening and weekend work to complete work given the new, compressed schedule) and the scope (decreased scope as not all originally planned features may be implemented given the reduced time).
- **Cost.** If the cost allocated to the project is reduced, this could result in reduced scope, since there is not enough money to pay for the full scope originally planned, and increased time, since there may be fewer resources working on the project, thereby requiring a longer time to delivery.
- **Scope.** If the project sponsor (representing the customer and end user) increases the scope of the project by requesting additional functionality or significant changes to planned functionality, this scope creep would typically require additional time and additional cost to design, implement, and test the added changes.

The beauty and simplicity of this model is that the mix of constraints, and any changes to the constraints, affect the overall quality of the software solution. The question always is how can an acceptable level of quality be maintained given changes to the schedule, budget, and/or functionality? This challenge always awaits the project team, especially the project manager, who is responsible for managing the project given the three constraints, and the test manager, who must ensure that high quality is preserved despite changes in the constraints. This is why it is imperative that any constraint changes mandated by the project sponsor be immediately discussed with the project manager who in turn will rely on both the development manager and test manager for consultation on what the true effect of the constraint changes will be to the project and its goal of meeting its objectives (which often are scope, cost, time, and quality or producing the functionality within the agreed-upon budget and timeframe while meeting quality expectations).

While the above holds true for those projects following a more traditional approach, for Scrum projects, time and quality are generally fixed; the schedule is not elastic, allowing for additional (or fewer) sprints, and quality considerations cannot be comprised. Therefore, the only variable on Scrum projects that can change is scope, or user stories, as more stories can be added to or current stories removed from the sprint backlog to properly meet expectations.

Preferably at the start of a project, it would be ideal to understand from the project sponsor which constraint is the most important. Is the sponsor interested in a well-defined set of functionality and features at the expense of a slight variation in schedule and budget? Or, is a particular deployment date most important, perhaps to gain the advantage in getting to market before the competition, given minimal changes to functionality and budget? Or, is the budget cast in stone and is more important than the full set of desired functionality and overall timeframe in completing the schedule? Knowing this important information up front will help the project manager and functional areas better plan the project, understanding what is really of paramount importance to the sponsor.

Unfortunately, this information is not always known at the start of the project, but may eventually come to light somewhere during the course of the project. In fact, the sponsor herself may not know the proper mix of constraints until the project is well under way. This requires the team to be as flexible (dare I say "Agile"?) as possible. This means that, from a testing and overall quality perspective, the test manager must be aware of the interdependencies between project components in order to make decisions on the impact of trade-offs. It is an unfortunate reality that, at times, quality may suffer due to the trade-offs in constraints that are required. For example, it may be determined during the testing phase that key functionality, which is essential to the overall product, was missed at the requirements stage. This may result in a decrease in overall quality, since the test team could not have planned for this additional functionality and may not be able to adequately test given the existing time and cost constraints. The test manager must clearly explain the impact of the reduction in testing time and associated risk to the product quality, noting that this new functionality may result in other areas not receiving adequate or even any testing time.

5.2.6 Change Management

Change on a project is a given, a constant, something that inevitably will occur if not once then several times on typical projects. Change is so prevalent that the Agile development methodology acknowledges change as one of the key principles in its Agile Manifesto: "Welcome changing requirements, even late in development, Agile processes harness change for the customer's competitive advantage."[4] The test manager must therefore have a flexible way to quickly understand the change, assess the impact of the change, and adapt to the change accordingly.

Change can occur in areas such as requirements, timeline, and budget (the project management triangle's triumvirate of scope, schedule, and cost), and overall quality. Risks to projects that can affect the test team include unanticipated issues with test environments, shortening the overall testing time; unavailability of hardware infrastructure, such as a necessary server, hampering the development team's compatibility testing, resulting in additional testing by the test team; and the like. (Risks are covered more extensively below.) It is important for the test manager to be able to perform an impact analysis in order to truly determine the ramifications of changes to the testing aspects of the project. This should be done more broadly by the entire team and include all changes and not necessarily only those that impact testing. If the project team does not have a process for impact analysis, it behooves the test manager to establish one for her test team to benefit the overall quality of the product to meet project objectives.

The individual impact analysis for each change is part of a larger, change management process that tracks, schedules, and assesses each change regarding impact. Given proper impact analysis, non-mandatory change (such as in what-if scenarios) can be discussed by the team before accepting, again with overall consideration of the affect the change will have on the project's out-

---

4   Beck Kent, et. al., "Twelve Principles of Agile Software," from the "Manifesto for Agile Software Development," 2001, www.agilemanifesto.org/principles.html. This is the definitive authority on understanding all things Agile.

come. The information that the change management process captures can also be used toward the end of the project (or at the end of each Agile Scrum sprint closeout) during project retrospectives and can serve as useful information for future projects.

5.2.7 Time Management

Experienced test managers and test teams, those who have invested years working both together as a team and within the testing field, will discover ways to make best use of everyone's time on projects. A good test manager, besides protecting, supporting, and growing her test team, will ensure that the test team is making the most efficient use of its time. This in part includes the test manager attending meetings, including project status meetings with the project manager and functional area managers and leads, providing her team's overall status and challenges, and then briefly sharing project highlights from the status meetings with her team. This ensures that the team can focus on their primary tasks and does not need to attend meetings that the test manager can and should attend as the representative of the test team.

Aside from insulating the team from additional meetings, the test manager can help the team make most efficient use of their time in the following ways:

- **Communication.** The test team should not be isolated (or perceived as isolated) from the rest of the project team, yet attending every meeting to ensure "face time" or representation is neither efficient nor wise. So, while the test manager may attend most meetings, this does not preclude test team members from offline, individual discussions, phone calls, or email exchanges. In fact, a test team that does not communicate with other project team members will prove to be less effective, even if more efficient, jeopardizing the overall quality of the product. If the project uses an offshore test team or testing team members in other time zones, communication and understanding is especially important, and the test manager needs to ensure that this communication works effectively for all. Since communication and collaboration are unofficial ingredients for a successful project, the test team is certainly encouraged to meet and discuss issues with other team members. However, the test manager must find the correct balance between her team's participation in meeting time versus test activity time. One Agile Scrum technique, intended to limit every team member's time in meetings, is daily Scrums. These meetings, often no more than 15 minutes per day, require each team member to stand (sitting tends to make participants more comfortable and prone to discuss issues beyond the meeting's time limits) and, one at a time, briefly report what he accomplished in the previous day, what he plans on working on that day, and any obstacles he has faced so the Scrum master can help remove project impediments. This is an excellent example in practice of enabling meetings to be more productive by intentionally limiting the time spent by the team in meetings.

- **Timeboxed periods.** Just as the time allotted to daily Scrum meetings is respected and preserved by the team, the test team (and in fact all team members) on Agile projects should conform to the timebox established for each sprint (iteration), which usually is from two to four weeks. If there are any untested items (user stories) or those that the team believes have not been adequately tested, the sprint should not be extended. Rather, in this case, those items should be moved to a later sprint, and the team should not get credit for those items until they are properly tested.

- **Requirements issues.** The test team should factor adequate time to resolve questions and issues in the requirements with the business analyst, project stakeholder or product owner (in the case of Agile Scrum, this is the project stakeholder responsible for user stories/requirements) as they affect test design. This additional time should be taken into account when the test team performs estimates of their testing tasks.

- **Test case automation.** Executing test cases takes time. Manually executing test cases and recording results, especially repetitive tests as included in a regression test suite, can be a less than optimal use of valuable testers' time. Test execution automation tools can help relieve the test team from performing repetitive testing, thereby allowing them to do more challenging and interesting work. However, test automation itself comes at a cost, including researching the best tool for the team's organization, budgeting for software licensing and any vendor services, infrastructure considerations, tool training, and development and configuration of the tool. As with most things in life, the benefits of a test automation tool need to be weighed against the overall costs.

- **Regression testing.** Related to test case automation, an effective regression testing strategy is to automate as many regression test cases as feasible since regression testing, by its very nature, is repeatable. This automation of regression test cases relieves the test team of monotonous, repeated manual testing, which can be error prone and thereby negatively impacting quality, allowing them to do more interesting and value-added work.

- **Smoke testing.** It's always a good idea to sample something before accepting it. Some beachgoers sample the ocean by slowly getting accustomed to the temperature of the ocean water, determining how rough or calm the water is, etc. Similar to this, testers should smoke test, or perform basic functionality, before accepting the code received from development and propagating it to multiple testers. If there are issues with the quality of the code and overall functionality, it makes most sense to catch this early and fix it before wasting valuable testers' time testing poor-quality code.

- **Training.** Keeping the skill sets of the test team current not only benefits their careers but also increases their value to the department. One way to do this is for the department to invest in continual training. However, this training, such as in Agile testing concepts and practices or learning how to be proficient in a test automation tool, ideally should not occur when key projects require testers to focus on testing tasks and should not be charged to a particular project's budget unless this training is directly applicable to the success of a project.

5.3   Project Risk Management

Learning objectives

LO 6.3.1   (K4) Conduct a risk assessment workshop to identify project risks that could affect the testing effort and implement appropriate controls and reporting mechanisms for these test-related project risks.

It is said that the only things absolutely certain are death and taxes. Therefore, life itself involves risks or uncertainties. You've probably heard of the mythical bus that wipes out employees; in our careers we've heard managers stating that it always made sense to mitigate the risk of key employees getting "hit by a bus" (variations include cars, trucks, or trains, but never boats for some reason) by providing training and hands-on experience to other employees to ensure coverage and maintain continuity in operational tasks (basically providing backups). Projects are no different in that they too contain risks or uncertainties. The Project Management Body of Knowledge (PMBOK) defines project risk as "...an uncertain event or condition that, if it occurs, has a positive or negative effect on one or more project objectives such as scope, schedule, cost, and quality."[5] Since project success is usually assessed by the sound balancing of the constraints within the Project Management Triangle (see Figure 5-1), consideration and management of uncertain events or conditions are key to a successful delivery of a product, service, or result (that is, a *project*). When we consider risks, we tend to think of only the unplanned negative things that can happen to a project, such as a vendor going out of business or a cyber-security breach of a key integration system, or, in the testing realm, sudden unavailability of a test tool that hampers progress in executing test cases. For purposes of our discussion, we'll only consider **negative** risks (threats) or risks that, if they do occur, will have negative consequences on the project. This definition of risk is absolutely aligned with that found in the ISTQB syllabus, which defines risk as "a factor that could result in future negative consequences" with the focus on the negative impacts of risk. In fact, as risks are assigned a risk level either quantitatively (for example, 1 (low) through 5 (high)) or qualitatively ("low," "medium," "high") based on their potential impact and likelihood of occurring, appropriate emphasis and mitigation strategies and actions can be taken. Positive risks, outside of the scope of our discussion, are often considered opportunities, such as a project completing substantially under budget. While on the surface this may seem like a wonderful project outcome, a project that comes under budget is often a reflection on the team (and especially the project manager) not properly estimating project effort. As credibility issues come into play, sponsors may be reluctant to fund future projects if the project manager and team have previously done a poor job of estimating a project's efforts.

Using a SWOT Analysis

On a side note, it is interesting that risk as both positive opportunity and negative threat appears in two of the four quadrants included in a standard strengths, weakness, opportunities, and threats (SWOT) analysis, which is a simple yet helpful method to determine factors that can affect not only a project's outcomes, but also individual career assessments and planning.

The project manager and project stakeholders including the test manager can collaborate to develop and maintain this grid pertaining to a project. Notice that the grid groups these aspects of the analysis in positive/negative as well as internal/external categories.

- **Positive:** Strengths and opportunities have positive effects on a project.
- **Negative:** Identified weaknesses and threats have the potential to harm a project.

---

5   Project Management Institute: *A Guide to the Project Management Body of Knowledge (PMBOK Guide) – Fifth Edition*, 2013, p. 310. Of course, the Project Management Institute's PMBOK is the definitive guide on everything related to project management.

	Positive	Negative
Internal	**Strengths** • Project members have previously worked well together as a team • Test team members are all ISTQB certified with many years of testing experience	**Weaknesses** • Project members inexperienced in new Agile-certified methodology • Chance that project funding will get reduced
External	**Opportunities** • New production version of partner's automated test tool includes features beneficial to the test team on this project	**Threats** • Key vendor's financial and corporate reputation are suspect

Figure 5-2   *Sample SWOT analysis on a hypothetical project*

- **Internal:** Strengths and weaknesses are typically considered internal to a project.
- **External:** Opportunities and threats pertain more to external factors affecting a project.

For example, a project strength such as an experienced team who has worked well on prior projects is both positive and internal.

After the SWOT analysis has been completed, the project manager and team should look to:

- **Capitalize** on project strengths, such as allocating key people resources to a project to make best use of their talent in order to help the project be as successful as possible.
- **Improve** upon weaknesses, for example through training or hiring experienced test team members to make them more proficient.
- **Exploit** opportunities, such as upgrading a test tool in order to realize much-needed functionality improvements.
- **Eliminate** or **reduce** threats, perhaps by investing in backup plans in case key external resources become unavailable.

The beauty of the SWOT analysis lies in both its simplicity and application. SWOT is a simple tool to develop, apply, and maintain, requiring no training or special skills. SWOT is also applicable and can be used on a project level tied directly to risk identification and management; by a specific team, such as the test team to evaluate the effectiveness of its team members; and even in individual career management. In fact, Jim has developed his own professional career SWOT analysis and has taught on this to employees to help them manage their own careers.

While managing project risks is ultimately the responsibility of project managers, they are heavily dependent on their functional area colleagues, such as the test manager, to help identify risks, assess their impact and likelihood, and work through viable mitigation plans for each risk.

5.3.1 Managing Project Risks

Project risk management is all about identifying, assessing, and controlling potential project risks that could have a negative impact on a project and its overall goals and objectives.

Although each company/department/shop may use slightly different names to identify the stages or phases a project undergoes in its life from beginning to end, the standard project lifecycle includes the following phases as shown in Figure 5-3:

Initiation	Planning	Execution	Closing
Starting the project	Organizing and preparing	Carrying out the work	Closing the project

Figure 5-3   *A generic project lifecycle*

- Initiation (starting the project)
- Planning (organizing and preparing)
- Execution (carrying out the work)
- Closing (closing the project)

When a project is in its planning phase, one of the deliverables a project manager develops is the project management plan. This plan includes a series of smaller, focused management plans that support the overall project management plan (e.g., communications, stakeholder, scope, etc.), including a risk management plan. The full list of project management plan components includes:

- Change management plan
- Communications management plan
- Configuration management plan
- Cost baseline
- Cost management plan
- Human resource management plan
- Process improvement plan
- Procurement management plan
- Scope baseline
  - Project scope statement
  - Work breakdown structure
  - Work breakdown structure dictionary
- Quality management plan
- Requirements management plan
- Risk management plan
- Schedule baseline
- Schedule management plan
- Scope management plan
- Stakeholder management plan

Although in a perfect world, we'd aim to eliminate all risks, in reality there are only a few main ways of dealing with risk, which apply to all risks, including test-related risks, identified in the risk management plan. These strategies include:

- **Avoidance.** Some risks can be eliminated, but usually not without consequences. For example, if a new risky feature cannot be developed and tested as planned without potentially adversely affecting other features in the product, this risky feature can be deferred to a later release once the product has matured and is more stable. However, this would impact the project objectives of delivering the full scope in the planned timeframe and the project sponsor obviously must agree to this change. This risk strategy in effect avoided the risk and potential negative consequences of introducing poor quality into the product.
- **Mitigation.** Risk occurrences and responses can be proactively planned and then monitored to reduce the overall probability of the risk occurring at all. If, for example, the testing effort for a major component (or even the entire testing effort) is outsourced, it is a good idea for the test manager to provide the due diligence in maintaining a strong relationship with the

outsourced partner to ensure that the testing staff is ready and able to begin testing as planned. Obviously, trust in and the reputation of the outsourced partner is key to managing this relationship in order to help manage the test effort and ultimately drive the success of the overall project and quality of the product, service, or result.

- **Transference.** Some risks can be shifted from one team to another, perhaps even a third party. An example of this is the test manager insisting that any delay in the start date for test execution will result in an equivalent delay in the end date for test execution. In essence, the test manager has then transferred the risk of test execution delay onto the rest of the project team. Of course, on projects where the end date is fixed and cannot be compromised, this results in a squeeze of the testing timeframe, resulting in the potential of fewer than the full plan of test cases executed, contributing to additional risk to the quality of the product. To mitigate this, the tester may need to work additional hours during the testing phase, additional short-term testing resources (e.g., developers) can be used to run test cases, and developers can be placed on immediate standby to work through production issues as soon as they are discovered.

- **Acceptance.** In some cases, it is either impossible or impractical to mitigate a risk, resulting in the project team willingly receiving the risk. For instance, if there is only one test server available to the project and it is not cost-effective or time-effective to purchase, install, and configure an additional test server to act as a backup, the team accepts the risk that the sole test server may crash, resulting in a potential delay in the test schedule and overall project schedule until the server can be repaired and made operational again.

- **Contingency.** This involves having a plan in place to effectively reduce the impact of a risk should it occur. Retaining a team of technical support and help desk personnel acts as a contingency against the risk of software defects delivered to customers and end users.

The project manager begins building the risk management plan by meeting with the applicable functional area managers/leads, including the test manager, to identify and document the various risks that could negatively impact the project. Often, a project manager may consult lessons learned or retrospective documents from similar projects to see whether any risks affecting previous projects may rear their ugly heads again and negatively affect this current project. Additionally, a project management team may include a template of common risks and successful mitigation strategies based on prior project experience and, when applicable, common sense. This initial research helps the project manager by setting her off on a good start to risk management. Jim had the early experience in the late 1990s of being involved with a company that achieved a Capability Maturity Model (CMM) Level 5 rating, the highest within Carnegie Mellon's Software Engineering Institute's maturity framework. As part of this rating, our quality management department developed a risk management template with appropriate job aid documentation that captured key risk identification information, pre-mitigation analysis, mitigation steps, and post-mitigation analysis. Let's review a similar template in Figure 5-4.

Risk Identification			Pre-mitigation Analysis			Mitigation Steps			Post-mitigation Analysis		
Number	Type	De-scription	Probability of Occurrence (%)	Cost of Occurrence ($000s)	Initial Impact ($000s)	Actions	Status	Additional Cost ($000s)	Probability of Occurrence (%)	Cost of Occurrence ($000s)	Remaining Impact ($000s)
4	project, schedule, cost	Key resource leaves the project	50	$200	$100	HR and management discuss job satisfaction and career management with key resource	Open	$0	30	$200	$60

Figure 5-4   *Sample risk management template*

- **Risk identification.** This section includes basic and unique information concerning each risk. For instance, risk number 4 documents the scenario where a key resource may leave the project. Notice that this risk, if it becomes reality, would affect the following risk types: project, the project schedule, and project cost. Each risk can map to one or more risk types.
- **Pre-mitigation analysis.** The team estimates a 50% probability or chance that this may occur. This percentage may be due to prior experience with the department or company, or even knowledge about the resource's intentions based on his/her current level of job satisfaction and even any prior company history of job change. This example assumes a fully loaded cost (including benefits and overhead allocations) of $200,000 per year. So, if absolutely nothing is done to address this risk, the impact of this occurring

has a dollar value to the project of $100,000, given the employee's cost and probability of risk occurrence. The project manager and project sponsor determine whether there should be any actions and/or costs taken to mitigate this risk.

- **Mitigation steps.** The team identifies actionable steps that can be taken to mitigate the risk either fully or more usually partially. In this example, HR and management address the person to get a better sense if he/she might be looking to leave based on overall satisfaction or dissatisfaction at work. Although this action isn't foolproof, the team notes that this action, which is still open (that is, hasn't begun or been implemented yet), would not cost anything other than internal labor costs that aren't generally listed here. While the mitigation is specifically targeted to the risk of the person leaving the company, there could be other actions taken if the resource stays within the company but either transfers to another department or is reassigned to another project. The project team would decide if these other scenarios with applicable actions should be defined and managed through this risk management file.

- **Post-mitigation analysis.** The team assumes that taking this specific action will result in a reduction in the probability of occurrence from 50 to 30 percent; however, the cost of occurrence remains the same at $200,000. Given the actions and resultant reduced probability of occurrence, the real impact to the project is now estimated at $60,000.

This approach was a practical and honest way of managing project risks. Since the mitigation actions did not always entirely mitigate the risk, the template had provisions to show the remaining impact from a financial perspective of the impact of risks that could not be fully mitigated; this was the impact of residual or remaining risk after all necessary mitigating controls were put in place. Related to the previous discussion on the risk mitigation strategy of risk acceptance, our template and process, although not necessarily reflected in Figure 5-4, included a contingency reserve, which was a small percentage of the overall project cost reserved to handle risks. The ISTQB defines *confidence intervals* as the period of time within which a contingency action must be implemented in order to be effective in reducing the impact of the risk. Often, there are trigger dates that act as indicators to both start and stop the contingency plan of action; the trigger dates are those dates within the confidence intervals. For example, the aforementioned scenario of the inoperable test server would pose a risk to the project prior to the start of the test phase, when the server is configured

ISTQB Glossary

confidence interval: In managing project risks, the period of time within which a contingency action must be implemented in order to be effective in reducing the impact of the risk.

properly to anticipate the upcoming testing activities, through the test phase, and possibly for some time after the test phase if post-deployment defects are found, requiring retesting using the test server and redeployment. These timeframes denote when the risk could be realized so the proper mitigation plans and actions could be taken; outside of this window, the risk is not realistic and, if it does occur, would have minimal to no impact on the project.

The best and most comprehensive risk management plan does absolutely no good to the project if, after it has been developed, it sits on a shelf and gathers dust. The key to good risk management is to actively review it with the functional areas, including the test team, periodically through the life of the project. Risk review includes reevaluating risks that exist in the plan to assess any changes to the likelihood, impact, and contingency and mitigation plans as the project progresses and any new information is known. Additionally, during risk review, the team should consider adding any new risks that have surfaced since the previous risk review. Lastly, if currently tracked risks that have passed have not been properly dispositioned as closed, this should be done during the course of the risk review. Aside from the mechanics and discipline of reviewing, updating, and actually using the risk management plan and associated deliverables to lead to a successful project, there are benefits to project team members meeting periodically, collaborating together, and wrestling with current and potential issues that could adversely affect the project. Often, as a good practice, project managers include schedule and action item review with the team periodically, as often as every week. Depending on the dynamics and particulars of the project, the risk management plan may be reviewed at each weekly project status meeting or in a less frequent manner, such as every two weeks or monthly. The project manager, with the buy-in from the project sponsor and team, would determine the review frequency. The key point is that manager/lead representatives from the applicable functional areas, such as system architecture/engineering, system/business analysis, software development, testing, deployment, operations, training, help desk support, and documentation, on software development projects collaborate periodically on project issues and risks including test risks.

5.3.2 Participating in Project-wide Risk Management

As a key stakeholder on the project team, the test manager must play an active role in the entire risk management process, including initial identification of risks and mitigation plans as well as periodic risk reviews. In fact, Jim has seen places where the key stakeholders on software development projects were the development manager, the test manager, and the project manager. This is why it is so important for a good project manager to include, as mentioned earlier, periodic review with the functional area representatives of not only the schedule and action items, but of the risks documented in the risk management plan or risk register.

While test managers are clearly involved in test-related risks, there are many other types of risks not necessarily tied directly to the testing effort, which will nonetheless impact testing. This makes sense when you think of the broad definition of software quality assurance. We often think of quality assurance as predominantly testing tasks and activities within the context of a project that are undertaken to ensure that the product has high quality. While this is certainly one important aspect of quality assurance, there is much more to quality assurance than testing alone. Other areas affecting overall quality and potentially incurring additional project risk include:

- **Requirements stage.** Poorly documented requirements, incomplete requirements (e.g., lack of non-functional requirements such as performance, usability, security, etc.), ineffective requirements gathering methods, and unavailability of key customers to help understand requirements can all affect testing, the overall quality of the product and the overall success of the project, so test managers must be cognizant of overall poor quality of requirements. While requirements are often a key basis for the development of test cases, requirements are not the only possible test basis document. In fact, quality risk registers, user documentation, defect taxonomies, the current application's functionality (if the project is intended to replace an existing application), and other documentation all serve as test basis documents. It may sound harsh to say that the old computer adage of garbage in/garbage out applies here; poor requirements lead to poor test cases. Even the best level of traceability, which is the matching of test cases to requirements to ensure test coverage, cannot ensure overall quality if requirements and other test basis documentation are sorely lacking. Of course, training business analysts and hiring those with experience and certification help in the requirements gathering and documenting efforts.

Additionally, the Scrum mind-set addresses requirements gathering as an iterative and interactive process, where the product owner (the face of the customer, representing customer needs) plays a key role throughout the software development project. The product owner defines requirements in the form of what's known as *user stories*. The product team (developers and testers) interacts with the product owner to clarify ambiguities in the user story requirements.

This way the developers know what to design and develop, and the testers know what to test. The beauty of this approach is that a small subset of requirements is defined and resulting software is developed and tested in a short period of time, usually two to three weeks. This means that the product owner sees tangible, working software early and has time to request changes to help the software evolve to better meet user needs. Where many Scrum projects fail is due to the inability of the product owner to devote sufficient, focused time on the Scrum projects; generally, the more user involvement, the better-quality software is produced.

- **Design stage.** Although poor requirements have a ripple effect and can adversely impact testing, inadequate requirements likewise can affect the quality of the system design. Poor design, including incorrect choices in architecture/platform, programming languages, and databases, as well as beginning the design stage before requirements have completed can all prove problematic for the test manager and test team. One reality check here is that, in order for a software development project to remain on schedule, it is often necessary to allow the design stage to begin before the requirements stage has completed. Jim has seen this in practice such that the project methodology for software projects included a threshold that a minimum of 85% of the requirements needed to be

What Makes for a Good User Story?

A good Scrum user story has several, general characteristics. You can think of these characteristics as following the INVEST[6] acronym, as solid user stories are:

- Independent (stories are separate and can be scheduled and implemented in any order)
- Negotiable (story details are based on collaboration between the product owner and team members)
- Valuable (stories have value to the customer)
- Estimable (stories contain enough information in order for a high-level estimate to be completed)
- Small (stories are the correct scope and can be implemented in no more than one month's time)
- Testable (stories contain clear acceptance criteria)

---

6   Bill Wake, http://xp123.com/articles/invest-in-good-stories-and-smart-tasks. Although this handy acronym appears in many Agile references, Wake's explanation is concise and even touches upon the SMART model (also covered in Chapter 2) which helps bring meaning to the development of goals.

completed before the project was allowed to move to the design phase. In this case, based on project history, it was determined that the risk of premature and faulty design to some extent outweighed the risk of the project running late.

- **Development stage.** Since testing is dependent on the quality of the software delivered from the development stage, poor (and especially no) unit testing, lack of adequate code reviews, absence of static code analysis, poor coding practices, and other risks affect testing in a negative way, often increasing the burden of testing or rejecting the code delivery until the quality of the delivered software is improved.

- **Integration stage.** The following are just some items occurring during the integration stage that can adversely affect testing: inability to or inaccurate capture of outstanding errors; insufficient or unavailable integration tools; an inadequate integration test lab; a poor integration procedure that is not done methodically. Continuous integration, where developers integrate their code into a code repository up to several times a day, can help mitigate the risk of integration issues.

- **Other.** Of course, there are inherent risks outside of the standard SDLC areas, including project resource risks (e.g., lack of qualified resources, redeployed resources), vendor risks (e.g., key vendor going out of business), etc. Additionally, there can be risks based on methodology, such as Scrum's focus on a sufficient, comprehensive level of documentation. This may pose an issue if the test team struggles with what they may see as insufficient documentation, especially in terms of requirements and design documentation; testers may feel that they just don't have enough documentation on which to base solid test cases. This risk can be mitigated by the working team setting documentation expectations up front, as the team would agree early on what constitutes the correct level of documentation for all stakeholders in order for them to do their work adequately; anything less constitutes a valid risk to the overall quality of the product.

To help keep the test manager aware of these risks, which are generally outside of his control, the project manager can supplement the risk management plan or risk register by listing the functional areas, such as software engineering, software development, as well as the test organization, potentially impacted by each risk. Additionally, the test manager or delegate, such as a test lead, should take a proactive role in participating in periodic project risk reviews usually conducted by the project manager so the test manager is aware of the impact to the test team and testing phase of the project given risks and issues identified by other functional areas. Here the test manager can be considered the liaison between the project's functional area team members and her test team. For example, at the project status meeting, the test manager, representing the test team, testing phase, and associated testing activities of the project, learns of an issue delaying development. The test manager would note at this meeting the potential risk to the testing phase. After this meeting, the test manager shares the issue raised at the project status meeting and plans a course of action with the test team to deal with this real or potential issue.

Although quality is everyone's responsibility, the buck often stops with the test team. In fact, quality seems so closely linked to the test team that, in some organizations, delegation of the quality responsibility lies with the test team such that the testing senior leader must sign off on the test plan, ensuring that adequate testing has occurred and the test results have met the overall test strategy and plan before the product can be deployed to production. We'll discuss how quality assurance and testing relate in the next section.

5.4   Quality Management and Testing

Learning objectives

LO 6.4.1   (K4) Define how testing fits into an organization's overall quality management program.

At the time of this writing, Jim teaches a college class in systems analysis and design. During a lesson on managing a system implementation, he asked the class three questions:

- *What is software quality assurance?*
- *What one word do you most associate with software quality assurance?*
- *How do you ensure software quality assurance?*

How would *you* answer these questions?

The class answered this way:

- *What is software quality assurance?* The answers ranged from the broad "Anything that ensures quality in the product" to "When you call a company's help desk and before the rep starts to speak you get the message, 'This call may be monitored for quality assurance.'"

▨ *What one word do you most associate with software quality assurance?* Not much of a response due to the class's background and experiences.

▨ *How do you ensure software quality assurance?* One surprising answer was "Continual testing, even after the product is in production."

Let's look at each of these questions and answers separately.

What is software quality assurance? The very broad answer of anything done to ensure quality in the product (and, by extension, the service or result) is nonetheless accurate. The ISTQB defines "quality assurance" as "part of quality management focused on providing confidence that quality requirements will be fulfilled."[7] "Quality management" itself, according to ISO 9001:2015, is based on a set of principles, including customer focus; leadership; engagement of people at all levels; a process approach, where interrelated processes work together as a coherent system; and an ongoing focus on improvement.[8] This has many manifestations and can be seen beyond software projects to include anything from customer surveys on the receipt of takeout purchased items from fast-food restaurants to that very familiar message on the help desk call, "This call may be monitored for quality assurance." Software quality assurance includes any intentional activities taken to ensure that quality exists in software in particular. The concept of quality assurance can be extended to any of the products we buy and the services we use. But what, really, is "quality"? The ISTQB defines quality as "the degree to which a component, system, or process meets specified requirements and/or user/customer needs and expectations."[9] Noted quality gurus defined quality as fitness for use, meaning a lack of defects or bugs (J. M. Juran[10]) and conformance to requirements (Philip Crosby[11]).

Quality is not the run-of-the-mill, the mediocre, the mundane, or the everyday. The pursuit of quality is the pursuit of value, excellence, even superiority. Test managers (and others, as we'll soon see) are responsible for con-

---

7   www.astqb.org/glossary/search/quality%20assurance.

8   www.iso.org/iso/home/standards/management-standards/iso_9000.htm   and   www.iso.org/iso/pub100080.pdf. This is a short, focused overview on key quality management principles which, when taken together, form the framework for performance improvement and operational excellence.

9   ISTQB Glossary, www.astqb.org/glossary/search/quality.

10   ASQ website, asq.org/about-asq/who-we-are/bio_juran.html. The ASQ, or American Society for Quality, distinguishes itself as a global community of people dedicated to quality who share ideas and tools, similar to what communities of practice do.

11   ASQ website, asq.org/about-asq/who-we-are/bio_crosby.html.

tributing to excellent software. Test managers do this through building a solid team of test professionals, by not only participating in requirements, design, and test reviews, but also by challenging the concepts, ideas, and reasoning used in these artifacts not for the sake of building solid documentation, but in order to ensure superior quality software.

What one word do you most associate with software quality assurance? Most people in the software industry equate "testing" with "quality assurance." In some organizations, there are separate departments for the test team and the quality assurance team. In other organizations, the test team is known as the QA team or quality assurance team. This is unfortunate because, not to overuse a cliché, but quality really is everyone's job and responsibility on the project. There is often a prevailing mind-set that the test team (those poor souls who are the last in line before the product goes out the door) has the sole responsibility for building and ensuring quality in the product. This view is seriously outdated. As mentioned earlier in the section on project risk management, the quality of the product produced as a fully functional, operational system is dependent on the quality of the requirements gathered from the user and documented for the team; dependent on the quality of the designs built that are themselves dependent on a solid understanding of user requirements; dependent on the quality of the software code that is built and the database architecture that is implemented; dependent on the test strategy, plans, and actual test cases, using the requirements and other project artifacts to ensure quality in the test phase; and dependent on ancillary services and documentation developed in support of the product, such as user, help desk, operational documentation, training material, and so on.

How do you ensure software quality assurance? As the response to the previous question shows, ensuring software quality assurance occurs in each stage of the SDLC. At a CMM Level 5 company, we had much training and documentation concerning our model, processes, and procedures. Every project stakeholder, including the test manager and project manager, was required to review and eventually approve all necessary project documentation from the requirements through design and testing documentation as well as attend and participate in various reviews. This ensured that project team members were committed to the project and all understood what was being built through the requirements, design, development, and testing phases. While there is post-production verification after a product has deployed to production, we often don't continually test the product, since project team members and other resources are allocated to new projects. However, we should be vigilant in soliciting input from users and customers regarding the continual value (i.e., quality) of the product long after it has been initially deployed.

We previously discussed that, in a project's planning phase, the project manager develops the project management plan that itself includes several smaller, focused management plans, including the risk management plan. One other focused management plan developed during the planning activities is the quality management plan (see Figure 5-5 for some of the major components used to develop the quality management plan). The essence of the quality management plan is to minimize variation and deliver results that meet requirements. In order to do this, the quality management plan includes various baselines, which act as starting points for comparisons or deviations, such as the scope, schedule, and cost baselines. Since scope, schedule, and cost represent the key indicators of project success and quality (remember Figure 5-1's project management triangle?), variations from each component's baseline indicate potential quality issues.

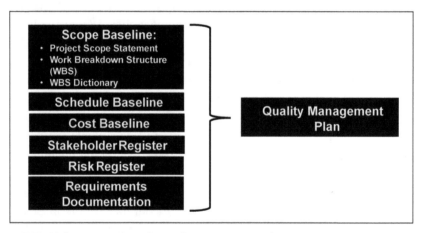

Figure 5-5   *Major components of a quality management plan*

Since quality management extends beyond testing, it is important to differentiate the responsibilities of each area; if one team handles both areas, it is crucial that testing activities be distinguished from overall quality management activities, so the test policy and test strategy expand into the broader quality policies and quality strategies that include much more than testing. The quality management discipline would be responsible for ensuring an integrated and consistent set of quality assurance and quality control processes, activities, and metrics. You can think of quality management (QM) as consisting of both quality assurance (QA) and quality control (QC).

$$QM = QA + QC$$

QA establishes the process for managing for quality and includes **preventative** measures such as establishing appropriate policies and guidelines taken to "assure quality" in software, such as reviewing test plans, selecting defect tracking tools, and training personnel in the various policies and guidelines (one of the companies Jim worked for invested in much training and documentation concerning the overall project and software methodology, helping them to achieve CMM Level 5 certification). The goal of QA is to prevent defects from entering the software. QA is more proactive.

QC on the other hand includes **detection** measures to determine the level of quality in the software. The goal of QC is to gauge and monitor the level of quality inherent in the software, assessing variation against requirements. QC is more reactive.

Think about quality assurance as defining the necessary quality requirements, such as standards, processes, procedures, and policies with an eye towards continuous improvement (enhancing and adapting those policies to fit the needs of the organization and business) and overall vision. Quality control then applies the quality assurance standards, processes, procedures, and policies against the product to check the product's level of quality. Any variations, deviations, or inconsistencies should include a plan to resolve and, given management approval, will be instituted in order to raise the level of quality.

5.5   Sample Exam Questions

In the following section, you will find sample questions that cover the learning objectives for this chapter. All K5 and K6 learning objectives are covered with one or more essay questions, while each K2, K3, and K4 learning objective is covered with a single multiple choice question. This mirrors the organization of the actual ISTQB exam. The number of the covered learning objective(s) is provided for each question, to aid in traceability. The learning objective number will not be provided on the actual exam.

Criteria for marking essay questions: The content of all of your responses to essay questions will be marked in terms of the accuracy, completeness, and relevance of the ideas expressed. The form of your answer will be evaluated in terms of clarity, organization, correct mechanics (spelling, punctuation, grammar, capitalization), and legibility.

Question 1

LO 6.2.6

As test manager on a project, you have been informed that the test environment won't be ready until three weeks after the original planned date of availability due to infrastructure issues. This could seriously impact both the time to execute and analyze planned test cases as well as the scope of test cases necessary to produce a quality product.

Which of the following statements best describes the role of the test manager in this situation?

A. Schedule delays are managed by the project manager so, while informed of this decision, it is the project manager's responsibility to effectively deal with this situation.

B. Since this delay will affect the test schedule and the functionality tested by your team, you voice your concern to the project team, including the project manager and project sponsor, explaining the effect this issue will have on your test team's ability to test the planned functionality, offering documented alternatives with resulting impacts.

C. The project manager works with the vendor who provides various options to get the necessary infrastructure on time, but the project manager is not very confident of the vendor's plans. You therefore are at the mercy of the project manager and vendor and take their direction.

D. The IT team responsible for building and maintaining the environment thinks they have some options to bring the project back on track. You rely on their guidance and hope for the best.

Question 2

LO 6.3.1

As a test manager, you conduct a risk assessment workshop to identify project risks that could affect your team's testing effort. As your workshop progresses, you and the functional area leads identify several potential risks with controls and monitoring or reporting mechanisms.

Of the scenarios below, decide which identified risk, control, and reporting mechanism directly addresses test-related project risks.

A. You learn that your department head has nominated your project to be the first to use a new agile scrum methodology. You and your team are very familiar with the conventional Waterfall technique. To mitigate the risk of project failure given a methodology with which the team is unfamiliar, you advocate additional training, hiring an agile coach, and postponing the project for another six months until the team is comfortable with this new approach. You take monthly assessments to gauge the team's comfort level with agile and take the next steps to begin the project using agile when ready.

B. You learn that the company will be undergoing a major reorganization that could affect your project. Since the reorganization may not affect your department or project for another year, you and the team plan on starting this project quickly with the goal to complete the project before the upsetting reorganization occurs. Given your "political connections," you plan on closely monitoring the progress of the reorganization, aiming to keep your project way ahead of the upcoming reorganization.

C. There is a risk that a key vendor will go out of business. The team suggests mitigating this risk by also engaging into a contract with a competitive vendor; in case the first vendor goes out of business, your company still has a viable contract with the second vendor. Your project team will periodically check on the progress of both vendor contracts to execution.

D. You have heard that your test lead on your project has been unhappy and may be looking for other employment opportunities. You take steps to continue training a strong test team member to act as a backup and work closely with the test lead on this project. Additionally, you work with your HR department to conduct stay interviews with your test lead to help discourage his/her potential leaving. You monitor the progress of these interviews along with the progress of your backup resource plan.

Question 3

LO 6.4.1

As a test manager, consider how your testing team can play an active role in the overall quality management program of your company.

To that end, select the one scenario below where you and your team are **not** actively involved in this quality management program.

A. You and your team take the active role in training others on the various testing policies and guidelines concerning quality assurance.
B. Your test team tests for defects in software as part of quality control detection measures.
C. You and your test team are asked to take a survey regarding choice of the best project management methodology, including Waterfall, agile, and other choices.
D. As part of an overall quality management program, your team contributes to building the test policy and strategy as well as working on projects, testing software to help determine the overall quality of the software prior to release to production.

Question 4

LO 6.2.1, LO 6.2.2

Scenario 3: Test Estimation

Assume you are a test manager involved in developing and maintaining a suite of products centered on a family of programmable thermostats for home, business, and industrial use to control central heating, ventilation, and air conditioning (HVAC) systems. In addition to the normal HVAC control functions, the thermostat also interacts with applications that run on PCs, tablets, and smartphones. These apps can download data for further analysis as well as actively monitoring and controlling the thermostats.

Three major customer types for this business are schools, hospitals and other health-care facilities, and retirement homes. Therefore, management considers its products as safety critical, though no FDA or other regulations apply.

The organization releases new software, and, when applicable, hardware, quarterly. It follows a Scrum-based Agile lifecycle, with five two-week iterations, followed by a three-week release finalization process. For the upcoming release, assume that there are five teams, each with one tester and four developers. The testers report in a matrix structure to you, the test manager. You also have two small teams within your test organization, one that focuses on test automation and another that creates and maintains test environments.

You follow a blended test strategy that includes requirements-based testing, risk-based testing, reactive testing, and regression-averse testing. During release planning, test estimation is done based on the number of requirements (user stories) and the number of risk items identified across those user stories for the entire release backlog. These estimates are used to avoid overcommitting in terms of overall release content. During iteration planning, test estimation is done on the number of requirements (user stories) and the number of risk items identified across those user stories selected for the iteration backlog.

Consider Scenario 3.

Assume that there have been three releases so far, all following the same Agile lifecycle, with similar (though in some cases differently-sized) teams, working on the same product line. The historical defect metrics for each release are as follows: Three major customer types for this business are schools, hospitals and other health-care facilities, and retirement homes. Therefore, management considers its products as safety critical, though no FDA or other regulations apply.

User Stories	Risks/Story	Defects Found	Defects Fixed	Defects Delivered
100	7.2	450	400	100 (50 undiscovered)
200	6.3	900	800	200 (100 undiscovered)
250	7.9	1,150	1,025	225 (100 undiscovered)

Part 1: Describe the process for release test estimation.

Part 2: Describe the process for iteration test estimation.

Part 3: Describe the use of the historical information presented above to create a model for estimating the number of defects found, resolved, and delivered in each release.

Question 5

LO 6.2.3

Continue with scenario 3, as described earlier, and as extended in the previous question.

After the first two iterations, you find that the following defect metrics apply so far.

User Stories	Risks/Story	Defects Found	Defects Fixed
80	9.6	500	320
200	6.3	900	800
250	7.9	1,150	1,025

Part 1: Identify deviations that have occurred from historical metrics.

Part 2: Discuss how these deviations will affect your iteration estimation process.

Question 6

LO 6.2.4, LO 6.2.5

Continue with scenario 3, as described earlier, and as extended in the previous two questions.

Assume that, at the beginning of the third iteration, three of the senior developers quit and take jobs with one of your company's main competitors. You are scheduled to have a meeting with management to discuss the impact of these resignations on testing and quality, and to make recommendations. Outline the key points you'll address in your meeting.

6   Test Project Evaluation and Reporting

Keywords: None

6.1   Introduction

Learning objectives

No learning objectives for this section.

In Chapter 5, we used a scenario of planning a summer vacation as a way to introduce the project management topics of planning, risk management, and retrospectives. Following with this analogy, once the vacation has begun, it's important to track and evaluate several areas to help ensure that our vacation is successful. For example, from a project perspective, we'd need to determine our budget beforehand and, throughout the trip (without getting too exacting) we could do periodic variance analysis. This analysis could compare our actual expenses to date against both our overall budget and budget to date. We could report to our family where we are from a vacation expense perspective and, if we were way over budget, we could discuss ways to help us get back on budget (e.g., we might need to rely on tuna sandwiches over filet mignon for dinner for the rest of the trip). Also, to get to our vacation spot, we could consider comparing our current traveling time against our overall travel plans. If it takes, for instance, six hours of driving time, we could take checkpoints to see if we're on schedule. If not, our family could determine whether corrective action needed to be taken…or we've just encountered too much traffic on the road and will arrive at our destination late.

This vacation analogy is one of several examples in our everyday lives of tracking a project or any major activity or initiative, taking periodic checkpoints to assess variance from a plan and overall performance. Truly, students are concerned with determining how well they are performing in class via their graded assignments and exams throughout the course and will look to take different tactics to raise their level if below expectations (e.g., studying harder, forming a study group, getting advice from their instructor, etc.). Similarly, employees are encouraged to have periodic performance reviews with their managers to ensure that they are meeting expectations concerning their goals; if not, corrective action can be taken early to get back on course. Lastly, similar to the information a project manager uses to assess project performance, a test manager needs to objectively track a project's test components in progress, evaluate the data, and take any necessary corrective actions to bring back performance to an acceptable level. This also includes reporting the appropriate data at the correct level to the correct internal and external stakeholders.

In this chapter, we'll explore some specific testing information that a test manager would be interested in tracking; delve into internal and external reporting to meet a variety of constituents' needs; discuss test reporting considerations at each of the primary testing stages within a project; and close with an overview of key quality control techniques essential for a test manager. While some people think of test metrics as purely a Waterfall project consideration, interspersed throughout this chapter, we'll see some Agile-specific metrics and ways to report on progress.

6.2   Tracking Information

Learning objectives

LO 7.2.1   (K4) For a given level of testing determine the most
effective metrics to be used to control the project.

As a project progresses through its lifecycle and approaches its testing phase, project stakeholders—in particular the project sponsor, project manager, and test manager—will need to know test progress to gauge the quality of the project. In order to do this, test managers develop metrics and report on such.

The ISTQB defines key reporting terms as below. In Table 6-1, I've included two realistic examples for each of the terms defined.

What are the overall purpose and true value of the metrics that you and your test team will develop for projects? In general, your metrics focus on three major areas: the quality of the product being developed; the progress of the project in meeting its goals; and the quality of the test process. Your various testing metrics will help determine the level of quality in the product as it

Table 6-1 *Basic reporting terms and definitions*

Term	Definition	Testing Example	Non-testing Example
Metric	A measurement scale and the method used for measurement	Defects detected	Speed
Measurement scale	A scale that constrains the type of data analysis that can be performed on it	Defects pre-release; defects post-release	Miles per hour
Measurement	The process of assigning a number or category to an entity to describe an attribute of that entity	Integer values, ranging from 0 to some maximum based on defects per prior project	Integer values, ranging from 0 to 120
Measure	The number or category assigned to an attribute of an entity by making a measurement	Defect detected percentage (DDP) = specific number of defects detected during testing, pre-release (50); specific number of defects detected by customer post-release (10), yielding a DDP of 83% or 50/(50 + 10)	Specific speed value at a given point in time (for example, on Saturday, June 18, 2016, the police officer clocked me as driving 65 miles per hour in a 55 miles-per-hour zone)

develops in terms of overall and point-in-time defects discovered/fixed/retested/ confirmed. Additionally, your metrics will yield information indicating how well the project will meet its key performance indicators, such as completion on schedule, in part by showing the test team's progress in executing planned test cases. Lastly, metrics can show high or low levels of quality in the test process through lessons learned sessions, offered at the end of major milestones or phases or the completion of the project in Waterfall projects or during sprint retrospectives at the end of each sprint in Scrum projects.

As a test manager, how do you best determine the metrics on which to periodically report? To begin, your metrics should align with and support the overall project objectives as well as specific testing objectives defined in the test policy. The objectives can include proper exit criteria from the test plan. Therefore, each metric should correlate to a key project objective, and you should be able to explain that correlation. For instance, at one place Jim worked in the project management office (PMO), from a project governance perspective, he was responsible for generating and distributing reports to project managers and their managers regarding conformance to the standard process and templates. These reports aligned with the overall management objective that all projects needed to follow the PMO-defined project process and use the prescribed templates.

Bear in mind that all metrics should include the following considerations:

- **Objective.** Metrics should not be unduly biased to favor one position over another. That is, metrics should never be used to project a false sense of progress when there are clearly issues nor a sense of undue concern when there is none.
- **Informative.** In one place Jim worked, senior leadership described a project as a way to tell a story. In this story, a project is like a journey with a purpose and well-defined beginning and ending; along the journey, periodic checkpoints help determine how well the project is progressing. These periodic checkpoints are metrics reports and should contain sufficient information (not too little and not too much) to inform and, as necessary, guide the audience in making any necessary decisions on course correction so the project can stay on its journey.
- **Understandable.** Although your metrics should be clear and as simple as necessary, given both the information presented and the target audience, each metric should be explained to ensure proper understanding and remove any ambiguities in interpretation. As best as possible, educate your audience in each metric and show the clear alignment of the metric to overall project and/or test objectives. In particular, explain where the metrics could indicate warning signs that either quality or project progress may be jeopardized.
- **Ease of gathering data.** Metrics that are extremely difficult or time-consuming to obtain from team members may be inaccurate or simply not provided at all. Such metrics that are cumbersome and arduous to produce on a regular basis may have diminishing returns; surely, if a tester spends even 10 percent of her time (e.g., 4 hours per week) gathering data and producing and distributing management reports, the team could decide on a more efficient (albeit skinnier) set of metrics to better utilize her time by running test cases.

Keeping these considerations in mind will go a long way to making metrics useful. If appropriate project decisions cannot be made based on reported metrics, they lose their application and usefulness and become an exercise in futility.

One useful approach to consider when developing a small set of metrics is the Goal-Question-Metric (GQM) approach, which begins with a set of goals defined by the organization/department/project and then characterizes a way to assess the achievement of those goals, resulting in a set of data per question in order to answer each question in a quantitative manner to assess performance.[1]

Since metrics are generally shared on a periodic (usually weekly) basis, it is highly recommended that any tools that can be used to both generate and distribute reports, relieving managers and/or staff from these tedious and repetitive tasks, be considered for use.

Typical testing data that could be tracked for a project include the following:

- **Test cases designed.** Similar to a variance analysis that a project manager performs on projects, including a comparison of budgeted or planned costs versus actual costs, the test manager would track the overall planned test cases designed for a project versus the actual test cases developed.
- **Defect metrics.** There are a variety of metrics involving defects, including these:
  - **A breakdown by status** (e.g., open, fixed, retested, confirmed, closed)
  - **A categorization by severity or priority** (e.g., number of defects related to high-, medium-, and low-risk tests based on a risk-based testing strategy)
  - **A breakdown by area** (e.g., number of defects discovered in different functional areas of the product)
  - **Trending** (e.g., increased number of daily defects discovered over time could indicate increasingly poor product quality and should be investigated)
  - **Convergence** (e.g., convergence or moving toward a desired goal or criterion, such as the total number of tests executed to the total number of tests planned for execution)
  - **Resolution turnaround** (e.g., how quickly it takes the development team to resolve defects and the test team to retest and confirm these fixes)
  - **Reopen rate** (e.g., if the rate that defects are closed and then reopened after testers retest increases over time, this could be indicative of poor code quality perhaps due to misunderstood requirements, design flaws, unskilled/untrained developers, etc.)
  - **Rejection rate** (e.g., defects created either in error or due to ignorance and measure wasted effort with an opportunity for improvement)

---

1   www.cs.umd.edu/~mvz/handouts/gqm.pdf

- **Test execution metrics.** Similar to defect metrics just addressed, test execution metrics include these:
  - **A breakdown by status** (e.g., number of tests run, passed, failed, blocked, etc.)
  - **Automated versus manual** (e.g., number of automated tests run, number of manual tests run)
  - **Execution rates** (e.g., how quickly tests are run)
  - **Convergence** (e.g., convergence or moving toward a desired goal or criterion, such as the total number of tests executed to the total number of tests planned for execution)
  - **Planned versus actual** (e.g., the number of actual tests run compared to the number of planned tests to be run at a point in time to see if test execution is on, ahead of, or behind plan)
  - **Number of test cycles** (e.g., how many test cycles or passes through the test set)
- **Coverage metrics.** The following metrics pertain to understanding the degree to which the test basis has been tested and, if possible, more than one type of coverage metric should be used:
  - **Code** (e.g., an indication of how many parts of the software have been tested or covered by tests within the test suite, including statement, decision, and condition coverage)
  - **Requirements** (e.g., the number of requirements that have been tested and, of those, how many are known to have problems)
  - **Risks** (e.g., the amount of test coverage depending on the level of risk, such as the amount of coverage on high-risk, medium-risk, and low-risk items)
- **Management metrics.** The following metrics focus more on test management-related items as opposed to test basis concerns:
  - **Resource hours** (e.g., the number of planned versus actual resource hours devoted to testing)
  - **Setup time** (e.g., the planned versus actual time to set up the testing environment, create test data, user accounts, etc.)
  - **Downtime incurred** (e.g., the expected and unexpected downtime incurred on a project due to issues related to the test environment, test infrastructure (such as servers), etc.)
  - **Planned versus actual** (e.g., while planned versus actual metrics are covered under defects and test cases execution categories, at the management level, this can include schedule and cost metrics by comparing the plans against the actual either at a point in time or in a cumulative sense at the project level or at the testing stage)

6.2.1 Burn Baby Burn

The Agile methodology often uses burn charts to represent project status over time. For instance, burndown charts are common and typically show story point movement over the course of a sprint or iteration. Similar to the risk burndown chart in Figure 6-4 to be addressed later, the sprint burndown chart in Figure 6-1 shows the amount of work remaining at the beginning of the sprint and the downward trend over the course of the sprint with the goal of zero story points remaining by the end of the sprint. Here, we can see that actual progress in completing story points during the sprint varies, with some days falling below plan (e.g., days 2, 3, 7, 8, 9, 10, and 11) and other days progressing above plan (e.g., 5, 6, 12, and 13); overall, all story points planned for the sprint have been completed. At the end of each sprint, the Scrum master updates the release burndown chart which, similar to the sprint burndown chart, reflects the progress the team has made in completing story points; the difference pertains to the scope as the sprint burndown chart focuses on the progress within the sprint while the release burndown chart reflects overall progress at the release level.

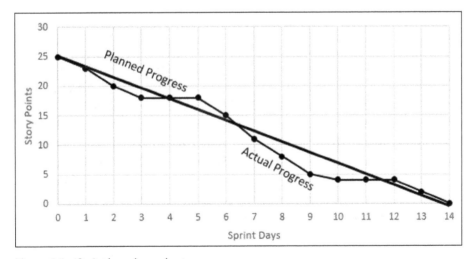

Figure 6-1   *Sprint burndown chart*

Burnup charts are also somewhat common with Agile projects. These typically depict functionality as represented by completed story points over time (see Figure 6-2). From this perspective, the trend increases over time as more and more functionality or user stories via story points are completed. Assuming a straight-line, linear approach in terms of an even allocation of completed story points, represented as planned progress, we can see that the actual progress, although never exceeding the plan within any one sprint, overall, achieves the goal of 200-story-point completion by the final, tenth sprint.

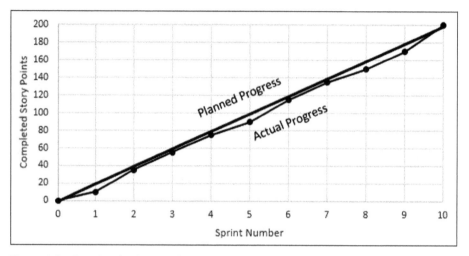

Figure 6-2   *Functionality burnup chart*

The above lists include metrics that capture information both point-in-time as a snapshot view or as trends to see how the information changes over time. Often, point-in-time information can be adequately represented in tabular form or as a histogram, such as the number of defects per status as of yesterday. In order to effectively see emerging trends over time, such as the number of defects per status per day over a 20-day period, a time-based graph such as a histogram would come in handy. Trends help uncover important information concerning schedule, resource, or quality issues. Obviously, trending information relies on and is derived from detailed information that is tracked accordingly.

   In order to properly track this data, the test manager must ensure that the data being reported is correct. Incorrect or invalid data can make the status and interpretation of the data unrealistically positive (resulting in a false sense of security with no action taken when there may indeed need consideration and a planned course of action to be developed) or unrealistically negative (causing inappropriate and unnecessary action to take place). Either situation would poorly reflect on the test team and leave egg on the face of the test manager.

6.3 Evaluating and Using Information — Internal Reporting

Learning objectives

LO 7.3.1 (K6) Create an effective test results report set for a given project for internal use.

As mentioned at the end of the previous subsection, the accuracy and validity of the reported metric data are critical. When comparing actual values to expected outcomes and variances arise, there will undoubtedly be further investigation and corrective action taken to reduce the variances to bring future actual results in line with planned results. For example, if the plan is to find 100 defects per week but the project is trending at an actual rate of 50 defects per week, management will want to know why. Some possible causes could be better-than-expected software quality, resulting in fewer defects discovered. Also, this result could be due to the fact that testers are unexpectedly out sick or because of a downed test environment, preventing testers from executing test cases according to plan.

As previously mentioned, it is important to educate your audience in the metrics that you present. That assumes of course that you, as test manager, properly understand the information yourself. Understanding this information requires expertise. Over time, this experience includes the ability to effectively extract or derive the information, interpret it, and research any variances. Again, reporting raw data that is flawed not only is misleading but also will seriously undermine your credibility as a test manager.

After you have verified the reporting information for accuracy, the information is ready to be distributed internally to your project team for review and consideration of any necessary action plans. Accompanying the reporting information should be a clear explanation of what the metrics represent and how to interpret them; this preferably should be done via meetings or conference calls to allow dialogue rather than through a less interactive means such as email. Different project team members will need to see different reports. For instance, management may wish to see high-level testing efficiency reporting of actual versus planned test-case execution. The development team may be interested to see more detailed defect metrics as defects affect the development team; such reporting may be shared internally before releasing to project managers or external team members in order to better understand the reason for the information reflected in this metric report.

The test manager uses internal reports to manage and control the testing aspects of the project. Some of these internal reports include:

- **Daily test design/execution status.** –This report lists the number of test cases executed on a daily basis and can show meaningful trends over time. The planned test-case execution on a daily basis can likewise be plotted and the gap, if any, between the planned and actual daily test case execution can be displayed (Figure 6-3).

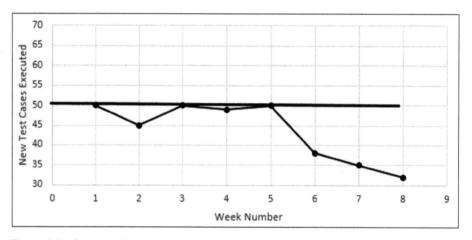

Figure 6-3   *Test execution status report*

The test manager can look at other reports or question her team to help understand any significant gaps between actual versus plan. For example, assume that the test manager has determined that the number of test cases to be executed by her team is 50 per day. The team performs as expected on the first of eight days. However, productivity dips a bit on days 2 and 4; productivity takes a nosedive beginning on day 6 and lasting through day 8. What could account for this? After researching the possible causes of this dip in productivity, it was discovered that there was an inordinate number of defects detected by this test team after the first few days of testing. The testers then were refocused on retesting the test cases related to the defects and thus were not focused on testing their planned, previously unexecuted test cases for the day, reflected in their poor performance on this internal report.

6.3.1 The earlier the better

One particular reality of many software development projects is that testing, positioned at the tail end of traditional, sequential models, often gets squeezed in terms of time in order to maintain the project schedule. This results in either stressed testers working extra hard and long hours to complete their testing tasks or some testing tasks being sacrificed and not getting done, compromising the quality of the product. If testing could somehow occur earlier than planned on projects, this concern may be reduced or even eliminated. One approach is to intentionally shift the testing design and execution as early as possible. Following an Agile approach called *test-driven development,* where requirements are turned into test cases first and then the code written and refactored until the test cases pass, this method moves testing much earlier into the process with the aim to produce better-quality products.

Additionally, given the general rule that it is easier and cheaper to fix a defect the earlier it is detected, the goal is to move test preparation and design, test execution, and overall risk mitigation as close as possible to the start of sprint cycles on a Scrum project. Often, for planned user stories per sprint, tests are not always designed and executed on day 1. There is sometimes a lag, and proper tests in support of stories contained within the sprint do not start for one or even several days into the sprint, causing this rush to test toward the end of the sprint cycle. Ideally, the following would happen:

- Tests for those cases planned for an upcoming sprint would be *designed* at the start or even prior to entering the sprint.
- At the start of the sprint, the goal is to *execute* all test cases in order to obtain the maximum time to test within the timeboxed sprint.
- Appropriately assessed higher risk user stories are addressed at the start of the sprint.
- All user stories and risks are covered by the end of the sprint.

In theory, this all makes sense. But how can the team do this in practice, especially when the team may be too occupied with closing activities of one sprint to expend time and energy designing test cases for the next sprint(s)? How can all planned test cases in support of the user stories (especially more important stories from a risk perspective) be executed on day 1 of the sprint before developers have coded to support the stories?

Test-driven development, noted above, can help, as user-story test cases can be executed on day 1 of the sprint since testing precedes actual development with this approach. Additionally, just as some time is allocated for future sprint planning, some time prior to the actual sprint can be used to design the test cases for user stories so, when the actual sprint begins, appropriate test cases are already predesigned before entering the sprint. Lastly, outside of the sprint cycle, the team can assess each user story from a risk perspective. This means that each story would be considered from a risk likelihood and risk impact perspective. Given a numerical assessment scale (e.g., 1 = low likelihood/impact, 2 = average likelihood/impact, 3 = high likelihood/impact), each story is assessed and assigned a risk priority number (RPN). For example, a story with a relatively high-risk likelihood of occurring and high impact if the risk does occur would be assigned an RPN of 9 (3 = high likelihood × 3 = high impact). Those stories with higher RPNs should be planned to be written and tested earlier in the sprint than later since these stories are more important to the product from a risk perspective and the overall mitigation of risks occurs by addressing the largest risks in the sprint first.

We can measure the effectiveness of this approach of test design, test execution, and risk mitigation as early as possible using metrics.

For example, as the risk burndown chart in Figure 6-4 shows, over the life of the sprint, as each user story is completed (the definition of done being executed and passed test cases associated with the story), there is a decrease in the overall risks associated with the sprint. For example, assume we begin with, for simplicity, 20 user stories assigned to the sprint, each with an RPN of 9 (high likelihood of occurrence times high impact or 3 × 3 = 9), with a total sprint RPN of 180. Day 1 of the sprint reflects this starting point. The second-day value of 162 is the starting point for that day, and the difference from the previous day (180 – 162 = 18) reflects completion of two user stories, since each has an

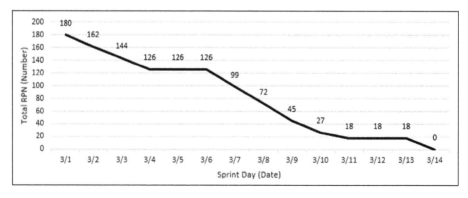

Figure 6-4   *Risk burndown chart*

RPN of 9. It helps to note that the sprint begins on a Wednesday (3/1), so we can see that the plateau from 3/4 to 3/6 is so because 3/4 and 3/5 are weekend days with no testing work accomplished, and we begin the week on Monday, 3/7, with a sprint backlog of 126 RPNs. This plateauing also occurs on the second weekend of the two-week sprint (3/11 and 3/12). Those stories with the larger RPNs should be planned to be completed toward the start of the sprint to best mitigate risk in case not all stories complete within this sprint as planned; obviously, in this example, each story has the same RPN so this prioritization would not make as much sense here, since all 20 user stories were assessed as high-risk items.

▨ **Daily defect status.** This report shows the various statuses of defects on a daily basis. Figure 6-5 shows the number of defects per status at the end of each day over an eight-day testing period. For example, at the end of day 1,

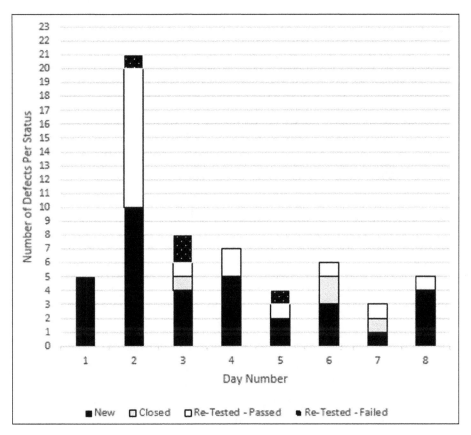

Figure 6-5   *Daily defect status report*

five new defects were created. During day 2, ten defects were retested and the associated test cases were then passed. Since there are four statuses that are being reported, this report can get a little difficult to read as it is and including an accompanying data table may help with the interpretation.

■ **Weekly defect trending.** As Figure 6-6 shows, the arrival rate of defects per week, with the exception of week 4, shows a trend toward declining defects over time. If an exit criterion for the project were to have at least one week without any new defects identified, then we see that we have satisfied this constraint on week 8 (assuming everything else remained the same and the team executed their planned number of test cases that week). The test manager may question why the number of defects discovered increased in week 4.

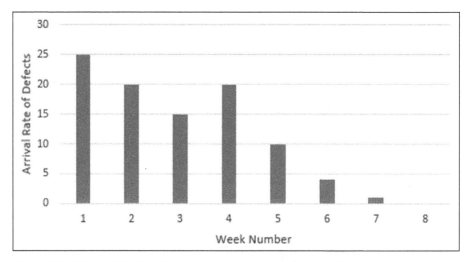

Figure 6-6   *Weekly defect trending report*

■ **Daily test environment reports and status.** This type of report can show a trend over time regarding the availability of the test environment. If, for example, test execution progress is down for a period of time, the test manager can consult this test environment report to see if there were any test environment downtime during the period of slow execution progress. The point is that these internal reports can work in tandem to better understand and interpret information that singular internal reports alone may not reveal.

- **Resource availability.** As its name implies, this type of report shows the availability of resources over a period of time. Let's assume that we have an eight-week testing cycle and we plan on a full staff of 10 testers dedicated to the entire project, including this eight-week cycle. The upper limit shows a target of 10 testing resources; if the full set of 10 testers is available each week, then we have achieved 100 percent testing resource availability. In interpreting the information in Figure 6-7, the project is at full capacity during weeks 1 and 2, but two testers in week 3 unexpectedly are out sick. While one of the sick testers returns to work by week 4, the other sick tester is out sick for this week as well. By week 5, we are at full capacity again, only to dip to 80 percent capacity the final week (week 8). This simple metric can be helpful to better understand if, for instance, our actual test case execution drops below plan in weeks 3 and 4, as consulting this report can help explain lower productivity due to tester illness. This metric can also apply to the Scrum approach and may shed light on why burndown charts are misaligned with a team's historical velocity; the team could very well experience less-than-planned velocity in a sprint if team members are unexpectedly out sick.

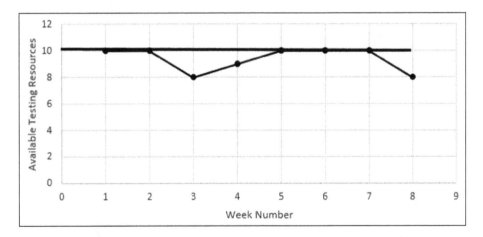

Figure 6-7   *Testing resource availability report*

While some may think that internal reporting does not need to be as formal as that intended for external consumers, the quality and accuracy of the information is just as essential, especially if management and the project team will make decisions based on the information in these reports. A word to the wise then is to invest the proper amount of time to ensure that the information is sound and to use good reporting tools and methods to make this reporting as easy and as accurate as possible.

6.4   Sharing Information — External Reporting

Learning objectives

LO 7.4.1   (K6) Create an accurate, comprehensible, and audience-appropriate test status dashboard.

LO 7.4.2   (K4) Given a specific project and project team, determine the proper level and media for providing weekly test reports.

Similar to internal reporting, the purpose of external reporting is to inform project stakeholders of the testing status of the project. The audience for external reporting often involves senior leadership or executives far removed from the day-to-day, operational work that the test team and other team members perform. At times, testing status may be a bit different from the status reported by other aspects of the project. This doesn't mean that one report is more correct than another, but rather that the reporting often comes from different perspectives.

As with any form of communication, external reporting must take into account its audience and that audience's needs and communicate status appropriately. For instance, the development team may require a detailed defect report to help better understand the level of quality software they deliver to the testing team. However, an executive may best be served by a high-level dashboard status of testing on the project. Generally, senior levels in a company require higher-level, trending information over information found in specific detailed reports. The quick visuals and trending information inherent in dashboards allow busy executives to quickly and easily interpret the metric data to inform them quickly and accurately of project and specifically test status.

Aside from tailoring the appropriate message to the target audience, another factor to consider is the amount and level of information to provide. For example, if the presenter will be available to answer specific questions, then this level of detail does not need to be in the material presented. However, if the presenter does not accompany the material, and reports appear for instance as a dashboard on the company intranet, it is advisable to create a facility to both display summary information and provide access to associated detailed information if the audience wishes to see specific details. Providing both the summary along with the capability to drill down for details adds credibility to the presenter.

External reporting will vary depending on the importance and criticality of the project and the expertise of the audience. However, some common examples of external reports for testing include:

- **Dashboard showing the current testing and defect status.** Probably the first items of inquiry for a senior leader as a consumer of an external report is to understand both the current testing status (where are we versus where should we be?; are we on target?) and the current defect status (how many defects are there and what are their statuses?). A dashboard that reflects the number of planned test cases to be executed and the actual number of cases executed as well as a breakdown of defects by status and trends over time will help the audience get a gauge on the quality of the product.

- **Resource and budget reports.** These reports help shed light on the planned and actual test resources assigned to the project and can assist if other reports indicate problem areas. For instance, if the actual test execution status is behind the plan, the resource report could explain this as several testers may have been unexpectedly out sick, setting the test team behind in its planned test execution. Regarding budget reports, again variance analysis can be used to show any major deviations of actual financial expenditures beyond the budgeted and planned expenditures, especially in terms of testing assets, environments and infrastructure, etc.

- **Risk mitigation chart.** Senior leaders often wish to see how the project mitigates risk. One simple way is to chart a grid of risks considering each risk's likelihood of occurring as well as overall impact if it does occur. Given a risk-based testing strategy, test cases in the high category (Figure 6-8), which are considered riskier test cases in terms of both high likelihood of occurring ("likely" or "near certain") with a corresponding high impact ("major" or "critical") if they do occur, should be planned to be tested first to allow sufficient time earlier in the cycle to fix potential defects. This planning and early execution of priority test cases help mitigate the risk of uncorrected defects adversely impacting product quality.

Figure 6-8   *Risk mitigation chart*

Test coverage chart (requirements- or risk-based). This chart provides a way to see which requirements have been tested via appropriate test cases and can be based on requirements ranking or risk ranking (addressed in the previous reporting example of the risk mitigation chart). As a traceability matrix ensures that test cases are built to satisfy each requirement, this chart shows the progress in executing test cases that relate to the requirements, indicating how much testing of the requirements have been achieved along with any defects related to those executed test cases.

- **Defect trends.** As previously shown in Figure 6-6, metric reporting can include the trends in new defects discovered per day or per week, the daily or weekly number of defects in each status, and other defect information.
- **Milestone achievement.** Meeting key project and specifically test milestones is important to communicate to project stakeholders. Milestones denote important points of progress in a project and achieving such gives greater confidence to stakeholders that the project is on track. From a testing perspective, key milestones could include completion of the test suite, completion of necessary test reviews, and completion of testing phases.
- **Project health indicators (red, yellow, green).** Project managers generally report the health of a project based on key performance indicators (KPIs). These indicators often relate to meeting defined objectives around cost, schedule, scope, quality, and customer satisfaction. Each KPI's actual information can be assessed against its plan and, given any threshold allowance, a health indicator can be determined. Figure 6-9 reflects an example of this: the project is doing fine in terms of project scope, product quality, and overall customer satisfaction at the expense of the project cost and more so the project schedule. This concept certainly applies to testing, and health can be assessed on achievement of milestones (although this might be packaged along with the overall project schedule KPI) or variance from specific testing targets and objectives. For instance, if the actual defects detected are more than 25 percent of the planned defects, the test manager can provide a

yellow health assessment. Generally, a green assessment indicates that variance analyses show actuals performing against plans within a given threshold; a yellow assessment means that, although actuals are beyond plans, the team is confident that they will meet the established plans through some recovery mechanism; and red assessment shows trouble in meeting plans such that no current recovery plans are in place and additional help is needed.

Cost	Schedule	Scope	Quality	Customer Satisfaction
Yellow	Red	Green	Green	Green

Figure 6-9 *Key performance indicators*

- **Predictive metrics.** Predictive metrics help look at the past as a way to consider what may happen in the future. For example, based on the weekly number of defects and their level of criticality, it may be possible to predict the number of high defects per total defects in future weeks.
- **"Go/No go" recommendations.** Generally, just before release of a product to the production environment, a project manager conducts a meeting with the necessary project stakeholders to assess if the product is ready to be released. Various questions need to be addressed at this meeting, the answers to which will influence the overall recommendation to move forward with the production deployment. In line with this, the team may address the number of any outstanding defects and their level of criticality to the product's quality. The team may also consider the number and relative importance of any test cases that have not yet been executed. The test manager and applicable test metrics play an extremely important part in determining whether the product is ready to be deployed, influencing the final "go" (release to production) or "no go" (defer the release until some steps are taken to ensure readiness) recommendation is made.

Similar to internal reporting, external reporting should be done on a regular basis, usually weekly. This helps set audience expectation in terms of anticipating what and when they will receive metric reports so they can best use that information for their own planning and necessary decision making. As a project manager, Jim has developed and used project-level templates such as a communication plan. Although the communication plan is intended to set expectations from the project manager to the project stakeholder in terms of what, when, and how project status and other communications will be handled, the concept applies here as well. If the test manager develops a similar communication plan (or is involved in influencing the project-level communication plan specifically for test status), this helps set the expectation for all project stakeholders.

Once the frequency and level of communication have been established based on the test manager's target audience, the test manager may have several options in terms of communication vehicles used to publish and distribute metrics reports. These include:

- **Real-time dashboard.** Software tools can display a dashboard of metrics at the appropriate level (usually high level with a capacity to drill down to specifics) and offer real-time updates if the metrics are linked to source testing information, such as defect statuses, test execution statuses, etc.

6.4.1 Kanban Boards

The Agile methodology offers some interesting and unique metrics related to test performance and progress.

One type of performance monitor is a Kanban board. Having its roots in manufacturing and engineering from the 1940s, the Kanban technique is a way to visually see team progress; in fact, the Japanese word "Kanban" means "visual signal" or "card." Jim was a product owner proxy on a Scrum project and worked with the project's Scrum master to develop a Kanban board that was used at each daily sprint stand-up meeting. At this meeting, aside from each team member reporting on work completed the previous day, work planned for the day ahead, and reporting any obstacles, each team member also showed movement of user stories across from left to right as the story progressed from "to do" through "to be tested" to "done" (see Figure 6-10). Since Scrum methods were new for us at that time, this manual method of recording progress in a public way for the team to see served our needs. (This Kanban board served as an information radiator, which is a publicly posted dashboard for others to quickly see and assess progress and can include information such as user-story progress within a sprint.) The Scrum master would then record the changes in status from the physical Kanban board to a tool so overall status and progress at the project level (including completed, current, and future planned sprints) could be reported or analyzed.

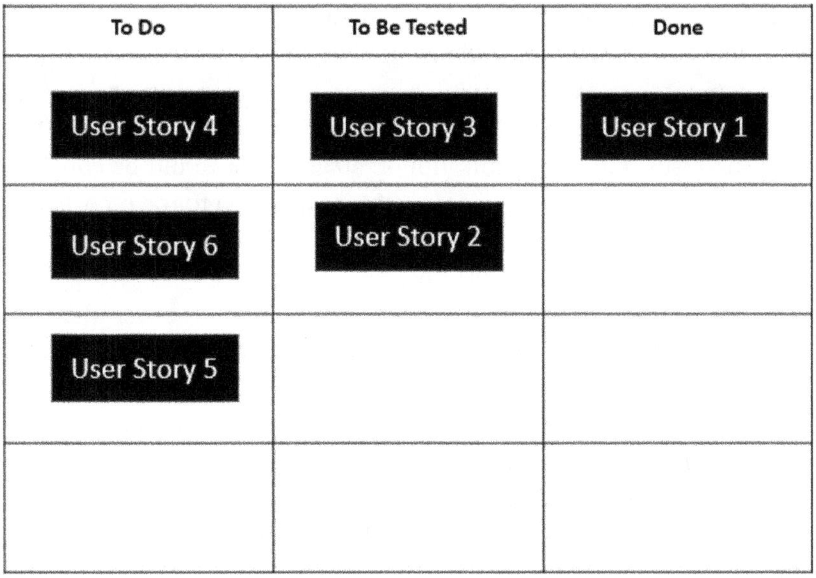

To Do	To Be Tested	Done
User Story 4	User Story 3	User Story 1
User Story 6	User Story 2	
User Story 5		

Figure 6-10   *Kanban board*

Jim has broadened the use of this simple but effective means of reporting progress to both present and manage his annual performance goals. Very simply, he wrote his goals on sticky notes and, over time, moved the notes from the "planned" column to the "in-progress" column to the "completed" column. This acted as a way for him to easily show anyone the current progress of his planned goals. Since most goals were due on a quarterly or even annual basis, he didn't complicate matters by maintaining history or tracking any trends in his progress or lack thereof. However, if necessary, he could have taken snapshots in time (e.g., monthly) to see if there were issues of concern with blocked goals over time. The advantage of this method is a simple way for management and fellow colleagues and (of course him!) to outline his work and progress toward completing goals.

- **Publishing to a known site on the intranet.** One task Jim had was to publish weekly reporting updates to a project collaboration site for other team members to see. While this was certainly not in real time, once the appropriate metrics were developed, the weekly updates did not require too much effort.
- **Emailed out to a distribution list.** Another task of Jim's involved generating monthly and weekly reports, sourced from a project management tool

and copied via a nightly job to the company's data warehouse. The report generation effort was not difficult or time-consuming; however, the cut-and-paste work to extract the information from the report and place in an email to a specified distribution list was tedious and error-prone. In terms of push versus pull communication strategies, this would be considered a push form of communication as he sent information to the report consumers; they did not access a website or intranet in order to get status updates whenever they wanted such updates.

- **Included in regular project status meetings.** Here, the test manager can periodically supply the project manager with test metrics to be included in the larger project status report. Typically, project managers will include schedule highlights, discuss risks and action items, and entertain updates from each functional area, including testing.

- **Physically posted in an office window.** While this may seem to be the low-tech method of communicating testing metrics, Jim has seen instances where project schedules were posted outside of the project manager's office or cubicle. Additionally, at one company where the Agile methodology was very popular and well-supported, one conference room was dedicated to an Agile project team, where, during story time, the Scrum master would post user stories along the glass walls of the room, so those outside could easily see many small slips of paper adorning the room. The point is that metrics reports in the form of graphs and charts can certainly be posted outside of the test manager's office. However, this should be only one of several other ways to periodically communicate test status to the project team.

Communication involves not only conveying information from the sender but also understanding information by the receiver. External reporting therefore is only effective when the target audience receives and understands the communication well enough to make plans and take the necessary action (if necessary). The reporting must include the proper level of detail to suit the needs of the intended audience. Providing too much information and details, when not necessary or warranted, can overwhelm the target audience, hampering their overall understanding and possibly discrediting not only the report but also its provider, you.

So, in order to be a successful test manager, one of the primary tasks is to adequately communicate test status to the intended audience at the appropriate level of detail so the audience can make informed decisions.

6.5 Test Results Reporting and Interpretation

Learning objectives

LO 7.5.1 (K6) Given a particular lifecycle, project, and product, design appropriate test results reporting processes and dashboards, including metrics, taking into account the information needs and level of sophistication of the various stakeholders.

LO 7.5.2 (K4) Analyze a given test situation during any part of the test process, including appropriate qualitative interpretation, based on a given test dashboard and set of metrics.

In addition to including different test metrics reports for internal and external reporting, different reports make sense at various phases of the software development lifecycle, specifically in the testing phases.

Planning and Control

Test planning involves identifying and implementing all activities and resources needed to meet both the mission and objectives noted in the test strategy. This could include identifying the features to be tested, the necessary testing tasks, who is assigned to perform each testing task, information on the test environment, entry and exit criteria, and any risks involved along with any mitigation plans.

Test control, an ongoing activity, is similar to performing the variance analyses mentioned previously. Although variance analyses exist at the project-management level, comparing budgeted or planned schedule, cost, and scope against reality or actuals at the time, they also can be extended to the testing realm in comparing planned test-case execution or expected defect discovery against actuals. While the test schedule and other monitoring activities and metrics are defined during the planning process, comparison of actual information against these plans occurs during test control in order to measure success. During test planning, traceability is established between the test basis, the test conditions, and other test work products that can be monitored during test control and monitoring. Traceability will help determine the extent to which quality risks are mitigated, requirements are met, and supported configurations work properly; this reporting goes beyond that of mere test-case status and defect counts.

Typical metrics in these phases include the following, which allow the report consumer to quickly determine significant variance analyses, where actual status deviates from planned status:

- **Requirements or risk coverage.** Coverage helps indicate how well the test manager is managing the test effort. This includes comparing actual test execution status against planned status in terms of requirements or risk coverage, which provide test cases aligned with either requirements (given a requirements-based strategy) or risk (given a risk-based strategy), with the test cases associated with the most important requirements or highest-risk items to be tested earliest. If less important requirements or lower risk items are addressed first, the testing approach should be reviewed and corrected. If inadequate risk coverage is occurring, the test manager should meet with the test team, development manager, and project manager to not only understand why, but also take measures to bring risk coverage back in line to meet planned expectations.

  Note that, if formal documentation of the system isn't available, coverage must still be established and should be based on targets set in collaboration with stakeholders. Given a risk-based testing strategy, this is done in terms of risks. Coverage metrics are still necessary and helpful even if system documentation is absent.

- **Test case development and execution status.** As with all other tasks in a project, the development and execution of test cases follow a plan. As the plan is carried out, the team can easily see if the development of the test cases is behind, on, or ahead of the planned development. Similarly, after the test cases have been crafted, the rate of test case execution could be compared with the planned rate and any significant variances, as leadership and management team define significant, should be reported and corrective actions taken to bring the actual in line with the planned.

- **Defect discovery trends.** The quality of the software can be gauged depending on the planned versus actual defect discovery trends. If the trend shows discovery of a great number of defects, or a larger proportion of critical defects, at a higher rate than anticipated, this could be indicative of significant quality issues or even a poor estimation job by the testers in not anticipating as many defects as occurred. Defect discovery can also be used as a test management metric. For example, in risk-based testing, the goal is to find most of the high-severity defects early in the test execution period. Then, during test control, you can monitor defect discovery to see if that pattern held. If the pattern does not hold, you can take steps to rectify, as generally there was probably a failure to properly assess quality risks.

- **Planned versus actual hours for testing activities.** If not carefully watched by the test manager, the actual hours can far exceed the planned hours for testing activities. The test manager should weekly check her budget and work breakdown structure to see if variations or deviations from plan are beginning to occur. The sooner this is detected and fixed, the better.

    There can also be cases where actual hours are less than planned hours as the test team is not as productive as planned. This could occur for several reasons, including unavailability of the test environment and/or systems, poor quality or missing test data, automation tool anomalies, unavailability of human resources, ill-prepared documentation or poor quality of incoming code. Regardless of the reason(s), the test manager must devise a plan and take action to rectify the lack of productivity and insufficient test coverage.

Analysis and Design

During the test analysis phase, the team is determining what to test based on the test objectives defined in the test policy, strategy and plans, taking into account stakeholders' perspectives on project and product success, including factoring in product quality risk analysis. The ISTQB calls "what to test" the test condition. Test analysis sets out to create a set of test conditions for a project using test basis documents and work products such as requirements specifications and, on Agile projects, user stories.

Typical metrics for the test analysis phase include:

- **Number of identified test conditions.** The actual number of identified test conditions can be compared to an expected number of conditions based on historical data. For example, prior data can indicate that, for each test basis element such as an individual requirement or quality risk, there should be five test conditions. If, for a particular project, there are fewer test conditions, is this a problem? If you are discovering more than five test conditions, is that necessarily a problem? The answer, of course, is that it depends. The ratio of test conditions per test basis element may be different from the historical data; the important point is that the test manager can substantiate the fewer or additional test conditions based on the characteristics of the product and the needs of the project.

■ **Defects found.** With an analytical test strategy, where the test team analyzes the test basis to identify test conditions to cover, there is an emphasis on reviewing requirements and analyzing risks. This analysis often uncovers defects in work products such as requirements specifications, design specifications, product plans, project plans, marketing documents, etc. Defects found in these various documents and work products against expectations based on historical data can be reported to management.

The test design phase then determines how to test those test conditions developed during test analysis.

Typical metrics for this test design phase include:

■ **Coverage metrics.** While coverage was addressed primarily in terms of risk in the planning and control phases, it takes on a much broader context in the test design phase. Here, coverage metrics include coverage of the risk items by the test cases but also coverage of the requirements likewise through the test cases. Other coverage types include quality characteristics as well such as functional interoperability, security, compliance, and reliability, ensuring these and other characteristics pertaining to the quality of the product are covered via appropriate test cases. Any coverage gaps that are not satisfactorily covered by one or more test cases expose risk, which in and of itself must be assessed according to potential impact and likelihood. An analysis of these gaps or deviations from the plan should be addressed with appropriate corrective actions before moving out of the design phase.

■ **Defects found during test design.** Defects can be discovered in the various test basis documents such as the requirements document, functional specifications documents, design documents, risk analyses, configuration document, and so on. These defects should then be tracked and reported against their sources and amendments and repairs made to those sources appropriately.

■ **Defects found during review cycles.** Phase containment indicates the percentage of defects resolved in the same phase in which those defects were introduced. Thus, defects discovered during various reviews, such as requirements reviews, design reviews, etc., and that are fixed before moving on to the next phase increase the quality of the product. If the defect cannot be fixed in the current phase and does escape to the next phase, it certainly will incur additional work in terms of documentation, status reporting, investigating and applying possible workarounds, and so on. However, the time, effort, and cost in managing these defects are still less than that spent detecting a previously unfound defect. The clear indication here is find early, fix early. Generally, defect trending may uncover quality problems if a higher than expected number of defects are found in the review cycle. This may require multiple review cycles in order to achieve an acceptable level of quality before the work products and the project in general can move to the next lifecycle phase.

On the flip side, if defect trending shows fewer and fewer new defects being discovered and reported each day, assuming there is sufficient test execution and test coverage, this may indicate sufficient quality in the product.

Lastly, if defect trending shows the largest number of defects found early in the lifecycle, this could very well indicate an efficient test execution process.

Implementation and Execution

The test implementation phase organizes the test cases, finalizes the test data and associated test environments, and creates a test execution schedule. This includes assessing risks, prioritization, the test environment, data dependencies, and constraints in order to devise a workable test execution schedule. This schedule must align with the test objectives, test strategy, and overall test plan.

Typical metrics at this test implementation phase include:

- **Percentages of environments, systems, and data configured and ready for testing.** We don't live in a perfect world and we need to make trade-offs. Often, we must begin testing without all test environments, systems, and configured data ready to go. This may not necessarily be a bad strategy. However, if the highest-risk items that should be tested earliest require setup, configuration, and data that are just not available, this could hurt and hamper the overall testing effort. Assessing readiness percentages alone isn't sufficient, so the test manager must determine the impact of less than 100 percent availability along with any schedule impacts or other changes, balancing all variables in order to product an acceptable testing effort and quality product.

  An example of data configuration readiness is an application requiring 100 configurations (to use round, easy numbers). As each configuration is completed, this contributes 1 percent to the total percentage of data configuration completeness.

▓ **Percentage of test data created and used.** The availability and accuracy of test data can also impact the order of test execution, resulting in a less-than-optimal testing schedule and test team efficiency. This could result in repeated reuse of the test data that are available as well as changes to automated tests by resetting them to their state of inactivity after each test case use.

An example of test data readiness is if source data can be directly loaded into the test environment. If so, after the data load, there is 100 percent test data availability. However, if the data needs to be massaged, changed, transformed in any way, the test data availability is not there until this transformation is complete. Just loading the raw or source data alone does not achieve this 100 percent test data availability since it is not yet ready for use.

▓ **Percentage of test cases that are automated and results of automation execution.** The test manager must ensure that the test case automation effort is achieving its goals as originally planned and documented. Additionally, the automation effort must also include results that are being integrated into the overall testing results. While it may seem great that for instance the 10 percent of the testing effort covered by test automation detects 50 percent of the defects, the test manager should be skeptical and question the types of defects that automation is finding, checking to ensure that the automation is indeed performing the correct validation, and lastly determine why manual testing is not uncovering a sufficient number of defects.

One caveat is not to expect that 100 percent of the regression test suite can or should be automated (for example, some tests are too complex, take too long to automate, or are not run enough to justify automating them).

In the test execution phase, as its name states, the actual execution of tests occurs with appropriate results recorded.

Test execution phase metrics include:

▓ **Percentage of test conditions and cases covered by test execution and the results of that execution.** This is basically coverage again. Obviously, if the coverage is not moving along according to plan, unexpected risks may show themselves. For example, a blocked test can prevent bringing to light defects that would result in architectural changes to the system and could adversely affect the performance testing schedule. Additionally, the test manager must monitor test case pass/fail information to determine whether the expected rate is being accomplished. If too many test cases are failing, indicating poor product quality, this may require a need for additional test cycles. Conversely, if too many test cases are passing, the test manager should question if adequate testing really has occurred, where focus should be applied given the extra time in the schedule, and if plans need to be modified for future testing cycles.

- **Percentage of test cases that are marked for inclusion in the regression test suite.** The number of test cases that should be included in the regression test suite varies depending on each product. In general, test cases that are expected to remain constant are good candidates for consideration for the regression test suite. These test cases can begin to be evaluated, if not at the design or implementation phase, then definitely during the execution phase.

- **Time spent maintaining automated and manual test cases.** The time devoted to maintaining the set of automated and manual test cases may not be trivial on a project. Changing requirements will undoubtedly contribute to the maintenance time beyond the scheduled time to maintain the documentation appropriately. There can be additional maintenance time if the delivered code doesn't match requirements, the data or environment has changed, the interfacing systems have changed, or due to several other factors. While this maintenance time will be assigned to the project and isn't really considered productive test time, it may have a sizeable impact on the testing project.

- **Breakdown between types of testing—e.g., black box, white box, experience-based.** The test manager needs to determine the risk coverage, defect detection, and test skill usage for each type of testing. After analyzing the information, the test manager may redirect testing resources toward a specific type of testing if this type is resulting in an inordinate amount of defects. If, for instance, scripted testing is finding fewer defects, this could be because the software has stabilized. Or, if white box testing is finding fewer defects, the test manager can investigate what code coverage levels are being achieved.

Evaluating Exit Criteria and Reporting

At the evaluating exit criteria phase, the test manager relates the test results to the exit criteria. In fact, throughout the project, the test manager is checking test results to ensure steady progress toward meeting the exit criteria. The test manager must consider removing any obstacles that could prevent the project from meeting its exit criteria. For Scrum projects, there is consideration here of examining the product, user story completion, and feature sets against their definitions of done.

Although the test manager monitors this progress on a detailed level, she reports to testing stakeholders at a summary level from a total project perspective. At this point, no new metrics are developed or introduced in the testing project.

Metrics that are finalized at this stage, unless the testing phase has been extended, help with process improvement on future projects. These metrics include:

- **Test conditions, test cases or test specifications executed versus planned and the final status of each.** The test manager can compare actual versus planned test cases executed with the assumed exit criteria of 100 percent test case execution, 100 percent test cases passing, and 0 percent test cases failed. Some projects do allow some number of failed test cases and defects, such as only low defects are allowed to be unresolved, as appropriate exit criteria. Although this may seem stringent, the test team and management can review the results against these criteria in order to waive, if necessary.
- **Number of testing cycles used versus planned.** The test manager can compare the number of test cycles used versus the number planned and determine if additional testing cycles could have improved the results.
- **Number and complexity of changes to the software that were introduced, implemented, and tested.** Typically, there is an agreement to freeze the code and not introduce any changes to the testing environment in order to offer stability. If too many complex changes have been allowed, this could seriously affect the test results and outcomes.
- **Schedule and budget adherence and variances.** These summary metrics are usually considered project management metrics. However, the test manager is responsible for the testing tasks in the schedule as well as the testing budget. The prudent test manager throughout the project keeps a careful eye on progress as measured through the schedule as well as cost via budget versus actual expenditure variance analyses. Nonetheless, the test manager

must pay particular attention to the variance analyses at test entry, at major testing milestones during test execution, and at test exit. The earlier variances are detected, the more time the test manager and other project stakeholders can take corrective action to rectify issues. At this point, the test manager provides overall variance analyses for summary reporting.

- **Risk mitigation.** The test manager can report any mitigating actions taken during the course of the project to lessen the impact or likelihood of test-related risks. Please reference the *Risk* section in Chapter 5.
- **Planned versus actual effective testing time.** This metric shows productive testing time and may exclude documentation updates, attending project meetings, automating tests, and supplementing the regression test suite. The report can show effective test time for individual testers or the entire test team.

Test Closure Activities

Similar to the closure of the entire project, the testing cycle includes a test closure phase that follows the completion of the test execution phase. Not unlike project closure, where the project manager ensures that all tasks on the project schedule are complete, the product is deployed to the customer in the production environment, a retrospective or lessons learned session is conducted, and all necessary project documentation is archived, the test manager and test team embark upon similar activities. From the test manager's perspective, she would ensure that all test-related tasks are complete, the final work products have been delivered, actively participate in retrospective meetings, and archive necessary test data, test cases, system configurations, and the like for the project.

Typical metrics in this phase and its associated closure activities include:

- **Percentage of test cases that can be reused on future projects.** Reuse is a strong benefit to help other, similar future projects. The test manager and test team can help determine which test work products can be reused not only on future internal projects but also to help the internal support team or external customers. Test cases that can be reused are a better investment in time compared with those used once and then discarded. For example, the test manager can transfer tests and test environments to the team who will handle maintenance testing. Also, the test manager can deliver automated or manual regression test suites to customers if they are integrating her system into a larger system. The extra work to hand off these work products should be factored into the overall project schedule as real work.

- **Percentage of test cases that should be moved to the regression test suite.** As discussed during the test execution phase, test case candidates for the regression test suite should be identified as early as possible and then finalized and added to the test suite during the test closure phase. Test cases that are expected to remain constant are good candidates for review for possible automation.

- **Percentage of the defects that have reached the end of their lifecycle.** Defects that will not be resolved in this project, including those defects that the team collectively agree will be deferred to another project, accepted as a permanent product restriction, or reclassified as an enhancement request rather than a defect or bug.

As part of test closure activities, the test manager may also look for process improvements. In fact, during retrospective sessions, the facilitator not only asks the team what went well and what didn't, she also probes for any process improvements, born usually from items that didn't go as well as planned or expected. The purpose of the retrospective is to help future, similar projects to be more successful since the "boat has already left the dock," so to speak, for the current project. Additionally, if team members will work on future projects together, retrospectives help uncover gaps in working relationships and can help foster better teamwork on future projects. For example, if on the current project defects seemed to be clustered around a certain area or functionality, future projects may consider including additional rigor in its quality risk analysis in part by including additional participants. Or, if there is an inordinate number of defects, the team could decide to do additional static testing, such as reviewing code through code inspections, or additional reviews of requirements, specifications, and designs. Also, if there were overall quality issues shown perhaps through a large number of defects, the team could brainstorm on ways to improve quality on future projects via process or tool improvements, or even training or certification to raise the skill level of project stakeholders, including the test team. Additionally, if the team seriously underestimated the amount of productive time to test, the number of test cases, or the number of defects discovered, this could indicate issues in estimating and management may seek training or other improvement measures. Lastly, if not all test cases have been successfully executed or defects successfully resolved by the project's end, a retrospective can help determine the reason(s) why, often leading to efficiency suggestions for improvement, a reevaluation of the test strategy, and possibly reexamining exit criteria.

Jim does note that, as a project manager in several different organizations, as solid as intentions are for not repeating prior mistakes or inefficiencies, most projects do not perform the due diligence in reviewing retrospective results from prior projects during the planning stage of the current project. Aside from the overall project perspective, this lack of applying lessons learned can also affect testing specifically, especially during test planning. Sometimes this lack of consulting lessons from prior projects is due simply to a lack of discipline; the PMO or project management office can help here by intentionally adding lesson reviews as a task during the planning stage of a project. Another reason for neglecting lessons learned is that there just have not been solid knowledge management tools to capture and classify this information allowing easy access. As knowledge bases and technology continue to improve, this should be less of a reason not to plan accordingly and prevent history from repeating itself.

Also during the testing closure phase, the test manager and test team must decide which test cases and other work products should be retained and reused for efficiency on other projects. The test manager should consider the percentage of overall test cases that can be reused and then appropriately register them in a repository. Similar to the discussion on project-level retrospectives, there should be an easy way to find the reusable components for future projects; otherwise, the effort to catalog and add work products to a repository will be useless unless those artifacts are found and used.

Additionally, the test team should be considering the number of test cases that should be added to the regression test suite. There should be a careful strategy in managing the size and growth of this test suite as the addition of too many tests could lead to very large testing cycles on projects. One way to tackle this problem is to ease the burden of regression test suite execution by automating as many of these tests as possible.

Lastly, aside from saving valuable test cases for later reuse, the test artifacts should also be archived. These artifacts include test cases, test procedures, test data, final test results, test log files, test status reports, and other documents and work products. These should be placed in a configuration management system for easy access.

6.6   Statistical Quality Control Techniques

Learning objectives

LO 7.6.1   (K2) Explain why a test manager would need to
understand basic quality control techniques.

Since testing is closely linked to quality control, the test manager should have a
firm grasp of the basic statistical quality control techniques, charts, and graphs
used to provide indications of testing progress for overall success. Quality control is aligned with what's been termed the Deming Cycle or Plan, Do, Check,
Act (PDCA) Cycle (Figure 6-11). Although introduced by Walter A. Shewhart,
it was W. Edwards Deming who popularized this process improvement model.
The model is based on the following four iterative steps:

- **Plan**   – Consider improvements to a process.
- **Do**   – Implement those process improvements.
- **Check** – Evaluate the improvements.
- **Act**   – Where the improvements fall short of expectations, take correc-
              tive action to further improve, which could include appropriate
              planning for the next iteration.

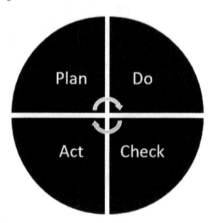

Figure 6-11   *PDCA Cycle*

Two things are relevant concerning this model: Based on its simplicity, it has
widespread process improvement application in terms of change management,
project management, employee performance management, and obviously quality management. Secondly, the steps in the PDCA Cycle, taken together, have

an overarching theme of continuous improvement. Continuous improvement involves a mind-set of ongoing efforts to evaluate processes with the goal of making them more efficient and effective.

Walter Shewhart has also contributed to one of the seven basic tools of quality. Of this collection, Shewhart introduced the concept of control charts, which are used to determine whether a process is in statistical control (Figure 6-12).

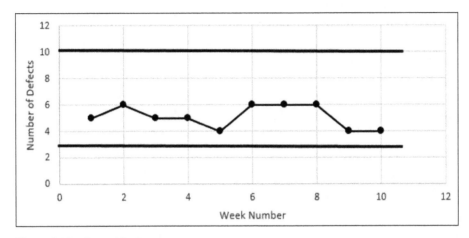

Figure 6-12   *Control limits report*

Specific limits, called *upper control limits* (UCL) and *lower control limits* (LCL), define the maximum and minimum thresholds. If a process contains measured points beyond these boundary control limits, those points are considered unacceptable variations. This can best be used by the test manager to help determine whether defects discovered during a project's test phase are within proper control limits or are indeed beyond acceptable thresholds and require additional attention to determine the root cause.

To determine the root cause of issues, another primary quality tool from the set of seven basic quality tools is simply called the *cause-and-effect diagram*. Also known as the *Ishikawa diagram* after its creator, Kaoru Ishikawa, as well as the fishbone diagram since completed diagrams resemble the bones of a fish, this tool identifies possible root causes for problems in order to help the team focus on problem resolution. For instance, Jim has used root cause analysis and incorporated the technique in a course on quality and project management. For a typical root cause analysis (RCA) session, the facilitator assembles key people who were involved in or are knowledgeable about the issue, preferably a work group rather than management. After stating the problem, the facilitator highlights a few probable areas, such as people/personnel, machinery/tools, process, and so on. Of course, given the specific situation, more meaningful areas can be included. Then, the facilitator brainstorms with the team, looking to identify possible causes of the issue. A simple technique, called *5 Whys*, can be used to generate more information or to get the team thinking about additional possible causes.

For example, if an issue is the reliability related to automated testing, one possible area to investigate is related to the unreliability of the automated tool in use (see Figure 6-13). Narrowing in on tool-related issues, the facilitator can ask the team why the tool is unreliable. When asked why it is unreliable, one answer could be that it is on an old server that is known to be unreliable. When asked further why the tool is on an old server, one response could be that management would not authorize the tool to be installed on a more reliable server due to cost issues. If it is determined that running the tool on an old, unreliable server is the primary or root cause of automated test reliability issues, a proposal can be made to migrate the tool to a more reliable server in order to help the success of this and potentially other projects that use the tool.

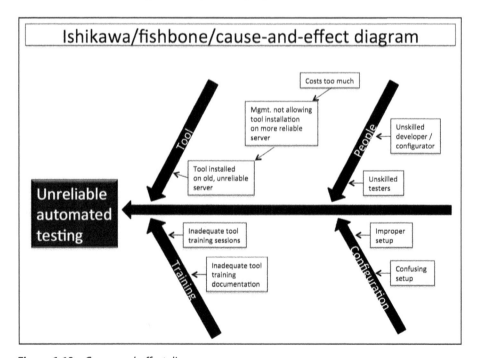

Figure 6-13   *Cause-and-effect diagram*

Successful test managers use quality tools to help uncover problems as well as make process improvements as part of a continuous improvement mind-set to make future projects more and more successful.

6.7   Sample Exam Questions

In the following section, you will find sample questions that cover the learning objectives for this chapter. All K5 and K6 learning objectives are covered with one or more essay questions, while each K2, K3, and K4 learning objective is covered with a single multiple choice question. This mirrors the organization of the actual ISTQB exam. The number of the covered learning objective(s) is provided for each question, to aid in traceability. The learning objective number will not be provided on the actual exam.

Criteria for marking essay questions: The content of all of your responses to essay questions will be marked in terms of the accuracy, completeness, and relevance of the ideas expressed. The form of your answer will be evaluated in terms of clarity, organization, correct mechanics (spelling, punctuation, grammar, capitalization), and legibility.

Question 1

LO 7.2.1

In order to properly track and control a project, you need to determine the right metrics to collect and present. Decide which grouping would help you most achieve the goal of proper project tracking.

A. Test environment, test systems, and test data readiness
B. Test cases, defects, and coverage metrics
C. Test resource availability, percentage of test cases that are automated, time spent maintaining automated and manual test cases
D. The number of areas for improvement discovered during testing lessons learned sessions, the efficiency of archiving testing work products, and the percentage completion of tasks at the end of the project.

Question 2

LO 7.4.2

Your project sponsor informs you that, as test manager, you must begin preparing and presenting weekly reports to senior leadership concerning the test progress of your team on this project. Determine which of the report choices is best for this audience.

A. Prepare a detailed defect report showing lots of information and trending over time since senior leaders like to analyze trends.
B. For the first few meetings, conduct information sessions with the executive leadership to best understand what information they are looking for.
C. Present one simple, very high-level metric to indicate overall project test status.
D. Provide one slide containing a dashboard of no more than four high-level reports that show trends over time.

Question 3

LO 7.5.2

During the test implementation phase, your test lead presents you with the following readiness for testing report (see next page). With the plan to formally begin testing in two days, what would your recommendation be?

A. Formally begin testing as planned since the percentage readiness components are never 100% complete prior to the start of test.
B. Accept the release because you have some test resources dedicated to nothing other than environment and data readiness and maintenance.
C. Since those test cases assessed as the riskiest will be executed earliest, you can begin as planned and worry about stabilization and readiness later.
D. Unless the readiness for each of the components reaches close to 90% readiness in two days, do not accept the release into test and continue to monitor readiness progress on a day-per-day basis.

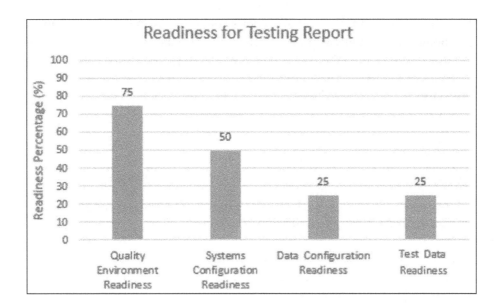

Question 4

LO 7.6.1

A test manager needs to understand basic quality control techniques because

A. every manager on a project team needs to understand both quality control techniques and project management fundamentals in order to effectively contribute to project success.
B. testing is closely related to quality control techniques that can help the test manager understand testing progress for overall project success.
C. test managers may be asked by senior executives about quality control techniques during project metrics presentations.
D. doing so will make her more credible with the management team.

Question 5

LO 7.3.1

Scenario 4: Set of Core Metrics

As test manager on a project to develop a new website for your global company, you need to create a set of core metrics for internal use by your project stakeholders.

Please list and describe the primary reports you would include, noting the main data points, reporting frequency and as much information as would be helpful for your test team to gather the data and prepare the reports for you.

Question 6

LO 7.4.1

> **Scenario 5: Dashboard of Test Status Metrics**
>
> You are the test manager on a project to launch a new companywide website.
>   To meet senior leadership's reporting expectations concerning the test status of the project, you must develop a dashboard of test status metrics that is accurate, comprehensible, and appropriate for your audience.

Please describe what would be included in this dashboard in terms of level of detail, taking into account your target audience, access methods for the report, frequency of report updates, etc.

Question 7

LO 7.5.1

> **Scenario 6: Processes and Dashboards**
>
> You are a test manager and you and your team have been assigned to a software development project to create a companywide portal.
>   Senior leadership expects you to design the necessary reporting processes and build dashboards with the appropriate test metrics for them.

For each of the five major testing phases of:

- planning and control,
- analysis and design,
- implementation and execution,
- evaluating exit criteria and reporting, and
- closure

select two metrics and explain why you feel they are important.

For each report, be sure to take into account the specific information needs and level of sophistication of your reports' target audience.

7 Testing Considerations for Domain and Project Factors

Keywords: feature-driven development, test-driven development

7.1 Introduction

Learning objectives
No learning objectives for this section.

When you have been a test manager for quite some time, you'll probably recognize this: each and every software development project is different from the previous one! This is so even when these projects claim, or maybe more accurately appear, to use the same software development approach, like Waterfall or an Agile approach as Scrum. Most likely the moment and level of involvement as a test manager and the testing goals will differ from project to project, often depending on the software development approach used. The same applies to both the amount of already existing documentation and the amount of documentation to be produced. In the first section of this chapter we'll take a closer look at test management considerations for lifecycle models.

Another challenge you might recognize is being a test manager of a project for which all or part of the development is being done by an external team. In the second section of this chapter we'll take a deeper dive at how to manage these partial lifecycle projects. Although you can think of many kinds of such projects, we limit ourselves to an explanation of the following four examples: integration projects, maintenance projects, hardware/software and embedded systems, and safety-critical systems.

The last section of this chapter addresses a typical test manager dilemma: When to release? Although it is almost never the test manager herself who makes such a decision, she should have a voice in the release considerations. As a test manager yourself, you might have been in a situation where you gave negative release advice, but your advice was overruled by for instance a business, marketing, or product manager. Leo has been there several times. Although our release advice is not always followed, it still makes sense to be aware of the considerations for the different release methods. We'll explore in more detail the following methods: market demand, ease of maintenance, and ease of installation.

7.2 Test Management Considerations for Lifecycle Models

Learning objectives

LO 8.2.1   (K6) Evaluate and report advantages and disadvantages associated with each lifecycle model in given situations.

LO 8.2.2   (K2) Describe the concepts usually found in Agile projects which may influence the testing approach.

The first project Leo worked on as a programmer he was responsible for creating the design, programming, and testing. This was a long time ago, but you could say this already looked a little bit like the T-shaped[1] professionals Agile teams are looking for nowadays. (Leo finds this a very amusing observation.) But between then and now the (soft) skills of developers have changed and many types of software lifecycle models have seen the light. And to make it even more complicated, in actual practice, organizations tend to implement parts of different models and combine them into one hybrid model that should satisfy their specific needs. So virtually each and every organization has another separate approach to software development. These models can strongly influence a test manager's approach to a given project. A test manager needs to know the

---

1   If you imagine the letter T being a representation of a person's skills, the vertical part of the T represents the core skill or expertise. In testing we would naturally suggest this is the core skill of testing (of which there are many variations and subskills). The horizontal part of the T represents the person's ability to work across multiple disciplines and bring in skills and expertise outside of the core skills (like designing or programming). The simplest definition of the characteristics of a T-shaped person is given by Jim Spohrer: *"A T-shaped person is that they are better at team work than I-shaped people. I-shaped people are good at talking to other I-shaped people like them. T-shaped people can talk with I-shapes in their area of depth, but they can also have productive conversations with specialists from many other areas. Beyond productive conversations, T-shapes also have empathy or an attitude that makes them eager to learn more about other areas of specializations."* Want to know more about T-shaped professionals? Refer to www.service-science.info/archives/3648.

differences between and similarities with these lifecycle models and should be able to play with it, because it determines the moment of involvement, the level of involvement, the amount of documentation (both available and produced) and the testing goals. In addition to that, the test manager must also be familiar with Agile approaches and how to participate effectively in an Agile project. In this section we'll not only look at the different lifecycle models and their testing implications, but we'll take an even closer look at the Agile methods, since they are fundamentally different from traditional models such as the V-model.

7.2.1 Comparison of Lifecycle Models

Have you ever asked the development team which development method they are using? Leo has several times and expects you won't be surprised by the answers he got. They just don't know! Asking for the development method didn't help him. However, there are some generic (test) aspects of development methods you could look at. As a test manager in such situations you could, for instance, find out at what moment and to what level you'll be involved in the project and how much time you'll get and/or need for testing. Ideally you are involved as soon as possible, but that might be hard, because in the situation of a traditional Waterfall project you might not get the chance to be heard at the beginning of the project. You might not even be on the project yet! On the other hand, in an Agile project it is common practice to be involved as soon as the project starts. Other aspects the test manager has to investigate as soon as possible are the amount of documentation available and the amount of documentation to be produced. This has, of course, a strong relation to the project's lifecycle. In Agile development environments the amount of both available and produced documentation is often less compared with that of traditional environments. The testing goals in terms of test levels will also differ from development method to development method. In the end the test manager has to deal with all these different aspects and come up with an appropriate test approach for a specific development situation. The following chart (Figure 7-1) might help by establishing this approach. The chart provides a comparison of the lifecycle models and their testing implications for five testing aspects.

7.2.2 Waterfall and Agile Models

In Figure 7-1 several lifecycle models are mentioned. The most used models are the Agile models and the Waterfall models. The other two models, V-model and iterative/incremental, are certainly still out there, but are less important

	Moment of Involvement	Level of Involvement	Documentation Supplied	Documentation Created	Testing Goals
Waterfall	After code is complete	None until code complete	Complete specifications	Complete test documentation	System testing, some acceptance testing
V-model	Reviews during requirements phases, planning during code development, testing when code is complete	Planning early, reviews of requirements documents, testing when code complete	Complete specifications	Complete test documentation	Integration, system and acceptance testing
Iterative/Incremental	Involved for first testable iteration of code	"Just in time" planning and testing for the iteration, emphasis on regression testing	Iterative specific documentation	Iteration test plans, iteration relative test cases, some automation	Integration, system and acceptance testing
Agile	Project initiation	Embedded in project team from initiation	Light, if any	Test automation, test checklists	All levels of testing, including some unit testing

Figure 7-1   *Comparison of lifecycle models and their testing implications*

and further can be seen as lying along a spectrum between Agile and Waterfall. Most test managers have worked, or are still working, in Waterfall environments and would be familiar with the model. Therefore only a brief refresher of the Waterfall model and a little more elaboration on the group of Agile software development approaches will follow.

Since most sections of this book apply to test managers working in a Waterfall environment, there is no need for extra elaboration about test management in such an environment. However, concerning working as a test manager in an Agile environment we've added two sections in which we'll take a deeper dive in the testing concepts as well as in the changed role of the test manager in Agile approaches.

Waterfall

The first formal description of the Waterfall model is often cited as a 1970 article by Winston W. Royce, although Royce never used the term Waterfall in that article.[2]

The Waterfall model is a sequential (non-iterative) software development process, in which progress is seen as flowing steadily downward (like a Waterfall) through the phases of requirements elicitation, analysis, design, coding, testing, production/implementation, and maintenance (see Figure 7-2).

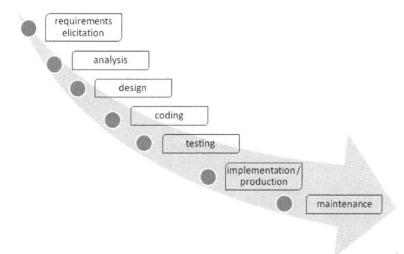

Figure 7-2   *Waterfall model*

The Waterfall model is derived from the traditional way of working in major projects in the construction industry. The purpose of this way of working is that you divide the project into several phases. You start with the first phase and do not start the second phase until you have completed the first. *Completed* in this situation means that phase 1 is reviewed and verified. And when you discover a defect in one of the phases you have to go back all the way to correct that phase and perform the following phases all over again.

Some people are fond of the Waterfall model, while other people hate it. At any rate, when you want to apply the Waterfall model you may consider the following advantages as well as the disadvantages (this is obviously not an exhaustive list).

---

2   Although Royce presented the Waterfall model as an example of a flawed, nonworking model, it became a very popular software development model that nowadays still is one of the most used models. If you're interested in his paper, refer to www.cs.umd.edu/class/spring2003/cmsc838p/ Process/waterfall.pdf.

■ **Advantages:**
- Time spent early in the software production cycle can reduce costs at later stages. After all, you only move on to the next phase after finalizing ("without defects" is the general idea) the phase at hand.
- There is a focus on documentation, which supports profound knowledge transfer to other project members as well as to new people to the project.
- It is a straightforward model, with clear phases. Therefore all project members know exactly what the current project phase is and what is expected of them.
- The model provides easily identifiable milestones in the development process.
- The Waterfall model is well-known. Many people have experience with it, so they can easily work with it.

■ **Disadvantages:**
- When a requirement is changed in, for instance, the coding phase, a large number of earlier phases must be done all over again.
- The phases are often very long and therefore time and costs are difficult to estimate.
- Within the project, the team members are often specialized. One team member may be active in the designing phase only, while a programmer may be active in the coding phase only. This could lead to waste of different resources. Often this is time. For example, the designer is working on the "perfect" design. Although the programmer could have started coding against the not-perfect version of the design, the programmer has to wait until the design phase is completed. This is a typical example of a waste of time.
- Testing is only done in one of the final phases of the project, so the project gets late insight into the quality of the software.
- There is much emphasis on documentation, which could lead to inefficiency.

Agile

Before we take this aforementioned deeper dive in the testing concepts as well as in the changed role of the test manager in Agile approaches, we first have to understand the basics of Agile: These are written down in the Agile Manifesto (2001) for software development.[3] This manifesto describes the four values and 12 principles for software development:

---

3   www.agilemanifesto.org. For US readers for whom the word *manifesto* sounds rather pretentious or stilted, it is a common term in Europe that is used to describe what would be called political platforms or position papers in the US.

■ **The four values:**
- Individuals and interactions over processes and tools
- Working software over comprehensive documentation
- Customer collaboration over contract negotiation
- Responding to change over following a plan

■ **And the 12 principles:**

1. Our highest priority is to satisfy the customer through early and continuous delivery of valuable software.
2. Welcome changing requirements, even late in development. Agile processes harness change for the customer's competitive advantage.
3. Deliver working software frequently, from a couple of weeks to a couple of months, with a preference for a shorter timescale.
4. Business people and developers must work together daily throughout the project.
5. Build projects around motivated individuals. Give them the environment and support they need, and trust them to get the job done.
6. The most efficient and effective method of conveying information to and within the development team is face-to-face conversation.
7. Working software is the primary measure of progress.
8. Agile processes promote sustainable development. The sponsors, developers, and users should be able to maintain a constant pace indefinitely.
9. Continuous attention to technical excellence and good design enhances agility.
10. Simplicity—the art of maximizing the amount of work not done—is essential.
11. The best architectures, requirements and designs emerge from self-organizing teams.
12. At regular intervals, the team reflects on how to become more effective, then tunes and adjusts its behavior accordingly.

The group of Agile software development approaches has become very popular because, in general, they should help organizations (at least compared to traditional approaches) in reducing time to market, being responsive to changing business and customer needs, and in delivering higher quality. All Agile approaches are based on short, timeboxed iterations that deliver increments of working software, through adaptive change, as more information comes to light in a communicative and collaborative manner.

> **ISTQB Glossary**
>
> **test-driven development (TDD):** A way of developing software where the test cases are developed, and often automated, before the software is developed to run those test cases.
>
> **feature-driven development:** An iterative and incremental software development process driven from a client-valued functionality (feature) perspective. Feature-driven development is mostly used in Agile software development.

The most commonly used Agile approaches are:

- **Kanban**[4]
  An approach to incremental, evolutionary process and systems change for organizations. It uses visualization via a Kanban board of a list of work items. It also advocates limiting work in progress, which as well as reducing waste due to multitasking and context switching, exposes system operation problems, and stimulates collaboration to continuously improve the system (Figure 7-3).

- **Scrum**[5]
  A framework within which people can address complex adaptive problems, while productively and creatively delivering products of the highest possible value. The Scrum framework consists of Scrum teams and their associated roles, events, artifacts, and rules.

- **eXtreme Programming (XP)**[6]
  A humanistic discipline of software development, based on principles of simplicity, communication, feedback, and courage.

---

4   *Kanban: Successful Evolutionary Change for Your Technology Business*, by David J. Anderson, and Donald G. Reinertsen. In this book you'll find answers to questions like: What is Kanban? Why would I want to use Kanban? How do I go about implementing Kanban? How do I recognize improvement opportunities and what should I do about them?

5   Definition as given by the authors of "The Scrum Guide," Ken Schwaber and Jeff Sutherland. www. scrumguides.org/docs/scrumguide/v1/scrum-guide-us.pdf. This is where it all started. If you haven't read it yet, just do it, so you know what Scrum is all about. It is less than 14 pages, so the size of the document cannot be an excuse for not reading it.

6   *Extreme Programming Explained: Embrace Change, 2nd Edition (The XP Series)* by Kent Beck and Cynthia Andres. XP principles are often seen as the basis for Scrum. For instance, user stories are mentioned in XP, but not in the Scrum guide, although many people mention user stories and Scrum in the same breath.

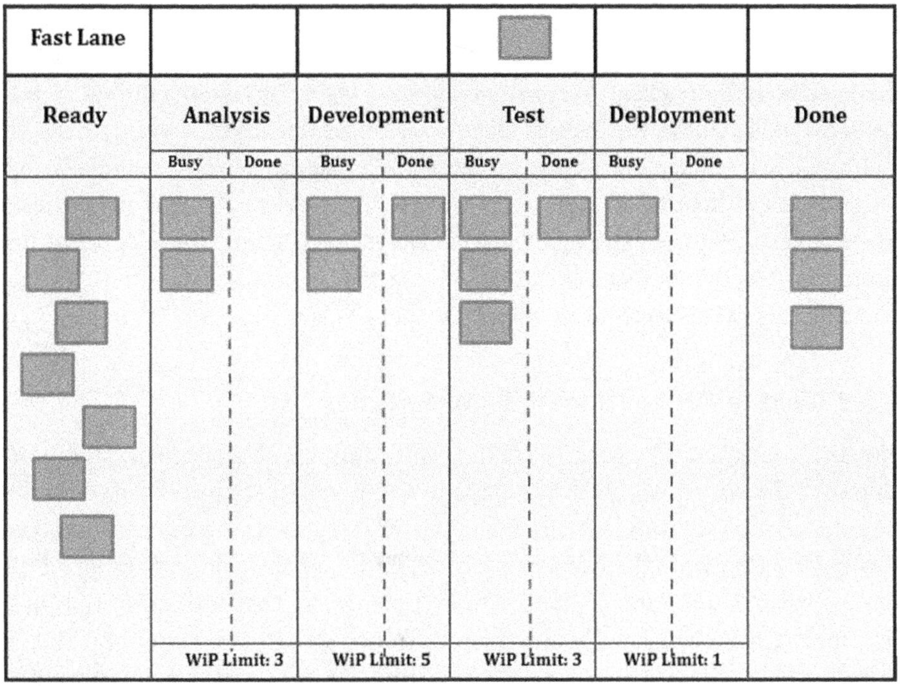

Figure 7-3 *Kanban board example*

As with all approaches, it is rarely the case that the approach is used as originally intended. Usually, aspects from various approaches are combined to form an approach that works best in a particular situation. The one combination we see often is a Scrum team using Kanban boards. Other concepts are also used in Agile environments. Think of behavior-driven development, acceptance test-driven development, feature-driven development, and test-driven development and of testing approaches like exploratory testing and context-driven testing.

Of course you as a test manager will need to adapt to all these (combined) Agile approaches, but it is also important to remember that many good practices in testing, common to other models, still apply. We've been involved in many situations where organizations working with a certain testing approach ceased with this approach when they switched from a traditional way of developing to the Scrum approach. Leo's first reaction always was and is: "So, you think you don't need something like conducting a risk assessment or a test design technique in whatever form anymore?" When you have a sprint of two weeks, the team more than ever needs—due to the short period of time—to find a way to focus on, and to cover, the most important risks. A risk assessment certainly would support the team in identifying and focusing on the most important risks. And when applying the appropriate test design technique (related to the specific risk to cover), you will be able to create the fewest number of test cases and still achieve the highest chance of finding defects or covering risks. In short, as a test manager don't forget all the proven approaches from the past but reuse or adapt those to the new situation. For instance, we know many projects where an exploratory testing approach is integrated with some—adapted to the situation—test design techniques and where they are very happy with this combination that seems to work very well for them.

7.2.3 Testing Concepts in Agile Approaches

The four values and 12 principles of the Agile Manifesto have a neutral relationship with the test approach. And Scrum too, which is an approach based on the Manifesto, scarcely provides any guidance on integrating testing and an Agile approach, or on what the consequences might be for the role and responsibilities of professional testers. It will also be no surprise that the integration of a test approach with the Agile approach does not always run smoothly. This is rather strange, as testing is not only an extremely important activity but must also be fully integrated with the chosen Agile approach. In particular, the following concepts are usually found in Agile approaches:

- **The test process must be integrated in the Agile approach.**
  - The test activities must be integrated in the development process itself. This means that testing is no longer a separate phase but is rather a continual activity of the Agile teams. Cross-training within the group is necessary to provide the best coverage of all tasks in an iteration.
  - All team members must be prepared to perform test activities. Although the team must contain a professional tester, this does not mean that all test activities must be carried out by this tester. Skilled testers and test managers learn more about other processes, such as design and development, and help other team members to understand the need for testing.
  - More communication is needed.
    With Agile methods, the emphasis lies on direct communication, preferably face-to-face, rather than on written modes of communication. It is best for Agile teams to be housed at a single location in order to make this possible. If possible, all the people needed for the project should be

accommodated together in a team at one location. If the team cannot be colocated, easy and quick communication methods must be established. For example, a daily status meeting via video-conferencing tool and project documentation exchange via a (cloud) tool.

- Testing is the driving force behind the quality of the project.

  Testing is no longer the last safety net before the software is implemented. Now the tester collaborates with all team members to provide continual information on the product's quality and its satisfaction of the business requirements. In fact the whole team, including each individual team member, must assume responsibility for quality.

- Test automation is necessary.

  The use of automation is becoming increasingly important and indispensable in the realization of a successful Agile project. Test automation must be utilized effectively to minimize the cost of regression testing. Regression testing is more important than ever, because the continuous change of Agile development incurs significant regression risk. Tests should be run frequently. When testers do have the skills for it, they could develop and maintain the automated test suite themselves. In practice they are often working together with the developers of the team.

- Testing must be incorporated into the definition of done.

  The project or the iteration is not yet done when the software has been built. It is only when this has been tested and all defects have been rectified that one can say that it is done. Accordingly, it is important to include the test aspects in the definition of done and be sure they are measurable and understandable.

Find the right balance by making conscious choices.

- Working software is more important than extensive documentation, which means that the "lack" of information must be compensated by more communication. For cases in which it is not absolutely clear if something should be documented or not, we always pose the following questions:

  - Why are we creating documents: does this documentation have value for the business?

  - For whom are we creating documents: does the team benefit from this documentation?

The answer is context-specific, of course, but if the entire team responds negatively to both questions, documentation would appear to be unnecessary.

- (Re)use the strength of proven test approaches
  Adapt and adjust this approach geared to the Agile environments. Best practices in testing such as defining test conditions and selecting appropriate testing techniques are still applicable.
- Improve continuously.
  Continuous test approach improvement must be implemented and planned approaches should change as needed to react to project realities.

7.2.4 Changed Role of Test Manager in Agile Approaches

Agile methods often work with a variable scope, but with fixed timeboxes and fixed quality. This is a huge change compared to the old Waterfall approach. In that approach often the scope was fixed and the release date flexible, although the latter initially was not meant to be flexible. Traditionally the test manager—and tester—were and still are critical to the success of the projects, especially in respect to establishing the quality of the products. But the roles are somewhat altered. The role of the "traditional" test manager changes when an organization adopts an Agile way of working. Sometimes test managers become more of a staff manager rather than a manager within a project of work. They will, for instance, support a Scrum master and/or a project manager (if there is still one) in the overall delivery. There is no reason, depending on the type of project and the skill set of the individual, why a test manager cannot be part of the team, however, in some cases this may cause issues as the test manager will no longer be the "manager," as the Agile team itself needs to be self-managing.

The fact that several traditional roles on a development project such as project manager, business analyst, etc. are not adopted directly in Scrum does not mean that the test management activities should not be executed. On the contrary, these remain unfailingly important. But they may be executed by any random team member with the appropriate expertise and skills. Nevertheless, it is advisable to have a professional tester on the team, to guarantee test expertise in the team. This tester has knowledge of the execution of a risk analysis, static and dynamic testing, test design techniques, the creation and execution of test cases, test automation, etc. But this does not mean that all test activities must be executed by this tester. Other team members may be requested to provide support in the creation and execution of the test cases, for example. In such a situation, the professional tester can act as a coach.

Test managers will need to mentor those persons who are undertaking testing activities and to provide guidance on the skills and competencies required by the tester in the Agile project. We may facilitate the formation of the Agile team at the onset of the project. The test manager will have a more hands-off role. Instead, she must be mentoring the testers within the team to be self-managed.

Test managers could also facilitate, along with the Scrum master, the management and removal of roadblocks. In some instances the test manager may anticipate a roadblock and ensure that it is removed before the team identifies it. Our experience can also be used during the risk identification and analysis during the initial reviews of the user stories. This of course can be used as input into assessing the technical difficulty of implementation of the user stories during the estimation period. The test manager may also work with the team on the test strategy/approach during the planning meetings at the release and sprint levels. Often the test manager will be part of the testing specialist group that will be called upon at various times throughout the project.

7.3   Managing Partial Lifecycle Projects

Learning objectives

LO 8.3.1   (K6) Compare the various partial project types, discussing the differences between these projects and pure development projects.

The test manager is often involved in projects for which all or part of the development is being done by an external team. This type of project brings its own test management challenges that are sometimes caused by late involvement, sometimes by lack of documentation, and sometimes by multiple ownership. In this section, we'll take a closer look at some of these partial lifecycle projects: integration projects, maintenance projects, hardware/software and embedded systems projects, and safety-critical systems projects.

7.3.1 Integration Projects

In many situations the test manager has to handle testing lifecycle changes that may be required when dealing with an integration project. The moment of involvement for externally developed software (or partially externally developed software) is often later than software that is developed in-house. The software is usually fully developed and assumed to be at least unit tested at the time it is received for integration. This means the test team may not have been involved in requirements and design reviews, and that the planning, analysis, and design time for the project are significantly reduced. In this section, we'll look in more detail at two of the most common integration project situations: a situation in which we've to deal with a supplying and accepting (demanding) party of the software, and a situation in which an organization implements commercial-off-the-shelf software.

Supplying and Accepting Parties

While developing software, a separation can be made between the responsibilities of client, user, manager, and system administrator on the one hand and system developer and supplier on the other. In the context of testing, the first group is collectively known as the accepting (requesting) party and the second group as the supplying party. The supplying party could be both an internal IT department and an external software supplier. Other concepts that are also referred to in this context are the demand and supply organizations. At a general level, there are two possible aims in testing:

- The supplying party demonstrates that what should be supplied actually is supplied.
- The accepting party establishes whether what has been requested has actually been received and whether they can do with the product what they want to/need to do.

In practice, the separation is often less concrete and sometimes system developers (from the supplying party) will offer their help to the accepting party. For instance, in the information analysis, when writing the specifications and in the acceptance test and vice versa, the expertise of users and administrators may also be employed in the building activities. On the other hand, often the situation occurs in which the supplying party and the accepting party don't cooperate properly. In both situations it is important to define the various responsibilities clearly. This certainly applies to testing. Who acts as the client of a test, who accepts it, who wants advice on the quality and who will test what, and when? So, what must a test manager consider in this situation?

- **Define expected quality.**
  What is the expected quality of the software delivered by the supplying party? The test manager and the accepting party have to think about this

up front and share these expectations with the supplying party as early as possible.

▨ **Define additional tests.**

What has already been tested by the software supplier and with what coverage?

◉ When "lucky," the supplier will show you—the test manager—their test strategy and maybe some test reports. In that situation you can establish an acceptance test strategy covering the still outstanding risks.

◉ When "unlucky" or when the supplier isn't willing to share their testing information, you have to think of another approach to establish the quality of the delivered software. You could for instance start with a smoke test or a kind of exploratory testing to gain an initial assessment of the quality of the software and take it from there. Software that shows significant defects at this point will probably need additional system testing, although this might have been the responsibility of the software supplier.

▨ **Define intake tests.**

Leo has been a test manager for many international testing projects. In most situations the software was built and delivered by an external (often foreign) party. Of course, we asked for their test cases, test reports, etc. But we hardly received anything useful. They just didn't want us to "look in their kitchen." But we, as the accepting party, didn't want to waste our time—especially not valuable end user time—on software that wasn't ready (due to poor quality of the software) for the acceptance test. So what we did was define 15 to 20 (end-to-end) test cases that covered the most important processes of the organization. We gave these to the supplier with the demand they had to run—after the delivered software was installed on our acceptance test environment—these test cases successfully, before we would even think about starting our acceptance tests. In Germany, where Leo's been working, they call it the *Demonstrationstest*. Many organizations adopted this idea and some organizations even made this a section in their contract with the software supplier.

Commercial Off-the-Shelf (COTS) Software

A large number of organizations are implementing commercial off-the-shelf software. Although the concept of COTS software suggests that there is not much that can go wrong, in practice things turn out to be different. Often implementations take much longer than planned, expected advantages for the organization have to be downscaled considerably during implementation, and at the time of deploying to production many things turn out not to be working correctly yet. Obviously organizations run big risks with such implementations. The question is, of course, where exactly risks are to be found when implementing COTS software:

- **Meeting the supplier's specifications.**
  In contrast with customized applications, the risk that COTS software will not meet the supplier's specifications is likely to be small. This holds at least if (this specific version of) the package has been delivered to tens, if not hundreds, of other organizations.
- **Tuning parameter settings and adding customized applications.**
  A much greater risk lies in the fact that several people have been working for weeks or months to tune the COTS software (parameter settings) and to add customized applications in order to make the COTS software work for the organization. Such complex activities can hardly be performed without making errors.
- **Adapting the working procedures and processes.**
  Together with the implementation of COTS software, the working procedures and processes of the organization are usually adapted. In this case, the risks are that new procedures are not described well, or that people cannot handle these new procedures, or that new procedures are not compliant with the way the COTS software is supposed to be used.
- **Involving the end users.**
  The end users are often insufficiently involved in the implementation of the COTS software and the modification of the processes. The risk of this is insufficient user acceptance.

Therefore, the risks hardly concern the functionality of the COTS software, but rather the implementation of this software in the organization. Since most COTS software supports a (large) number of organizational processes, risks are usually huge. These risks must be considered by the test manager, especially in the development of the test strategy. In case of COTS software, the test manager is much more focused on *not testing*. Everything that is standard and is frequently used by many users (in other organizations), and therefore has proven itself, does not have to be tested again. The question for testing COTS software is: what is considered low or very low risk, especially in terms of likelihood of failure? *These aspects consequently do not need to be tested.*

7.3.2 Maintenance Projects

The use and development of information systems and technical infrastructures have grown more than ever. The dependency between business processes and automated information systems becomes increasingly stronger. Besides this, existing information systems often need to be adapted to new wishes. The awareness has grown that the costs during use and maintenance of information systems exceed the initial development costs by far. The existing literature on testing and test methods provides a sufficient grip on testing of new software applications. Practical experience has proved that it is still difficult to apply this approach to testing of software during maintenance. If we assume that the average life expectancy of an application is 10 years, we can safely state that testing during maintenance happens more often than the testing of new software. Consequently, it is not surprising that more money is involved in testing during maintenance than during the development period of software applications. Testing during maintenance is not a new work area. On the contrary, for many people it is a daily routine. This also applies to us, and below you'll find a few of our own practical pieces of advice:

- Organize a kickoff session with all relevant parties to obtain clarity on various subjects.
- Create a standard maintenance test plan containing all reusable test aspects.
- Set up, use, and maintain a regression test set that can be adjusted in size.

But first, here is a short introduction to maintenance, just to avoid misunderstandings regarding the concepts. A part of application management that occurs on an operational level is called maintenance. In general, a distinction is made between three types of triggers for maintenance: modifications, migration, or retirement of the software. Maintenance can be performed ad hoc or in a planned way. Ad hoc maintenance is performed to fix defects that cannot be delayed, because they cause unacceptable damage in production. Corrective maintenance is the only form of ad hoc maintenance. Planned maintenance comprises all other types of maintenance. These are performed in accordance with regular development processes per release, which usually start with an impact analysis. Some types of corrective maintenance can also be performed in a planned way. This concerns defects that do not need to be resolved immediately, because they cause acceptable or no damage in production.

Let's have a closer look at the previously mentioned practical advice:

- **Organize a Kickoff Session**

  When making an inventory of the test basis it sometimes happens that changes are not very well-documented and, in the case of ad hoc maintenance, the actual cause for the change is not described. A well-tried method to gain clarity on this is to organize a kickoff session with all parties concerned (business information management and management of technical infrastructure, developers, users, and testers). Defining the impact, identifying risks and defining and/or adapting the test strategy, are topics that fit very well into such a kickoff session. Don't forget taking the non-functional quality attributes into account as well in that session, and also keep the existing situation in mind when collecting these non-functionals. Improving, for example, a performance requirement from 3 seconds to 1 second is very hard to realize in a maintenance release, if this was not a prerequisite in the original design. Specifically in case of ad hoc maintenance, the kickoff session can be used to discuss ways to reproduce an error in a test situation. The challenge in organizing a kickoff session is getting the desired participants together at the same time, in view of the usually very limited timeframe for testing.

- **Create a Standard Maintenance Test Plan**

  It is advisable not to repeatedly invent a new way of working. Both the test process and reusable test aspects such as test specification techniques, required infrastructure, organization, communication, procedures, and a regression test set can be worked out and written down once in a standard maintenance plan. A (limited) test strategy needs to be included in this as well. By, for example, performing a risk analysis on a system, both the very risky and less risky parts can be distinguished. A change to a risky system part requires more test effort than on less risky parts. In case of ad hoc corrective maintenance, solving the production problem has top priority. Even though this results in not taking all necessary steps of a structured test approach, it is vital just then to have a standard maintenance test plan available, since it describes which test activities are essential in an ad hoc situation and should always be performed. If, besides this, a calibrated regression test set is available that can be easily adapted to the test strategy, it is possible to perform a high quality test, even in an ad hoc corrective maintenance situation.

▨ Set Up, Use, and Maintain a Regression Test Set

The most important difference between the test strategy for new development and maintenance is the likelihood of occurrence of the risk. A number of changes are implemented in an existing system, mostly as a result of problem reports or change requests. These changes can be incorrectly implemented and need to be tested. With the adjustment there is also a minor chance that faults are introduced in the unchanged parts of the system, as a result of which the system deteriorates in quality. This phenomenon of quality deterioration is called regression and is the reason why the unchanged parts of the system are tested as well. In fact, risk classifications of subsystems during maintenance can differ from those of new development. Let's look at an example. A new-build high-risk subsystem is tested thoroughly during building and after that released into production. Later, in a maintenance release some new functionalities are added, but the high-risk subsystem hasn't changed. Because the chance for regression for this high-risk subsystem is the only risk involved, a less thorough test can be performed compared to the situation when it was build. This type of strategy determination is called (test) impact analysis. Per change (an accepted request for change or a solved problem report) an inventory is done on which system parts were changed, which system parts may have been influenced by the change and which quality characteristics are relevant. There are various possibilities for testing each change, dependent on the risks (see Figure 7-4):

1. A limited test, focused on the change only
2. A complete (re)test of the function that is changed
3. The testing of the coherence of the function that is changed and the adjacent functions
4. Testing the entire system

In addition to this, you might consider executing a regression test for the entire system. The regression test focuses mostly on the coherence between the changed and the unchanged parts of the system, since these are most likely to suffer from regression. If the test strategy for the new development is available, the levels of importance attributed to the subsystems play a role in the construction of the regression test. A regression test can be executed in part or in full, depending on the risks and the test effort required. The use of test tools is most effective in the execution of regression tests. The

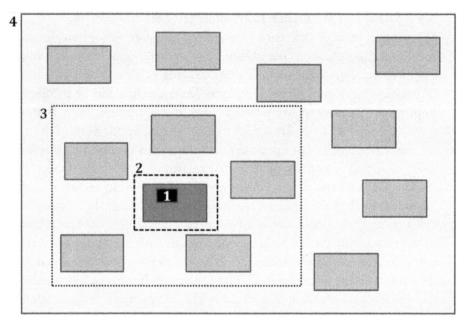

Figure 7-4   *Test strategies*

main advantage of automation of regression tests is that a full test can be executed each time with limited effort and it is not necessary to decide which parts of the regression test will, and which will not, be executed. The choice to formulate the strategy either in terms of subsystems or change requests is affected by the number of change requests and the system part affected by the changes. The more changes and the larger the part of the system affected, the stronger the preference goes to determining the test strategy at the subsystem level, rather than basing it on change requests.

Keeping the regression test set up-to-date is likely to be forgotten. It is therefore advisable to incorporate updating the regression test set as a clear activity in the test phase. While executing the test it may have happened that the system did not react in the way assumed in the test case. If that was an incorrect assumption, the test case has to be adjusted in accordance with the production situation. Furthermore, a decision has to be made if new test cases need to be added to the regression test set. This can be done simply by using the changes and possible defect reports as a basis. It has to be taken into account that the correct classifications used for the calibrated regression test set have to be added.

Besides test cases resulting from planned maintenance paths, test cases can result from ad hoc corrective maintenance as well. Although it is often stated in the latter case that it just concerns the solving of a problem for which the functionality remains unchanged and therefore does not have to be included in the regression test set, it can be useful to include them for the following reason: the problem was solved in one particular software version, but the change has to be implemented in the following software versions as well. Often this does not happen for some reason, and therefore it is advisable to add a specific test case to the regression test set.

Finally, it could be desirable to adjust the risk analysis in the standard maintenance test plan. This mainly applies to the chance of failure of the tested subsystems, which can be adjusted based on the number of detected defects.

7.3.3 Hardware/Software and Embedded Systems Projects

As you might expect, testing hardware and software combination projects and embedded systems projects require a somewhat different test approach compared to testing of "traditional" software projects. You could say that embedded systems is the ultimate form of a hardware and software combination project. However, embedded systems means many different things to different people. It covers a broad range of systems, including mobile devices such as mobile phones and tablets, keyless entry, cameras, robots, thermostats, etc. Although the list of embedded system examples can be endless, they all have a common factor—namely, a combination of hardware and software that interact with the surrounding physical world. On the other hand, "There is no general consensus about what an embedded system is, nor is there a complete list of characteristic properties of such systems," as stated by Bas Graaf, Marco Lormans, and Hans Toetenel from Delft University of Technology in the Netherlands.[7] Whatever the definition you prefer or make up yourself, testing embedded systems will

---

7   Graaf, Lormans, and Toetenel present in their paper, "Software Technologies for Embedded Systems: An Industry Inventory," some results of the MOOSE (software engineering MethOdOlogieS for Embedded systems) project. MOOSE is a project aimed at improving software quality and development productivity in the embedded systems domain. One of the goals of this project is to integrate systems and software engineering, requirements engineering, product architecture design and analysis, software development and testing, product quality, and software process improvement methodologies into one common framework and supporting tools for the embedded domain. For more reading refer to virtual.vtt.fi/virtual/proj1/projects/moose/docs/graaf_in_template_springer.pdf.

always be a challenge for the test manager! Let's look into a few of these challenges: test environment, integration test strategy, and test organization.

Test Environment

The three most important elements of the test environment are:

- **Hardware, software, and network**
  In contrast to "traditional" software, embedded systems can have different physical appearances in the different development stages, which often require different test environments. Besides the production type itself, you might have to test models of prototypes in the early stage of system development.
- **Test databases**
  The need for tests to be repeatable with reproducible test results also applies to embedded systems. So tests—along with the storage of test data—must be designed to support this.
- **Test tooling**
  Like testing traditional software, it is not always possible yet to run the software in the real world. In that situation, simulation (e.g., stubs, drivers) and measurement (e.g., for detecting and analyzing output) equipment may be required.

As test manager, you must be aware that these test environments tend to be complex, so more time must be allotted in the schedule for setting up and testing these test environments. The complexity of these environments may result in more frequent equipment failure and replacement issues, which may cause unexpected downtime. The testing schedule must allow for outages of equipment and provide ways to utilize the test resources during system downtime.

Prototype is mentioned above. Using a prototype for testing has many advantages as long as you are aware of the following risks. Prototypes may show behavior that the production models will not show. This can be either good or bad. Maybe a prototype defect is reported, although this can't happen in a production environment. The other way around is of course also possible. The prototype is working fine, but the production version shows different, maybe even abnormal, behavior. Often it makes sense to apply for an "at least two of each" rule for prototypes. With this rule you could mitigate the problem of an individual prototype with a "bad unit" in it.

Even more difficult to find with testing is the situation in which the prototype shows incorrect behavior but the software accepts that incorrect behavior when it should raise an error. This will mask the problem that will only appear when working in the production environment. When using a prototype in a testing environment, the tester must work closely with the prototype developers to understand the status and behavior of the prototype at hand. When working together, the occurrence of aforementioned risks should not happen.

Integration Test Strategy

An integration test strategy is necessary because of all the dependencies between different software modules, different hardware parts, and between the software and the hardware. Of course, this test strategy depends on the integration approach chosen by the project. Top-down, bottom-up, and big bang integration are the three fundamentally different approaches. Because these three approaches are not mutually exclusive, there is a variety of approaches due to combinations of these three. Which approach will be the chosen approach depends on these factors:

- Architecture
- Availability of the integration items (software or hardware from external suppliers)
- Size of the system
- Whether it is a new system or an adjusted existing system

The test manager has to determine the integration test strategy for one (or a combination) of the following integration approaches:

- **Top-down integration.**
  In this approach, the backbone structure of the system is crucial. This backbone (also called control) structure is developed in a top-down sequence, which creates the opportunity for a top-down integration of the modules. This naturally starts with the top-level control module. Per level and after integrating all connected modules for that specific level this level must be tested. As with testing traditional software, modules that are not ready or available yet will be replaced by stubs. A disadvantage of this approach could be that changed requirements with an impact on low-level modules may lead to changes in top-level modules. This may lead to a (partly) restart of the integration process and its testing. As a test manager you should think of a regression test in order to support this. Another disadvantage

might be the number of stubs necessary to test every integration step. An advantage of top-down integration is that, even though major parts of the system are still not available and may be substituted by stubs, an early look and feel of the entire system can be achieved.

- **Bottom-up integration.**
  This integration approach starts with low-level modules with the least number of dependencies. Often drivers are developed and used to test these modules. This approach can be used to incrementally build the system and may (maybe even will) lead to an early detection of interface problems. By building the system incrementally, these problems can be isolated rather easily and are therefore much cheaper to resolve compared to when they are discovered when the complete system is ready. Although this is a huge advantage, you have to take a few disadvantages into account as well. Often you need a lot of drivers to execute this approach and—because of the iteration of the tests—this approach can be very time-consuming.

- **Big bang integration.**
  This integration approach is a very simple approach; after all modules have been integrated, the system can be tested as a whole. A huge advantage is no stubs and drivers have to be used, and the strategy is quite straightforward. An obvious disadvantage of this approach is that it could be difficult to find the causes of defects. And another disadvantage is that integration can only start when all modules are available.

Test Organization

Testing embedded systems has its own demands on the test organization. As a test manager you might consider these factors:

- The degree of technical expertise needed in the testing team (or training needed)
- Solving issues (e.g. downtime) in the testing environment can be difficult and time-consuming
- Retesting can also be very time-consuming
- Collaboration with the developers (knowledge sharing)

All of this will influence the time schedule. As a test manager it is smart to play a role in establishing the project (test) schedule to make sure enough time is planned, for instance, for solving (unexpected) issues in the testing environment and retesting.

7.3.4 Safety-critical Systems Projects

What is a safety-critical system?[8] Generally you could say a system is a safety-critical system when a failure can cause serious damage to people's health (or worse). Safety-critical systems are often embedded systems. Examples of such systems are in avionics, medical equipment, and nuclear reactors. But other systems could also be safety-critical, for instance an application that runs on a network of PCs and mobile devices that supports doctors, nurses, and physicians' assistants in making diagnostic decisions. With such systems, risk analysis is extremely important and rigorous techniques to analyze and improve reliability are applied.

Building a safety-critical system involves dealing with law and certification authorities. Some of the regulations and/or requirements related to safety critical systems are very strict. In order to fulfill these requirements, there has to be a well-structured process with clear deliverables. For instance, a standard for certification of commercial avionics applications can be used (in the United States DO-178C and the European analog ED12C),[9] or the IEC 61508 guideline,[10] which describes a general-purpose hierarchy of safety-critical development methodologies that has been applied to a variety of domains ranging from medical instrumentation to electronic switching of passenger railways. Another standard, developed by the British Ministry of Defence, is a standard for safety management called MOD-00-56.[11] Part of this standard is a description of a structured process for developing and implementing a safety-critical system. The process shares some products and activities with the test process.

---

8   Are you interested in practical lessons that can be applied for building safety-critical systems based on what is currently known about building safe electromechanical systems and past accidents? If yes, refer to Nancy Leveson's book *Safeware: System Safety and Computers*.

9   The Federal Aviation Administration (FAA) is the national aviation authority of the United States, with powers to regulate all the aspects of American civil aviation. These include the construction and operation of airports, the management of air traffic, the certification of personnel and aircraft, and the protection of US assets during the launch or reentry of commercial space vehicles. Refer to www.faa.gov.

10 IEC stands for International Electrotechnical Commission for all electrical, electronic, and related technologies. IEC uses the following definition of functional safety: "Freedom from unacceptable risk of physical injury or of damage to the health of people, either directly, or indirectly as a result of damage to property or to the environment."
    Learn more about this at www.iec.ch/functionalsafety.

11 When you are interested in an introduction to system safety management concepts, terms, and activities, refer to the introduction booklet as written by the British Ministry of Defence: www.gov.uk/government/uploads/system/uploads/attachment_data/file/27552/WhiteBookIssue3.pdf.

Also, the safety process includes several test activities. If the shared activities and products are not coordinated well, then both processes can frustrate each other. The result is then a product that is not certifiable or a product that offers the incorrect functionality.

Let's take a closer look at a typical safety lifecycle process and what a test manager could do when taking part in such a process.

Safety Lifecycle Process

Let's consider—at a high level—a typical safety lifecycle process. The objective of this process is to develop from some global requirements a system certified for safety-related use.

▨ **Prerequisites to successful safety management.**
  Successful safety management requires that organizations and project teams must follow good practices in areas such as:
  ● Quality
  ● Configuration management
  ● Use of suitably qualified and experienced personnel
  ● Management of corporate and project risk
  ● Design reviews
  ● Independent review
  ● Closed-loop problem reporting and resolution (e.g., take corrective actions to prevent similar problems in the future)

▨ **Setting safety requirements.**
  One of the most difficult elements of the safety process is setting the level of required safety risk for the system. Individual projects will be guided by departmental safety policy but must develop and record their own justification for the targets and criteria which they use. The requirements for safety will vary according to the system size, function, or role, but will include one or more of the following:
  ● Legal and regulatory requirements
  ● Certification requirements
  ● Safety-related standards
  ● Policy or procedural requirements
  ● Risk targets (quantitative and qualitative)
  ● Safety integrity requirements
  ● Design safety criteria

▨ **Safety management planning.**
If the safety requirements define where we want to reach, the safety management plan sets out how to reach the destination.

▨ **Safety stakeholders.**
Safety management is most successful when the decision makers have good engagement with stakeholders from an early stage of a project. The stakeholders must be identified, and then there should be consultation to understand their requirements, with support where necessary from subject matter experts.

▨ **Safety monitoring and audits.**
There is never certainty that the risks of accident occurrence have been fully controlled or that a positive safety culture is prevalent within an organization. The non-occurrence of system accidents or incidents is no guarantee of a safe system. Safety monitoring and safety audit are the methods used to ensure that the "safety system" does not decay but is continually stimulated to improve the methods of risk control and safety management.

▨ **Safety compliance assessment and verification.**
  ◉ Safety compliance assessment is concerned with checking whether the system achieves, or is likely to achieve, the safety requirements. It uses both design analysis and auditing techniques. If the requirements are not achieved, then corrective action has to be taken and the safety must be reassessed.
  ◉ Safety verification aims to provide assurance that the claimed theoretical safety characteristics of the system are achieved in practice. This will involve reviewing all safety incidents that occur and testing that safety features operate as they should.

Test Management Considerations in a Safety Lifecycle Process

As a test manager you must expect—even demand—to be involved in all of the above phases of the lifecycle. Let's take a closer look at these phases and what your considerations could be per phase.

▨ **Prerequisites to successful safety management.**
Think of how to organize design reviews by the test team or by an external—independent—party and risk assessments. Actually, determine a quality assurance approach in general you want to use.

▨ **Setting safety requirements.**

The requirements (functionality, security, performance, usability, etc.) are the test basis for the test. This is the time to start reviewing and executing the risk assessment. Obviously safety-critical systems provide some special challenges, including the need for additional testing for conformance to regulations, certification, and published standards. For tracing and tracking purposes don't forget to implement and maintain traceability matrices, which are very helpful aids to use.

▨ **Safety management planning.**

The test team will spend significant time on reviewing and verifying documentation, including test documentation. Allocating both time and people with needed skills and knowledge is key. The allocated test time should be part of the overall project plan and be clear to everyone involved.

▨ **Safety stakeholders.**

Make an inventory of your principal stakeholders. Involve them as much as possible in the testing activities, when executing the risk assessment and when determining the exit and acceptance criteria.

▨ **Safety monitoring and audits.**

Monitor the test safety aspects by executing audits, and give advice based on the results of the audits. Sometimes compliance to industry-specific regulations and standards may influence some test aspects:

- The level of (test) documentation required
- Which (test) tool must be used
- The thoroughness of testing, whether automated or not
- The level of code and requirements coverage
- The manner of defect classification
- Whether all defects must be documented or not

▨ **Safety-compliance assessment and verification.**

During test execution defects will occur. Of course, these defects need to be analyzed and probably resolved. The correction of a safety defect can have influence on the functioning of the system and vice versa, as a correction of a functional defect can influence safety. In order to overcome this problem the impact analysis and the corrective actions should be centralized. As a test manager, be aware that a corrective action for a safety defect can lead to a functional retest.

7.4 Release Advice and Considerations

Learning objectives

LO 8.4.1   (K4) Analyze the business context with respect to deployment, installation, release management, and/ or product road map and determine the influence on testing.

As a test manager, it could be difficult to give accurate release advice. Often, you must look at it from two angles—the quality of the software, and considerations of the product such as market demand, ease of maintenance, or ease of installation. In this section, we'll take a closer look at both angles.

7.4.1 Release Advice

Often, the release advice is created at the end of the test execution stage. The purpose of the release advice is to provide the client and other stakeholders with a level of insight into the quality of the software that will allow them to make informed decisions on whether the software could be released. The information in the release advice should not actually come as a surprise to the client. She has been kept abreast of developments relevant to her by means of reliable progress reports and, where necessary, risk reports. In order to supply the client with the information necessary at this stage, the release advice must cover at least the following subjects:

▨ **Release recommendation.**
A recommendation as to whether, from the point of view of the testing, it would be advisable to release the software. The final decision, however, on whether or not to release the software does not lie within the test process. Many more factors are at work here, other than those relating to the test process. For example, political or commercial interests that make it impossible to postpone the release, despite a negative release advice, should be considered. In the next section this will be discussed in more detail.

▨ **Obtained and unobtained results.**
Which test goals have been achieved and which have not, or only to a certain degree? On the basis of the test results, the test manager gives her opinion and advice on the test goals set by the client. It is also indicated whether the exit criteria have been met. The number and severity of the

open defects play an important role here. Per defect, it is indicated what the consequences are for the organization. If possible, risk-reducing measures are also indicated, such as a workaround, allowing the software to be released without the defect being resolved.

- **Risk estimate.**
  At the beginning of the test process, an agreement is made with the client about the extent to which product risks will be covered, and with what degree of thoroughness. For various reasons, it may be decided to cover certain parts less thoroughly with testing than the risk estimate indicates. Moreover, during the test process, all kinds of changes are still usually being made to the original strategy; additionally, the original risk estimate has possibly been adjusted, perhaps resulting in additional or different risks. The test manager points out which characteristics or software parts have not been tested or have been less thoroughly tested than the risks justify and so present a higher risk. The associated consequences are also shown.

7.4.2 Release Considerations

As opposed to the release advice, the test manager may or may not be able to have a voice in release considerations. This is often the domain of the business, marketing, and product managers. The test manager does, however, need to be aware of considerations for the different release methods, products, and customers. A few examples of possible considerations are the market demand, ease of maintenance, and the ease of installation.

Market Demand

In one of Leo's projects as a test manager, he worked for a bank where an Internet banking application was developed. At the time the software had to be released into production, it turned out that the front-end and back-end of the system couldn't communicate with each other. Obviously, he gave a negative release review. But the client ignored this because they knew other banks were also working on this feature. And when those banks were able to offer this feature to their customers before "his" bank could, the bank would lose customers for sure. As a temporary measure, workers were hired to enter the incoming transactions to the back-end system and vice versa. This was not an exceptional situation, because depending on market demands it may make sense to release a product before a feature was complete. Some obvious considerations may be competitive products are already in the market, a replacement for a product is already problematic, or the organization wants to get early feedback on a new concept. Whatever the reason, the test manager may have to adjust the exit criteria for the testing phases to support this type of partial release. Exit criteria adjustments should be done only with the approval of the project team as this can have quality and support implications. As in the example above, a real-life simulation with the temporary workers was carried out, before releasing the software into production.

Ease of Maintenance

In the past we were always a little bit hesitant in releasing faulty software into production. Of course that depended on the type of software. We wouldn't do that with safety- or mission-critical software. But nowadays in some environments it is hardly an issue anymore. When we examine apps on our mobile phones, we often have to deal with a few issues. But we also know that we'll get a new version of the app in a matter of hours or days. So a release decision may consider the ease of delivering fixes to the customer. Depending on the type of software, fixes may be automatically downloaded, may require media delivery, or may be available for the customer to download as needed. The ease of both obtaining and installing fixes may determine the acceptability of releasing a product prior to final testing approval.

Although it could be very easy to install fixes, you still have to think about risks such as—when the product fails in production—image loss, loss of income, damage claims, or unhappy customers. As in the app example, software may be released in this way with the assumption that the user would rather deal with some defects that will be resolved quickly than wait for a more solid release. Of course this decision depends—again—on the type of software. This would apply more to non-critical software than it would to safety- or mission-critical software. Although the decision of releasing the software into production is made by others (e.g., business, marketing, or product manager) rather than the test manager, the test manager needs to be able to supply accurate information regarding the outstanding risks, the known issues, and an approximate schedule for the delivery of fixes.

Have you ever been in the situation where the software supplier fired one after the other software fixes at you? We have. Those need not be a problem as long as those fixes are easy to install. On the other hand, installing those fixes may require additional coding by the customer's development team, making them less likely to quickly install changes and fixes. As a test manager in a project where a software package was implemented by a third-party software supplier, the package supplier sent Leo and his team one after the other software updates. The problem they had was that the package was incorporated in the client's software landscape with many tailor-made interfaces. The almost continuous stream of software updates led to the situation that the client's software engineers were almost constantly busy adjusting the various interfaces. But in the end they refused to install all these updates. The consequence of this was that support by the software supplier became difficult because—in the end—they had a lot of customers running multiple different versions of the software.

Ease of Installation

Sometimes it can be hard to install a fix or a new version of the software, and sometimes it is a piece of cake. Some considerations involve the consequences of the installation of a maintenance release, a series of fixes, and the deployment mechanism.

- **Maintenance release.**
  When considering a maintenance release, the test team must understand any effects the fixes will have on the existing software and user organization.
  - Is a data conversion required? If so, the test team has to test this conversion as well.
  - Will additional coding in adjacent software systems be required? When this is the case, probably more testing will be required by the test team.
  - Will the customer need to adjust procedures? Again, if so, this has to be tested before the maintenance release is released to production.
  - Will the customer need to retrain their users because of a change to the user interface? Maybe the user needs additional training in the test environment.
  - Will the customer incur downtime during the installation and implementation of the fix? This is something that must be taken care of by the project or business manager.
- **Series of fixes/updates.**
  Some updates are easy to install, and others are difficult. If you are familiar with installing updates, you probably know that the supplier assumes that you already have installed previous updates. And when you have not installed all previous updates, you probably experienced problems when installing the newest update. Right? So, often customers should not have

the possibility to choose which updates they want to install and which ones they do not. The newest update might not work on their system when skipping previous updates; it also makes support of installation and testing more complicated. To avoid the problem of customers picking the updates they would like to have and to ignore others, sometimes the supplier of these updates combines these updates in one package, which must be installed as a whole. This could lead to a greater testing effort.

■ **Deployment mechanism.**
Cool, the update is tested and works perfectly according to whatever specification. But that was still in a testing environment. As a test manager, don't forget to pay attention to testing the deployment mechanism, preferably together with the operations people. Ensure it is the correct version of the update in the required format for the proper system. This may include testing the installation procedure, any automated wizards, various upgrade paths, deinstallation procedures, and mechanisms used to actually deliver the fix to the user.

7.5 Sample Exam Questions

In the following section, you will find sample questions that cover the learning objectives for this chapter. All K5 and K6 learning objectives are covered with one or more essay questions, while each K2, K3, and K4 learning objective is covered with a single multiple-choice question. This mirrors the organization of the actual ISTQB exam. The number of the covered learning objective(s) is provided for each question, to aid in traceability. The learning objective number will not be provided on the actual exam.

The content of all of your responses to essay questions will be marked in terms of the accuracy, completeness, and relevance of the ideas expressed. The form of your answer will be evaluated in terms of clarity, organization, correct mechanics (spelling, punctuation, grammar, capitalization), and legibility.

Scenario 7: Experiment

In an organization the software development department would like to start an experiment. This experiment involves two different software development approaches. The department is split up into two groups. Both groups will develop the same software product, but one group will be using a Waterfall approach and the second group an Agile approach (Scrum).

Question 1

LO 8.2.1

Refer to Scenario 7.

Compare and elaborate for both the Waterfall and the Agile (Scrum) approach on the moment of involvement as a tester, level of involvement as a tester, and level of supplied system documentation.

Question 2

LO 8.2.2

A Scrum team has adopted the following approach:

- A sprint lasts for two weeks.
- The sprint starts with a team of architects designing the system for three days.
- Then this team of architects is replaced by a team of software engineers who will write the software for five days.
- Finally, the test team comes in and tests the product for two days.

The test team is complaining they can't get the job done.

What should be done to make Scrum work in this situation?

A. Add more professional testers.
B. Extend the sprint length up to four weeks.
C. Integrate test activities in the development process itself.
D. Remove user stories from the "doing" column on the Scrum board.

Scenario 8: Implementing COTS Software

An organization is experiencing problems with its customer relationship management (CRM) software. It was designed and built a long time ago. The organization has decided to look for a commercial-off-the-shelf (COTS) replacement for the CRM software. After a selection procedure, they picked one that would suit their needs. They visited a lot of other organizations using the same CRM COTS software in order to hear more about their experiences with this COTS software. All these organizations were unanimous in their experiences. They were all extremely satisfied.

Question 3

LO 8.3.1

Refer to Scenario 8.

Which risks do you see or do you not see when implementing this CRM COTS software?

Question 4

LO 8.4.1

Near the end of the software development project the test manager provides release advice to the project team. Although the test manager gave negative release advice (due to some severe defects), the software was released into production anyway.

What could be a reason to ignore the test manager's release advice?

A. A safety-critical product does not allow any delays.
B. Being first with this product on the market.
C. The product can be installed very easily.
D. The test manager has a history of giving incorrect advice.

8 Evaluating Effectiveness and Efficiency

Keywords: feature-driven development, test-driven development

8.1 Introduction

Learning objectives

No learning objectives for this section.

As a test manager, I often get questions:

- Why do you need so much time for testing?
- When do you start executing tests?
- Why are you still not done testing?
- What is the test coverage you've achieved?
- How many defects have you found?
- What is the severity of the still-open defects?
- What is the quality of my system?
- How do you know when to stop testing?
- When can I release the software into production?
- How many defects can I actually expect during production?
- What did you test anyway?

Sound familiar? Answering these types of questions with well-founded, factually based answers is not easy. Most questions can be answered with reference to the regular evaluation and reporting mechanisms as described in Chapter 6. To create such reports, you need relevant and correct data which is—unfortunately—often hard to gather. But when you've succeeded in gathering this data, you should be able to answer most of the above-mentioned questions. Metrics on both the quality of the system under test and on the test process are of great importance in order to substantiate your test advice and improve the test process. In order to improve the test process, you need a well-balanced set of metrics with which the consequences of a particular implemented improvement measure can be compared, considering the situation before the measure was adopted. As test managers, we really need such a set of metrics, since we must continually evaluate the effectiveness and efficiency of the testing activities both to monitor the on-going test activities as well as to look for improvement opportunities.

A structured approach for defining a set of test metrics was covered at the beginning of Chapter 6. This chapter also addressed test reporting in-depth. So in this chapter, we will mainly look at the metrics for measuring the effectiveness, efficiency, and satisfaction of the test process, along with some example sets of metrics for some specific test objectives. In the last section of the chapter, we'll explain how a retrospective meeting can be used to improve the test process for subsequent projects.

8.2   Effectiveness, Efficiency, and Satisfaction Metrics for the Test Process

Learning objectives

LO 9.2.1   (K2) Explain the purpose of tracking effectiveness, efficiency, and satisfaction metrics, and give examples that would apply to a test project.

It is not always easy to explain the difference between effectiveness and efficiency. Efficiency and effectiveness are two related concepts with a delicate but nevertheless important difference in meaning. They are often mistakenly used interchangeably. Here is an explanation of the differences based on Joris in 't Veld's work.[1]

■ **Effectiveness** indicates whether the outcome of the process has been realized or not. (A helpful metaphor here is determining whether the destination was reached.) Unlike efficiency, effectiveness does not relate to the process itself, but to its outcome.

---

1   As said, the differences between effectiveness and efficiency are for many people often hard to grasp. Joris in 't Veld made a study of this in the context of system engineering. For a more scientific study of this, refer to one of his books about this topic, such as *Analysis of Organizational Problems.*

▧   **Efficiency** is the degree of utilization of resources to achieve a particular goal. (A metaphor such as how short the route is to the destination may be helpful.) A process is said to be efficient when few resources are used in relation to the common, agreed-upon standard. These resources could be, for example, time, effort (person-hours), commodities, or money.

Generally, one tries to organize processes in such a way that they are both efficient and effective—in other words, increasing productivity (Figure 8-1). Obviously, this is easier said than done, because efficiency targets may conflict with effectiveness.

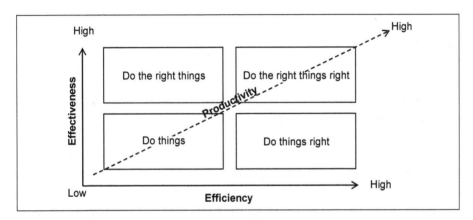

Figure 8-1   *Relation between effectiveness, efficiency, and productivity*

Another, maybe softer, metric is the satisfaction metric. With this metric, we try to examine how (test) stakeholders have experienced the value of the testing process. How did they perceive it? Since this is such a soft metric, many different definitions, or actually descriptions, exist.—for example, Pearson's[2]:

▧   **Satisfaction** with the overall quality of the product and its specific dimensions is usually obtained through various methods of customer surveys. For example, the specific parameters of satisfaction in software monitored by IBM include the CUPRIMDSO categories (capability, functionality, performance, usability, reliability, installability, maintainability, documentation/

---

2   In Pearson's Software Quality Metrics Overview (https://www.pearsonhighered.com/program/ Kan-Metrics-and-Models-in-Software-Quality-Engineering-paperback-2nd-Edition/PGM31), you'll find some interesting software metrics—product metrics, process metrics, and project metrics—that are very well described and explained. You can use this to define your own set of metrics. Refer to http://fac.ksu.edu.sa/sites/default/files/software_quality_metric_overview.pdf

information, service, and overall); for Hewlett-Packard they are FURPS (functionality, usability, reliability, performance, and service).

A general warning regarding metrics is in place here. It is human nature that people change their behavior to meet the desired metrics, which could cause unintended side effects. For example, Leo worked on a project for which they had an agreement (metrics) about the amount of test cases that they (as a team) would execute per hour. (He doesn't even remember now why they had this metric, but they had to deal with it nonetheless.) While executing the tests, they bumped against not being able to fulfill this metric. Since the programmers were finished coding, the test team asked them to help with executing tests, and they agreed. In the end they accomplished the metric. "All's well that ends well," one might think. However, after the software was released into production, one after the other production failures occurred, and management blamed the test team. After some investigation, the test team found that the programmers had executed the tests and ticked them off. However, they didn't bother to check the expected results of the test cases with the actual outcomes of the system under test! Apparently, the test team didn't give the programmers enough instructions. So although we fulfilled the metric, it caused a huge unintended side effect. Therefore, the test manager should carefully plan the introduction of metrics and constantly monitor for unintended side effects.

Another important consideration is the fact that testers are not working on an island, meaning that the defined set of test process metrics (effectiveness, efficiency, and satisfaction) are strongly affected by overall project and organizational behaviors, activities, and attributes. Obviously a successful delivery of requirements, user stories, use cases, code, and so on might have significant positive impacts on these test process metrics. And of course the opposite also applies, as an unsuccessful delivery of these software lifecycle products might have a negative impact on those metrics. The test manager has, often by nature, a good overall view of all the processes and should be able to use that information to help improve the overall process flow.

When you as a test manager are asked to define a few metrics, you might take the following best practices into account before or while defining those metrics:

⬜ **Start small.**
Start with a limited set of metrics and build it up slowly.

⬜ **Keep the metrics simple.**
The definition should appeal to the intuition of those involved. The more complicated the metrics, the more difficult they are to interpret and to use.

⬜ **Define easy-to-gather metrics.**
Choose metrics that are relatively simple to collect. The more difficult it is to collect data, the greater the chance that it will not be accepted.

⬜ **Avoid data errors.**
Collect data electronically as much as possible. This is the quickest way of data collection and it also avoids the introduction of manual errors into the data set as well.

⬜ **Record accurately.**
In the case of billable time registration, for example, it sometimes happens that incorrect billing codes are used. For example, software engineers especially tend to book time against testing codes when they actually are solving a defect.

⬜ **Keep presentations simple.**
Avoid complicated statistical techniques and models during presentations. Just use easy-to-understand figures like tables, diagrams, and pie charts.

⬜ **Be transparent.**
Provide feedback to people who have handed in the data as quickly as possible. Show them what you did with the information.

It is almost impossible to define a list with all possible metrics you can think of. Below we present a (non-exhaustive) list of metrics for effectiveness, efficiency, and satisfaction (refer to Table 8-1). These are just examples. Refer to Chapter 6 for even more examples of metrics, including some metrics that you can use in an Agile development environment. Use or adjust those metrics, or create new metrics that suit you best in your specific situation. Often the best way to define a set of metrics is to start thinking about which goals you want to achieve with the set of metrics first, as promoted by the Goal-Question-Metric (GQM) approach, discussed in Chapter 6.

Table 8-1   *Effectiveness, efficiency, and satisfaction metrics (examples)*

Effectiveness Metrics:

Metric	How to Measure
White box statement coverage	Ratio between the number of tested program statements and the total number of program statements. Tools that can produce such metrics are available.
Requirements coverage	Percentage of requirements covered by identified test conditions.
Number of tests	Ratio between the number of tests and the size of the system (for example, expressed in function points). This indicates how many tests are necessary in order to test a part.
Percentage of test conditions covered by tests	Ratio between the covered test conditions and the total number of test conditions defined.
Percentage of tested conditions	Ratio between the tested and the total number of test conditions defined.
Defect detection effectiveness	The total number of defects found during testing, divided by the total number of defects—estimated partly on the basis of production data.
Appropriate use of testing techniques	Ratio between actual test coverage and the planned (or needed, or agreed-upon) test coverage.

Efficiency Metrics:

Metric	How to Measure
Test costs	Ratio between the test costs and the total development costs. A prior definition of the various costs is essential.
Savings achieved by reusing test products	Effort, duration, and/or resource savings achieved on the current project based on testing work product reuse from previous projects.
Cost per detected defect	Total test cost divided by the number of defects found.
Budget utilization	Ratio between the budget and the actual cost of testing.
Test efficiency	The number of required tests versus the number of defects found. (You should strive to find defects with the least possible number of test cases.)
Number of defects found (relative)	The ratio between the number of defects found and the size of the system (in function points or KLOC) per unit of testing time (e.g., 5 defects/KLOC per hour). (KLOC: Kilo [thousand] lines of code.)
Savings of the test	Indicates how much has been saved by carrying out the test. In other words, what would the losses have amounted to if the test had not been carried out?[3]

---

3   Calculating this can be difficult. You could use the cost of quality and compare the cost of production failures against the cost of failures found during testing. Refer to these articles by Rex Black and Leo van der Aalst when making calculations: www.rbcs-us.com/site/assets/files/1345/what-it-managers-should-know-about-testing-roi.pdf and http://leovanderaalst.nl/Article%20Testing%20expensive%20-%20Not%20testing%20is%20more%20expensive.pdf

Satisfaction Metrics:

Metric	How to Measure
Stakeholder satisfaction	Distribute surveys to be filled in by project stakeholders.
Alignment with business objectives	Investigate to what extent plans and schedules are aligned with the business objectives.
Clarity of test reports	Distribute surveys to be filled in by the recipients of the test reports.
Tester satisfaction	Organize and execute a test process evaluation.

How to set up and run a survey

Surveys? Probably we all are prompted to fill out a survey on a regular basis. Right? It is so commonplace that you hardly think about how to set up a survey, how to run it, and how to process the results. If you wish to set up a survey yourself, you'll find some useful tips in this section. Leo compiled these tips from teaching, consulting, and experience.[4]

Consider these four steps:

1. Decide on the boundaries of the survey
2. Set up the survey
3. Run the survey
4. Process the results of the survey

1. Decide on the boundaries of the survey

- **Be specific in what you want to know.**
  For instance, don't ask the customer about his feelings about the finished project, but ask his feelings about the collaboration with the developers.
- **Determine the participants.**
  Ensure that you invite the intended group of stakeholders you wish to complete the survey. If you, for instance, want to know what the feelings of the customer are, you likely don't want the developers to participate in this survey, unless you want to investigate the different views of both parties on the same topic.

---

4   When you want to know more about how to set up and run a survey, a good start is here: www.wikihow.com/Execute-a-Successful-Survey. You'll find an overview on how to set up and run a survey, as well as its sources for further investigation.

░ **Determine the number of participants.**

When the number of participants is low, the conclusions will—of course—be debatable. So, try to involve enough participants with which you could give a substantiated conclusion.

░ **Decide on the manner of collecting survey data.**

Make it easy for the participant to fill out the survey. You could pay a visit to all participants (face-to-face), or call them, but having them fill out an Internet survey might be more efficient. Just think about what would work best for you.

2. Set up the survey

░ **Determine the format of the questions.**

Are you going to use "open questions," which may take a lot of time to process the answers? Or are "closed questions" (multiple-choice) more suitable in your situation?

░ **Decide on the length of the survey.**

Think about how many surveys you're asked to fill out that will take "less than an hour" and how willing (or not) you're willing to spend that time. Think very carefully about the size of your survey before sending it out. If it is too long, your response rate may be low. Alternatively, if it is too short, you probably won't get enough information to come up with a thoroughly substantiated conclusion.

░ **Determine question ordering and wording.**

Again, make it as easy as possible for the participant. Think of a logical order of the questions, and use clear wording. For instance, how do you—the customer—think the communication went with the developer during the project? And then provide the participant with five possible answers that can be ranked by the participant.

░ **Test the survey.**

It is always good to have someone else take a look at the survey before you are going to deploy it. Better yet, ask some colleagues to actually fill it out and remove imperfections in the survey.

3. Run the survey

▢ **Distribute the survey.**
Distribute the survey to the previously identified participants.

▢ **Decide what's in it for the participant.**
Ensure that you explain to the intended participants why it is useful for them to complete this survey. You can do this via email together with the survey, but note that people may miss the email or just don't take the time to read it. Think about calling people before sending the email with the survey and explaining to them over the phone that they should expect this survey email and why it is important for them to fill it out. This results in a higher response rate.

▢ **Set a time frame.**
Think of the time frame within which the participants have to respond (which should be made clear to the participants, of course) and about how long in total the survey period will last (a week, a fortnight, a month?).

4. Process the results of the survey

▢ **Collect the results.**
You have to combine all results from all participants per question. In practice it is often easier to work with numbers than with text. So make sure you've thought about how to combine the results when you created the survey.

▢ **Process the results.**
Perhaps you can draw a conclusion per question. Maybe you will correlate the answers of two or more questions and draw a conclusion. Besides drawing conclusions, you may define some improvement suggestions. Think of possible follow-ups based on the conclusions or improvement suggestions as a result of the survey.

▢ **Distribute the results.**
You have run this survey for a reason, so make sure that you notify the participants about the results of this survey. This is best accomplished via a presentation. If that's not possible, just ensure they get the results anyway, through whatever means are possible. When you don't do this, the participant might not be that willing to invest time to complete another survey in the future.

8.3   Effectiveness, Efficiency, and Satisfaction Metrics for the Test Policy Objectives

---

Learning objectives

LO 9.3.1   (K6) For a given test policy, define, evaluate, and report effectiveness, efficiency, and satisfaction metrics.

As we all know, different projects will have different (test) objectives. In one situation, the main objective could be risk reduction, while in another early time to market, and in a third cost reduction. Often, one has to find a balance between all of those aspects. The identified test objectives are often documented in a project plan, test plan, definition of done, or test policy. A set of applicable metrics—measuring effectiveness, efficiency, and satisfaction—can be very useful in both providing insight into the status of the process and in supporting decision-making in relation to the stated test objectives.[5] As stated, each test project is different, so the set of metrics will differ from one project to another and even from one test objective to another. When defining a set of metrics we, as test managers, still have to be aware of possible unintended side effects as discussed in the previous section.

An example often clarifies things. So let's consider a few example test objectives, more or less in the same way as the GQM approach describes it:

- **Objective 1**
  - Goal: Optimal customer/user satisfaction
    - Question: Are the most important defects found that could affect customer or user satisfaction?
    - Question: Is enough information produced about these defects so they can be fixed prior to release?
- **Objective 2**
  - Goal: Reduce risk to an acceptable quality level prior to release
    - Question: Are the most important risks covered/found early in the testing process?
    - Question: Are the most important risks covered/found in the testing process?

---

5   For a detailed discussion on derivation of metrics for test objectives refer to the book *Beautiful Testing: Leading Professionals Reveal How They Improve Software (Theory in Practice)*, by Tim Riley and Adam Goucher. Twenty-seven testers and developers contributed to this book by sharing their personal stories with respect to a wide range of testing qualities and techniques.

◼ **Objective 3**

◦ Goal: Provide the project team with important (test) information

▪ Question: Is the information appropriate?

▪ Question: What are the costs to produce this information?

Looking at these three objectives, we can assign the following metrics with respect to effectiveness, efficiency, and satisfaction (refer to Table 8-2):

Table 8-2   *Effectiveness, efficiency, and satisfaction metrics related to test objectives (examples)*

Metric (Effectiveness)	How to Measure	Objective		
		1	2	3
Percentage of defects detected	Ratio between the number of defects detected and the total number of defects.	x		
Percentage of critical defects detected	Ratio between the number of critical defects detected and the total number of critical defects.	x		
Percentage of critical defects that escaped to production	Ratio between the number of critical defects detected and the total number of production defects caused by escaped critical defects.	x		
Percentage of critical defects found early in test execution	Ratio between the number of critical defects detected in the first quarter of the test execution stage and the total number of critical defects found in the test execution stage.		x	
Percentage of critical tests run early in test execution	Ratio between the number of critical tests run in the first quarter of the test execution stage and the total number of critical tests run in the test execution stage.		x	
Percentage of identified risks covered by (executed) tests	Ratio between identified risks and the total number of (executed) tests in relation to these risks.		x	
Percentage of useful information provided by testing	Ratio between useful information and the total amount of information in a test report. (Useful information is information relevant to the individual stakeholders. When calculating this, you could ask yourself the following three questions: (1) Should it be in this report because it is relevant for me, the test manager? (2) Should it be in this report because it is relevant for the testers? (3) Should it be in this report because it is relevant for one of the stakeholders? If your answer would be no to all of these three questions, it is apparently a non-useful section in the report.)			x

Metric (Efficiency)	How to Measure	Objective		
		1	2	3
Percentage of defects rejected by development	Ratio between the number of rejected defects by development and the total number of defects.	x		
Cost per defect found during testing (you may distinguish between average cost of detection [also called cost of appraisal] and cost of internal failure[6])	Total test costs divided by the total number of detected defects.	x		
Average cost per risk item covered during testing	Total test costs divided by the total number of risk items.		x	
Percentage of costs associated with producing test reports	Ratio between the costs of producing test reports and the total test costs.			x

Metric (Satisfaction)	How to Measure	Objective		
		1	2	3
Stakeholder perception of accepted risk prior to release and after it has been released into production	Survey of risk perception prior to release to be completed by the stakeholders, and the same survey after three months of production. Make a comparison between both survey results.		x	
Project team perception about sufficiency, importance, and timeliness of information provided by testing	Survey of project team about sufficiency, importance, and timeliness of information provided by testing.			x

6   Average cost of detection is something the test team can influence (by decreasing the cost to achieve adequate coverage), but average cost of internal failure is mostly determined by development and other bug repair efficiency issues. When you want to calculate this refer to this article by Rex Black: www.rbcs-us.com/site/assets/files/1345/what-it-managers-should-know-about-testing-roi.pdf.

8.4   Project Retrospectives

The aim of a test retrospective—regardless of the development approach such
as Waterfall when working traditionally or Scrum when working in an agile
way—is to learn from experience gained during the completed testing phase(s)
and to document the lessons learned and improvement suggestions for future
projects or sprints. As a test manager, you should be able to organize and lead
evaluation sessions. These are possible ways of organizing these sessions:

- Identify and gather evaluation topics
- Require each team member to participate
- Ensure mutual trust (open exchange of ideas, no personal attacks)
- Collect all issues and group them
- Form pairs and give them three minutes to think up as many actions as possible per group
- Rotate the pairs after three minutes, having them move on to the next group
- Run through all actions
- Provide each participant with three votes, and ask them to select their favorite actions
- Identify the most popular actions and determine the action owners
- Set a maximum time limit, for example, of 60 minutes for an Agile retrospective (could be a few hours in a traditional environment)

These 60 Agile retrospective minutes apply to the effective amount of time
needed. I often have combined such an evaluation session with a lunch, because
it was the end of a project and the people had done their best to make a success
out of it. Personally, I think it is important to pay some attention to this
achievement and thank the people who have done such an excellent job.

You could extend the evaluation session with a more personal feedback
when useful (such as for resolving any interpersonal issues):

▨ Tips and tops[7] for the team and for each other:
  - Stick notes onto the board (at least one tip + one top) for the team.
  - Offer feedback to the team member via a note (at least one tip + one top) per team member.
  - Feedback is always constructive!

Another structure for outlining an evaluation in an Agile environment (retrospective) is given by Esther Derby and Diana Larsen[8]:

▨ Set the stage.
▨ Gather the data.
▨ Generate insights.
▨ Detect what to do.
▨ Close the retrospective.

Often these retrospective sessions are held at the end of a project or sprint, but it is a smart thing to organize these on a regular basis during the project or sprint as well. This is the best way to continuously improve what has been learned. During the retrospective sessions, you might take the following feedback rules into account:

When you are the sender of the feedback:

▨ The feedback should be wanted by the receiver and of good quality so the receiver finds it useful and would like to have more of it.
▨ The feedback atmosphere should be one of mutual trust.
▨ Describe briefly, without judging or interpreting, what you observed and start with something positive first.
▨ Remember, it is your (subjective) feedback, so use "I" instead of "one" and "you," and make sure your feedback is as specific as possible (don't make it universal).
▨ Provide concrete and realistic improvement suggestions (don't say that you might think of another approach, but rather come up with a possible other approach yourself).

---

7   Tips and tops is a feedback method where the tips are recommendations and the tops represent what you did well.

8   Esther Derby and Diana Larsen (with coauthor Ken Schwaber) explain in their book *Agile Retrospectives: Making Good Teams Great* how to use tools and which tricks and tips you can use to organize a retrospective in general and how to organize a retrospective specifically for your team and organization.

▒ Don't wait to give feedback until the organized retrospective session; provide it during the project or sprint whenever you think it is useful or necessary.

When you are the receiver of the feedback:

▒ People have thought about it, so value the feedback, listen to it, learn from it, and thank the feedback provider for giving the feedback.
▒ Accept the feedback as it is. You can ask questions for a better understanding of the feedback, but don't start defending yourself.

As the organizer of the evaluation session, you can think of possible topics yourself or ask the intended participants of the evaluation session which topics they want to discuss. Often, evaluation topics such as the following are addressed:

▒ Test process
▒ Test result (maybe also root cause analysis)
▒ Stakeholder involvement
▒ Test infrastructure
▒ Results from implemented improvement suggestions from previous evaluation sessions

Of course, each project or sprint requires its own list with appropriate topics/questions. For inspiration, see the sample evaluation checklist in Figure 8-2 and on www.tmap.net.[9]

When you as test manager want to focus merely on test process improvement you can choose from the various test improvement approaches described in the ISTQB Advanced Test Manager and Expert Improving the Test Process syllabi, such as CTP, IDEAL, TMMi, and TPI NEXT.[10]

---

9   Figure 8-2 shows a part of an example evaluation checklist. For the complete list refer to www.tmap.net/downloads. If you're interested in checklists for other topics like Internet testing or mobile apps testing, these are here as well.

10   In the book *Test Maturity Model integration (TMMi) - Guidelines for Test Process Improvement* written by Erik van Veenendaal and Brian Wells, you'll find an improvement model largely based on the CMMi model. You can also use the approach as described in the book *TPI NEXT - Business Driven Test Process Improvement* written by Alexander van Ewijk and others. In this approach, key areas, maturity levels, and checkpoints together with clusters and enablers are concepts that are used when identifying improvement suggestions. Both *TMMi* and *TPI NEXT* have developed an approach aimed toward use in Agile environments. The book *Critical Testing Processes: Plan, Prepare, Perform, Perfect,* by Rex Black provides a non-prescriptive (i.e., business-oriented rather than maturity-model-oriented) framework for test process improvement as well.

CHECKLIST TEST PROCESS EVALUATION

This checklist can be used during and after completion of the test process to assess the process quality. Its use during the test process may be a good way to prevent problems.

- *Is the client sufficiently involved in the product risk analysis and test strategy?*
- *Is the test process running under pressure of time? If so, are concessions being made towards the original test strategy?*
- *Are the users involved in the test process on time?*
- *Do the users believe that the acceptance test is given sufficient time?*
- *Are concessions being made during the test process with respect to the planned test volume and intensity?*
- *Is the test team receiving support from experienced (external) advisors and test specialists?*
- *Is there sufficient subject knowledge available in the test team?*
- *Has defect handling been organized properly and does version control work adequately?*
- *Are the connections to existing systems and the organization receiving sufficient attention?*
- *Is there sufficient co-ordination with other projects?*
- *Does the prescribed test method, as established in the test handbook, provide enough information and support in the case of any problems?*
- *Is there a check whether the guidelines are being observed?*
- *Is there a procedure for possible deviations from these guidelines?*
- *Has a test plan been created according to the regulations?*
- *Is there a critical end date when testing must have been completed?*
- *Has the test plan been specified in greater detail and/or maintained during the execution of the test?*
- *Are the requested supporting aspects (tools, appliances, et cetera) being made available in sufficient quantities and on time?*
- *Is it possible to complete the intended test plan within the limits set?*
- *Is the test plan clear and can it be executed by the members of the test team?*

Figure 8-2   *Part of an evaluation checklist*

Organizing and executing the retrospective is one thing, but delivering outcomes that result in actual change is another thing. Successful retrospectives involve the following:

▨ **Keep track of history.**
Use a library of data (e.g., a Wiki), reports, and minutes from past retrospective meetings, which could serve as readily available information (for instance, what were the improvement suggestions and what were the results after implementing these?) as a resource for future retrospectives.

▨ **Eliminate the cause of the problems.**
Identify the source of the problems encountered and suggest solutions that likely will eliminate the causes of the problems in the future.

▨ **Make improvement suggestions visible.**
A pitfall we often encounter in practice is that a retrospective is executed as planned and improvement suggestions are identified, but they don't get

implemented. Besides the obvious prerequisite "management commitment" as described next, it could help to visualize the identified improvement suggestions. In Scrum environments Leo sees improvement suggestions translated into user stories that not only are visible to everyone but also can be taken into account when executing Planning Poker (refer to Chapter 5 for a longer explanation).

- **Get management commitment.**
  Implementing improvement suggestions often consumes time and resources, so make sure you've got management commitment and support to implement these suggestions.

8.5   Sample Exam Questions

In the following section, you will find sample questions that cover the learning objectives for this chapter. All K5 and K6 learning objectives are covered with one or more essay questions, while each K2, K3, and K4 learning objective is covered with a single multiple-choice question. This mirrors the organization of the actual ISTQB exam. The number of the covered learning objective(s) is provided for each question, to aid in traceability. The learning objective number will not be provided on the actual exam.

The content of all of your responses to essay questions will be marked in terms of the accuracy, completeness, and relevance of the ideas expressed. The form of your answer will be evaluated in terms of clarity, organization, correct mechanics (spelling, punctuation, grammar, capitalization), and legibility.

Question 1

LO 9.2.1

Four test team members are discussing the meaning of effectiveness, efficiency, and satisfaction. They are using aerospace metaphors to support their thoughts. John, the test engineer, says: "Effectiveness is when you launch a rocket to Mars and it gets there via the shortest route and by burning the least amount of rocket fuel as possible." "Actually," says Mary, another test engineer, "This would be an example of efficiency." Andrew, the test automation guy, joins the discussion. "No, you got it all wrong. Efficiency could be reaching the desired planet Mars instead of, for instance, Pluto." "Well, I would say reaching Mars using the least possible rocket fuel is an example of satisfaction," says Annie, the test data specialist.

Who gave the correct metaphor?

A. John
B. Mary
C. Andrew
D. Annie

Scenario 9: Safety-Critical Project Metrics

In a safety-critical project, the following test objective is defined:

Reduce risk to an acceptable quality level prior to release.

The test manager of the project talked with some stakeholders, and he was able to define some questions supporting the test objective:

1. Are the most important risks covered/found early in the testing process?
2. Are the most important risks covered/found in the testing process?

Question 2

LO 9.3.1

Refer to Scenario 9.

Define and elaborate on metrics for effectiveness, efficiency, and satisfaction with respect to the described test objective.

Scenario 10: Sprint Retrospective

At the end of the first sprint of a Scrum project, a sprint retrospective has been held. Below is a list of comments/feedback given by the Scrum team members:

- User stories were not clear.
- Not enough domain knowledge present in the Scrum team.
- Not enough time for testing.
- Programmer is missing testing skills (when defining/executing unit tests).

Question 3

LO 9.4.1
Refer to Scenario 10.

Which improvement suggestion would you define?

Appendix A: The Expert Test Manager Exams

This appendix is written for those of you who are using this book to prepare for the ISTQB Expert Test Manager exam. In order to fully prepare for the exam, in addition to mastering the learning objectives and material in the syllabus, you need to understand the structure of the exam itself as well as practice with exam questions. In the first section, we'll describe the structure of the exam, which you should read before reading the eight chapters of this book.

Each chapter of the book contains sample questions that cover all the learning objectives for that chapter, and you should work through those questions after reading each chapter. The answers to those questions, along with complete explanations of the answers, are provided in Appendix B. You should check your answers carefully against the correct answers, including the explanation for the answer. If you get the right answer but for the wrong reason, the chances are very good that you will not be so lucky on the real exam.[1]

As with all ISTQB exams, the Expert Level exams are based on learning objectives. You are familiar with learning objectives from the Foundation and Advanced Level exams. However, one of the unique characteristics of the ISTQB Expert Level syllabi and exams is the presence of learning objectives with highly sophisticated cognitive difficulty. The six levels of learning objectives relevant to the Expert Level exams are:

- K1: remembering. Being able to remember some technique, fact, or definition. You won't see any K1 level questions, but your ability to recall basic facts, concepts, and definitions is essential to the questions you will see, as was also the case with Advanced Level exams.

---

1   In addition to the sample questions provided in this book, you should try the comprehensive practice exam, covering all three exams, provided by the ASTQB on their website, www.astqb.org. The Expert Level exams are extremely difficult and challenging—as they well should be—and you should fully leverage this book's resources, the ASTQB's resources, and the ISTQB's resources to help you prepare.

- K2: understanding. Being able to compare, contrast, and cite examples related to some technique or fact. You will see multiple-choice K2 level questions.
- K3: applying. Being able to solve a problem using a technique or fact. You will see multiple-choice K3 level questions.
- K4: analyzing. Being able to analyze a scenario or situation and select the right solution to the given problem. You will see multiple-choice K4 level questions.
- K5: evaluating. Being able to analyze a scenario or situation and select the right solution to the given problem based on various criteria that may be internal or external to the given scenario. You will see essay-type K5 level questions.
- K6: creating. Being able to construct a new solution to the given problem from a deep understanding of the problem, the available (partial) solutions, and the internal and external criteria that influence the appropriateness of the solution. You will see essay-type K6 level questions.

What's new at the Expert Level are the K5 and K6 learning objectives and their associated essay questions. These essay questions, along with some of the multiple-choice questions, are frequently based on scenarios.

The multiple-choice questions are graded in the same way as the Advanced Level exams—i.e., mechanically by comparison to predetermined correct selection. The essay questions are graded by a panel of experts. These experts read your solution and compare it to a standard, called a rubric, that provides guidance on what should be present in the answer. However, in addition to having the correct content in your answer, your ability to present your answer in a clear, compelling way also matters.

Details about the structure of the three Expert Test Manager exams are available on the ISTQB website, and we encourage you to read that information carefully. We're not going to restate the contents of those documents, but we do want to highlight some key points for you.[2]

The multiple-choice and essay sections of the exam are cleanly partitioned in two ways. First, the multiple-choice questions, which are found in one section, cover the K2, K3, and K4 learning objectives. The essay questions, which are found in another section, cover the K5 and K6 learning objectives. There

---

2   At the very least, download and read the "ISTQB Expert Level Exam Structure and Rules" found at www.istqb.org/downloads/send/12-expert-level-documents/79-istqb-expert-level-exam-structure-and-rules.html.

is no overlap in coverage. However, scenarios can be common across multiple-choice and essay questions.

Second, the multiple-choice and essay sections are partitioned in time. You may have a set period to complete each section. Prior to taking the exam, you should ask whether you can move time between the two sections. For example, if you finish the multiple-choice section early, you can certainly move on to the essay section, but can you transfer the remaining time on the multiple-choice section to the essay section? When Rex took the three exams, he was not allowed to do so. He found that this created time constraints on the essay sections that were a real challenge. To provide a complete answer, and to retain enough time to review and revise his answer before the time expired, required careful time management.

Like the Advanced Level exams, the number of points varies for the questions. For the multiple-choice questions, the usual rules of thumb apply:

- K2 questions receive one point.
- K3 questions receive two points.
- K4 questions receive three points.

As with the Advanced Level, simpler K3 and K4 questions might receive fewer points, but usually these rules of thumb should work.

While the multiple-choice questions are valuable, they are a relatively small portion of your score. Usually, most of the points—i.e., around two-thirds to three-fourths of the total points—will accrue to the essay questions. Not only does that point distribution alone make the essay questions high stakes; further, you have to select two out of three questions to answer. No extra points are awarded for answering all three. So, you must read the three essay questions, decide which two you will do best on, and then spend your time answering those. Time is limited, so read the questions thoroughly but efficiently, and make your decision about which two questions to answer crisply and decisively.

You almost certainly won't have time to change your mind about which two questions to answer midway through answering the second question. On one exam, Rex *did* change his mind about which second question to answer midway through answering the first question, because he realized there was a synergy between the two questions he ultimately answered. There's a risk to selecting essay questions that have synergistic elements, because, if you are on the wrong track on one question, that will probably lead to mistakes on the other question too.

For the exams, the Expert Test Manager syllabus is broken down into three sets of logically related topics and subtopics, as shown here:

- Part 1: Strategic Test Management
  - Missions, Policies, Strategies, and Goals: Mission, Policies, and Metrics of Success; Test Strategies; Alignment of Test Policy and Strategy Within Organization
  - Evaluating Effectiveness and Efficiency: Effective, Efficiency, and Satisfaction Metrics for the Test Policy Objectives
  - Managing Across the Organization: Integrating Tools Across the Organization; Quality Management and Testing
  - Managing External Relationships: Merging Test Strategies with Third-Party Organizations
  - Domain and Project Factors: Test Management Considerations for Lifecycle Models; Managing Partial Lifecycle Models
- Part 2: Operational Test Management
  - Managing External Relationships: Types of External Relationships; Contractual Issues; Communication Strategies; Integrating from External Sources
  - Project Management Essentials: Estimating Effort; Balancing Quality, Schedule, Budget, and Features Implemented; Performing Risk Assessment; Monitoring and Controlling a Test Project
  - Test Project Evaluation and Reporting: Tracking Information; Internal Reporting; External Reporting; Test Results Reporting and Interpretation; Statistical Quality Control Techniques
  - Domain and Project Factors: Release Considerations
  - Evaluating Effectiveness and Efficiency: Project Retrospectives
- Part 3: Managing the Test Team
  - Managing the Test Team: Building the Test Team; Developing the Test Team; Leading the Test Team
  - Managing Across the Organization: Advocating for the Test Team; Placing the Test Team in the Organization; Creating and Building Stakeholder Relationships; Handling Ethical Issues

In spite of the apparent sequencing of the exams through the part numbers, you can take these exams in any order you like. If you study for the exams all at once—e.g., by reading the syllabus, checking the glossary definitions of terms in the syllabus, and going through this book's material and sample questions in their entirety—then you should take the exams as quickly as possible afterward, one after another. If you study for the exams one at a time, you should read and study the relevant sections for one exam, take that exam, and then move to the next exam.

Of course, you are not required to take all three exams. Each exam has its own certification. If you only need one or two of the certifications at this point in your career, feel free to just take those exams. It may be a bit more time-consuming to come back later and study for the exam(s) you skipped. Whether you study for all three exams and then take all three exams in rapid succession, or you study for and take one exam after another, it's probably more efficient to do all three exams within the space of a month or so, rather than, for example, take one, then take another a year later, and then take the last one a year after that.

That said, training providers will provide courses that involve hands-on application of these concepts at work. If you are using this book in concert with such a course—or just using this book for self-study while making sure you have tried the concepts out in real work—you'll need to be in a position to use the relevant concepts on the job. That could take a year or two. Will you gain a deeper level of knowledge from applying these concepts in your daily work? Yes, of course. So, a slow-but-steady, one-exam-at-a-time, real-world approach to gaining your full Expert Test Manager certification is likely to be more effective at teaching you the ideas in this book and on the exams.

Ultimately, the choice is up to you. It depends on what you want to achieve with this certification, as with all ISTQB certifications. The ISTQB program is a rich, varied, and ever-expanding one, designed to support you, the professional tester, in your career path. As those of us who have been professional testers for decades know, there is no single true and immutable path to where you want your career to go. There are many paths. We hope you enjoy your own, personal career path, and that this book has been a helpful guide along the way.

Appendix B: Answers and Explanations for Chapter Sample Questions

To help ensure a sound understanding of the chapter material as well as better prepare for the ISTQB exam, consider taking the sample chapter exam questions and then checking your answers in this appendix. Each question pertains to the learning objectives identified within each chapter. All K5 and K6 learning objectives are covered with one or more essay questions, while each K2, K3, and K4 learning objective is covered with a single multiple-choice question. This mirrors the organization of the actual ISTQB exam. While the number of the covered learning objective(s) is provided for each question to aid in traceability, the learning objective number will **not** be provided on the actual exam.

It is advised to tackle these questions after reading the applicable chapter. Try to answer each question on your own as if you were taking the exam. Then, refer back to this appendix to explain the correct answer for multiple-choice questions and the rationale for essay questions.

Chapter 1: Test Missions, Policies, Strategies, and Goals

Question 1

Multiple-Choice

Learning objective 2.2.1

D is the correct answer because reliability and availability are clearly the highest goals for the customer. A is incorrect because testing can detect some defects but not all defects (of whatever type) and cannot force the removal of the defects it finds. B is incorrect because the focus is primarily on bugs that would cause reliability regression. C is incorrect because it is part of the strategy (the "how we accomplish the mission") rather than the mission itself (the "what is to be accomplished").

Question 2

Multiple-Choice

Learning objective 2.2.3

Option B is correct because test defects should cost less than production defects. Option D is correct because you want to focus on customer-impacting defects. Option G is correct because you want to find the highest possible number of defects. Option A is incorrect because this is related to efficiency of coverage, not to defect detection. Option C is incorrect because cost of quality is an efficiency metric, not an effectiveness metric. Option E is incorrect because a high level of test coverage ensures confidence building, but the focus of testing on defect-prone areas is ideal for defect detection. Option F is incorrect because regression testing does not typically find many defects.

Question 3

Multiple-Choice

Learning objective 2.3.1

A is the right answer. Risk-based testing can be used because you have access to the stakeholders, whose participation in risk analysis is an essential success factor. Reactive testing can be used because you have tests with business domain and technical expertise. Requirements-based testing cannot be used effectively because you don't have written requirements specifications. Directed testing might not be useful; there is no discussion in the stem about whether someone is available on the project who can provide test conditions. Model-based testing might not be useful; there is no discussion in the question about whether automated performance or reliability testing is required, and the inputs for model-based functional testing are not available. Automated testing might not be useful; we don't have any information in the stem that indicates the need for automated testing or the suitability of automated testing on this project.

Question 4

Multiple-Choice

Learning objective 2.3.2

C is correct because the test team was not able to use requirements-based and risk-based testing due to time constraints. A is not correct because the test conditions given by the developers might have been correct, but developers will almost never give a complete set of test conditions. B is not correct, because reactive and directed strategies will often, by themselves, not find most defects, even when the testers are competent. D is incorrect because, when adequate attention is given to quality and testing, any lifecycle model can support quality delivery.

Question 5

Essay

Learning objectives 2.2.2, 2.3.3, and 2.4.1

For part 1, you should list at least risk-based testing (to manage the risks). Listing reactive testing (to find defects not found by analytical techniques) is also correct. Automated testing (to manage regression risk) would also be important. Given the auditing requirements, requirements-based testing (to demonstrate completeness) should also be listed.

For part 2, the objectives are not entirely adequate. Building confidence in the system and creating information that will allow intelligent release decisions and support auditing are also important. If these objectives are not included, the remuneration plan will reward testers for doing an incomplete job, one that does not meet the needs of the organization. In addition, you might have noted that the remuneration policy given does not include metrics or goals for those metrics and so is not measurable.

For part 3, you should list building confidence and providing information as additional test objectives needed in the policy. The remuneration policy should include metrics and goals that map to the objectives.

Chapter 2: Managing the Test Team

Question 1

Multiple-Choice

Learning objective 3.2.3

D is the right answer. About two-thirds (but not all) of the staff do not have ISTQB certification, which is a possible explanation for the inconsistencies in approach. Some of the staff already have sufficient technical skills. A is wrong because inconsistent testing approaches are known to be a bigger issue than insufficient technical knowledge. B is wrong because some of the staff already have ISTQB certification and sufficient technical skills. C is wrong because the staff already has application domain experience.

Question 2

Essay

Learning objectives 3.2.1 and 3.2.2

For the first part of the question, the correct answer should explain why Candidate B is more closely aligned with the stated situation and goal in the scenario. However, if an excellent rationale can be provided for why Candidate A can learn game testing—or perhaps might have gaming experience from their free time, which is not indicated on the résumé—that can also be an acceptable response. Candidate C is not a good fit because this person too closely resembles the given profile—including the weaknesses in technology and testing—of the existing team; you should hire people who bring the team closer to the overall goals. Candidate D is not a good fit because this person is inconsistent with your goal of standardizing on the ISTQB program.

For the second part of the question, the answer should mention the need for multiple rounds of interviews, a mixed interview team, and an understood interview process. It should mention using interviews to explore the candidates' problem-solving and critical-thinking skills, their ability to communicate in spoken and written form, a team-oriented work approach, their curiosity, and the appropriate skills and experience with technology, the application domain, and testing, though mentioning only two or three of these is sufficient. It should also mention the use of the interview to evaluate attitude, presentation of self and skills, organizational skills, and interpersonal skills. Finally, it should mention types of interviews, ideally including at least two of the types listed in the syllabus: telephone screens, group and panel interviews, behavioral questions, situational questions, technical questions, puzzle solving, specialized questions, team dynamics, exams, and audition interviews or assessments. If you said that Candidate A should be interviewed, the answer should mention the need to evaluate this person's ability to test games.

The second part of the question is clearly much harder than the first because it involves remembering a sophisticated set of concepts and applying them to this specific situation.

Question 3

Multiple-Choice

Learning objective 3.2.4

A is a good answer because poor performance also includes antisocial behaviors that affect team capability. C is a good answer because the test team must be able to carry on its essential tasks after termination has occurred. B is not a good answer because, except in cases where personal animosity toward the manager has made a person ineffectual, how you feel about individuals should not determine how you treat them. F is a good answer because a tester must be effective within the test team in the future as well as in the past and the present. D is not a good answer because there are a number of reasons, beyond personal performance, that could result in tests taking longer than planned. E is not a good answer because it does not apply in across-the-board layoff situations. G is not a good answer because defect metrics are rarely good measures of individual performance.

Question 4

Multiple-Choice

Learning objective 3.3.1

A is the right answer; the improvement is gradual because you are gradually improving skills through training rather than hiring people with those skills already (which would result in rapid improvement). B is wrong because the goals are said to conform to the SMART guidelines, and there is no information indicating unfairness. C is wrong because this was presumably already done as part of identifying the skills gaps. D is incorrect because formal training is often one important part of a development plan.

Question 5

Multiple-Choice

Learning objectives 3.3.2 and 3.3.5

B is the right answer because it fits with the tester's résumé, the test strategy (since the ATA course would cover risk-based testing), and the development plan. A is not the right answer because technical skills growth is not as appropriate as testing skills in the scenario and because the goal is not readily measurable. C is not the right answer because it is not realistic to expect that someone can learn risk-based testing in a single lunchtime training session. D is not the right answer because, while the ATM course would cover risk-based testing, it is not appropriate because there is no indication that the individual tester is on a test-management career path at this time.

Question 6

Multiple-Choice

Learning objective 3.3.3

C is the right answer because, given alignment between the roles and responsibilities and the mission of the test team, testers can know how to act to be consistent with that mission. A is not the right answer because roles and responsibilities can be defined for both generalized and specialized test groups. B is not the right answer because it relates to the test manager's understanding rather than the individual tester's understanding. D is not the right answer because, while testers who act inconsistently with their defined roles and responsibilities may need to be terminated, it is far preferable that testers be given good guidance to act correctly.

Question 7

Multiple-Choice

Learning objective 3.3.4

D is the correct answer because extroverts like to engage with the world around them and the people in it. A is not correct because a thinking individual will tend to apply consistent reasoning to their review work. B is not the right answer because a feeling individual might not consistently apply the SLAs and requirements for the offshore team. C is not correct because a judging individual is well suited for following the clearly defined expectations for the offshore team's work.

Question 8

Multiple-Choice

Learning objective 3.4.3

A is the best answer because it allows people to learn new skills and avoid tedious testing activities. B is incorrect because, while public praise is motivating, manual regression testing is tedious. C is incorrect because public criticism is demotivating and manual regression testing is tedious. D is incorrect because it simply moves the motivation problem offshore and might lead to layoffs within the current team.

Question 9

Essay

Learning objectives 3.3.6 and 3.3.7

Correct answers should mention the following points:

- Both performance reviews should show clear evaluation of performance against goals and objectives for each employee.
- The high-performing individual should receive a positive evaluation, with clear and specific praise directed at work done well.
- The high-performing individual should have SMART goals set that will grow her technical leadership, perhaps by sharing what she knows with her colleagues, through cross-training, brown-bags, and so on.

- The poor-performing individual should receive a negative evaluation, with clear and specific feedback on what is not being done properly.
- The poor-performing individual should be directed to receive training in testing and technology, with SMART goals set regarding the training and outcomes of the training.
- Both performance reviews should consider input from other test stakeholders, not just the test manager.
- Both performance reviews should be based on data and facts, not just opinions, and should consider the entire period of the review, not just the period right before the review.
- Both performance reviews should mention the need for regular, periodic feedback on SMART goals set in the reviews.

Correct answers may also mention that the poor-performing individual might be placed on a preliminary path toward termination if skills and results do not improve. If termination is mentioned, the positive personality and behavior attributes of the individual should also be mentioned as mitigating factors.

Correct answers may mention that the reviews should adhere to any specific requirements and forms from the human resources department.

Question 10

Multiple-Choice

Learning objective 3.4.1

D is the correct answer because weekly reporting to you and your manager should suffice and cross-communication within the team is important. A is incorrect because informal communication might not capture all the information needed for the group status report and because testers need to be aware of each other's status. B is incorrect because testers need to be aware of each other's status. C is incorrect because the information from the meetings early in the week will be stale by the time the weekly group status report is released.

Question 11

Multiple-Choice

Learning objectives 3.4.2 and 3.4.4

B is the correct answer because these programs can be implemented quickly (given budget) and can specifically target trust issues. A is incorrect because a lack of trust usually involves a feeling of alienation from someone or some group and reading about that person or group will not resolve that feeling. C is wrong because people tend to congregate with friends and people they already trust at such meals, so existing trust issues will not be resolved. D is wrong for the same reason as C and because the question did not mention anything specific to celebrate.

Chapter 3: Managing External Relationships

Question 1

Multiple-Choice

Learning objective 4.6.1

D is the correct answer because the outsourced testing service provider must know what its objectives are and must have a test oracle available. A is incorrect because the engagement has a well-defined, limited scope; ordinary due diligence in these situations does extend to comprehensive assessments. B is incorrect because the vendor will work in its own environments and only needs to be integrated with test result reporting tools. C is incorrect because, in this situation, the provider simply provides test results; the client decides what those results mean in terms of project progress.

Question 2

Multiple-Choice

Learning objectives 4.3.1 and 4.4.1

C is the correct answer because it minimizes communication overheads for your team and provides quick, uniform access to the test results for the entire project team. A is incorrect because of the overhead imposed on your team. B is incorrect because the delay associated with learning about any defects could impact project schedules. D is incorrect, because it is not difficult for any competent, well-equipped testing service provider to integrate with a client's existing systems.

Question 3

Multiple-Choice

Learning objectives 4.2.1 and 4.5.1

D is the right answer for three reasons: (1) a thorough acceptance test is justified based on the lack of an established track record with this vendor, (2) the test must be against clear requirements in the contract in order to be fair to both sides and to avoid evasion of responsibility by the vendor, and (3) the vendor should be held accountable for delivering a quality product. A is the wrong answer because, even if the testers are competent, there is no guarantee that vendor management will provide them with the time and resources needed to do their job. B is the wrong answer because your company wants to purchase a complete, tested product; system test has as a typical objective the finding of defects that need to be fixed. C would be correct if the product were critical to the business, but given that it is a nonessential, complementary product, such expense (and acceptance of the vendor's costs of external failure) cannot be justified.

Question 4

Essay

Learning objective 4.7.1

For part 1, the entry criteria should include (a) checking that the vendor's planned testing is complete according to the specified contractual criteria; (b) one or more criteria related to the readiness of the acceptance test environment, tools, and test data; and (c) delivery of an installable, testable video system by the vendor.

For part 2, the exit criteria should include (a) a review of the acceptance test results by project management and the vendor, (b) sign-off or other formal acceptance by client management, and (c) coverage of the stated requirements and other contractual elements, in a way that will satisfy auditor needs.

Other criteria mentioned in the Foundation, Advanced, and Expert syllabi may also be mentioned in both parts. However, it is important that both parts not show signs of confusing the test levels; that is, the criteria should clearly be focused on acceptance testing, not system integration testing. They should also not be confused with the vendor's internal entry and exit criteria—for example, for their own unit testing or system testing.

Chapter 4: Managing Across the Organization

Question 1

Multiple-Choice

Learning objective 5.2.1

A is the right answer because it allows you to respond to the owner's request by demonstrating the suboptimization inherent in it. B is not the right answer because the team is already highly effective. C is not the right answer because there's no indication that the test group has made mistakes. D is not the right answer, in part because there is no one single standard ratio, but also because successful organizations do vary in these ratios.

Question 2

Essay

Learning objectives 5.2.2 and 5.3.1

The correct answer should indicate an independent test organization that reports into a senior level of management above the level accountable for delivery dates and budgets. The answer may include a discussion of how to use a matrixed organization to retain the flexibility and responsiveness of embedded testers (especially in an Agile organization) while preserving the independence of judgment necessary in a safety-critical world. The answer should tie this approach to cost of quality analysis, which will show quantitative benefits because of the high cost of external failure in safety-critical systems. The answer should also tie this approach to reduced risk of injury or death of users as a qualitative benefit, which will also sustain a positive reputation. In addition, the answer should mention that a centralized approach will create common test work product deliverables, which will better support auditing, reducing the risk of failed product delivery.

Question 3

Multiple-Choice

Learning objective 5.6.1

D is the right answer because requirements engineers and system architects will be involved in specification reviews; then developers will be involved in code reviews and unit testing; then the testing services group will run test levels such as component integration testing, system testing, and system integration testing—and finally, selected customers will participate in the beta tests. A is wrong because executive managers are typically not involved in testing, other than as recipients of summary test results reporting. B is wrong because requirements reviews will typically precede design reviews. C is not as good an answer as D because specification reviews are omitted.

Question 4

Multiple-Choice

Learning objective 5.2.3

C is correct because testing is being reorganized without test management input. F is correct because the development team introduced the bugs to begin with. H is correct because it is an example of micromanagement. A is wrong because a test manager should be ready to explain reasons for an unexpected number of bugs. B is wrong because cost of quality is a best practice to determine testing efficiency. D is wrong because test stakeholders should be invited to give input on test scope. E is wrong because test stakeholders should participate in quality risk analysis. G is wrong because regular reports on such process metrics are expected from test teams.

Question 5

Multiple-Choice

Learning objective 5.4.1

A is correct: programmers and technical support staff both need details about what works and what doesn't work; project managers, executive managers, and UAT managers need to understand high-level test status; executive managers may need to understand how effective and efficient various groups are; and business analysts, project managers, and UAT managers need to understand how thoroughly the tests covered the requirements. B is incorrect because while technical support staff might be interested in requirements coverage reports, they also especially need access to detailed defect reports for all deferred defects prior to release. C is incorrect because project managers and executive managers need to see test summary reports, certainly more so than the typical business analyst or programmer. D is less correct than A because peer managers such as project managers and UAT managers typically do not have the right to audit the test manager's group.

Question 6

Essay

Learning objectives 5.7.3 and 5.7.2

The answer should include the following components:

- A selection committee of stakeholders
- Integration with other tools (can include examples such as configuration management)
- Defining user and administrator roles
- Defining ownership of the tool and tool-related tasks
- Planning for conversion of the existing defect data
- Planning for continuity of testing and development tasks during the migration

Question 7

Essay

Learning objectives 5.8.1 and 5.5.2

In the first part of the answer, the response should address the following:

- Public: Safety-critical defects should not go untracked because they are more likely to escape to production elevators.
- Client and employer: Executive and senior management has mandated the use of this defect tracking tool for all defects, and testers should not contradict such directives unless they are in conflict with the public interest.
- Product: Defect reports are important test work products, and failing to submit such work products where appropriate does not meet the highest professional standards.
- Judgment: If the test findings are skewed for whatever reason, integrity and independence of testing suffer.
- Colleagues: The system of using process metrics to evaluate people is unfair, and the testers are being placed in an ethical bind through this system.
- Management: As a manager, all these ethical issues must be resolved in a way that promotes ethical behavior in the future.

In the second part of the answer, the response should recommend a discussion between the test manager and the development manager about the undesirable side effects of the new performance evaluation system. The test manager should hold this conversation in such a way that it is not possible to determine the programmer who approached the tester or the tester involved. The objective of the discussion should be to arrive at alternative ways of evaluating programmer work products without making the testers into villains who have to inflict personal damage on colleagues simply by doing their job.

Question 8

Multiple-Choice

Learning objective 5.5.1

C is the right answer because it establishes a positive relationship with your two most important peer managers in this situation and at the same time makes it clear that you want to work collaboratively with them. A is not a bad idea, but it's not the first step; rather, it would need to build on C. B is the wrong answer because such a discussion could easily come across as criticizing the work of your development and tech support colleagues. As for D, a gap analysis on the current process isn't a bad idea either, but the approach given here could seem as "ganging up" on the development manager.

Question 9

Multiple-Choice

Learning objective 5.7.1

A is the correct answer because some of the data (but not all) is failing to import properly. B is not the correct answer because there's no information about a lack of clarity in responsibilities. C is wrong because requirements importing is not a change but rather a basic initial requirement that wasn't implemented properly. D is wrong because there is no indication that the requirements management tool is being retired in favor of the test management tool.

Chapter 5: Project Management Essentials

Question 1

Multiple-Choice

Learning objective 6.2.6

B is the correct answer since the test manager is playing an active role in determining alternatives with resulting impact in order to track any changes to the schedule and scope of testing. A is not the correct answer since this choice puts the test manager in a secondary, passive role rather than as a strong project team member to drive effective solutions. C is incorrect since this choice places the test manager in a passive role rather than as an active team member, who should be responsible for documenting the effect of this change to the test team, the scope of what can be tested, and the impact on the overall quality of the project given this change. D is incorrect since the test manager needs to take more of an active role in documenting and determining alternatives and trade-offs given the change in schedule.

Question 2

Multiple-Choice

Learning objective 6.3.1

D is the correct answer since the future of your test lead's involvement with this project will directly address a risk that affects testing. A is incorrect since methodology choice affects more than testing and the mitigation of project postponement is more widespread than on the test effort alone. B, if it occurs, is not the correct answer since the reorganization may not directly affect testing on this project; you and your test team may remain intact. Not only is the scenario and suggestion to pursue two vendor contracts in C not realistic or cost-effective, it does not necessarily directly impact the test team.

Question 3

Multiple-Choice

Learning objective 6.4.1

C is the correct answer since project management methodology is not part of the quality management program. A is incorrect since testing policies and guidelines are part of quality assurance and quality assurance is part of quality management. Similarly, B is incorrect since testing is part of quality control and quality control is part of quality management. D is incorrect since test policies and strategies are part of quality assurance and testing is part of quality control, and both quality assurance and quality control are part of quality management.

Question 4

Essay

Learning objectives 6.2.1 and 6.2.2

For part 1, release planning, the main techniques should include at least two of the following, based on historical data: test effort per user story or developer-to-tester effort ratios (possibly using historical velocity); quality risk analysis (though at this point it can only identify major risk areas, not specific risks); possibly function point analysis and test point analysis (given a relatively stable release backlog). A work breakdown structure can be used for resource estimation, but specific tasks can't be estimated during release planning. Since the release backlog is subject to change, more detailed estimation techniques are probably not useful.

For part 2, iteration planning, the answer should include at least two of the following: brainstorming such as planning poker; historical data related to test case iteration (e.g., every bug fix requires two tests to be rerun); and quality risk analysis for the stories in the iteration (see also below). Function point analysis and test point analysis could possibly be used, given good historical data. If a work breakdown structure were created during release planning, it could be updated to show details for a given iteration, especially if the tool used to do so allows display of an electronic task board.

For part 3, model should indicate the consistency of the historical defects metrics:

Five defects are introduced per user story, with the number of risks per user story also stable and not seeming to change that.

Of those defects, about 90 percent are detected during testing. Developers remove about 90 percent of the bugs found by testers. However, including bugs undiscovered by testers, only 80 percent of all bugs are removed during testing.

Extra points if the answer mentions that these metrics do not include defects detected and removed during reviews and lower levels of testing.

Extra points if the answer mentions investigating whether the number of risks per story is stable on an iteration-by-iteration basis, and using the results of that investigation to fine-tune the iteration planning process mentioned in part 2.

Question 5

Essay

Learning objective 6.2.3

For part 1, the answer should discuss the following points: (1) the number of user stories per iteration is consistent with the second release; (2) there has been a significant increase in the number of bugs found per user story; (3) the number of defects fixed per user story is consistent with earlier releases, which means a lower percentage of test-discovered bugs are fixed in each iteration. Extra points for recognizing that the increase in bugs per user story is roughly consistent with the increase in risks per user story.

For part 2, the answer should mention that the increased number of bugs found during iterations is putting extra load on the test team. In addition, the answer should mention that the higher-than-normal number of bugs left unfixed in each iteration is accumulating technical debt, which increases the effort required to test each subsequent release. Iteration estimation going forward must allow for more bugs in each user story, allow for more time to be spent finding these bugs, and more time to be spent executing each test due to the higher likelihood of problems due to technical debt. (Extra points for noting that, given a fixed head count and fixed iteration time, these two situations will have the effect of reducing test coverage. Even more extra points for noting the importance of escalating this situation to management, especially if the answer includes a metrics extrapolation to show the much-higher number of bugs per user story that will be delivered to the customers.)

Question 6

Essay

Learning objectives 6.2.4 and 6.2.5

The answer should include the following observations: (1) the rate of developer bug introduction is already too high (see previous question); (2) the rate of developer bug resolution has fallen significantly from previous releases; (3) technical debt has accumulated already, so the upcoming release is already in trouble from a quality standpoint; (4) accumulated defects and technical debt are reducing test coverage, increasing risk to system quality; (5) the resignation of these three key individuals, senior people comprising 15 percent of the development staff, will significantly exacerbate all four of these problems.

Recommendations should include at least two of the following: (1) schedule one or more stabilization or hardening sprints to resolve bug backlog and reduce technical debt while also catching up on any coverage omitted in the first two iterations; (2) reduce the planned user stories per iteration for each team to match the actual velocity that can be achieved with quality; (3) replace the lost developers as quickly as possible, but take into account the impact of Brooks's law on team productivity when you do; (4) make contingency plans to extend the release window beyond the usual 13 weeks if necessary to maintain quality. Recommendations should not include any compromises to quality, due to the nature of the product as mentioned earlier, nor should they include significant increases to the size of the test team, as the test team is not the bottleneck in this situation.

Chapter 6: Test Project Evaluation and Reporting

Question 1

Multiple-Choice

Learning objective 7.2.1

B is the correct choice:

- You are explaining both the planned and actual test cases designed and executed, showing how well actual design and execution compare with the plan.
- You are showing defects created from failed test cases by various criteria, including status, priority, and functional area.
- You are describing the amount of test coverage related to requirements and risk, to ensure that adequate test cases are being designed and executed.

A's metrics will be useful, but they are generally used prior to the release entering the test execution phase and reporting on such would be less effective afterward.

While each of C's metrics has a proper place of importance, they are less applicable in determining project progress and control.

D's tasks and metrics pertain predominantly to test closure activities and would be less effective in providing information on project progress or control.

Question 2

Multiple-Choice

Learning objective 7.4.2

D is the best choice since you are presenting only a few high-level trending reports.

A is incorrect. While trending may be important for senior leaders, since they are far less removed from the details of the projects, it is best to communicate high-level rather than detailed information.

B is incorrect. Since executives have little time to devote to reviewing reports, let alone determining report specifics, it is better to prepare the necessary high-level project test information, learning what has worked well from other, similar projects, and present that information.

C is incorrect. While it is true that simplicity may make sense for presentation to executive leadership, possibly one metric may be too little information and may evoke many more questions than planned, potentially damaging the credibility of you as the presenter.

Question 3

Multiple-Choice

Learning objective 7.5.2

D is the best choice since the environment, systems, and data are not ready to begin test execution. It is better to sacrifice a day or two in the schedule with the confidence that the test components are solid.

A is incorrect since some components may be 100 percent complete at the start of test so this reasoning is faulty.

B is incorrect since it is not a good testing practice to allocate some of your scarce test resources to anything but test case execution during the test execution cycles.

C is incorrect. While it is true that test cases with the highest assessed risks should be executed first, it could be risky, even foolhardy, to begin testing when not properly prepared.

Question 4

Multiple-Choice

Learning objective 7.6.1

B is the best choice since it correctly ties quality control techniques and testing to understanding testing progress.

A is incorrect. Although an understanding of both quality control techniques and project management fundamentals are important, knowing such doesn't really explain why test managers should understand basic quality control techniques.

C is incorrect. Although this may be true, it alone is not a sufficient reason to be knowledgeable about quality control.

D is incorrect. While this may be true, credibility alone is not a valid reason for knowledge and understanding.

Question 5

Essay

Learning objective 7.3.1

One should look for a list of reports along with rationale for selecting the reports and an identification of what would appear on the horizontal and vertical axes to include:

- Daily Test Cases Designed Report
- Daily Test Cases Executed Report
- Daily Defect Status Report
- Weekly Defect Trending Report
- Resource Availability Report

Question 6

Essay

Learning objective 7.4.1

The answer should include the following considerations:

- Tool sophistication, such as an electronic dashboard or website that includes real-time metrics, cutting and pasting into a webpage from manually developed reports)
- Level of detail (e.g., high-level or detailed)
- Reports showing trending or simply snapshots in time
- Key testing areas that the target audience would be interested in (e.g., test cases, defects, coverage) with variance analysis between planned versus actual information
- Notification mechanism (e.g., manually generated email or automated email from a scheduler)
- Frequency of report distribution

Question 7

Essay

Learning objective 7.5.1

The answer should include the following considerations:

- Two reports per phase, focusing mainly on reports related to test cases, defects, risk or requirements coverage, and preparedness or readiness
- Variance analysis between planned versus actual information, as applicable per report
- The level of detail given the reporting level and degree of sophistication of the target audience;
- The method of report distribution and notification (e.g., emails with links to the dashboard of reports)
- The frequency of report distribution

Chapter 7: Testing Considerations for Domain and Project Factors

Question 1

Essay

Learning objective 8.1.1

The answer should distinguish between the Waterfall and the Agile (Scrum) approach. The moment of involvement should indicate that the testers in the Waterfall approach will be involved late in the project (often after the coding is completed) and in the Agile approach as early as possible in the project (often from the start). Regarding the level of involvement, the following difference should be mentioned: in the Waterfall situation after the coding is completed, while in the Agile situation the testers and the test activities are embedded in the team from the start of the project. In respect to the level of supplied system documentation, the answer should mention that the documentation in Waterfall approaches is often more comprehensive than in Agile approaches.

Question 2

Multiple-Choice

Learning objective 8.1.2

C is the correct choice. Testing—as all other development activities—is not a separate phase in Scrum anymore, but is rather a continual activity. So, test activities should be carried out from the beginning of the sprint and not only by the testers, but by all team members.

A is incorrect. The problem is not the lack of (professional) testers. The problem is the fact the development activities are not integrated. Besides that, adding more testers still wouldn't get the job done in two days.

B is incorrect. The problem is not the length of the sprint, but the fact that the development activities are not integrated.

D is not correct. The problem is not the number of user stories at hand, but that testing is not integrated in the development process.

Question 3

Essay

Learning objective 8.2.1

The answer might involve a discussion about meeting the client's functional demands/specifications. Since this CRM software is proven technology with proven working functionality, the discussion should conclude with the statement that it will be unlikely the CRM software wouldn't meet the client's expectations. The answer should mention possible risks introduced by tuning (setting up organization-specific parameters) the COTS software and by adding customized applications. The discussion probably should mention that this risk is exacerbated if the user organizations that were visited differ significantly from your company in terms of line of business, size of business, org structure, etc. Another risk might be adapting existing working procedures to the new situation, which could be wrongly described. A discussion might be set up on the involvement of the end users. If they are involved late in the process or even not all, this could lead to the risk of insufficient user acceptance.

Question 4

Multiple-Choice

Learning objective 8.3.1

B is correct. A market demand could make sense to release a product that might not work entirely correctly. Such a demand could be being the first with this product on the market.

A is incorrect. When releasing a safety-critical product, it doesn't make sense to release when the product contains defects. The opposite is actually more appropriate. Don't release when containing defects.

C is not correct. The fact that a product can be installed easily doesn't reduce the risk when installing a product with defects. This could lead to image loss, compensation claims, etc. The ease of installation doesn't avoid this.

D is incorrect. In the situation where a test manager gives incorrect advice all the time, it doesn't make much sense still letting him do the job. It would be better to find a replacement for the test manager. Besides that, the test manager could be right this time.

Chapter 8: Evaluating Effectiveness and Efficiency

Question 1

Multiple-Choice

Learning objective 9.2.1

B is correct. Shortest route and burning the least amount of fuel as possible is an example of efficiency.

A is incorrect, as John is describing efficiency.

C is incorrect. Meeting the target (Mars) would be an example of effectiveness.

D is not correct. Satisfaction is about how the process was perceived by the stakeholders, not about a combination of effectiveness and efficiency.

Question 2

Essay

Learning objective 9.3.1

The answer should distinguish metrics between effectiveness, efficiency, and satisfaction. From the set of metrics it must be clear the candidate knows the difference between effectiveness, efficiency, and satisfaction. Examples of effectiveness metrics could be: Percentage of critical defects found early in test execution, percentage of critical tests run early in test execution and percentage of identified risks covered by (executed) tests. An example of efficiency could be: Average cost per risk item covered during testing. An example of satisfaction could be: Stakeholder perception of accepted risk prior to release and after it has been released into production.

Question 3

Essay

Learning objective 9.4.1

With respect to the unclear user stories, you might expect suggestions like planning refinement sessions, or extending the user story with more, but limited, documentation, or more communication with each other (knowledge transfer). More documentation and more communication would also apply to "not enough domain knowledge present in the team." And besides that, you might expect improvement suggestions aiming for more product owner involvement or more stakeholder involvement in general. When there is not enough time for testing, you might expect improvement suggestions as test automation or emphasizing testing as a whole-team approach. When a programmer is missing testing skills, you might get improvement suggestions such as pair programming, which means a programmer and a tester working together on defining and executing tests (knowledge sharing).

Index

Printed in the USA
CPSIA information can be obtained
at www.ICGtesting.com
JSHW051456221024
72172JS00010B/87